# THE BIRD
# WATCHER'S
# AMERICA

*books by Olin Sewall Pettingill, Jr.*

GUIDE TO BIRD FINDING EAST OF THE MISSISSIPPI

GUIDE TO BIRD FINDING WEST OF THE MISSISSIPPI

LABORATORY AND FIELD MANUAL OF ORNITHOLOGY

# THE BIRD WATCHER'S AMERICA

Edited by

## Olin Sewall Pettingill, Jr.

*Laboratory of Ornithology, Cornell University*

*Illustrated by John Henry Dick*

THOMAS Y. CROWELL COMPANY
New York    Established 1834

Apollo Edition 1974

*The Bird Watcher's America*

*Published by arrangement with*
*McGraw-Hill Book Company.*

*Library of Congress Catalog Card Number: 73-20835*
*ISBN 0-8152-0356-X*

ABOUT THE EDITOR:
*Olin Sewall Pettingill, Jr., one of*
*the nation's leading ornithologists, is Director*
*of the Laboratory of Ornithology at Cornell University,*
*contributing editor to* Audubon Magazine,
*and author of the famous Oxford guides*
*to bird finding.*

# CONTENTS

## Alaskan Islands

## The North Country

## The Wetlands

## Prairies, Deserts, Desert Mountains, and Canyons

## The Lower Rio Grande Valley

## Migration Spectacles

## Some Avian Specialities

# INTRODUCTION

In the process of gathering information and preparing the text for my *Guides to Bird Finding* east and west of the Mississippi I soon realized that the books could not begin to do justice to some of the exceptionally fine areas for birds and, for that matter, could not even include certain areas simply because they did not come within the geographical scope. As it happened, the books were designed to cover only the forty-eight contiguous states—political limits which birds do not recognize.

Following the publication of the books and the enthusiastic reception which they have enjoyed, I came to the conclusion that there should be a sequel, a book that would concern itself with details on some of the best areas. Then I had to make a few decisions. Should the book stay within the forty-eight states? If not, what should it encompass? Should I write the book myself, more or less in the style of the guides, or should I enlist the authorship of others better qualified than I to present the subject matter?

The book, I decided, should cover North America north of Mexico so as to include some of the exciting places for birds in Canada and Alaska. This made a suitable selection more difficult because, in more than doubling the geographical scope, I greatly increased the number of attractive opportunities. My selections would have to be more limited and arbitrary than ever.

If the book were to deal with the areas in any detail and have the distinct flavor of authority, it would require more than my personal knowledge (actually limited to a small percentage of the areas), the literature, and correspondence. My guides had to be impersonal, written from accumulated information—there was no other way. Other persons should write this book, speaking from their own experiences and endowing it with their own enthusiasm.

I first listed the places that I should like to have in the book and then proceeded to find the persons who could and would write about them. A few places had to be deleted from the original list for want of qualified authors.

Early in 1962 I began writing prospective authors about the book I proposed. I stated what I would like to have them cover in one 2,500-word chapter—heretofore unpublished; I briefly described the general style and invited them to participate. On receiving their acceptances—and thus having a team of authors, so to speak—I wrote all of them again, enclosing a list of themselves, so that each one would know who the others were, and two pages of precise suggestions as to subject matter and the approach to readers. As these suggestions were carefully followed and are now pertinent to the contents of this book, I am quoting them below.

1. The book is not to be a guide to bird finding as such. Authors may use their own judgment on what to say about route directions, transportation, accommodations, clothing, and special equipment. If areas are remote and generally inaccessible to the public (e.g., sea islands), have no accommodations, require advance arrangements and permission to visit, and offer hazards to one's safety and health, then some indication should be given and, if possible, advice on what to do. No doubt Roger Peterson and Olaus Murie, in writing about Alaska's Pribilof Islands and Brooks Range, respectively, will have something to say about problems of access and living.

2. The book is to cover a wide variety of notable environments and their ornithological peculiarities. The pine barrens of Michigan (by Harold Mayfield) and a virgin prairie (by W. J. Breckenridge) are examples. Because the selection of places is limited by the availability of authors (i.e., persons who can write authoritatively and well), anything approaching a comprehensive coverage of all environmental types is impossible.

3. The book is aimed at the audience of bird watchers who, knowing the commoner species in at least their home region, are ready for encouragement in seeking other places for different birds. Authors may assume that their readers are acquainted with a large proportion of the widespread North American bird families and species (birds as likely to occur in New England as California) and know how to use guides to identification. If the occasion arises when an author wishes to point out something noteworthy about a species peculiar to his area by comparing it with a widespread species, he may assume that the reader will know what the widespread species is.

4. The author may feel assured that, in writing for the bird watcher, he is also writing for ornithologists. There will be much interest among all of us in knowing, for instance, what Ira Gabrielson will have to say about Malheur and Klamath Lakes, and Bob Allen about the Florida Keys.

5. I am not concerned about uniformity of presentation. I should like to have each chapter reflect the author's particular interests and personality, and convey to the reader his enthusiasm for the area, its birds, scenery, and potentialities for enjoyment and study. I hope he will write in the first person, if it is easy for him to do so. In 2,500 words, all an author can hope to do is give the reader an impression—enough to stir his imagination and create in him an urge to go and see for himself.

6. The author should not attempt to describe an area in detail —just say enough about it to give a quick picture. Similarly, he should not include all the species—just bring in those peculiar to the area or about which something should be said. A few comments on one or more species' habits, ecological relationships, and survival problems would be in order.

7. Scientific names will generally not be included.

8. The author should not hesitate to include personal reflections, anecdotes, and experiences, or touches of humor.

9. The author may include items of information on vegetation (e.g., flowering plants likely to be in bloom), mammals and other vertebrates, insects, etc., but should not stray too far from birds.

10. When possible, the author should point up opportunities for investigation, so as to provide a challenge. We want readers to

realize that there are still frontiers of knowledge for bird watchers.

11. Finally, no author should miss the opportunity to emphasize an area's uniqueness and value as a natural resource or to point out any known threat to its perpetuation.

The forty-four authors of this book represent many fields of endeavor. The majority are well known in the annals of ornithology, wildlife management, natural history, or conservation. A score are teachers in high schools, colleges, or universities. Three are novelists and one is a newspaper columnist. Three are businessmen. Three are housewives. All have one thing in common—an insatiable love of finding, studying, and enjoying birds in natural environments and the great ability to write about it, thus sharing their happy fortune with thousands of others.

In order that readers may know about the authors and may better appreciate what they are writing about and against what background, I have introduced each of their chapters with a biographical sketch. It is intentionally informal, sometimes anecdotal, in the spirit of the chapter that follows.

It has been a deep sorrow and great loss to me and to all of us in the field of natural science and conservation that three of the authors, Robert P. Allen, Paul L. Errington, and Olaus J. Murie, have just recently passed away. Their chapters are among their last writings for publication.

Names and terms used in this book need only a few words of explanation. All the bird names of *species* are capitalized and follow those designated in *The A.O.U. Check-List of North American Birds* (5th edition, 1957, and supplementary corrections). No names of other animals and no plant names are capitalized. Names of life zones follow those customarily used in most ornithological works. If the reader desires a fuller explanation than given in several of the chapters (for example, in "The Sierra Nevada" by Verna R. Johnston, "Great Smoky Mountains National Park" by Arthur Stupka, etc.), he may refer to my *A Laboratory and Field Manual of Ornithology* (1956, Burgess Publishing Company, Minneapolis) or most any other text.

Guides to field identification that will be useful to any reader inspired to explore the bird watcher's America for himself are those by Roger Tory Peterson—*A Field Guide to the Birds* (for eastern United States and Canada) and *A Field Guide to Western Birds* (published in 1947 and 1961, respectively, by Houghton Mifflin Company, Boston); and by Richard H. Pough—*Audubon Bird Guide: Eastern Land Birds, Audubon Water Bird Guide: Water, Game, and Large Land Birds,* and *Audubon Western Bird Guide* (published in 1946, 1951, and 1957 by Doubleday & Company).

Finally, I should be a traitor to myself if I did not recommend *A Guide to Bird Finding East of the Mississippi* and *A Guide to Bird Finding West of the Mississippi* (published in 1951 and 1953 by Oxford University Press, New York). Both books have detailed information on the routes, accommodations, habitats, and birds, that will supplement those chapters in this book concerned with the areas in the forty-eight contiguous states.

Olin Sewall Pettingill, Jr.

Ithaca, New York
February 17, 1964

# *Atlantic Coast and Coastal Islands*

# BONAVENTURE ISLAND

## Hugh M. Halliday

*The day has all but passed when a boy can have his very own natural area in which to play and explore and perhaps to dream. Hugh Halliday had just that on the undeveloped acres of his father's farm, about seven miles west of Toronto, Ontario, where he was born in 1896. And his early adventures in those lush woods and meadows and along the peaceful river with its adjoining marshes engendered a consuming interest in natural history, particularly birds.*

*Huge MacKenzie Halliday grew up in the era of the hunter-naturalist, egg collector, and muskrat trapper, all of whom found this undeveloped property in the midst of farming country singularly attractive and were always welcome to hunt, fish, or collect there. Thus young Halliday was exposed to a variety of people "from poets to tramps" who were concerned with some aspect of wildlife but not necessarily conservation.*

*Like many a country boy he gravitated to the city where he joined the staff of the* Toronto Daily Star *in 1918 and has been connected with its successors, the* Daily Star *and* The Star Weekly, *in one way or another ever since. In the* Star *for the last twenty-five years he has published a regular Saturday column, "Bird Life," and illustrated it with his own photographs. More recently he has initiated a column, "Bird Land," for five other days of the week.*

*On his own assignments he has traveled in nearly all sections of North America, taking pictures and collecting material for his columns, magazine articles, and four books, including:* Adventures among Birds (*1959*) *and* Adventures among Animals (*1960*). *A fifth book is in the hands of the printers.*

*One of Hugh Halliday's assignments took him to Bonaventure Island because it is "one of the focal points among the bird islands. . . . I could scarcely avoid stopping there." His story here explains why, after that first perfunctory visit, he has returned to this extraordinary place again and again.*

    Bonaventure Island lies in the Gulf of St. Lawrence, three miles off the little fishing village of Percé on the eastern side of the Gaspé Peninsula. Perpendicular cliffs, rising as high as 280 feet above the sea, compose most of the island's six miles of coastline. Abandoned fields, overgrown pastures, and some coniferous woods blanket its interior of two square miles. From its highest point, 400 feet in the southeast corner, the surface slopes northwestward toward the landward side and the village of Percé.

At one time Bonaventure Island was an active fishing center with a human population of 200. With the advent of the motor boat, which made water travel so convenient, many people moved to the mainland. Only seven families now live there the year round. But in the spring and summer seabirds of several species return to Bonaventure to nest and hordes of visitors come year after year to see them, particularly Gannets—the great, white, goose-like birds with black wing-tips.

In recent years, at least since World War II, Bonaventure Island—in fact the whole area—has lost much of its quaintness and charm, for it has become a focal point for bird watchers, photographers, and just plain tourists, and the resulting industry has had its effect on the region and the people. But the Gannets and their way of life have not changed. They remain the same as they were when Jacques Cartier first beheld their nesting cliffs.

It is real adventure to sail around Bonaventure Island in a small boat and view its towering cliffs which, during the nesting season, are white with huge communities of Gannets. And all about, the Gannets are sailing, diving, fishing. If the bird finder is fortunate to be at Bonaventure during the herring and capelin season in late May and early June, he will have the thrilling experience of witnessing a thousand or more Gannets in a mad riot of plunging into the sea for their favorite food.

There are other birds too. Below the cliffs, on rocks projecting just above the surf, Common Murres congregate by the thousands. As the boat approaches, they waddle over to the edge of the rocks and, like elfin Dutchmen, topple into the sea. In addition to the thousands of Murres associated with the island are lesser numbers of Razorbills as well as Black Guillemots, Common Puffins, Leach's Petrels, Herring Gulls, and—a special for any bird watcher's list—the little gulls known as Black-legged Kittiwakes.

Bonaventure Island is ideal for nesting seabirds. It gives them suitable isolation from the mainland while its cliffs, with ledge shelves and niches formed by the uneven erosion of hard and soft rock strata, provide them with nest sites inaccessible to island intruders. The winds, striking the cliffs, create powerful updrafts of air, which allow the birds to land and take off easily. And the outlying sea holds a plentiful supply of their principal food—fish—so necessary when there are vast numbers of hungry youngsters to satisfy.

The Gannets—the most spectacular of the resident birds because of their number, impressive size, and gleaming white plumage—tend to monopolize the shelves of the cliffs and even the fields directly above. Indeed they practically eclipse all the other resident birds.

It is mainly on the southeast side of the island and around toward the southwest where the cliffs are high and sheer that the Gannets nest and rear their young. In early times as many as 100,000 Gannets were said to have nested on Bonaventure Island, but in 1887 only 3,000 individuals were reported. Man had almost succeeded in exterminating them. By 1915 the colony had increased to an estimated 4,000 pairs. Then came the Migratory Bird Treaty between Canada and the United States which made the molesting of these birds and their nests an offense. In 1918 the island became a federal bird sanctuary, and, shortly thereafter, the late Captain Willie Duval, a native of the island, was appointed bird-protection officer, a post which he held until 1956.

In 1947 there were approximately 19,000 breeding Gannets

which reared some 4,000 young, but the following year the population had increased by only 500. Old age and the general hazards of life had taken their toll. At the present time Mr. John Paget, also a native of the island and bird-protection officer, esteemes the population at 65,000. Apparently the Gannets have been gaining and, if the rate of increase continues, they should be back to their former numbers within a few years.

Though by no means among the largest seabirds, Gannets nonetheless weigh between eight and ten pounds and have a wing spread of six feet. Like gulls, they have long, pointed wings, and they are masterful gliders.

Gannets winter along the Atlantic Coast, south to the Gulf of Mexico, and occasionally some—usually immature birds—stray across the ocean. The adults commence arriving at Bonaventure Island in early April before the frost is out of the ground. Rocks and ice falling from the cliffs sometimes take a toll of birds before the nesting season starts.

In building new nests or remaking old ones the Gannets use materials easiest to obtain—seaweed, grasses, and odd bits of this and that. So concentrated are the communities that the nests are just far enough apart to prevent the occupants from pecking one another.

The single bluish-white egg, deposited about the middle of May, is overlaid with a calcareous substance which becomes a dirty brown by the time the egg hatches—in roughly six weeks. Should anything happen to the first egg while it is still fresh, it is usually replaced. However, if the incubation is advanced, no second egg is laid.

Both parents incubate the egg and brood the nestling. Before changing places on the nest, the parents normally cross their bills and mutually stage a pretty bowing ceremony. The bird, being relieved from nesting duty, then plunges from the cliff, gaining momentum by a downward glide before regaining elevation and assuming the standard pattern of flight.

At first the young are blind, helpless, naked, and dark-skinned—strongly suggesting chunks of black rubber. But in a week their eyes are open and they have started to sprout a covering of fluffy white down. They are fed on predigested fish obtained directly from the throat of the parent. At first the parent takes each wobbly head in its bill and, half-swallowing it, lets the nestling mouth down the semi-liquid diet. A few days later the young begin to take the initiative and beg to enter the parent's throat. And before they have left the nest, the young become so demanding that they try to swallow the parent's head if the mouth isn't opened promptly.

An unforgettable performance is the Gannet's method of fishing. Circling its objective, usually forty or fifty feet above the water, but sometimes 200 or even 300 feet, each bird straightens its head and neck, folds its wings, and, in one great power dive, strikes the water with such impact that a geyser shoots up to fifteen or thirty feet. In a moment or two the bird reappears, its throat bulging. It may have swallowed a full-sized mackerel or as many as five herring in just one plunge, and it may lie on the surface of the water for as long as half an hour before attempting to fly.

In their spectacular dives the Gannets are said to penetrate the water twenty-five or thirty feet, but the late Captain Duval, with whom I spent considerable time, was sure that they never went deeper than ten or twelve feet. They are after fish, not diving records, and can be observed from the cliffs as they zigzag through the water. Gannets apparently are unable to dive from the surface of the water as do loons, sea ducks, and many other waterbirds.

By September the nestlings, having been stuffed on fish, are larger than their parents because of excessive fat. While they stretch and strengthen their wings, their parents lose interest in them and desert them for a week or ten days at a time. Before the month is out, they take to the sea by a flapping downward plunge, sometimes bouncing off the cliffs. Still unable to fly, they get away from land by swimming and drifting. Fishermen report seeing them exercising on low rocks and pattering over the water on their big black webbed feet. Eventually they are able to rise from the crest of the waves. Like any young bird, the young Gannet does not have to be taught how to catch food. When physically able, it instinctively follows the inherent pattern—taking to the air and diving straight down.

When young Gannets finally take to the sea, their plumage is a sooty brown. Later it becomes flecked with white. Their fully adult, white coloration does not appear until their fourth year, when they reach breeding age. Since very few immature birds are ever seen on the nesting ledges, probably they spend their youth traveling far and may not even return to land until ready to nest. Their slowness in reaching maturity suggests that their life is a long one.

The conventional way to view the cliffs and the Gannet colony is from a boat, but if one wishes to visit the colony, he must go to the boat landing on the low landward side of the island and walk back for a mile or so, following meandering cowpaths through a thick, half-grown forest of white and black spruce and balsam. There are sufficient cattle on the island to keep the paths passable, yet not enough to affect the woodlands. Although cowpaths may not be the shortest route, they are sure to be the most pleasant.

As you tread the paths, often bordered with Canada dogwood (bunchberry) and the sweet, odorous twinflower, you will hear the croaking of a Common Raven and the *ts-ts-ts-ts-ts-ts* of the Black-poll Warbler. Pine Siskins nest in the evergreens and, during the morning and evening, the fluty melodies of Veeries and Swainson's Thrushes can be heard. Robins and White-throated Sparrows seem to be everywhere.

Suddenly you break through the evergreens amidst a deafening blare of Gannet voices. The cliffs below you and the fields above are dotted with Gannets, and the air is filled with their snow-white forms as they sail about and fly back and forth between sea and cliff to feed and change places with their mates. The Gannets have a language which blends with the wild roar of the sea. When alarmed, their raucous notes rise to a metallic shriek. But around their nests they communicate in friendly, two-syllable phrases and while gracefully soaring they repeat their *craw-aw*. Sometimes, with bills locked in combat, they fall from the cliffs. During nesting time, rivals may battle for hours and even fight to the death.

The photographer should be sure to take along an abundance of film. Certainly getting pictures of Gannets poses no problems, for they are extremely photogenic and the most cooperative of wild birds in that they show little fear. Sometimes they will defend their nests against human intruders.

For flight pictures one is often able to stand overlooking the cliff while a Gannet continues to fly in a circle level with the cliff, passing approximately the same distance from the photographer each time. Possibly the photographer is standing a trifle too close to the nest to which the bird is attempting to return. In that case, if he moves back a short distance, he can get a perfect picture of a Gannet coming in for a landing. This same bird may well take off again and go through the same performance, providing the photographer with a second opportunity.

Discretion should always be observed in the nesting colony. Normally, while one parent is away, the other is guarding the egg or young. At no time should the human intruder keep the guarding parent away from the nest, as its contents then become exposed to marauders such as gulls.

In summer more than fifty species of land and sea birds can usually be seen on Bonaventure Island and, occasionally, a rarity for this latitude—for example, a Mockingbird—turns up. There are no rats, toads, frogs, or snakes on the island. Every third or fourth winter an ice bridge forms to the mainland and a fox may cross over, causing trouble when the birds return to nest.

Near the mainland, in view from Bonaventure Island, is Percé Rock. For more than a century no one had been able to scale the 250-foot cliffs of this upthrust although a helicopter landed successfully on it in 1962. Double-crested Cormorants breed on Percé Rock along with Herring Gulls. Like Gannets, the cormorants feed on fish but they dive for them from the surface, not the air. Like Gannets, they too may dive deeply. Once, while in a small boat, I saw a cormorant come to the surface with a sculpin, a fish of the sea bottom. My companion immediately dropped a line to measure the depth. It was seventy-five feet!

Since a highway follows the shoreline completely around the Gaspé Peninsula, you can reach Percé from either direction. It is some 650 miles from Montreal whether one takes the northern route which follows the south side of the St. Lawrence or the southern route along Chaleur Bay. Many tourists make a loop through this picturesque part of old Quebec Province, allowing time to stop at Percé for a visit to Bonaventure Island and its Gannets.

# NOVA SCOTIA

## Harrison Flint Lewis

*Harrison Flint Lewis was born in 1893 in Sag Harbor, New York, and lived there until 1911 when his family moved to Yarmouth, Nova Scotia. He graduated from Acadia University in 1917, received an M.A. degree from the University of Toronto in 1926, and a Ph.D. from Cornell University in 1929.*

*His interest in birds extends back to 1897 when his maternal grandfather gave him a subscription to* Birds, *a periodical illustrated with color pictures and published in Chicago. This interest, quiescent for some years, was greatly stimulated during the summer of 1909 by close association with the late E. Chesley Allen of Yarmouth.*

*After a year of teaching school in Nova Scotia, two years in the Canadian Army during World War I, and two years as civilian auditor in Canada's Department of Militia and Defence, Harrison Lewis became Chief Federal Migratory Bird Officer for Ontario and Quebec, 1920 to 1943. His next two positions were natural steps—superintendent of Wildlife Protection for Canada, 1944 to 1947; Chief, Canadian Wildlife Service, from 1947 until his retirement in 1952.*

*He has been editor of two publications—*The Canadian Field-Naturalist, *1922 to 1925, and* Sportsman's Province, *1956 to 1958—and a number of books. He wrote* The Natural History of the Double-crested Cormorant (*1929*), *has published over 300*

17

*articles and notes in scientific journals, and served as president of
several conservation organizations.*

*Anyone who thinks that Dr. Lewis has retired is wrong. Any-
one who reads this chapter will suspect—and rightly so—that his
present home in Sable River, Nova Scotia, is near Cape Sable
which he describes in his restrained manner as a "jumping-off
place" for south-bound migrants. It seems pretty certain that from
early spring until late fall Dr. Lewis is out-of-doors, busy observing migrants or finding nests, encouraging local cooperators, and
always keeping an eye out for the occasional "strays." And the rest
of the year—reading, organizing his notes, and writing up material
recently gathered. No ornithologist ever retires.*

In Nova Scotia the ardent bird watcher will find a
happy concentration of interesting contrasts. Since the province is
almost surrounded by the ocean and its broad inlets and, at the
same time, is wide enough to have extensive inland tracts, seabirds
and landbirds live in close proximity.

In Nova Scotia, "winter birds" such as Pine Grosbeaks, Winter
Wrens, and Golden-crowned Kinglets build their nests and spend
the summer, while Willets and Semipalmated Plovers, Veeries, and
Gray Jays nest almost side by side.

The western extremity of Nova Scotia, the part nearest to New
England, is Brier Island, on the southern side of the mouth of the
Bay of Fundy. In the spring Brier Island is a landing-place for
large numbers of migrants and frequent "strays" from the south,
and, beginning in August, a take-off point for a substantial stream
of warblers, sparrows, thrushes, and other south-bound birds.
When the weather is right, this is an excellent place to observe the
fall migration.

In the autumn many landbirds leave Brier Island, heading
northwest on a course which brings them to the shores of Grand
Manan, New Brunswick, in the Bay of Fundy, and New England
by the shortest over-water flight. When the winds are southerly,
this migratory movement is not apparent. But in fine weather with
a northwest wind to block their passage, great numbers of landbirds
accumulate on Brier Island and are very conspicuous.

Under such conditions it is easy to see what birds form the

majority of the migrating companies. At one time a bird watcher may find the island crowded with Eastern Kingbirds; at another, it may be alive with Yellow-shafted Flickers, or Baltimore Orioles, or Black-capped and Boreal Chickadees. Occasionally there is a modest hawk flight crossing Brier Island and heading for New England.

In some years, tanagers and Indigo Buntings are conspicuous strays in April, and in late summer and fall such wanderers as Western Kingbirds, Brown Thrashers, Yellow-breasted Chats, Dickcissels, and Rufous-sided Towhees often occur. The Yellow-billed Cuckoo, Lark Bunting, and Lark Sparrow have been found.

A highway that includes two short crossings on government car ferries connects Brier Island with the town of Digby. Although there is no regular public accommodation in the attractive village of Westport on Brier Island, visitors may be able to obtain food and lodging in pleasant private homes by making local inquiry. There is public accommodation in Freeport, just across Grand Passage from the island; camping is entirely practicable.

The North Point of Brier Island, easily accessible by road, is the best vantage point for observing the fall migration. Pond Cove, at the southwest end of the island, and the area around the main light station frequently yield birds of unusual interest.

A few miles offshore from Brier Island and other coastal points in the general vicinity, Greater and Sooty Shearwaters and Wilson's Petrels—birds that breed in the Southern Hemisphere—may often be found in summer, idly passing their non-breeding season.

Another interesting "jumping-off place" for south-bound migrants, especially shorebirds, is Cape Sable, the southern tip of Nova Scotia. This outer point of a small, low, treeless island sheltering extensive tidal flats and marshy areas is inhabited only by government employees at the light station and their families.

Cape Sable is reached by boat from Clark's Harbour on Cape Sable Island which is connected to the mainland by a causeway. Cape Sable Island is much larger than the island that forms the actual cape. A good deal of confusion revolves around the names Cape Sable, Cape Sable Island, and Sable Island which is far out at sea. All of these places are sandy and were named "sable" (meaning sand) by the early French explorers.

Cape Sable Island, jutting as it does into the North Atlantic tides that race to and from the Bay of Fundy, has remarkably cool summers. This coolness probably accounts for the fact that Cape Sable Island is the southernmost nesting ground of the Least Sandpiper and the southernmost station for the cloudberry, or baked-apple berry, a northern fruit of modest fame.

Other shorebirds that nest in this vicinity are the Willet, the Semipalmated and Piping Plovers, and that old friend, the Spotted Sandpiper. The big, vigorous Willets are conspicuous with their loud cries and flashing black and white wings. They nest among bushes or other low cover on the upland near the shore, hatch their young about the middle of June, and promptly conduct them to the marshes and tidal flats. The Piping Plover prefers to nest on sandy beaches, while the Semipalmated Plover generally chooses a beach with pebbles.

Since this southern extremity of the province provides extensive feeding grounds for shorebirds, it is frequented from early July to the end of November by south-bound flocks building up energy for the overwater flight they must make. The number of species and of individuals increases to a maximum in the first half of August and then gradually dwindles.

Both the Hudsonian Godwit and the Whimbrel occur among the shorebird flocks in the Cape Sable area in August. Other shorebirds observed here in their appropriate periods of passage are American Golden Plovers, Black-bellied Plovers, Ruddy Turnstones, Greater and Lesser Yellowlegs, Knots, Pectoral Sandpipers, White-rumped Sandpipers, Dunlins, Short-billed Dowitchers, Semipalmated Sandpipers, and Sanderlings. The Killdeer, Common Snipe, Upland Plover, and Solitary Sandpiper may be expected to occur occasionally. Purple Sandpipers winter in the area.

Many stray birds, probably uncertain as to what is best to do next, pause for a time in the vicinity of Cape Sable. Yellow-breasted Chats, Western Kingbirds, and Mourning Doves occur almost every year. The Yellow-crowned Night Heron, Cattle Egret, and Yellow-headed Blackbird have been found and the remains of a Green-tailed Towhee were picked up.

Some 200 miles east of Cape Sable and close to the ocean shore of Nova Scotia is the Eastern Shore Bird Sanctuary, a small group of coastal islands maintained by the Nova Scotia Bird Society. The nearest villages on the mainland, Harrigan Cove and Necum

Teuch, are on Route 7, the main highway running eastward from Halifax. There are hotel accommodations in Necum Teuch and the neighboring community of Moser's River. Motorboats are available for hire in the villages, but in rough weather one cannot reach the outer islands.

The Common Eider nests in substantial numbers in this refuge and may be readily observed. In May the ducks make their nests, lined with soft eiderdown (guaranteed genuine!), in sheltered places on the islands and lay four or five eggs apiece.

The eggs hatch in June, usually in the first half of the month. The watchful, anxious mothers soon lead their lively youngsters to the shore where they launch out happily upon the sea. Frequently several females pool their broods in a single convoy and protect them in concert. From mid-June to mid-July numerous groups of Eider ducklings and their guardian mothers may be seen in coves, passages, and other sheltered waters among the islands. Meanwhile the adult male Eiders wander away by themselves and molt into dingy eclipse plumage.

The Eastern Shore Sanctuary includes a cluster of outer islands that are treeless and a number of wooded islands nearer the shore. Several pairs of Black Guillemots as well as a sizable colony of Leach's Petrels nest on the outer islands. The Leach's Petrels make their homes and lay their eggs in burrows that they excavate in the sandy soil. During the incubation period one bird of each pair remains in its burrow with the single egg while its mate flies far out to sea to feed. The members of the pair change places only during the night. Consequently, at the height of incubation, though hundreds of Petrels may be sitting on eggs in their burrows, not

one is visible during the day. Naturally, visitors are requested not to excavate the burrows.

Herring and Great Black-backed Gulls both nest in the sanctuary. There are many Arctic Terns in the vicinity, but they may or may not nest in the sanctuary. One can never be sure because terns are inclined to shift their nesting grounds frequently.

The wooded islands are fine habitats for some birds. A large colony of Double-crested Cormorants nests in the spruce trees on one. A pair of Ospreys and several Great Blue Herons also occur. And the only known nesting ground of the Fox Sparrow in Nova Scotia is on these wooded islands where the bird's rich, melodious song, "the expression of irrepressible joy," is at its best as it rings through the moss-carpeted glades. Blackpoll Warblers nest on these islands and Lincoln's Sparrows are found on the adjacent mainland.

Another seabird assemblage of great interest every year is on Hertford and Ciboux Islands, in the Atlantic four miles off the mouth of St. Ann's Bay on the northeast side of Cape Breton Island. Such notable birds as the Common Puffin, Razorbill, and Great Cormorant breed here together with the Black Guillemot, Double-crested Cormorant, Leach's Petrel, and gulls and terns.

Among the birds of the North Atlantic the Puffin is unique. Its gaudy, over-size beak and the bespectacled appearance of its eyes seem ludicrous to the observer but evidently not to the bird. A Puffin preserves a strictly sober air at all times—even when it seems to the observer to be playing with another Puffin. I have watched two Puffins grasp each other with bills interlocked, and then engage in most strenuous wrestling, like human hand-wrestlers. Such a contest ends as quickly as it began. Those that I watched fell over a cliff. Outside their nesting burrows these birds have little to say, but in their subterranean homes they utter at times a series of moans having a distinct pattern of emphasis.

The appearance and manner of the Great Cormorants bespeak an ancient lineage and a proper pride therein. The dignity with which they conduct themselves is not lessened by the fact that they live largely on sculpins. The highlights of their plumage are always restrained and in the best possible taste.

The quietness of some of the species of seabirds breeding on these islands is fully offset by the spirited clamor of a conspicuous multitude of nesting Herring and Great Black-backed Gulls and

Common and Arctic Terns. It has been repeatedly reported that a few pairs of Common Murres breed on one of these islands, but this is unconfirmed. If any visitor succeeds in finding Common Murres breeding here, or elsewhere in Nova Scotia, the author will greatly appreciate being notified.

Some of the most interesting birds that breed in Nova Scotia do not nest in colonies. They hatch and rear their young on individual nesting territories scattered through forested tracts, large or small, in the interior of the province. For the most part, ready access to the vicinity of their favorite habitats is provided by a network of main highways and secondary roads.

One bird that provides many a thrill is the Common Loon. Its bulky nest, often on a small island in a lake, is commonly unconcealed and close to the water's edge. Where a main road runs along a lake shore, loons may feed unconcerned within a few yards of passing traffic.

The Common Raven, another large bird of great interest, is fairly common throughout Nova Scotia. Although the Common Raven seems to prefer wild areas, it also occurs in towns. This great black bird seems to spend much time in play, taking advantage of the air currents, riding the updrafts, sailing, and tumbling. According to some authorities, it is "probably the most highly developed of all birds." Larger and more rugged than the Common Crow, it is most easily recognized by its hoarse, croaking notes.

The yellow subspecies of the Palm Warbler, a common breeding bird of the bogs wherein grow scattered, stunted black spruces, is most numerous near the ocean shore of the province. The handsome Pine Grosbeak, a bird usually associated with winter, is a moderately common breeding bird in various parts of Nova Scotia, especially in the southwest and on Cape Breton Island. It is particularly noticeable in July when it gorges on the seeds in the fruit of the shadbush or wild pear (*Amelanchier*).

Other passerines of special interest that are generally distributed in the interior of the province and vary locally from common to uncommon are the Yellow-bellied Flycatcher, Olive-sided Flycatcher, Gray Jay, Boreal Chickadee, Red-breasted Nuthatch, Brown Creeper, Winter Wren, Hermit Thrush, Swainson's Thrush, Golden-crowned Kinglet, Ruby-crowned Kinglet, and Northern Waterthrush.

Ring-necked Ducks breed not uncommonly in fresh-water

marshes. The Spruce Grouse, Goshawk, and Black-backed Three-toed Woodpecker, though not really common in any area, are widely distributed in the woodlands.

The Gray-cheeked Thrush that breeds in Nova Scotia is the subspecies *bicknelli*. It is a summer resident in the western end of the province, on the wooded parts of Cape Forchu, and on Seal and Mud Islands in Yarmouth County, and has been reported in summer on some of the forested mountains of Cape Breton Island.

The forests of conifers, especially the spruces, are home to a number of parulids: The Wilson's Warbler is found near the ocean from the vicinity of Halifax eastward. The Tennessee Warbler, which is of erratic occurrence as a breeding bird, may be at times fairly common almost anywhere. The Cape May, Bay-breasted, and Mourning Warblers are to be looked for, as nesting birds, chiefly in the eastern part of Nova Scotia, especially on Cape Breton Island. The Cape May prefers the tops of tall spruces where it nests among the clusters of cones. The Bay-breasted spends much of its time in the shaded interiors of coniferous woods or of individual conifers and places its nest on a limb usually within twelve feet of the ground.

Around the salt- and fresh-water marshes in various parts of the province the Sharp-tailed Sparrow nests and utters its gushing, unmusical song.

Pine Siskins and White-winged Crossbills act as they do elsewhere and breed erratically in most parts of the province. It is thought that Evening Grosbeaks nest on Cape Breton Island. Any evidence of this species breeding in any part of Nova Scotia will be most welcome.

Nova Scotia is fortunate in being one region where that majestic bird, the Bald Eagle, may still be observed frequently and fairly easily. Scattered pairs nest on the eastern mainland; greater numbers breed along the Cabot Trail and among the forest-clad mountains of Cape Breton Island where the Eagle is a common and inspiring sight. A few years ago an ornithologist counted a dozen Eagles along 150 yards of Baddeck River.

May every bird watcher who visits Nova Scotia be richly rewarded in the search for new and interesting species. Local members of the fraternity will be glad to welcome him and happy to lend a hand.

# DOWN EAST IN MAINE

## Allan D. Cruickshank

*Why do I even try to introduce Allan Cruickshank? Anyone who reads this book will know him well either as a photographer whose pictures have been used in over 175 books and countless magazines; as an author of over a half-dozen books and unnumbered short articles and parts of books; as a teacher at the Audubon Camp of Maine where he guided the instruction in ornithology and served with distinction as "dean of women" for twenty-two summers; as a lecturer who has introduced Audubon Screen Tours to many communities and entertained countless others with his films of Texas, the Suwannee River, and the Bear River Marshes; as the recipient with his wife of several medals and awards both for nature writing and leadership in conservation; or as the present editor of* Audubon Field Notes *who whips the Christmas Bird Counts into publishable shape and always makes certain that his home area in Florida has the maximum number of species.*

*Allan Dudley Cruickshank, born in the Virgin Islands in 1907, became a resident of New York at the age of two, and graduated from New York University. After brief periods of employment with the schools on Long Island and in the American Museum of Natural History, he went to work for the Audubon Society in 1935 and, except for a two-year stint with the U.S. Army Pictorial Service during World War II, has been on the staff ever since.*

25

*So much for the career data; now for a personal note. Among the twenty-five eager young students in my very first bird class—held at the Lost River Nature Camp in New Hampshire—was a slip of a girl named Helen Gere. On learning that I was photographing birds this quiet Quakeress showed me some pictures of Barn Owls taken, she said, by a friend named Allan who lived on Long Island. They were excellent shots and I praised them highly. The course lasted only two weeks but before it was over we were all as familiar with the habits, behavior, and talents of Allan Cruickshank as we were with the attributes of the Black-capped Chickadee which nested in a fence post outside the classroom door.*

*The next I heard they were married and in due time I met the man myself—friendly, effervescent, ever ready with a joke or a witty sally. And then I found out that he was a member of a gang—a tight, confident little group, including among others Roger Peterson and Joe Hickey, who ranged the wild country in and around New York City, weekend after weekend, season after season, looking for birds. They were a terror to all timid bird watchers who crossed their path. At first they terrified me, a loner at bird watching, but gradually I came to feel at ease in their presence and to trust them. It is obvious that my trust is complete now or I never would have asked Allan Cruickshank to write here about Maine— my native state.*

Maine, our northeasternmost state, is ideal vacationland. Its summers are relatively cool, the countryside is varied and picturesque, and a large portion of it remains attractive wilderness. Many summers spent exploring the Belgrade Lakes, Rangeley Lakes, Moosehead Lake, and the always exciting Mount Katahdin wilderness with its Spruce Grouse, Black-backed Three-toed Woodpeckers, Gray Jays, and Pine Grosbeaks have only increased my enthusiasm for the Pine Tree State.

Almost anywhere in Maine is superb vacationland, but for the bird watcher the most exciting areas lie along the coast. A straight line drawn from the southern tip of the state at Kittery to the northeasternmost point near Eastport measures only 230 miles. Yet this shoreline is so irregular that if the high-tide mark were traced along its deeply cut bays, harbors, and inlets, and around its islands, the length of shoreline would stretch to approximately 1,300 miles.

The mouth of the Kennebec River divides the Maine coast into two major sections. Southwest of this point the shore is essentially low with numerous sandy beaches and extensive saline marshes irregularly broken by rocky ledges. Northeast of the Kennebec the coast is more rugged with conifer-coated, granite promontories boldly pushing into the pounding surf, and a thousand or more islands and ledges adding to the scenic beauty. On Mount Desert Island, Cadillac Mountain rises majestically from the ocean to an elevation of 1,532 feet, the loftiest point on the Atlantic Seaboard north of Rio de Janeiro.

The majority of the outer islands are treeless, with grasses, ragweed, and seaside angelica growing profusely behind barnacle-coated rocky shores. On many of these islands are nesting colonies of gulls and cormorants. The Savannah Sparrow is usually the dominant, and often the only, passerine inhabitant.

Most of the inner islands are heavily coated with climax red and white spruces. Frequently these trees are picturesquely draped with delicate banners of gray-green usnea lichen, and there from mid-May to late July the Parula Warbler's sizzling trills rival the buzzes of Black-throated Green Warblers, and the tinkling songs of Slate-colored Juncos.

Anyone wishing a good comprehensive introduction to the biology of this coast should attend a two-week session at the Audubon Camp of Maine. Here teachers trained in the study of birds, plants, insects, and marine biology stress the ecological picture with emphasis on the interrelationships among all living forms. The camp is located on Hog Island, the Todd Wildlife Sanctuary in Muscongus Bay, one of the most beautiful areas on the entire Maine coast. It should be emphasized, however, that everyone attending this institution is expected to participate fully in three courses, a rather rugged but exciting and most worthwhile schedule.

Listen to any group of ornithologists talking about field adventures in Maine, and invariably Matinicus Rock leaps into the conversation. On this tiny oceanic island nest some of the most interesting birds in all North America. Bird watchers dream of visiting it and spending at least one night there in a tent or sleeping bag. Many have tried repeatedly to visit it and failed. A lucky few have sailed there on smooth seas, landed without difficulty, and departed as easily. But potential danger lurks in the wind and the sea, and a sense of adventure and uncertainty arises whenever plans to visit the Rock are made.

It is easy to go as far as Matinicus Island, the largest of eight islands comprising the Matinicus Archipelago, approximately fifteen miles from the nearest point on the mainland. Every Tuesday, Thursday, and Saturday at 7:30 A.M. a sturdy mailboat bearing passengers, freight, and mail leaves Rockland, sails southward between Owls Head and Vinalhaven in Penobscot Bay, and about 10 A.M. reaches the little fishing hamlet of Matinicus on Matinicus Island. The boat returns to Rockland the same day.

This is an exciting trip any day from early June through September. Within the first half-hour hundreds of Herring and Great Black-backed Gulls have been sighted. Small groups of Laughing Gulls and occasionally a few dainty non-breeding Bonaparte's Gulls are discovered. Most ledges as well as spar buoys, nuns, and other coastal markers are decorated with Double-crested Cormorants, many of them in picturesque spread-eagle pose. The experienced observer can usually pick out one or two of the larger, stockier Great Cormorants. Oddly enough, this rare summer bird is the only cormorant expected in winter along the Maine coast.

By the time the boat passes Owls Head, excellent studies of Common Eiders, Ospreys, Black Guillemots, and Common and Arctic Terns have been made. All three scoters are a possibility.

Usually the Surf Scoter predominates and the White-winged ranks second. By this time a few Common Ravens have sailed near, their long wedge-shaped tails and graceful soaring flight easily distinguishing them from the smaller Common Crows.

Beyond the Vinalhaven–Owls Head line the mailboat plows across open ocean, and possibilities of rarer oceanic species increase. The experienced observer immediately becomes more alert and carefully scans the water in all directions. Occasionally I have seen Sooty Shearwaters, Greater Shearwaters, Wilson's Petrels, and Leach's Petrels in this area. The stormier, foggier, and wilder the weather, the more chances there are that these pelagic birds will be driven in from their more normal feeding areas farther from shore. The Manx Shearwater probably occurs annually and you should always be on the lookout for this small black-backed visitor from the Old World.

From late July through September you are almost certain to see flocks of phalaropes riding on the waves. Normally the Northern Phalarope outnumbers the Red. The birds are most frequently found feeding near extensive rafts of floating marine algae. The greatest flights are usually correlated with unusual concentrations of whales, which in turn are correlated with great movements of fish. On several occasions I have seen many thousands of phalaropes in a single flock just outside Penobscot Bay. Thousands of chattering phalaropes erupting from the ocean to open a path for an oncoming boat is one of the most stirring sights I can remember.

Anytime during the summer you may see an occasional jaeger in determined falcon-like flight trying to rob a tern or gull of its food. But it is not until the major southward movement during August and September that you can be sure of seeing these exciting aggressive birds. Some weeks the Pomarine predominates, other times the Parasitic. At anytime you may consider yourself fortunate to see the more delicate Long-tailed Jaeger.

As the boat sails alongside of Matinicus Island the rich organ-like songs of Swainson's Thrushes, the sweet whistles of White-throated Sparrows, and occasionally the emphatic *Whoops! Three beers* of the Olive-sided Flycatcher are heard above the chugging of the motor. In the spruces near the docks Parula, Myrtle, Black-throated Green, and Bay-breasted Warblers are usually in evidence. But all such passerine birds may be found on the mainland surrounding Penobscot Bay, so slight attention is usually given them. Even ordinary oceanic birds do not hold the interest now, for five miles to the south appears Matinicus Rock. It looks like a fairy-tale castle rising from the sea, and to many a person access to it seems as unobtainable as the mythical pot of gold at the end of the rainbow.

But those who have laid careful plans and made the proper arrangements feel increasing excitement as they glimpse the tiny island. Anxiety mounts: Will the journey onto Matinicus Rock now be canceled by a suddenly rising sea? Will the lobsterman keep his appointment to transport the gear and bird watcher to the Rock?

Plans to visit Matinicus Rock should be cleared through the United States Coast Guard Station in Rockland. When the necessary permission is obtained, the next step is a telephone call to the Rock to determine the names of lobstermen who work in the waters near the Rock. Arrangements for transportation to the Rock may then be made with a Matinicus Island lobsterman. It is wise to telephone the Rock again shortly before boarding the mailboat to make sure landing is possible at that time.

If all goes according to plan, equipment is soon transferred from the mailboat to the small lobster boat swaying below it. Presently Matinicus Island recedes in the distance, and famous Matinicus Rock looms higher and higher. Arctic Terns constantly overtake the boat and fly on toward the Rock. Groups of Black Guillemots rise abruptly a few yards before the bow. Suddenly a Common Puffin whirrs by and the trip is already a success.

Well outside the surf, which even on a calm day surges high on the rocks, the lobsterman tosses an anchor overboard. A Coast Guard man smears grease on the tracks leading from the boat shed down a very steep grade and into the water. Suddenly a dory carrying another Coast Guard man leaves the shed, plunges down the rails, hits the water with a tremendous splash, and then rides easily beyond the surf. Once more the bird watcher and his equipment are transferred, and the Coast Guard man rows to a place in front of the runway. After watching the waves intently for a few minutes he suddenly thrusts the dory forward, steering it exactly between the rails. A hook is snapped on the dory, and a windlass slowly pulls it up the slope and into the shed. The bird watcher has achieved his goal and landed on Matinicus Rock.

The Rock is an impressive oval-shaped mass of granite jutting abruptly sixty feet above high-tide mark. While its twenty-three acres are mostly bare rock, interspersed above high tide are rich growths of grasses, harebells, yarrow, and sedum.

The lighthouse buildings are grouped tightly near the southwest end with the tower of massive granite blocks rising from the highest point of the island. Nevertheless several severe autumn and winter storms in the last century have swept waves completely across the Rock and even smashed the glass at the top of the tower. The seaward side of the Rock is protected by high broken cliffs, and from this rugged seawall there is a gentle downward slope toward the mainland. Even though this landward side is bordered with low rocks, landing is often dangerous or impossible and should not be attempted without the aid of the Coast Guard and their special landing equipment. The island is regularly pounded by heavy seas, swept by strong tides, and subject to sudden dense curtains of fog. It is not unusual for the fog horn to roar its warning for forty-eight or more hours at a time. While this trip demands careful plans and sensible precautions, no bird watcher should let these essentials deter him from visiting Matinicus Rock. It is an experience that will never be forgotten. The potential dangers, the necessary precautions, help make it even more indelible.

More than seventy-five pairs of Common Puffins now nest on Matinicus Rock, the southernmost colony of this species on our Atlantic Coast, and the only breeding place for this species in the United States. This clown-like alcid with its dignified upright posture, its trim black and white plumage, its over-sized gaily colored red, blue, and yellow bill, its deliberate rolling, pigeon-toed walk, is the favorite bird of many bird watchers. Puffins returning to their nesting cavities beneath giant rocks will often hold five to seven small silvery fish in their unique bills. Invariably I find myself staring at these birds in amazement, and wondering how any bird can hold several slippery fish in its bill and then pursue and catch others far beneath the surface.

I have never visited Matinicus Rock without seeing one or more Razorbills, and I have been assured that in recent years a pair or two have even nested here. A third alcid, the Black Guillemot, is the most abundant member of its family on the Maine coast. This species nests commonly on islands south to Muscongus Bay. Its glossy chocolate-black plumage, large white shoulder-patches, and bright red-orange legs make it an unusually handsome species. In flight its wings move so rapidly that it reminds me of a giant black-and-white bumblebee buzzing over the waves. In most areas along the Maine coast its favorite food is a small red rock eel, and these birds are frequently seen with bright rock eels dangling from the bill as they fly toward a crevice to feed the young.

More than 1,000 pairs of Arctic Terns sometimes nest on Matinicus Rock, some eggs placed in well-built grassy nests, others deposited in a mere crack in a rock. How exciting it is to watch these dainty, graceful "sea swallows" with their long deeply forked tails, their blood-red bills and feet, and their effortless, bounding flight. Little wonder that they are among the greatest migrants in the world. Some Arctic Terns nest within 450 miles of the North Pole. In winter they migrate to the southern parts of the Southern Hemisphere and a few may even reach antarctic waters. Those nesting on our islands cross the Atlantic before heading south. Young birds banded on the eastern coast of North America have been picked up dead in Europe and Africa.

Of all the birds nesting on the Maine coast the Leach's Petrel or "Carey Chicken" is probably the most exciting, romantic, and mysterious. To know it well, many a night must be spent on Matinicus Rock or another of the oceanic islands where it breeds. This bird's habitat is the open ocean. It seldom approaches the coast except during wild stormy weather. It comes ashore on isolated ancestral breeding islands only under cover of darkness, and only because it requires a place to lay and incubate its single, mostly white, dove-like egg. Even though a hundred or more pairs of Leach's Petrels nest on Matinicus Rock, the uninitiated could spend an entire day there and yet be unaware of the presence of these birds. Experts familiar with petrels can locate their burrows readily by sniffing the air for the characteristic musty petrel scent.

All day and sometimes for several days without relief, the incubating birds remain silently in their burrows. Not until about an hour after the final glow of light has vanished from the western horizon do the first incoming petrels bound like giant moths above the island. Later their mellow, staccato, half-purring songs fill the air. The muffled, chuckling responses of their mates underground can be heard if one is sitting near a burrow. After a brief ceremony the new arrival replaces its mate in the nesting hole, and the relieved bird bounds far out over the ocean to take its turn at feeding, often not returning for several days. Incubation takes an amazing six weeks—undoubtedly because there is intermittent incubation, both birds often leaving the egg unattended for days at a time.

Finally the young bird hatches, a bluish-gray, almost shapeless, fluffy mass, looking surprisingly like the sweepings from a vacuum cleaner! For nine or ten weeks this bird remains in its underground home, fed nocturnally by its parents. It grows quite plump, and appears to be exceeding its parents in size. Eventually the parents abandon it, the young bird grows restless, it loses weight, and finally under the cover of darkness a remarkable inherited rhythm of behavior sends it bounding out into the night and away from the island to join other Leach's Petrels on and above the endless waves. Probably not until it is old enough to breed will this bird return to land—its ancestral island, Matinicus Rock.

# THE NEW YORK CITY REGION

## John Bull

*Born in 1914 in New York City, reared and educated practically in the shadow of its skyscrapers, John Bull first became interested in birds as a Boy Scout—and has been actively interested in them ever since, in various ways.*

*From 1942 to 1959 he served the United States Customs as a feather specialist, concerned with the protection of wild birds by preventing importation of their plumage. In 1952 he studied tropical birds in Panama; in the winter of 1961 he led Audubon Wildlife Tours in Florida; and in the following winter conducted an elementary course in ornithology at the American Museum of Natural History where he is currently engaged as a research assistant. He has written a book,* Birds of the New York Area *(1964).*

*John Bull will tell you in the following pages about the astonishing number of bird species which have been recorded in the New York City area and the existing opportunities for bird watching. It would seem that a New Yorker need never travel to see birds. All he has to do is wait and the birds will come to him.*

Despite the fact that New York City is one of the world's largest metropolises with sprawling, thickly settled suburbs which monopolize the landscape for miles around, it has much of interest in the way of birds. As many as 412 species have been

reliably recorded in the New York area, and rarely a year passes when one or more new species are not added to this imposing list. At one time or another nearly one half, or 190 species, have bred in the area where, for over a century, many keen field workers have noted and reported assiduously the ever-abundant and diversified birdlife.

There are two reasons why the New York City area, even though in the Temperate Zone and relatively small, should possess such a rich avifauna. The first is that the city is strategically situated on the Atlantic flyway in the path of migrant hordes which use both its coastal and inland routes. The second is that it has a great variety of habitats ranging from the ocean and its beaches to inland wooded hills, some of which attain elevations of 1,800 feet.

In the New York City region, north meets south. The outer coast of Long Island is the summer home of the Great Black-backed Gull and the Glossy Ibis, the former on its southernmost nesting grounds and the latter at the most northerly outpost of its breeding range.

Long Island—extending 120 miles into the Atlantic—has always been famous for its rare birds. To its shores come strays from European waters, hurricane-borne vagrants from the tropics, and visitors from the north, south, and west. Long Island is the best area by far for bird watching within the New York City region. Of the 412 species reported in the New York area, all but a dozen have been recorded on Long Island. The south shore, from Brooklyn to Montauk Point, offers the bird watcher exciting rewards throughout the year. Besides the ocean itself, there are numerous bays, lagoons, and inlets; both sandy and rocky coastline with barrier beaches, salt marshes, and extensive tidal flats; coastal ponds and fresh-water marshes; and both deciduous and coniferous woodlands. The coniferous woods are known as the pine barrens.

There are five localities on or near the south shore of Long Island that are outstanding for birds. Proceeding from west to east, the first is Prospect Park in the heart of Brooklyn. Situated as it is, at the junction of the coast and the Hudson Valley, it receives many migrating landbirds from both routes in the fall. In spring it has a notable variety of warblers—thirty-eight species have been reported.

The Jamaica Bay Wildlife Refuge, a short distance to the east of Prospect Park and wholly within New York City limits, is a "must" for the visiting bird watcher. With the dramatic New York skyline as a backdrop, this refuge contains some of the best concentrations of waterbirds in the northeast and is attractive to the field ornithologist because of the relative ease with which birds may be observed. A walk around the elevated dikes enables one to scan the fresh-water pond on one side and the bay and salt marsh on the other. In the immediate vicinity of the dike are scattered plantings of shrubs and trees that grow well in sandy soil and provide food and shelter for many birds.

During the cooler months, Jamaica Bay Refuge is the home of numerous waterfowl. In summer, various marsh-loving birds —grebes, bitterns, ducks, and rails of several species—nest. On the open sandy areas Common and Least Terns, Black Skimmers, and Piping Plovers breed. Two kinds of egrets, several herons, and best of all, the Glossy Ibis, have reared their young in the refuge in recent years.

During both spring and fall, the flats on both the bay and pond sides of the sanctuary are frequented by enormous flocks of shore-birds. The list of species is long and some are quite rare. The Avocet, two godwits, all three phalaropes, the Buff-breasted Sand-piper, and many others have been reported from time to time. Usually seen every year are two Old World specialties—the Cur-lew Sandpiper and the Ruff. The Curlew Sandpiper should be looked for on the flats, preferably on an in-coming tide, during the last two weeks in May when it is almost invariably in bright-colored breeding plumage and easily distinguishable from its cus-tomary associates, the Dunlins, which are there in abundance. Oc-casionally it occurs in the company of Knots and is then not as readily discernible. The more unpredictable Ruff has been seen anytime from late March to June or even July. This species shuns the open flats and is found either in the marshy vegetation along the pond shore or, more rarely, on the upland consorting with Killdeers. Rarely is more than one Ruff reported each season, but one spring quite recently, two different males in full breeding rega-lia and a Reeve (female) were observed all on different occa-sions. In the winter months, Lapland Longspurs and Ipswich Spar-rows (both regular in this area) may be seen in the open fields. On calm days, the Ipswich Sparrows may be observed to advantage perching on snow fences.

To enter the Jamaica Bay Refuge the visitor must have a permit which may be obtained by writing the Department of Parks, Arsenal Building, Central Park, New York City.

For the fall migration of landbirds—in September and October especially—Riis Park, on the ocean front and just fifteen minutes drive west from Jamaica Bay, is particularly good for wind-drifted passerines. This is also a place where the introduced House Finch occurs the year round.

An hour's drive to the east brings one to Jones Beach. For an entry permit to this area's most outstanding spot, Tobay Pond, write Town Supervisor, Oyster Bay, Long Island. Tobay Pond is notable for its breeding Gadwalls and Yellow-crowned Night Her-ons. It is a good place for waterfowl. If one is lucky, he may see a European Widgeon among the hordes of other ducks. On the bay side, or in the vicinity of Jones Inlet, good-sized flocks of Brant may be observed. In late May and early June, if an onshore wind is blowing, Sooty Shearwaters may be seen usually inshore, close to the beaches.

It is in the autumn, however, that the birding is at its best anywhere along the south shore of Long Island. From late August through October, flights of landbirds occur with the passage of each cool front. All three falcons—the Peregrine Falcon, Pigeon Hawk, and Sparrow Hawk—are regularly seen along the beaches. The Pigeon Hawk and Sparrow Hawk occur in large numbers. On the outer coast the following woodpeckers and passerines are reported each fall, in small numbers to be sure, but nevertheless regularly: Red-headed Woodpecker, Western Kingbird, Mockingbird, Loggerhead Shrike, Philadelphia Vireo, Orange-crowned Warbler, Connecticut Warbler, Yellow-breasted Chat, Blue Grosbeak, Dickcissel, Lark Sparrow, and Clay-colored Sparrow. Of course, most of these may also be observed at certain other localities along the south shore between Riis Park and Montauk Point.

In the areas of Moriches Bay and Shinnecock Bay, the bays (especially the inlets), the dune road paralleling the ocean, and the beach front itself are all very productive places, particularly during the summer and fall. At least one pair of Oystercatchers nests here each year, and the extensive flats at low tide are excellent for the larger shorebirds—both species of godwits, Willet, and Whimbrel —and numerous smaller shorebirds as well. One may observe breeding Roseate Terns nearby and nearly every year, in late summer and early fall, a few Royal and Caspian Terns. In September and again in late May and early June, especially after storms, one should visit the inlets and the ocean itself for the possibility of seeing shearwaters, jaegers, and phalaropes. After hurricanes one should be on the lookout for tropical and subtropical vagrants.

The Montauk region, from the lighthouse on the bluff overlooking the ocean to the jetties at the inlet near the fishing station, is at its best, ornithologically, in the dead of winter from December to March. The colder and stormier the season, the better it is for bird watching, except during a northwest wind when it is a waste of time. A strong easterly gale, or the period immediately afterward, yields the most notable rewards. At that time one should stand on the bluff at the base of the lighthouse and face the sea. From late August to early November, if the wind is from an easterly direction, Cory's Shearwaters come in close to shore.

From about mid-December on, the populations of certain wintering seabirds build up. Vast flocks of scoters mill about the point in spectacular fashion. Among them a few eiders of both species may be seen, the colorful adult drakes in the minority. Gannets, gleaming white and jet black, plunge from high in the air into the sea after fish. More rarely there may be Harlequin Ducks or some of the alcids—perhaps Dovekies, Razorbills, Thick-billed Murres, or possibly even a Black Guillemot. Occasionally Black-legged Kittiwakes may be observed from the shore, particularly during or after storms. Perched on the jetties at the inlet to Lake Montauk are Great Cormorants which are seen to best advantage in February and March when the adults assume their breeding plumage. Purple Sandpipers occur on the rocks here as they do on almost every other rock pile along the entire shore. And on nearly all the coastal ponds and bays one sees the introduced Mute Swan.

In New York City itself is Central Park where the section, known as the "Ramble," is especially good during the spring migration when landbirds, particularly warblers, may be seen to advantage. In fact, it is quite possibly the very best place to observe small landbirds because the trees are low and the warblers concentrate in a few choice spots. Bronx and Pelham Bay Parks are noteworthy for owls during the colder months, although all of the regular woodland species have been seen in one or the other of these parks during the course of a single winter.

Highly odoriferous, but hardly scenic, are the sewer outlets and garbage dumps, so attractive to the gulls. The truth is, the more potent the stench, the more productive the area for the rarer gulls. At such places in and around New York Harbor, especially on Staten Island and in the "Jersey meadows," the observer, if patient and enduring, may hope to spot the two regular-occurring European species—the Little Gull and Black-headed Gull—almost always associating with the numerous Bonaparte's Gulls. "Black-headed Gull" is a misnomer; the adult in breeding plumage has a *brown,* not black, hood. Look for these two, and the Iceland Gull as well, at sewer outlets particularly. The Iceland Gull is usually in the company of the superabundant Herring Gulls and the less common Ring-billed Gulls. The Glaucous Gull may be seen on occasion at the garbage dumps and, if one is extremely fortunate, the rare but now regular Lesser Black-backed Gull, another visitant from the Old World. The best time of year to look for these rare gulls is between November and April, although the Little Gull may be observed in late spring and early fall as well.

In New Jersey, one of the outstanding areas for birds is Troy Meadows, a vast fresh-water marsh, possibly the finest in the region. An elevated boardwalk cuts through the heart of this marsh where, during April and May, one may see and hear Wood Ducks, American and Least Bitterns, Soras, Virginia Rails, Common Gallinules, Common Snipe, and many other marsh-loving birds. The bird watcher should start early in the day, preferably before dawn, and remain in the area until mid-morning. He should then go to the nearby Boonton Hills for woodland birds. This is one of the places where Blue-winged and Golden-winged Warblers nest and sometimes hybridize, thus providing an opportunity for one to see the hybrid forms—the Brewster's and Lawrence's Warblers.

Also worthy of note are the Bald Eagles which may be seen in winter along the Hudson River above Yonkers, chiefly when there is heavy ice on the river. The best locality is at Croton Point. As many as a dozen or more have been seen at one time from this spot. Occasionally, the Eagles may be observed, perched on cakes of ice, as far south as the George Washington Bridge.

Unfortunately the site at Massapequa, Long Island, formerly occupied by a colony of European Goldfinches, is now a housing development. There is no area today where one may be certain of finding these birds.

The visiting bird watcher is invited to attend meetings of the Linnaean Society of New York, held at the American Museum of Natural History at 8:00 P.M. on the second and fourth Tuesdays of each month, excepting June, July, and August when meetings are held on the third Tuesdays. Guests are always welcome. They may find out when and where to look for certain species, how to reach the choice areas, and, if interested, may participate in the field trips which are conducted several times each month.

# BULL'S ISLAND, SOUTH CAROLINA

## Alexander Sprunt, Jr.

*Alexander Sprunt, Jr., ornithologist, conservationist, author, and lecturer, is a Carolinian through and through. He was born in Rock Hill, South Carolina, in 1898, and has lived all his life in Charleston—except while attending Davidson College in North Carolina, serving in the U.S. Navy during World War I, and taking on numerous assignments for the National Audubon Society.*

*After returning from the Navy he joined the staff of the Charleston Museum and continued there until 1934. It was then that the National Audubon Society enlisted his help while still permitting him to keep his home in Charleston. For the next six years he was supervisor of the Society's southern sanctuaries, and thereafter, until he retired in 1963, he performed various other tasks for the Society. He led wildlife tours in Florida, Coastal Carolina, and elsewhere; he made a long lecture tour each year; he taught at the Audubon Camp of Texas; he undertook numerous research projects.*

*Over the years Alexander Sprunt has managed to find time for writing. His principal books are* Dwellers of the Silences *(1935),* South Carolina Bird Life *(1949)* with E. Burnham Chamberlain, The Warblers of America *(1957)* with Ludlow Griscom and others, and a revision, published in 1954, of *A. H. Howell's* Florida Bird Life *(1932). His contributions to technical journals and pop-*

41

*ular magazines total about 300. Recently Davidson College, his alma mater, awarded him an honorary doctorate for his "outstanding work in the field of ornithology."*

*I presume that all of us have our emerald isles—places that seem to us just about as close to paradise as places can be. Alexander Sprunt's emerald isle is Bull's Island off the coast of his home state. After you read here what he says about it, you will understand why.*

To the bird-watching fraternity Bull's Island stands as an exceptional place, a gem, and—to employ an overworked designation—a mecca, having been visited by hundreds and hundreds of observers from all over the United States. As far as the Atlantic seaboard is concerned, Bull's Island occupies a position at the top, or near the top, of any list of bird-finding areas and for good reason.

This barrier island, some seven miles long and a little more than a mile wide at its broadest point, lies off the South Carolina Low Country, some fifteen miles north of Charleston, and forms the southern horn of a crescent which is Bull's Bay. Salt marshes rim its landward side; the Atlantic Ocean washes its eastern beach; and between the ocean and the marsh are magnificent woodlands of giant magnolias, huge pines, and venerable live oaks, all wreathed in yellow jasmine, wild grape, and smilax together with graceful banners of Spanish moss.

This is historical country. Englishmen first looked on the shores of Carolina from Bull's Bay in 1670. Audubon, with his friend John Bachman, collected and observed birds on the nearby mainland and may have visited Bull's Island although there is no direct evidence. Of late years Bull's Island has been owned by Gayer G. Dominick, who built a comfortable house and maintained a duck-turkey-deer shooting preserve for fourteen years. In 1936 the house was sold to the government and the island, turned over to the U.S. Fish and Wildlife Service, became a unit in the Cape Romain National Wildlife Refuge which now encompasses 34,716 acres in Charleston County.

The house, Dominick House, is operated as a concession and has accommodations for fifteen to twenty guests. Visitors wishing to visit the island should make reservations in writing to Dominick House, Awendaw, South Carolina. You should always allow time for confirmation of specific dates so that you may be met at the mainland dock. Visitors coming by water in their own craft should follow the chart of the Inland Waterway.

Since the visitor must depart for this magnetic attraction from a mainland landing, directions are necessary. The Ocean Highway, US Route 17, is the key road either north from Charleston or south from McClellanville, headquarters for the Cape Romain Refuge. Fifteen miles north of the former or twenty miles south of the latter, a paved highway, See-wee Road, branches off Route 17 at a general store, the See-wee Supply Company.

Turning east on this adequately marked road you proceed for three miles to a dirt road forking to the right. Turn right and travel two miles to Moore's Landing, the take-off point for Bull's Island. At the Landing an acre of government property which is fenced and watched provides safe parking for the car. The boat will be waiting.

On the way in from Route 17 watch and *listen* for Brown-headed Nuthatches and Red-cockaded Woodpeckers in the bordering pinelands. If you are fortunate, you *might* see the unpredictable Bachman's Warbler which has frequented this area for the past few seasons and which all American bird watchers, including Roger Tory Peterson, would "give their shirts" to see.

Once on the boat, the run to Bull's Island is often hardly less than spectacular. If it is taken at half-tide or at least when some of the oyster banks and mudflats are exposed, the trip is a bird watcher's paradise. Most of the Oystercatchers of the Atlantic Coast concentrate in this area in the winter; scores may be seen at any time of year. I once told a visiting ornithologist that I would show him Oystercatchers at Bull's Island by the hundreds. He was polite, but his expression showed a disbelief that did not vanish until we were on our way to the island and he was counting Oystercatchers literally by the hundreds.

Marbled Godwits, multitudes of Black-bellied and Semipalmated Plovers, milling flocks of Dowitchers, Ruddy Turnstones, Willets, and "peeps," with an occasional Long-billed Curlew frequent the exposed bars and flats. Gulls, terns, and Black Skimmers cruise the air while grebes and mergansers skitter across the bow or vanish beneath the surface of the marsh-bordered channel. Red-winged Blackbirds and Boat-tailed Grackles chatter from the grasses, sometimes drowned out by the clacking calls of Clapper Rails, the "marsh-hens" of the Low Country. Ospreys and Bald Eagles, Turkey and Black Vultures patrol the sky with here and there a high-line formation of silhouetted ducks and shorebirds passing as if on review.

Once on the island, the visitor never fails to be awed by its semi-tropical, out-of-this-world aspect. The truck which meets the boat comes up to Dominick House, set in a wide lawn which is surrounded by venerable live oaks and stately pines. You go to your room, change to field clothes, and set forth.

You walk first, perhaps, down the Beach Road which runs from Dominick House to the ocean, a veritable tunnel beneath the trees except where it crosses the open expanse of House Pond. Here ducks leap upward on both sides, and squadrons of them move away in the grass. You enter the tunnel again to see, almost by the road itself, a wild Turkey gobbler raise its head from foraging and scratching among leaves, an antlered buck clearing the track with a bound while a jet-black fox squirrel, ensconced in the crown of a cabbage palm, stares intently at you, his white nose and ears gleaming from the shadows.

Another opening looms ahead, an arch of light beyond the trees. You come out amid the sand dunes which fringe the magnificent seven-mile beach. Low-growing grasses and plants contrast with clustering clumps of wax myrtle. Myriads of tiny tracks are delineated in the sand—those of beach mice, Ground Doves, and the ghost-gray Ipswich and Savannah Sparrows.

You walk to the beach. Ricks of shells lie along the high-water mark at the edge of hard-packed sand, and only the murmur of the surf breaks the stillness. Although there are numerous places on the island where one feels remote, perhaps none equals the beach. For miles, there is not a soul, not a house—nothing but the sun and the tide-swept sands. Far down the strand a flock of gulls stands at the edge of the surf. Nearby a Sanderling speeds along on invisible legs, instantly bringing to mind the delightful poem, "One Little Sandpiper and I." Gray and yellow sand crabs scuttle away in straight lines—sideways or backward—their pale colors and soundless activity well meriting the name "ghost crab."

On this beach too the great sea turtles come lumbering in from the surf under the June full moon to lay their eggs among the dunes. In the Low Country the full moon in June is known as the "turtle moon" because this is the only time of year that these huge creatures come ashore.

Later in the day you might explore the woodlands penetrated by a system of well-kept sandy roads. Deer, raccoons, and squirrels roam the pine-oak-magnolia forest. Otter and mink cruise the dykes and banks of the three main pond areas—Summerhouse, Middle, and Moccasin Ponds and the largest, Jack's Creek Basin, which covers many acres in the north end of the island. Alligators are completely at home in these ponds and some attain impressive size. For several years Summerhouse Pond was dominated by a monster fourteen feet long.

In and about these watery domains the show of ducks and, in recent years, geese is something to behold. There is probably no one place in eastern United States along the Atlantic flyway where so many species of waterfowl can be seen with so little effort. I have on many occasions seen as many as fifteen species in a day. The all-time record for the island is, so far as any of us know, twenty-three species recorded a few years ago by the artist-ornithologist John Henry Dick. The proximity of the ocean to the island's fresh-water areas and the adjacent salt marshes make such a list possible. Let us consider the ponds in order: From a high bluff, crowned with a screening of live oaks one can look down on Jack's Creek Basin where you may expect to see Mallards, Black Ducks, Gadwalls, Pintails, Blue-winged and Green-winged Teal, Ruddy Ducks, and Hooded Mergansers. From the deep woods that surround Moccasin Pond it is well to look for Wood Ducks, Ring-necked Ducks, Lesser Scaups, Redheads, and Canvasbacks. At Summerhouse Pond there is a dam which separates the fresh water from the salt marsh. This is the place to look for a few Buffle-heads, Red-breasted Mergansers, and Common Goldeneyes. And along the beach you may look out at flocks of American and Surf Scoters, rafts of Greater Scaup, and an occasional Oldsquaw. Where else could one view such a pageant in a day? And now we may add geese because Canada Geese occur in steadily increasing numbers every winter with always a scattering of Blues and an occasional Snow. So much for the waterfowl.

An unadulterated strain of the wild Turkey lives on Bull's Island. During the several winters that I conducted the Audubon Wildlife Tours here, Turkeys were seen on several occasions while we were at the dining-room table for breakfast. Of course this may not be some bird watchers' idea of the way to find wild Turkeys— without the slightest effort, while consuming bacon, eggs, grits, toast, and coffee—but it can still be done.

Pileated Woodpeckers are commonplace as are other members of the woodpecker family. Painted Buntings, known as "non-pareils" in the Low Country, are spring and summer residents.

Warblers and sparrows of various species, Chuck-will's-widows, flycatchers, swallows, wrens, thrushes, vireos, tanagers, Rufous-sided Towhees, and Cardinals are resident or seasonal.

Rarities of course cannot be predicted. They would not be rarities if they could. However, the following birds have occurred on Bull's Island in the past and may do so again: Frigate-bird, Roseate Spoonbill, European Teal, Swainson's and Rough-legged Hawks, Gray Kingbird, Ash-throated Flycatcher, Bachman's Warbler, and Black-throated Gray Warbler. You cannot expect to see these species, but some people have been that fortunate.

Before you leave the island, you must take a look at the guest book which reads like an ornithological directory. The American Ornithologists' Union was entertained on Bull's Island during its Charleston meeting of 1938. Status names liberally besprinkle the pages.

After your visit to Bull's Island, you will have no difficulty understanding why we sometimes call this lovely spot The Emerald Isle. Regardless of the time of year or the birds you may see, you will have one impression above all others—the impression of greenness, luxuriant greenness.

# THE FLORIDA KEYS: PAST AND PRESENT

## Robert Porter Allen

*Robert Porter Allen was born in South Williamsport, Pennsylvania, on April 24, 1905. Descended from a family that had settled in Lycoming County in 1760 and named for his paternal grandfather, who was for many years prominent in Pennsylvania legal and political circles, he had only to follow the pattern set up by the three generations before him and enter the family law firm.*

*But from the age of ten young Bob Allen had only one interest —birds. Everything else was secondary. High school was a bore, Lafayette College simply an ordeal. He broke all kinds of rules so that he could spend as much time as possible in the woods and fields. At first he was an avid hunter who could bag a dozen yellowlegs in one short trip along the river near his home. Later, on the campus of Lafayette, he spent more time banding birds than perusing books.*

*On the advice of Louis Agassiz Fuertes, to whom he wrote in 1925, he transferred from Lafayette to Cornell University where he remained for only three months before the death of his father forced him to look for employment. During the next three years he worked his way on tramp steamers twice around the world and to Europe, South America, and the Orient. In 1930, upon meeting his future wife in New York, he gave up the sea and joined the staff of the National Audubon Society as librarian and general handyman.*

*Eventually he became the Society's research director, a post from which he retired in 1960.*

*A self-trained field biologist, Robert Allen was one of the most competent and respected in the profession. Specializing on endangered bird species, his investigations took him from Alaska and the Canadian Arctic south to Yucatan, the West Indies, and the Caribbean Islands of South America. The results are embodied in his three research monographs published by the National Audubon Society: "The Roseate Spoonbill" (1942), "The Whooping Crane" (1952), and "The Flamingos: Their Life History and Survival" (1956). Besides these monumental reports he wrote three books—* The Flame Birds (1947), On the Trail of Vanishing Birds (1957), Birds of the Caribbean (1961)—*and a children's book,* The Giant Golden Book of Birds (1962). *In recognition of his skill in significant research and writing, he received the Nash Conservation Award (1955), the Brewster Medal of the American Ornithologists' Union (1957), and the John Burroughs Medal (1958).*

*In 1939 Robert Allen moved with his family to Tavernier in the Florida Keys. Here, after his retirement and until his death in 1963, he spent most of his time writing. In 1962 he wrote the following reflection on the Florida Keys, his home for the last twenty-five years of his life.*

On any grand tour of places in North America that are of major interest to the growing number of migratory bird watchers, the Florida Keys are high on the list. Because of the balmy climate, most visitors prefer to arrive during the winter months, and by now it is generally understood in birding circles that this is the best season in which to see those species that are of chief interest.

In January and February a number of birds are nesting on the multitude of mangrove keys that are scattered across the shallow green waters of Florida Bay, chiefly within the boundaries of Everglades National Park—Roseate Spoonbills, Great White Herons, Reddish Egrets, Ospreys, and Bald Eagles among them. For some years the National Audubon Society has conducted boat tours to the main nesting sites, while major feeding places in tidal sloughs along the Overseas Highway are becoming well known to most visitors. A few birders show up during the warbler migration, which under the right conditions of wind and frontal movements can be quite spectacular, especially in spring. Summer vistors find a relatively quiet scene, but the hot and often humid air of this season is enlivened by the cheerful dawn and dusk songs of our resident Cardinals and the chatter of the Gray Kingbirds, while the daylight hours are filled with the sweetly sad and endlessly repeated notes of the Black-whiskered Vireos. White-crowned Pigeons, nesting for security reasons on isolated keys in the bay, fly to the tangled hammocks that remain on larger islands like Key Largo, Plantation Key, the Matecumbes and others in the Big Pine Key area, there to feed on poisonwood berries, pigeon plums, and other fruits and seeds.

In addition to the resident species that are new on many a visitor's life list, there is always a possibility of rarities. In winter the Scissor-tailed Flycatcher and Western Kingbird are usually present in certain areas, but with such regularity that they can no longer be counted as rare. The colorful little Bananaquit shows up every now and then, and the Cuban Golden Warbler, first found nesting near Key West in 1941, is now a common breeding species on a number of keys in Florida Bay and is moving north to the mainland. White-winged Doves appear occasionally, and there is always an outside chance of finding a Zenaida Dove or even the elusive Key West Quail Dove. Offshore there are many possibilities, provided the visitor charters a boat that can go well out into the Gulf Stream.

Interest in the avifauna of the Florida Keys goes back many years, but the influx of large numbers of bird-minded visitors is rather recent. Beginning in a small way in the mid-1930's, there was a marked increase in the period immediately following World War II, thanks largely to Audubon Wildlife Tours. Christmas Bird Counts are now conducted each year in several Florida Keys locations—Key Largo–Plantation Key, Lower Matecumbe, Marathon–Grassy Key, Big Pine Key, and Key West—with a large number of enthusiastic participants, including visitors from other areas, who are always welcome. Some twenty years ago the writer had difficulty finding even one fellow spirit willing to join him on a Christmas Count! Considering the fact that the habitats are not very diversified, and that open water makes up a large part of most of the census areas, the number and variety of birds observed is quite respectable. The Key Largo–Plantation Key area is the only one that has produced more than 100 species on a single count day, and it is 80 per cent open salt water (ocean and bay), 10 per cent tropical hardwood hammock, 5 per cent mangrove swamp, and 5 per cent mudflats. It is the only count area of the 661 throughout the United States and Canada that consistently reports breeding species during the specified period of the counts.

Most of these and many additional facts are now fairly well known to the peripatetic bird watchers who travel hither and yon each year, from one avian mecca to another, and who have a way of gathering great stores of local information. Sometimes these expert and highly mobile birders, who usually know exactly what they want to see in any given area, move through at such a clip that the real atmosphere of a region may elude them. Very often this is unfortunate, for the local history of human events and ecological change may provide a backdrop against which the present flora and fauna can be seen in more interesting perspective. This is especially so in the Florida Keys where rather drastic changes are of recent date or still in progress and where both the past and the present, with all their color and interest, are frequently obscured by such modern improvements as neon lights and the many other distractions that seem to clutter a new and busy highway.

It is useful to remember, for example, that only a little more than a half-century ago the Keys were a long string of virtually unspoiled islands with very few inhabitants and no connection with the mainland of Florida except by sailboat, naphtha launch, or steamer from Key West. These islands have a marine origin, and the very ground we live on is superimposed on the remains of a Pleistocene coral reef. Geologists now tell us that during the Sangamon interglacial phase, approximately 100,000 years ago, this ancient reef lay beneath from ten to thirty feet of ocean. When the ice of the Wisconsin glacier receded, perhaps 20,000 years ago, the level of the ocean dropped to a point some 100 meters (328 feet) below present tide marks. At that time the shoreline was probably some eight or nine miles farther out than it is now. Actually, during this period, it comprised the coast of the Florida mainland, and the present bays and channels have been created by the slow and inexorable rise of ocean levels. The present offshore reef, with

its variety of living corals, came into being when the right ecological conditions were attained, for these creatures require certain
water depths and temperatures and clear sea water that is not
contaminated by alluvial deposits. The highest elevations built by
the ancient Sangamon Reef make up the islands we know today as
the Florida Keys.

Other changes have come with the introduction of plant
debris, seed pods, and other vegetation, carried ashore by the
combined action of the sweeping curve of the Gulf Stream, the
prevailing southeast winds, and the occasional violent hurricanes.
The flora of the Keys is essentially tropical, brought in by wind
and tide from Cuba, the Bahamas, and other parts of the West
Indies. Much of south Florida has benefited from these natural
introductions. But the Keys, being frost-free, have a unique variety, and the original hardwood hammocks must have been magnificent—mahoganies, lignum-vitaes, Jamaica dogwoods, mastics,
gumbo-limbos, strangler figs, and many others. Along with the plant
debris came the precocious seedlings of *Rhizophora,* the red mangrove, land-builder extraordinary and undoubtedly one of the earliest pioneers. Added to these was a fine array of palms and
palmettos and an infinite variety of tropical vines and shrubs.

Compared with the length of time required to shape these islands, cover them with vegetation, and populate them with animal
life, the arrival of man on the scene is rather recent. Who the first
Indians were and where they came from is only conjecture. It is
logical to suppose that they came by sea—wandering Lucayans,
Arawacks or Caribs—paddling large seagoing canoes hacked from
the giant trunk of the ceiba tree. When the first white man cruised
off these shores early in the sixteenth century, they were inhabited
by the Calusas, a tribe that dominated the west coast of the Florida peninsula from Tampa Bay southward and on through the
Keys. Here they lived in huts built of logs and the fronds of the
thatch palm. They hunted, fished, and even planted some vegetable
crops. Juan Ponce de León sailed from Puerto Rico in 1513 and
reached the Florida coast. As he cruised south along the Keys, his
were the first Western eyes to see and describe this region.

In the years that followed, many seafaring adventurers were
wrecked on the Florida Reef, including vessels from the Spanish
plate fleets. Wherever they met them on even terms, the Spaniards

saw in the natives a source of slave labor for their cane fields and other growing enterprises in New Spain, and it wasn't long before Indians on the Keys and elsewhere in Florida came to regard any white man as a deadly enemy. Most shipwrecked people who managed to get safely ashore on the Keys were tortured and killed by the natives, but a notable and very fortunate exception was Hernando D'Escalante Fontaneda. On his way from New Spain to school in Europe in the year 1545 or 1547, Fontaneda, at the age of thirteen, was captured by the Calusas somewhere on the Keys. His life was spared and he lived among these savage people for seventeen years, until rescued and returned to Spain, where he wrote his brief but highly interesting memoirs.

Most of Fontaneda's remarks about wildlife are on the practical side, being chiefly concerned with animals that could be used as food. He mentions the abundance of deer, the presence of "very large bears," and describes a form unknown to Europeans, the raccoon ("fat and good to eat"). Large on the Calusa diet were turtles, spiny lobsters, and fish of many kinds. There was also a creature that Fontaneda calls a "sea-wolf," probably because it yelped or barked and lived in the sea. When it came ashore on the rocks it was sometimes killed and eaten, but only by "principal persons," so it was a sort of gastronomic status symbol in this barbaric but highly class-conscious society. Most authorities believe that this animal was the West Indian seal, now apparently extinct.

It is our loss that Fontaneda was not interested in birds and does not mention them at all. The first visitor to the Keys who had any such interest was Bernard Romans, who rounded Cape Sable and sailed as far as the Lower Keys in the year 1771, more than two centuries after Fontaneda. In 1824, Titian R. Peale, the Philadelphia artist, apparently visited the Keys, for he brought back specimens of the Reddish Egret, Zenaida Dove, and the White-crowned Pigeon. But the first major ornithologist to visit the Keys was John James Audubon, who arrived at Indian Key near the present Islamorada on April 24, 1832. In the following weeks he was at Key West, then a bustling seaport, Mule Key, the Tortugas, and Sandy Key off Cape Sable. At Sandy Key he collected three Greenshanks, a European shorebird resembling our Lesser Yellowlegs. These are the only specimens of this species ever recorded on this side of the Atlantic. In the vicinity of Key West he found the Zenaida Dove and Key West Quail Dove in some abundance, two species that have virtually disappeared from this region. He also found and described the Great White Heron.

When Audubon went ashore on Indian Key 130 years ago, the presence of man had already made its mark. Although Audubon tells us something of the wreckers he met and transcribed the "Wrecker's Song" ("Key Tavernier's our rendezvous, at anchor there we lie . . ."), he fails to mention how sophisticated the wrecking community at Indian Key had become. From other sources we learn that Jacob Housman's Tropical Hotel, built in 1826, not only had a bar, but a billiard table and bowling alley! Of course, in spite of such luxuries, these were still pioneer days, and the bloody Indian massacre at Indian Key took place eight years after Audubon's visit, in 1840, when Housman's hotel, billiard table, and bowling alley, among other things, went up in smoke. But it takes more than an Indian massacre to discourage the determined enterprise of man. Indian Key was still a place of importance when Gustavis Würdemann of the U.S. Coast Survey stayed there in 1857. But the surrounding country was still a little-known wilderness and Würdemann saw large flocks of molting flamingos in upper Florida Bay, which he visited in early August with a half-breed Seminole as a guide.

In many respects the Florida Keys remained a wilderness until the Flagler railroad route was pushed through from the mainland all the way to Key West in the years 1906–1912. This enterprise ended the insular isolation of this unique area and virtually destroyed the last large tracts of virgin tropical hardwood forest. The development that we witness with sad and somewhat wistful eye today has inevitably followed. But one outstanding feature of this region has not been destroyed: the frost-free, tropical climate. With the exception of some of the wading birds, the avifauna in general continues to prosper, and some species have actually increased as a result of land clearing operations. A few West Indian forms may still be moving into this area and visiting bird watchers who are especially interested in rarities should keep their eyes open. Someday even the European Greenshanks may show up again somewhere in the Florida Keys. It has happened before!

# Eastern Mountains and Foothills

**IN NORTHERN NEW HAMPSHIRE**
Tudor Richards

**HIGH CHEAT OF WEST VIRGINIA**
Maurice Brooks

**GREAT SMOKY MOUNTAINS NATIONAL PARK**
Arthur Stupka

# IN NORTHERN NEW HAMPSHIRE

## Tudor Richards

*Tudor Richards grew up in Groton, Massachusetts, where he was born in 1915. His interest in birds, begun in New Hampshire where he spent his boyhood summers, was nurtured by courses under Ludlow Griscom and Glover M. Allen while he was an undergraduate at Harvard and under Josselyn Van Tyne at the University of Michigan from which he received a master's degree in wildlife management.*

*Following the war Tudor Richards returned from service in the Pacific to make his home in New Hampshire. Here during the first several years he worked for the White Mountain National Forest, carried on state-wide waterfowl surveys for the New Hampshire Fish and Game Department, and taught forestry and conservation at St. Paul's School. Since 1954 he has been employed by the University of New Hampshire Cooperative Extension Service as County Forester of Cheshire County. In the summers, since 1958, he has been instructor in wildlife at the Lost River Conservation Camp for Teachers.*

*Tudor Richards has provided a welcome "shot in the arm" to bird study and conservation in the Granite State. His writings, photographs, and lectures on natural history and conservation have been effective in making his conservation-conscious state ever more mindful of the need for preserving natural areas and wildlife resources. Under his guidance as president since 1953, the Au-*

*dubon Society of New Hampshire has been promoting field trips, taking bird censuses, compiling bird lists, acquiring refuges, establishing nature centers, and helping in other ways to save the state's natural resources.*

*As one will surmise on reading what he has to say here, a great interest of Tudor Richards is the distribution of birds in New Hampshire, a subject on which he hopes to publish at length in the near future. Meanwhile he continues to lead field trips at all seasons from the north country to the Isles of Shoals, several miles off the New Hampshire coast.*

The avifauna of northern New Hampshire's forests, bogs, lakes, and mountains includes many species nesting at or near the southern limits of their ranges. Since it has been investigated off and on by both professional and amateur ornithologists for nearly a century, it was once thought by us to be so well known as to need no further study. How wrong we were has been proven recently by our turning up something unexpected during almost every visit to the region.

Northern New Hampshire, the region of which I speak, is roughly triangular in shape—about 100 miles north and south by fifty miles east and west across its base. What we call the North Country is the blunt northern tip; the White Mountains comprise the larger southern portion. The region is bounded on the west by the Connecticut River that flows between New Hampshire and Vermont; on the east by Maine; on the north by Quebec; and on the south by the southern limits of the White Mountains.

Although the North Country contains a number of 3,000-foot mountains, it is distinguished chiefly by its extensive spruce-fir flats and sizable lakes and ponds. The best known of these, the Connecticut Lakes in Pittsburg, are drained by the Connecticut River. The largest lake in the area is Umbagog, the most westerly of the Rangeley Lakes, with about one-third of its fifteen-square-mile surface in Maine. It is drained by the Androscoggin River which courses south to the White Mountains and then east into Maine.

Far more scenic than the North Country are the White Mountains with about forty-six peaks exceeding 4,000 feet, including Mt. Washington—the highest peak in northeastern United States

—nearly 6,300 feet above sea level and 5,800 feet above the lowest land in the region. Clear, cool, rushing streams, small mirror-like ponds, and impressive, glacier-carved, U-shaped ravines are characteristic of these mountains. Much of the finest scenery can be viewed from the highways that go through the Notches—Pinkham, Crawford, and Franconia—all of which are close to 2,000 feet at their heights-of-land. Their only rival in the North Country is Dixville Notch.

Precipitation in the region is well distributed throughout the year and ranges from forty to sixty inches annually. Winter temperatures frequently drop to 30 degrees or more below zero and snow accumulations often exceed four feet. Summers are cool in the mountains, but warm in the valleys where agriculture, principally dairy farming, is still practiced on the better soils.

White pine, commonly associated with hemlock, is the most conspicuous tree of the valleys. On sites above 1,200 feet or so, red spruce and balsam fir are the predominant conifers. In the North Country white spruce is also common, while on consistently wet sites, black spruce and tamarack are characteristic of more acid conditions and northern white cedar of more limy areas. The most abundant of the broad-leafed trees are the "pioneer" species —pin cherry, gray and paper birches, and trembling aspen—and the "climax" northern hardwoods—beech, sugar maple, and yellow birch. Red oak is common in the lower valleys, red maple on many of the more moist sites at lower altitudes. Paper birch is the one hardwood that accompanies spruce and fir at the timber-line whose elevation averages about 4,500 feet.

Though the cutting of commercial timber has extended all over the region during the last 100 years, there are still remnants of virgin forest in many inaccessible places, especially at high altitudes. The timber-cutting practices of the several large paper companies that own most of the North Country, while not ideal, are a little better than those on many of the small private holdings in or near the valleys. Most of the White Mountain area is part of the White Mountain National Forest where multiple use and selective cutting are now the rule and where important natural areas are being preserved.

The Connecticut Lakes area embraces Pittsburg, the largest and most northern township in New Hampshire, and adjacent

Clarksville. With the exception of one year-round resident, Mr. Fred T. Scott, who has long been interested in the local birdlife, no serious bird students seem to have worked here until the 1940's. By that time Mr. Scott was already familiar with the more notable permanent-resident birds such as the Spruce Grouse, Black-backed and Northern Three-toed Woodpeckers, and Gray Jay, and had recorded the rare Barrow's Goldeneye in winter.

In the last fifteen years a small group of us have, with Fred Scott's help, learned still more about the birdlife of Pittsburg. Undoubtedly my most exciting day in the field was July 11, 1951, when Fred introduced me to the "Moose Pasture," a semi-open bog on the north side of a dammed-up stream, called East Inlet, above Second Connecticut Lake.

We left our car at the dam and were approaching the Moose Pasture by canoe when we heard young woodpeckers calling from a dead stub right beside the water. After paddling as close as possible, I stepped out of the canoe, and started to shinny up the stub. At that moment a bird popped out of the nest hole just above me and flew to the trunk of a nearby tree. It was a well-developed juvenile male Northern Three-toed Woodpecker, one of New Hampshire's rarest species and a "life bird" for me. While I was fumbling with my camera, trying to photograph the young bird, the larger and more clearly marked adult male appeared.

Not wishing to upset this family further we pushed on by canoe and soon landed at the edge of the Moose Pasture. Once well within it we could see all around us acres of small, widely-spaced black spruces and tamaracks, interspersed with cassandra and other low shrubs. A little farther away was a ring of taller spruces and, in the distance, the virgin spruce-covered slopes of 3,000-foot mountains. I felt as though we were deep in the wilderness of northern Canada.

As we stood there, we could hear the remarkably loud, rollicking song of a Ruby-crowned Kinglet coming from one of the taller spruces. This tiny species, a favorite of mine, was considered at that time to be a rare summer resident in New Hampshire. Soon afterward we came across a female Spruce Grouse with four young. Her chicks safely hidden, she perched in the top of a small spruce while I photographed her at short range. A few minutes later two Gray Jays flew by, gliding as usual at extraordinarily slow speed between wing flaps.

A suggestion of even better things to come was a pleasing, warbling trill, descending in pitch and then rising to a new high— the song of a Lincoln's Sparrow. Very shortly we heard others nearby and eventually counted six pairs—more than all the Lincoln's Sparrows previously recorded during the nesting season in the whole of New Hampshire.

I have returned often to the Moose Pasture. My last visit was with about twenty-five members of our state Audubon Society, walking, or perhaps I should say "bushwhacking," in from the logging road north of the bog to find Fred Scott waiting for us. We were lucky enough on that trip to discover some moose signs and to see two Pine Grosbeaks fly by. Before the day was over, we had recorded other northern birds such as the Black-backed Three-toed Woodpecker, Yellow-bellied Flycatcher (in deep, heavily-shaded conifers), Gray Jay, Common Raven, Ruby-crowned Kinglet, Philadelphia Vireo (aspens and alders), Wilson's Warbler (alder and brushy spots), and Rusty Blackbird (swampy places) —all between East Inlet and Scott's Bog, a similar impoundment close by.

Since the time of my first visit to East Inlet, the several thousand acres of virgin spruce on the flats and lower slopes have been reduced by lumbering to the bogs and one fine 125-acre block at Norton's Pool just above the Moose Pasture. Like all the rest of the area, this belongs to the St. Regis Paper Company which is preserving it for the time being and, we hope, permanently. Meanwhile, of the birds listed above, the Raven and Ruby-crowned Kinglet have increased while the Spruce Grouse, Gray Jay, and three-toed woodpeckers all seem to have become scarcer as their habitat has been reduced.

Apparently no one has found a nest of the Northern Three-toed Woodpecker in Pittsburg since 1954, though occasional adult birds are still seen. We and others have, however, come upon a number of nests of the Black-backs. Most of them have been in dead spruces and birches, rarely in living trees, from three to thirty feet (average ten to fifteen feet) from the ground. Although Black-backs are relatively quiet and easily overlooked, their nests are not hard to find if they contain young birds because these keep up a constant chatter that can he heard a great distance away.

There are many other good places to look for northern birds in the Connecticut Lakes area besides East Inlet and Scott's Bog. Common Loons and Common Mergansers still occur on the lakes despite increasing harassment by motor boats. In the vicinity of Back Lake there are several small ponds worth investigating. One, called Mud Pond, often has Common Goldeneye or Hooded Merganser families on it, and there are interesting landbirds in an adjacent bog.

The Lake Umbagog area compares favorably with Pittsburg for landbirds and is superior for waterbirds. A dam, built seventy-five years ago at a point four miles down the Androscoggin River from the Lake and two miles upstream from Errol, raised the level of the River, the Lake (to 1,245 feet), and the Magalloway River which joins the Androscoggin just below its mouth. It also flooded many oxbow ponds, bogs, and swamps, creating perhaps the best wetlands in the interior of New Hampshire.

Except for the pulpwood that often jams the rivers until summer and the log booms designed to keep it from getting sidetracked, the whole water area above the dam is ideal for exploration by canoe. As a matter of fact, canoeing here is a great challenge and crossing one of the log booms a rather sporting proposition. Actually these may soon be a thing of the past since reports have it that there will be no more log drives.

The great ornithologist William Brewster visited Umbagog almost every year from 1871 to 1909, his findings eventually being published in *The Birds of the Lake Umbagog Region of Maine* (1924–1938). Although he listed such rarities as the European Widgeon, Eskimo Curlew, Ruff, and Passenger Pigeon, his greatest contributions were in determining the status, and compiling information on the life histories, of the more regular residents and visitors.

To me the most fascinating spot at Umbagog is a bog which Brewster named "Floating Island." This is on the north side of the Androscoggin, about two miles above the dam, and can be reached by canoe from the edge of the highway, just above the dam, through a backwater paralleling the river. In or along the marshy edge of this bog I have been fortunate to find, during the nesting season, a number of birds unrecorded in summer by Brewster anywhere in the Lake Umbagog region. The list includes the Green-winged and Blue-winged Teal, Ring-necked Duck, Common Snipe, Ruby-crowned Kinglet, Long-billed and Short-billed Marsh Wrens, Palm Warbler, and Lincoln's Sparrow. Although we have found the Palm Warbler here during several different summers, it is unrecorded elsewhere in New Hampshire at this season.

Other noteworthy summer birds of the area are the Pied-billed Grebe, Common Goldeneye, Hooded Merganser, Bald Eagle, Osprey, Sora, Tennessee and Wilson's Warblers, and Rusty Blackbird. Of the rarer permanent-resident birds that Brewster found in the Umbagog region, the Spruce Grouse, three-toed woodpeckers, and Gray Jay are all apparently still present, but less common than in the Connecticut Lakes country. The Common Raven, on the other hand, has recently increased to an extraordinary degree. In February 1963, for example, I encountered thirty-one of these awesome birds in one flock.

Another dammed-up portion of the Androscoggin River that is excellent for waterbirds, and more accessible, is the Pontook Reservoir in Drummer, midway between Errol and Berlin. Though virtually the same marshbirds and waterbirds occur here in summer as at Lake Umbagog, a group of us were amazed in the summer of 1962 to see a Common Gallinule swimming around among the cattails. On an earlier visit to Pontook, crouching low in a canoe I drifted to within about 100 feet of a female Black Duck with a record number of young—no less than fifteen! They were diving repeatedly, presumably for some kind of food.

The best places for waterbirds and marshbirds in the White Mountain area are Cherry and Little Cherry Ponds in Jefferson. Both are quite inaccessible. The former can be reached by walking along one of the railroad tracks that passes by it. The well-known ornithologist Horace W. Wright used to visit these ponds in the course of his investigations of the local birdlife, and published the results in 1911. In recent years we have found these ponds even more rewarding than they were in his day, adding to the list of summer residents the Pied-billed Grebe, Green-winged Teal, Wood and Ring-necked Ducks, Hooded Merganser, Virginia Rail, both marsh wrens, and Rusty Blackbird. There is also a breeding season record of the Common Gallinule. Previously this list of summer residents included only the Great Blue Heron, American Bittern, Black Duck, and Sora. In the forest pond surrounding Cherry Pond one can expect to find in summer the Yellow-bellied Flycatcher, Boreal Chickadee, Ruby-crowned Kinglet, and Wilson's Warbler, and there is a good chance of finding such birds as the Evening Grosbeak and White-winged Crossbill.

Cherry Pond is also well worth visiting during migration. One late-April day a few years ago, I counted on its placid surface seven Red-necked Grebes and twelve Horned Grebes. On a more recent late-April day at dusk there were a dozen species of waterbirds on the pond and at its edge several Woodcock and one Snipe performing overhead at the same time. On another occasion, late in May, I was thrilled to see at the pond four Solitary Sandpipers, eighteen Greater Yellowlegs, one or two Dunlins, about fifteen Dowitchers, and a sizable flock of Least Sandpipers as well as two Black Terns.

The Audubon Society of New Hampshire has recently acquired the land around the two ponds and, with the cooperation of the state, has set up the Pondicherry Wildlife Refuge, using the old name of Cherry Pond.

The avifauna of the White Mountains is interesting among other things for the altitudinal distribution of such nesting birds as the thrushes and wood warblers. Though the Wood Thrush seems to have been unknown in our region before the 1890's, it is now common in the valleys along with the Veery and, to a lesser extent, the Hermit Thrush. The Hermit Thrush ranges up to at least 3,000 feet and the Swainson's Thrush, which is scarce below 1,000 feet, is common to abundant from about 1,500 feet to timberline at about 4,500 feet.

The minimum altitude at which the (Bicknell's) Gray-cheeked Thrush nests is higher than that of any other summer-resident bird of New Hampshire. The Gray-cheek nests only rarely below 2,000 feet and is most common in the vicinity of timberline. The only place, south of New Hampshire, where the Gray-cheek is known to nest is on Mt. Graylock in Massachusetts. Its song is somewhat similar to that of the Veery except that it goes up instead of down. Though not as musical, the notes have an eerie quality that is especially in keeping with the bird's wilderness setting and the dusky hour of the day when it is most often heard.

About two dozen species of warblers nest in northern New Hampshire, from the Pine Warbler, in the lowest parts of the valleys, to the Blackpoll Warbler, which is uncommon below 1,500 feet but abundant at higher altitudes. On any day in early summer the Blackpoll's insect-like trills can be heard from the dense stands of conifers on many mountain slopes below timberline. Another denizen of the mountain conifers but generally less common than the Blackpoll, except in the flats of the North Country, is the handsomer, yet hardly more musical, Bay-breasted Warbler. A third mountain species deserving special mention is the shy Mourning Warbler which prefers the shrubbery of semi-open areas and has an unusually liquid song. Three species of warblers—the Nashville, Myrtle, and Magnolia—are found at all altitudes below timberline.

Among the many other birds typical of the White Mountains are the Broad-winged Hawk, Yellow-bellied and Olive-sided Flycatchers, Boreal Chickadee, Red-breasted Nuthatch, Winter Wren, Golden-crowned Kinglet, Purple Finch, Pine Siskin, Slate-colored Junco, and White-throated Sparrow. Another summer resident that is turning out to be less rare than we have been regarding it is the Philadelphia Vireo. This bird sings so much like the Red-eyed Vireo that it is often overlooked. The Spruce Grouse, though uncommon to rare, is well distributed, especially at higher altitudes. The three-toed woodpeckers and Gray Jay are rare and not well distributed, but are reported more or less regularly.

Above timberline the birdlife of the White Mountains is disappointing. The only common nesting species are the Slate-colored Junco and White-throated Sparrow. In recent summers the Pigeon Hawk, Common Raven, and Water Pipit have all been reported at least once. The Raven, in fact, seems to be becoming regular and to be nesting. To make up for the general lack of birds above timberline are the lovely displays of alpine flowers, the most conspicuous being two arctic species, the Lapland rose bay and the diapensia, that bloom in early June, and a buttercup-like local species, the mountain avens, that blooms later.

Within the White Mountains the most rewarding of the highly-specialized bird habitats are the bogs and the ponds with boggy edges, such as Bog Pond and Lonesome Lake in Lincoln. One of my favorite spots is Church Pond Bog, in the Passaconaway Valley, off the Kancamagus Highway. The bog can be reached by a trail that starts at the U.S. Forest Service campground and makes a loop to beautiful Church Pond. One route goes through the bog; the other along the edge of it. The open section, sixty to seventy acres in extent, is one of the very few places in the mountains where the Lincoln's Sparrow is known to be a summer resident. Along the edge of the open section or in the nearby wooded part, just east of the main road from the campground, I have also found in summer the Spruce Grouse, Boreal Chickadee, Ruby-crowned Kinglet, Tennessee Warbler, Rusty Blackbird, Evening Grosbeak, Red and White-winged Crossbills, and Pine Siskin.

In the winter the countryside of the White Mountains and the North Country is enlivened by finches—Evening and Pine Grosbeaks, Purple Finches, Common Redpolls, Pine Siskins, American Goldfinches, and occasionally Red and White-winged Crossbills. Some of us think that northern New Hampshire is never more attractive than on a still, cold winter's day during a "northern finch" year, with White-winged Crossbills swooping in flocks around cone-laden evergreens, filling the sparkling air with their gay, canary-like songs, while the surrounding mountains, all dazzling white with snow, seem almost close enough to touch. In any case—winter or summer, spring or fall—there is much for the bird watcher to see and enjoy in northern New Hampshire.

# HIGH CHEAT OF WEST VIRGINIA

## Maurice Brooks

*Maurice Brooks, professor of Wildlife Management at West Virginia University and forester at West Virginia University Agricultural Experiment Station, fitted into his chosen career quite naturally. Born in French Creek, West Virginia, in 1900, the son of a naturalist and nephew of three others, he attended West Virginia Wesleyan College and received his A.B. and M.S. degrees at West Virginia University. Except when studying in Michigan, teaching in Minnesota and Virginia, and taking an occasional expedition, this true son of West Virginia has never been away from the state for prolonged periods. His eight years as a member of the West Virginia Conservation Commission, seven years as director of the West Virginia Conservation School, and eight years as chairman of the West Virginia Biological Survey Committee all testify to his devotion to West Virginia.*

*His special interest is in the Appalachians from Canada to Georgia, where he has worked throughout the whole range and explored most of the higher peaks of the entire system. He views all of this country, particularly his favorite spot, the Cheat Mountains of West Virginia, with the eyes of a veteran forester-ornithologist, knowing the forest types and the species of birds each forest type entertains, yet being continually baffled and intrigued by certain species which, at the northern or southern limits of their ranges, behave strangely by not nesting where they do*

67

*normally. Here Professor Brooks leads us on a leisurely ten-mile trip through his beloved Cheat Mountains. Expect no dramatic moments, but rather a gentle teaching, a quiet questioning, and—we shall forgive him—a little boasting. The boasting is justified when you consider that it comes from one who first camped in the Cheat Mountains as a boy of ten and has since been returning to them at every opportunity.*

The river, and the mountains which rise on either side of it, are both called Cheat. Just who first used the name, or why he chose it, is unknown, and seems likely to remain so. One theory has it that the river was named Cheat because of its tricky and deceptive waters—sudden floods, hidden eddies, and potholes that threaten canoeists and swimmers. A local historian, with more imagination than facts, once ascribed the name to a legendary French noble, the Marquis de Cheath. Unfortunately, no one else had ever heard of the titled Frenchman. Over along the Greenbrier, a rival stream with plenty of credits of its own, old-timers say that Cheat River naturally took its name from the character of the inhabitants who lived beside it, but they speak in prejudice.

No matter about the name. If its hidden origin adds a dash of spice, that is to the good. One thing is sure: outdoorsmen seeking birds, flowers, trees, salamanders, mammals, or just the scent and feeling of the North Country will not be disappointed. The river may deceive, but the mountains never.

Cheat River rises in eastern West Virginia and flows in a northwesterly direction until it joins the Monongahela a mile or so on the Pennsylvania side of the Mason and Dixon Line. Draining a complex series of mountain ridges, the river has five principal forks, the one to the west being longest and largest. If you will point your right hand, palm up, to the south, elongate the thumb, and part the fingers, it will help you to see the picture. The digits are, of course, the five forks; spaces between them represent mountain ridges.

The elongated thumb is Shavers Fork, epitome of the best that Cheat has to offer. Its source is a moss-rimmed spring at an elevation of 4,760 feet above sea level. On either side are spruce-clad ridges a few feet higher. It is many a mile before these ridges are crossed by a highway. By the time the river descends to 3,000 feet it becomes a respectable stream, perhaps the largest at that elevation in eastern United States.

To the east the next fork is Glady, fine trout water, draining some of the best wild Turkey country in West Virginia. Beyond Glady Fork is Laurel Fork, center in recent years of intensive beaver activity. In one three-mile stretch of this stream there were eighteen occupied beaver dams. Eastward of Laurel is Dry Fork, so-called because it flows over limestone into which the stream sometimes disappears. Dry Fork rises on the slopes of Spruce Knob, West Virginia's highest point. Gandy Creek, which flows through a spectacular cave, is a tributary. At the upstream entrance to this cave Barn Swallows, according to the ancient habit of their kind, still plaster their nests against the limestone ledges.

Farther north and east, Blackwater Fork, last of the five, gathers its waters in the great sphagnum bogs of Canaan Valley. This placid stream, darkened by acids from decaying vegetation, will not stay placid long; soon it plunges sixty-five feet to form Blackwater Falls, and then tumbles and roars through three-mile-long Blackwater Canyon.

Thus is Cheat River formed, and even to its mouth it flows through mountain country. Just east of its junction with the Monongahela is Chestnut Ridge, most westerly of the high Allegheny escarpments. It holds tenaciously to its North Country character also; a few miles upstream from the river's mouth Common Ravens nest on the sandstone cliffs and Veeries sing in hemlock thickets that border the stream.

Forests, most of them second-growth, clothe the ridges which Cheat River drains. This is not agricultural land; there is some open bluegrass where limestone outcrops, but for the most part the country is wooded. And as the forests vary at different elevations, so do the birds. We shall follow them from Tygarts Valley River on the west, up the slopes of Cheat Mountain proper to the summit of Barton Knob, then across the high plateau through which Shavers Fork flows, past the "blister swamp" with its northern balsam firs, and to the summits of the eastern ridge almost 3,000 feet higher than our starting point in the valley. Our journey will be only ten miles long, but it will go, figuratively, from the mideastern states to Canada.

Tygarts Valley is low enough and broad enough to have a considerable segment of oak-hickory forest, the "central hardwoods" of the forester. Once it was oak-hickory-chestnut forest, but the blight came and chestnut is now only a remnant (but hopefully increasing) series of sprouts. Along the streams are sycamore and elms; tulip poplar and black walnut were once common, but these trees are too valuable to have been left uncut. Taken all together, the forest here is not greatly different from those in the Lower Ohio Valley.

Breeding birds, too, are, with some notable exceptions, such as might be found along the Ohio. Orchard Orioles find homes suitable to their name; Acadian Flycatchers call from almost every forested ravine; Yellow-breasted Chats perform their antics by day and by night wherever briery tangles occur. There are Blue-gray Gnatcatchers about all the larger oaks, and Cerulean Warblers may be nesting in the same groves. Prairie Warblers like abandoned fields and farmsites; when undergrowth becomes thicker White-eyed Vireos move in. Hooded and Kentucky Warblers choose wooded borders; Cardinals and Carolina Wrens are everywhere, and where there are black walnut trees surrounded by grassy openings and low bushes there is an occasional sweetvoiced Bachman's Sparrow.

Here and there, however, are variants in the ornithological pattern. Bewick's Wren is locally common; it is a rarity in the Lower Ohio Valley. *Crataegus*-dotted fields and thick stands of orchard grass have Henslow's Sparrows, while more open and windswept grasslands afford homes for Savannah Sparrows. Rose-breasted Grosbeaks prefer denser woodland than do Cardinals, but these two often nest close to each other. Oak-covered slopes have their singing Black-throated Green Warblers, a circumstance which will appear strange to those who think of this bird only in connection with conifers.

Characteristic of the unglaciated Appalachians are forested coves which occur just upslope from the broader valleys. Where gradients ease off, water is slowed in its descent, and streams tend to spread out. Leaves from higher slopes wash or blow into these sheltered areas, adding their increment to the soil's fertility. When night comes, cool air currents pour down the ravines. Everything combines to produce deep and well-watered soil, with optimum conditions for plant growth. Wildflower enthusiasts regard some of these coves (Cade's Cove in the Great Smokies is a notable example) as among the finest natural gardens to be found in eastern North America.

So unusual is growth of trees in these coves that foresters have given it a special name, "cove type" hardwoods. There is more than a suggestion of the tropics in the wealth of woody plants found here; instead of dominant positions held by one, two, or three species, in a cove there may be twenty-five or thirty common trees, with perhaps an additional twenty species only slightly less common. So favorable are growing conditions that trees reach maximum dimensions; numbers of known size-records for American trees are held by these cove-dwellers.

Mature forests of the cove type do not support a wealth of birdlife. On the slopes of the Cheat Mountains these coves are good spots for Ruffed Grouse and wild Turkeys. Pileated Woodpeckers find homes here, and Red-shouldered and Broad-winged Hawks are summer residents. Black-and-white and Worm-eating Warblers abound, as do Ovenbirds. Every stream will have its Louisiana Waterthrushes. As forests are opened up, many bird species from the valley below move in.

When cool air drainage is an important climatic factor in these coves, we often get hints of things to come farther upslope. Rhododendron sometimes forms dense tangles; and in these, Black-throated Blue and Canada Warblers occur, even at modest elevations. Hemlock stands along streams provide nesting sites for Solitary Vireos. Veeries join Wood Thrushes, and where briery fields occur Chestnut-sided Warblers move downhill.

Upward from the coves almost to the crest where an elevated plateau begins, the Cheat mountainsides are forested with beech, maples, birches, and basswood, the "northern hardwoods" of the forester. This forest is typical of much of hilly New England, and of the south shore of Lake Superior. There are striking similarities in the birdlife of all three areas.

The fat-rich triangular nuts of beech trees are prime favorites in the diet of many birds. Unfortunately, however, beech is not a dependable bearer; one good crop in three years might be considered average. Since beech is the most important food-producing plant in this forest, there are wide fluctuations in bird populations from year to year. In summer this is not so apparent; many of the breeding species are regular in their occupancy, although game species such as the Turkey will not be. Autumn and winter tell a different story. When beechnuts are abundant, Evening Grosbeaks (now occurring as fall and winter visitors about every two years in the Cheat region) are found in tremendous numbers; flocks of several thousand have been reported. Red-bellied Woodpeckers sometimes move from lower elevations, and Red-breasted Nuthatches linger later than we might expect them at these heights. So long as this rich food lasts, birds abound; when it is gone they, too, disappear.

Wood warblers present striking evidence of the curious mixed nature of this forest's biota. Species whose centers of abundance are southward meet and mingle with some whose distribution is more northerly. I have recorded thirteen breeding warblers in this forest, a pretty rich list for any area. If you still find the life-zone concept useful (and most of us who dwell in mountain lands swear by it), this is the Alleghanian province of the Transition Life Zone beautifully exemplified.

Thus far in our journey up a Cheat mountainside we have chosen to drive eastward on US Route 250, making frequent stops and short side trips. As we approach the first crest (Cromer Top in local nomenclature) we are coming to the extensive plateau which lies between the eastern and western ridges of this mountain mass. We are approaching the 4,000-foot contour, and the paved highway leads downhill until in three miles Shavers Fork of Cheat is crossed. It is time to leave our car, and to go afoot to Barton Knob, one of the rewarding summits of the Cheat Range.

The state maintains a fire lookout tower atop Barton Knob, and there is a jeep trail to the top. The hike along this begins in an area of mixed forest with red maple, yellow birch, hemlock, and red spruce being the more important species. There is also a varied and dense understory of woody plants, with rosebay rhododendron, mountain laurel, deciduous hollies, viburnums, and other attractive species. Abundance of food, with the variety of nesting niches, guarantees a good breeding-bird population.

Where recent forest cuttings are growing into blackberry thickets, Mourning Warblers are common. Along the streams (and often at surprising distances away from them) Northern Waterthrushes sing. Black-throated Blue Warblers are especially abundant, and in the spruces one begins to hear Golden-crowned Kinglets, Red-breasted Nuthatches, and Brown Creepers. Occasionally there is a Yellow-bellied Sapsucker, although these have been inexplicably rare in recent years.

At the foot of the mountain Carolina Chickadees whistled their four-note call, but they are far below us now; here the two-note whistles tell of a high population of Black-capped Chickadees. Juncos are everywhere, and Winter Wrens sing in darker spruce and rhododendron tangles. I usually see one or more Barred Owls along this trail, and there is always a good chance of surprising Turkeys.

At the summit the forest is a pure stand of red spruce, the crown sixty or seventy feet from the ground. Blackburnian Warblers nest high in these, and Magnolia Warblers build at lower elevations. Swainson's Thrushes seek high ground, particularly as the last light of evening fades, and there are a few Hermit Thrushes. Downslope we can hear the Veeries and Wood Thrushes, so four species blend their voices.

Throughout the year there are wandering groups of Red Crossbills in the Cheat Mountains, and Barton Knob is as good a place as any to look for them, particularly when a full crop of spruce cones is set. Pine Siskins are commoner in winter, but they sometimes summer here also. During one glorious June there were hundreds of White-winged Crossbills, but those vagrants are unaccountable. I confidently expect that in some future summer the Evening Grosbeaks will decide to remain and nest, although this hasn't, so far as I know, happened yet.

To switch attention to another vertebrate group, it was just under the Barton Knob tower that Leonard Llewellyn collected, and handed to Graham Netting, the first specimen of the little gold-flecked Cheat Mountain salamander, a species which has never been found away from the Cheat range. Herpetologists may find this, along with Wehrle's, Allegheny Mountain, and red-backed salamanders, in the same decaying spruce logs.

When we return to the paved highway we follow it eastward for a couple of miles, and presently notice a Civil War historical marker commemorating Fort Milroy, highest permanent fortified point occupied by Union troops during the war. Here the old grade of the Staunton-Parkersburg Turnpike leaves the present highway, and a walk up it is worth taking. There has recently been a pretty destructive lumbering job along it, but in the dead snags that remain a few Olive-sided Flycatchers call. This is rich country for warblers also, and thrushes find an abundance of nesting sites.

Again returning to US 250, we follow it through natural gardens of rhododendron and mountain laurel to Shavers Fork which we cross at 3,556 feet elevation. It is well to leave the car once more, and to hike upriver along the railroad track. Swamp Sparrows will be trilling in the alders along the stream, and Mourning Warblers are particularly abundant. In swampy areas Traill's Flycatchers nest, and Purple Finches warble from the spruce tops. Plant collectors will have a field day if they follow fishermen's trails along the river; here are northern species that seem out of place in the latitude of Washington.

Just eastward of the river crossing we begin to pass the "blister swamp," one of West Virginia's few natural stands of northern balsam fir. This swampy area affords some of the best birding on the mountains. Almost any of the mountaintop species already mentioned may occur, but there are a few specialities. During April and May evenings Woodcock "sky-dance" above open areas along the highway. At dusk here one evening we listened to three Woodcock in flight, heard two Saw-whet Owls calling nearby, while across on the slope of Gaudineer Knob a Barred Owl screamed.

This swamp is a mammalogist's "holy ground"; big gray West Virginia flying squirrels, water shrews, star-nosed moles, red-backed mice, yellow-nosed voles, and woodland jumping mice have all been taken locally. To properly confuse the botanist, early coral-root, an orchid species from the north, and Fraser's sedge, a plant prize from the southern highlands, grow almost side by side.

Warblers particularly like the blister swamp, and what a variety one finds here! Golden-winged Warblers are common, and during some years there are Nashvilles in the alders. All the other northern species are found here, and such widely-distributed species as American Redstarts, Yellow Warblers, and even Yellow-breasted Chats occur. At this point I might as well restate a claim made elsewhere. I have recorded twenty-two species of breeding warblers in this section of Cheat Mountains; until further evidence is presented, I'll let that stand as the best list from any single mountain in North America.

Of course we shall end our Cheat Mountains journey at Gaudineer Knob, each year becoming better known to the outdoor brotherhood. This vast stand of young spruce trees is, in many respects, in a class by itself, but since it has been written about, and is being written about, elsewhere, I shall merely say, "Don't miss it. At any season it will reward you."

Why are the Cheat Mountains so good for birds? The area has four of the major forest types of eastern North America, with any number of fascinating gradations between them. It is well-watered, with dense understories under the forest crown. Fire has not been a major problem, and scars of lumbering are quickly healed.

Elevation ranges from valley to summit are nearly 3,000 feet, and there are extensive areas above the 4,000-foot contour. Exposed cliffs are scarce, but many other ecological niches occur—streams, swamps, open lands, and forests—in every stage of succession. Plant life is varied enough to afford natural foods at all seasons of the year. A surprising number of woody and herbaceous species have evergreen foliage providing winter cover.

Pleistocene glaciation may well have been a major influence in creating the present complex ornithological picture. These unglaciated mountains are far enough south to have a goodly representation of bird species which we have called "Carolinian." They are, however, only about 150 miles south of the Allegheny system's farthest advance of glacial ice. We can imagine that during glacial periods vast numbers of breeding birds were forced southward. Some of them, of necessity, must have learned to occupy unfamiliar breeding niches. Habits like these, once forced on them, have been retained during the comparatively few thousand years since glacial retreat.

There is another, and to me a fascinating, aspect of local bird distribution—one to which ecologists have, I think, not given sufficient attention. Many species reach, or are near, the periphery of their ranges in the Cheat Mountains; in such tension zones, birds—and other living things—often behave strangely. Parula Warblers nest in sycamore or oak trees, Black-throated Greens occupy dry oak-hickory ridges, Black-throated Blues build in clumps of chestnut sprouts. Many of these phenomena occur when the species are nearing their altitudinal limits. Why, we do not know.

Fortunately, much of the Cheat Mountain range is within the Monongahela National Forest, which means it may be preserved in good condition. It is accessible and within reach of urban centers in the East and Middle West. I think the visitor will like what he finds here.

# GREAT SMOKY MOUNTAINS NATIONAL PARK

## Arthur Stupka

*From his early teens Arthur Stupka has been a naturalist in the truest sense, no living thing, plant or animal, failing to stir his curiosity to learn more about it. To many of us today he is not so much a naturalist as the highly informed and hospitable ornithologist at Great Smoky Mountains National Park. Indeed, we are apt to think of him and the Great Smokies simultaneously. He is the author of a* Natural History Handbook, Great Smoky Mountains National Park *(1960),* Notes on the Birds of Great Smoky Mountains National Park *(1963), and numerous articles in ornithological journals.*

*Arthur Stupka was born in Cleveland, Ohio, in 1905, graduated from Ohio State University, and later received a master's degree from that institution. He was a ranger-naturalist for one summer in Yosemite National Park in California and for another summer in Acadia National Park in Maine. In 1933 he became a full-time park nauturalist at Acadia, the first to occupy such a position in eastern United States. Then in 1935 came what proved to be his momentous move—he was transferred to Great Smoky Mountains National Park in Tennessee, where he has been for the last thirty years, serving as park naturalist and, beginning in 1960, park biologist. He and Mrs. Stupka make their home near Gatlinburg on a hill overlooking Mt. Le Conte and other peaks of the Great Smokies. Here they will continue to live after his retirement.*

*In writing here of the Great Smokies, Arthur Stupka offers no spectacular aggregations of birds. As is the case in mountain areas, the birdlife is appealing more for its quality than quantity. What he does offer are mainly forest dwellers, resident and transient, to be found along the roads and trails at different elevations. As a further inducement he speaks of the incomparable floral displays and a backdrop of lovely scenery—and even suggests by indirection that some bird watchers may become so entranced by the environment that they will neglect to look for birds. Heaven forbid!*

Great Smoky Mountains National Park, virtually *terra incognita* less than two generations ago, is now the most visited national park in the country. Millions of Americans, coming from all points of the compass make their way to this vacationland where some of the highest mountains in the eastern United States are the dominating topographic feature.

Lying between the Little Tennessee River on the west and the Big Pigeon River on the east, Great Smoky Mountains National Park comprises some 800 square miles of mountainous terrain, with altitudes ranging from 857 feet to the summit of Clingmans Dome at 6,643 feet, the highest point. As many as sixteen peaks rise above 6,000 feet. The landscape is almost completely forested, even at the highest elevations. There is no timberline.

In the variety, number, and size of their trees, the forests of the Great Smokies are without equal in eastern North America. Their magnificence is accounted for in a large measure by the high annual precipitation which averages fifty-five inches in the foothills to eighty-five inches on the highest summits. Thanks to the moisture, trees not only grow luxuriantly but rapidly. Forests devastated by fire, lumbering, wind throw, landslide, or other destructive agencies recover with impressive speed. And trees seem to grow almost everywhere—arching over watercourses, taking root on fallen and decaying trunks in the forest, and some even growing on other living trees. Approximately one-third of the total acreage of the park has escaped all manner of human disturbances in the past and is consequently a particularly choice segment.

Shorebirds and waterbirds are for the most part scarce or absent in the Great Smokies. Of the few species recorded, one-half have been noted on only three or fewer occasions. Four—the Green Heron, Wood Duck, Killdeer, and American Woodcock—have been known to breed, but always very uncommonly to rarely. Reservoirs, created by the construction of huge dams to the west and southwest of the park, attract some migrating shorebirds and waterbirds, but the park itself is largely a home for forest-dwelling birds. The streams, all of great beauty, are mostly small, shallow, rocky, cold, and fast-flowing brooks or rivulets which drain the steep mountainsides. The Belted Kingfisher, a permanent resident, and the Louisiana Waterthrush, one of the earliest warblers to appear in the spring, are the only two intimately associated with these sparkling watercourses.

To the visitor the forests of the Great Smoky Mountains are likely to appear quite hard to classify since they contain over 100 kinds of trees, many of which are intermixed. Essentially, however, the forests are divisible into six major categories: the spruce-fir, northern hardwoods, cove hardwoods, oak forests, pine stands, and other forests the most distinctive of which are hemlock stands, heath balds, and grass balds.

One will have no difficulty recognizing the *spruce-fir forest,* a Canadian Zone environment which extends from the highest sum-

mits down to approximately 4,000 feet elevation and is characterized by red spruce and Fraser fir. Where the dense coniferous pole-
stands are interrupted, the openings are often taken over by pin
cherry, yellow birch, mountain ash, and mountain maple. This is
the home of the Saw-whet Owl, Olive-sided Flycatcher, Common
Raven, Black-capped Chickadee, Red-breasted Nuthatch, Brown
Creeper, Winter Wren, Golden-crowned Kinglet, Veery, Red
Crossbill, Slate-colored Junco, and such warblers as the Black-
throated Blue, Canada, Chestnut-sided, and Blackburnian. Some of
these are at or near their southernmost breeding limits in the eastern United States; others spill over into the mountains of northern
Georgia. A few, such as the Junco, perform a vertical migration,
nesting in the higher mountains and wintering in the foothills.

The *northern hardwoods* which form a rather narrow band
around the lower limits of the spruce-fir forest are dominated by
yellow birch and American beech with a number of trees including
various oaks, red and sugar maples, mountain silverbell, eastern
hemlock, cucumbertree, and black cherry reaching their highest
limits here. A number of the Canadian Zone birds already mentioned occur in these forests along with the Yellow-bellied Sapsucker, Solitary Vireo, Scarlet Tanager, and Rose-breasted Grosbeak.

The *cove hardwoods,* found mostly at altitudes ranging from
3,000 to 4,000 feet, are open, columnar-like stands of exceptionally large trees of various species. Usually represented are yellow
buckeye, basswood, yellow poplar, mountain silverbell, sugar
maple, eastern hemlock, white ash, northern red oak, and others.
A number of the record-size trees for which the park is noted grow
in these forests. Although there are few natural areas whose charm
can match these cathedral-like groves, the birds inhabiting them
are disappointing in variety and number. Even with good binoculars, it is difficult to observe the rather few, mostly small-sized,
species occupying the crowns of these forest giants. What there is
by way of a bird population is made up of species from the northern hardwood forest above—represented by the Black-throated
Blue Warbler and Junco—and the more heterogeneous growths
below—represented by such birds as the Red-eyed Vireo and
Wood Thrush. In the cove hardwood forests the Veery and Wood
Thrush overlap, while some species find their uppermost limits
here and others are at their lowermost breeding altitudes.

The *oak forests,* on intermediate to dry slopes at lower and middle altitudes, are made up of several species of oaks and hickories along with such trees as red maple, sourwood, sweet birch, yellow poplar, blackgum, and black locust. Until recently the American chestnut was an important component of these forests. Mountain laurel, rosebay rhododendron, and various other shrubs may form a fairly dense understory. The following birds, along with fifteen or sixteen species of warblers, nest in the oak forests: Yellow-billed Cuckoo, Whip-poor-will, Eastern Phoebe, Acadian Flycatcher, Carolina Chickadee, Tufted Titmouse, Carolina Wren, Brown Thrasher, Wood Thrush, Blue-gray Gnatcatcher, Yellow-throated Vireo, Red-eyed Vireo, Chipping Sparrow, and Field Sparrow.

Four kinds of pines, along with some oaks and a number of other trees that grow in dry and exposed situations, make up the *pine stands.* As a rule, the pines merge gradually with the oak forest above, their presence usually indicating a drier habitat. Blueberries and huckleberries often form an extensive understory. This low-and-middle-altitude forest is the least productive for the bird finder. Some of the birds of the oak forest may spill over into this drier, hotter area, but, generally, few birds are known to breed in the pines. The westernmost part of the park, just east of the Little Tennessee River, has extensive stands of second-growth pines where the Red-cockaded Woodpecker, one of the rarest birds in the park, was reported in 1935 and 1953.

The other forests are local and at varying elevations. At the low and middle altitudes fairly extensive stands of eastern hemlock occur and may grade into some of the forests mentioned above. The Parula and Black-throated Green Warblers frequent, but are not restricted to, these needle-bearing evergreens.

The heath balds, or "laurel slicks" as they are known locally, are high-altitude, treeless areas where plants of the heath family and a few others form low, extremely dense stands. The usual dominance of catawba rhododendron and mountain laurel gives these areas an evergreen appearance the year round and a spectacular floral display in June. The handsome Chestnut-sided Warbler, the most common high-altitude warbler in the park, is one of the most characteristic breeding birds of the heath balds.

Grass balds are high-altitude meadowlands, the origin of which has been a challenge to botanists and ecologists for years. These essentially treeless areas, for the most part of rather limited acreage, are confined largely to the western highlands of the Great Smokies. Although the variety of birds on the grass balds is not great, the chances of coming upon a wild Turkey are better here than in other parts of the park. And who, be he avid bird watcher or a hiker with no interest in natural history, would not be thrilled by the sight of a wild Turkey? Many of the birds of the spruce-fir forests occur along the margins of the grass balds where they are much easier to see than in the thick woods. Also on the open balds or along their forested edges are birds that may breed throughout the park from the lowest to the highest altitudes. Some of the species are the Ruffed Grouse, Bobwhite, Chimney Swift, Ruby-throated Hummingbird, Yellow-shafted Flicker, Hairy and Downy Woodpeckers, Catbird, and Rufous-sided Towhee.

The scarcity of diurnal raptors, which the eminent ornithologist, William Brewster, commented upon in 1885, still prevails. The Red-tailed Hawk is the most likely to be sighted, followed by the Turkey Vulture and, from April to October, the Broad-winged Hawk. For years Peregrine Falcons nested on the bare cliffs near Alum Cave Bluffs and were observed by many of the hikers who went to Mt. Le Conte in the late spring. Since 1961 a pair of Common Ravens have occupied this nest site and the Falcons are seldom seen. Neither the Golden Eagle nor the Bald Eagle breeds in the park—the almost unbroken forest cover excludes the former; the absence of suitable water the latter.

As for owls: The Screech Owl may be regarded as fairly common at low and middle altitudes. Statistics show that the red phase outnumbers the gray by at least four to one. The Great Horned Owl, probably one of the earliest nesters in the park, is mostly a bird of the low-altitude forests while the Barred Owl may be found at any altitude. In recent years the discovery of the Saw-whet Owl in the spruce-fir forests during the nesting season has extended the breeding range of this boreal species south to the park.

If we assume that the Swainson's Warbler, noted here in June on three occasions, has nested, twenty-three of the thirty-five warblers observed in the park may be regarded as breeding species. Of the non-breeding warblers, four—Nashville, Mourning, Magnolia, and Northern Waterthrush—have their southern limits in or near the West Virginia mountains. The remainder move still farther north. Ordinarily it is during the fourth week in April that one may encounter the largest numbers of these warblers in their spring migration. In the fall there are many migrating warblers to be seen although many more pass over at night, sometimes in concentrations. Joseph C. Howell and James T. Tanner, who examined 1,044 birds killed on the night of October 7–8, 1951, at the Knoxville airport ceilometer, twelve miles north of the park, reported that one half of the forty-six species represented were warblers and constituted 83 per cent of the total mortality.

Many changes in birdlife have occurred during my thirty years in the park. Recently the Horned Lark has been discovered nesting, while the Barn Swallow, House Wren, and Blue Grosbeak now nest in the immediate vicinity of the park. Perhaps the Traill's Flycatcher will eventually join them as a breeding species in the area. The Brown-headed Cowbird appears to be more plentiful; Red-headed Woodpeckers and Eastern Bluebirds have become scarcer. Evening Grosbeaks, whose initial appearance in the park occurred in 1951, have wintered here in considerable numbers during half of the ensuing ten-year period. They were absent in the winters of 1952–53 and 1953–54. Present again during the two winters that followed, they have appeared every other winter up to 1961–62.

Any area visited by bird watchers has its share of rarities or accidentals, and the list is bound to lengthen as the years go by. Here are some species belonging in these categories: A trio of White Pelicans observed flying over Clingmans Dome on September 21, 1937, by Edward S. Thomas and his brother, John; the Brant on October 22, 1939, and the Western Kingbird on October 1, 1957, by Joe F. Manley; two Pigeon Hawks on September 23, 1940, by Dean Amadon; two American Golden Plovers, by some of us along the transmountain road after a storm on October 29, 1953; The Laughing Gull by Roger Tory Peterson and James Fisher during their initial visit to the park on April 30, 1953; the Sooty Tern blown in by the great storm that lashed the Bahama Islands in late July, 1926; the Lincoln's Sparrow by George Miksch Sutton on April 24, 1952.

Each of these birds is so unexpected that one is inclined to remark that it will not occur soon again. This leads me to the Red Phalarope and a word of caution. On December 17, 1944, a

Christmas Bird Count party came upon the remains of a Red Phalarope near the park headquarters building, less than two miles from Gatlinburg, Tennessee. The bird had been dead for many days, if not weeks, and how it came there remains a mystery. On the evening of September 30, 1949, upon being asked by members of the Carolina Bird Club, meeting near the park boundary at Fontana Dam, North Carolina, about some of the most unusual birds on the park list, I dwelt at some length upon the Red Phalarope record and concluded that in all probability the species would not reappear in my lifetime. But, alas, the very next morning, while I was leading this same group down the ramp to the Fontana boat dock, I looked out over the water and there it was—a Red Phalarope spinning around in the water.

US Route 441 from Gatlinburg to Newfound Gap on the stateline ridge will give you a sample of the different ecological areas. Some 600 miles of graded trails lead into practically all parts of the park. Beginning in the northeast corner at Davenport Gap, the Appalachian Trail follows the high divide—the boundary between Tennessee and North Carolina—for approximately sixty miles before it drops down to Fontana Dam. Much of this trail remains at a high altitude where you can expect birds of the Canadian Zone. Five trails, varying in length from five to eight miles, lead to the summit of Mt. Le Conte (6,593 feet elevation) where overnight accommodations are available from May through October. There are shelter cabins on Mt. Le Conte, Gregory Bald, and at intervals along the Appalachian Trail.

When should the bird watcher visit the Great Smokies? Late April, at the height of spring migration, is a fine time. June, too, is good because breeding birds are on their nesting grounds and the catawba rhododendrons, flame azaleas, and mountain laurel are in bloom at the middle and high altitudes. July and August, the months when most people put in their appearance and when the mid-summer lull in bird activity takes place, is not the best time. September and October are delightful months, with the temperature cool, the mountains robed with gloriously colored foliage, and many birds lingering during their south-bound migration. Spring or fall, either time should be happily rewarding.

# Pacific Coast, Western Mountains and Foothills

FROM MONTEREY TO YOSEMITE
> Arnold Small

THE SIERRA NEVADA
> Verna R. Johnston

THE CALIFORNIA CHAPARRAL
> Howard L. Cogswell

OLYMPIC NATIONAL PARK
> R. Dudley Ross

GLACIER NATIONAL PARK
> J. Gordon Edwards

IN COLORADO—LAND OF THE LONG SPRING
> Alfred M. Bailey

THE BLACK HILLS OF SOUTH DAKOTA
> Herbert Krause

# FROM MONTEREY TO YOSEMITE

## Arnold Small

*In my younger years I harbored the illusion that all good ornithologists were born in New England, usually Massachusetts, and in due course were admitted to the sacred confines of the Nuttall Ornithological Club. Eventually I came to realize that a few other good ornithologists were born in New York and joined the Linnaean Society instead! In all seriousness, I am now aware that an early association with the Linnaean Society has been a major factor in shaping the bird-watching interests, ambitions, and proficiencies of a great many persons, including at least a half-dozen authors in this book. Arnold Small is one.*

*Born in 1926, Arnold Small grew up in New York City and attended the City College of New York. After the war he migrated West and received a master's degree from the University of Southern California.*

*Arnold began looking for birds at the age of fifteen. At seventeen he joined the Linnaean Society and, in his words, "has been going full steam ever since." Indeed he has, for by 1962 his life list of birds for the forty-eight contiguous states alone totaled 601.*

*For twelve years he has been teaching high school biology, the last eight in the school system of Los Angeles. He was ornithologist for three summers at the Audubon Camp of California and is currently president of the Los Angeles Audubon Society, an organization of over 1,000 members.*

*Five years ago Arnold Small took up photography, specializing in birds and other natural-history subjects. To this project he applied the same energy and enthusiasm that he has given to tracking down "life birds" and indeed has recently pursued them all the way to Africa. Since he prefers to have his subjects against a background of beautiful scenery, he is particularly fond of taking pictures in the vicinity of Monterey and Yosemite, two areas discussed in his article that follows.*

The Black-footed Albatross skims the giant swells that roll across Monterey Bay; the Great Gray Owl hunts its prey in the tree-bordered high meadows of Yosemite National Park; the Sage Grouse dances on the sagebrush plains of the Mono Basin. When you have seen Monterey, crossed the golden fields and vineyards of the Central Valley, climbed the almost imperceptible grade through the oaks and pines on the western slope of the Sierra Nevada, and stood before the majestic sequoias, towering cliffs, and magnificent waterfalls of Yosemite National Park; when you have reached the snowfields and glaciers of the crest of the Sierra Nevada, and, finally, viewed the hundreds of miles of sunswept desert around Mono Lake in the Great Basin to the east, you will have savored much of the best of California.

Since November 17, 1542, when Juan Rodriguez Cabrillo, a Portuguese navigator, first anchored his two small vessels in Monterey Bay and dispatched the first ecstatic description to the King of Spain, Monterey, "land of the cypress," has been the diadem in the jeweled crown of the California coast. Cabrillo stayed only two days; the bird finder needs much more time for, in addition to the glorious scenery of this attractive coast, Monterey offers a birdlife that is exciting any month of the year.

The strange attraction of seabirds for the Monterey coast seems to stem from the deep submarine canyon which extends into the sea from the end of Monterey Bay. Since there is no continental shelf in this area, the deep, cold waters, rich in dissolved nutrients, upwell in the Bay and provide fertilizer for the phytoplankton and the various food chains growing from them. For a study of tidepool life, one could hardly choose a better place. For migrating seabirds this food-rich bay is a natural avenue along which they linger to prosper on the products of the sea.

In the winter months, often windy and stormy, the harbor at Monterey, the rocks at the Hopkins Marine Station, and the coast near Point Pinos on the Monterey Peninsula are all excellent vantage points for observing seabirds, especially the alcids and shearwaters. Common Murres, Pigeon Guillemots, and Ancient and Marbled Murrelets are commonly seen from shore while the bay teems with six or seven species of gulls, three species of cormorants, Brown Pelicans, Fulmars, and shearwaters.

One of the best ornithological events of the year comes in March and April when thousands upon thousands of migrating Common, Red-throated, and Arctic Loons stream from near Point Pinos northward across the bay. The height of the seabird migration takes place in early May when there are always immense flights of Sooty Shearwaters making approximately the same crossing as the loons. Upwards of four million Sooty Shearwaters have been counted during a single day from Point Pinos.

My own preference for Monterey Bay is October when the seabirding offshore has no parallel in North America. By chartering a boat or boarding one of the numerous sport-fishing vessels at Fisherman's Wharf, you can be taken to the best of the birding waters only a few miles out. The sea is apt to be rough at almost any time of the year and the air will have a chill even in July, but for the land-locked bird finder, armed with anti-motion pills and a windbreaker, the trip will be a long-remembered experience.

Even before the boat is beyond the mouth of the bay, it will be surrounded by myriads of "tube-noses." Black-footed Albatrosses can be seen at almost any time of year and October is no exception. Often I have watched them from the rocks at Point Pinos. There will be Sooty Shearwaters by the hundreds and—the greatest attraction of all—white-bellied shearwaters in even larger numbers. In among them will be Pink-footed, Manx, and Gray-backed (New Zealand) Shearwaters. The Gray-backed—a trim little shearwater with a rather long tail, gray back, white belly, and a distinctive inverted "W" marking on the back and wings—is a certainty along this coast during the first two weeks of October. In smaller numbers will be the Slender-billed Shearwaters and Ful-

mars. One of the truly remarkable developments in recent years
has been the regular appearance here of Skuas during October.
You can also expect a fine flight of petrels—Ashy, Black, Leach's,
and Fork-tailed. Dozens will pass your boat all day long. Other
pelagic attractions include Sabine's Gulls, Parasitic, Pomarine,
and possibly Long-tailed Jaegers, various alcids, and Northern and
Red Phalaropes. And there is always the possibility of spotting a
really unusual bird such as a Pale-footed Shearwater, Wedge-tailed
Shearwater, Cape Pigeon, Wilson's Petrel, or Laysan Albatross.

For something of a slightly different flavor you should visit
Point Lobos Reserve State Park, an area of 355 acres along the
south shore of Carmel Bay and the most beautiful of all the state
parks in California. The Spanish called Point Lobos the "Point-of-
the-Sea-Wolves" because of the hosts of California and Steller's
sea lions found regularly along the rocky headlands. Herds of the
California sea otter, one of the rarest major mammals in the world,
float almost unnoticed among the strands of giant kelp in quiet
bays. By studying the kelp carefully with binoculars or telescope
you may see these hoary, five-foot-long creatures diving for aba-
lones and sea urchins. When surfacing with its catch the sea otter
also brings up some small flat rocks. Then rolling belly-up in the
water, it places a rock on its chest, and using it as an anvil proceeds to smash the tough-shelled invertebrates and devour the succulent organs within.

In the park also is one of the few remaining natural groves of
the picturesque Monterey cypress whose dark green foliage, wind-
scoured bark, and twisted forms accentuate the never-ending
struggle between land and sea. On the rocks are flocks of gulls,
pelicans, and cormorants, and—always—the striking red-legged
Black Oystercatcher which thrives along this coast. The quiet trails
that wind back from the sea among groves of Monterey pines are
bordered with dark green *Ceanothus*. Hidden among the rocks are
lichens and succulent "gardens" containing a number of endemic
forms.

This coast is truly matchless, and each change of date and
weather brings new birds to its shores. It will be difficult for any
bird finder to turn his back on the Pacific and follow a hypothetical
trail to the east.

Let us imagine a line drawn across California at right angles to the long axis of the state and intersecting Monterey, Yosemite National Park, and Mono Lake. If we could follow such a line, we would start eastward from Monterey and climb the several low, pine-and-oak-clad ridges, collectively called the Coast Range. As we descend from the Coast Range, the great Central Valley is spread before us as a grassy carpet. Here, in spring, grow solid masses of California poppies interspersed with lupine, owl's clover, fiddleneck, and Indian paintbrush. After some fifty miles across this basin we come to the first gentle foothills of the Sierra Nevada where the valley oaks and then the blue and golden-cup oaks invade the fringes of the grassland.

We climb ever so slightly now. The oaks grow thicker, the grasslands drop away, and very shortly grayish Digger pines are mixed with oaks. Higher now, at an elevation of about 4,000 feet, we find that the Sonoran Zone vegetation of the foothills has given way to black oaks, incense cedars, and yellow pines of the Transition Zone. The terrain steepens and, in the moist canyons, there are closer stands of yellow pine, Douglas fir, and incense cedar. Above 5,000 feet the cedar gradually becomes dominant. Along the watercourses, draining westward from the—as yet unseen—snowfields above, are cottonwoods, maples, alders, and redbuds.

At an elevation of 6,000 feet the Transition Zone forest reaches its peak and we enter areas where there are large stands of Jeffrey and sugar pines and white fir. Higher still are forests of red fir, white pine, and some lodgepole pine. On the windswept ridges above 8,000 feet we glimpse our first Sierra junipers—great gnarled and twisted masses clinging dizzily to the inhospitable ridges. Above 8,500 feet the denser forests and meadows give way to more open Hudsonian Zone forests of smaller trees. More lodgepole pines with their lance-like trunks are mixed with mountain hemlocks—rich green, spire-like trees with drooping tops.

Finally, at about 10,000 feet we reach the crest of Tioga Pass and enter the realm of the white-bark pine. Above us is tundra, granite talus, and ice, and 6,000 feet below and far away to the east lies Mono Lake, locked in a sagebrush basin.

The Sierra Nevadas, a great fault-block range about 80 miles wide, stretches north and south for some 400 miles on California's eastern side and rises to heights of over 14,000 feet. The gently-sloping western side, in the path of the moisture-laden winds from the Pacific, is clothed in verdant forests and cut by streams that tumble in waterfalls of unrivaled beauty. In their rush to the sea, they flow through glaciated canyons and deposit silt to fill in lakes and form park-like meadows. One such meadow is Yosemite Valley.

The towering cliffs of El Capitan, Half Dome, and the other ramparts which overlook Yosemite Valley and the Merced River stand more than one-half mile above the valley floor. Yosemite Valley, about 4,000 feet above sea level, is a forest-bordered meadow about seven miles long and a mile wide, its openness interrupted in places with a forest of yellow pine, white and Douglas fir, and black oak.

Although Yosemite has a special charm in winter, birdlife is scarce. Bird finding is best during the summer months when, along the trails and in the campgrounds of the valley floor, such birds as White-headed Woodpeckers, Steller's Jays, Western Tanagers, and Black-headed Grosbeaks are readily seen.

A special treat is the Dipper (Water Ouzel) which occurs along the Merced River, but is most frequently and easily found along Tenaya Creek near Mirror Lake. These grayish, wren-like landbirds are almost completely aquatic. Usually you see them buzzing along streams, alighting on rocks, and "dipping" in their characteristic fashion. If you watch carefully, though, you may see them dive into a riffle, swim under water by using their wings, or, perhaps, actually walk around on the stream bottom, searching for their favorite food, caddis-fly larvae. Later they will bob, cork-like, to the surface and swim shoreward in the manner of a miniature duck.

The crow-sized Pileated Woodpecker frequently nests along the trail which circles Mirror Lake. This delightful walk should also yield Winter Wrens, MacGillivray's Warblers, and Black Swifts. Scanning the dizzying heights above should reveal White-throated as well as Black Swifts as they wing their way along the beetling cliffs.

In contrast to the hubbub of the valley floor with its birds, cataracts, waterfalls, and river are the quiet groves of giant sequoias. Among these cathedral-like forests birdlife is sparse. If you hear Golden-crowned Kinglets and Brown Creepers lisping far above you or catch a glimpse of a Pileated Woodpecker or White-headed Woodpecker dashing from one giant to another, you should be content. There is no forest in the world to match these splendid sequoias, and quiet meditation comes naturally to the visitor standing among these enormous trees.

For mountain-forest bird watching at its best, you should drive from the valley floor to the rim of the gorge. The Glacier Point road leads through a Canadian Zone forest of red firs and white and lodgepole pine which is frequently interrupted by lush meadows. During June and July in these forest-rimmed meadows at about 8,000 feet, you may often hear the wren-like song of the Lincoln's Sparrow and see or hear Blue Grouse, Calliope Hummingbird, Evening Grosbeak, Pine Grosbeak, Pine Siskin, Red Crossbill, Fox Sparrow, and Hermit Warbler—species not found in the drier pine forests of the valley floor. Do not be surprised if you run onto mule deer, coyotes, porcupines, and black bears.

Probably the very best place in our forty-eight contiguous states for seeing Great Gray Owls is along the borders of these mountain meadows. They occur any time of the year but are most readily seen during October and early November. Early in the day or late in the afternoon these large diurnal owls often sit on small lodgepole pines or red firs along the fringes of the meadows, which they scan for pocket gophers, squirrels, and mice.

I recall my first experience with Great Gray Owls. We arrived at Peregoy Meadows about midnight one November 11, stopped the car, left the headlights on, and began to "squeak." Within a minute a pair of these big creatures flew into the trees nearby, while in the distance we heard two other owls, a Saw-whet and a Spotted, voicing their annoyance at the intrusion. Early the next morning we had little trouble locating more Great Grays—five in all. We approached to within ten feet of one individual as it uttered a very low *whoo,* swooped off its perch, caught a pocket gopher, returned to the same perch, and devoured its prey, seemingly indifferent to us.

The Tioga Pass Road takes you well above the Canadian Zone forest, through the Hudsonian Zone forest, and eventually crosses the tundra at Tuolumne Meadows. Near the shores of Tenaya Lake are fine stands of lodgepole pine, and higher still are mountain hemlocks and white-bark pines. The hemlocks often wear broad "skirts" of needles at their bases where the snow has compacted and protected them from the blasts of the winter winds which may bend the supple spires of the crown but do not easily break them. The wind-shedding adaptation of the slender crown is shown by other shallow-rooted mountain trees such as red firs. The white-bark pine shows another adaptation. Its branches are so flexible that, even though the tree itself bears a broad crown of needles, they do not break under a heavy weight of snow. As these trees approach timberline, they creep along the ground, bent and blasted by the wind and snow. Since they cannot raise their crowns above the skyline, they resemble shrubs more than trees at these extreme elevations.

It is in this Hudsonian Zone forest that you will meet a wide variety of birds, many with far-northern affinities. Red Crossbills are not uncommon in the white-bark pines; Clark's Nutcrackers fly from ridge to ridge, searching for pine cones and uttering raucous calls. Among the sparse conifer stands you should also encounter Black-backed Three-toed Woodpeckers, Williamson's Sapsuckers, and Hammond's Flycatchers. If you visit Tuolumne Meadows early enough (about late June), you may find Gray-crowned Rosy Finches feeding upon seeds and frozen insects along the edges of the melting snow.

A representative portion of Yosemite National Park can be seen by auto, but some of the finest of mountain scenery and the best bird finding is in the "back country," which may be reached only by the trails that crisscross the park. Later in the summer the Rosy Finches may be found only by hiking onto such tundra and talus slopes as are found on Mt. Dana and Mt. Lyell. All along the way you will be greeted by the shrill whistle of the yellow-bellied marmot, the inquisitive scream of the pika, and the guttural croak of the Common Raven.

From Tioga Pass, the highway descends into an arid region of Jeffrey pines, California junipers, and Great Basin sagebrush intersected by creeks lined with alder, birch, and cottonwood. The desert-like nature of the land soon becomes evident, even at an elevation of 7,000 feet. Gray Flycatchers, Say's Phoebes, and Mountain Bluebirds appear to prefer these drier slopes. Lower down, 6,000 feet below the pass, in the Great Basin, I have seen the surface of Mono Lake literally covered with thousands of Eared Grebes and Wilson's and Northern Phalaropes at certain times of the year. The Great Basin country is also the home of the Brewer's Sparrow, Black-billed Magpie, and Sage Grouse.

To be present on the strutting grounds of the Sage Grouse during the mating season is one of the bird watcher's highest experiences. I recall one particular visit we made to a dancing ground near Crowley Lake, some miles south of Mono Lake. We arrived at the snow-covered meadow one midnight in late March and entered blinds. By four o'clock the meadow was alive with over 100 strutting, booming cock Sage Grouse. By the light of the full moon we could see them as they erected and spread their stiffened tails, raised their white collars, and fluttered their wings in a peculiar drooping motion as they expelled air from their inflated yellow air sacs with a curious "popping" noise. The night air was filled with a steady chorus of poppings, cluckings, and cacklings. Each cock seemed to have his own particular strutting area and occasionally squabbles broke out as one bird trespassed on another's territory. We had glimpses of the hens as they fed among the displaying males.

This performance continued into the morning. As the sun climbed well above the distant mountains we fumbled with frost-numbed fingers for our cameras and began to adjust the delicate settings in the tricky light. Just as the exposure meter indicated enough light for filming, a pair of Golden Eagles coursed over the meadow and put every grouse to flight. The dance was over for the day.

Late that night we again closeted ourselves in the freezing blinds. At dawn all was in readiness and, as the sun mounted higher, we prepared to photograph. Also operating on schedule were the Golden Eagles. They appeared and repeated the performance of the previous morning.

Almost exactly two years later we attempted the same routine, but once again the Golden Eagles were there to greet the dawn. Thereafter we did a bit more field work and discovered that the Sage Grouse also displayed in the late afternoon when, most fortunately, the Eagles were occupied elsewhere.

From Black-footed Albatross to Great Gray Owl to Sage Grouse, these extraordinarily different birds represent the extremes in the environment that you will explore in the course of 300 miles from California's Monterey Coast to high Sierras to sagebrush plain.

# THE SIERRA NEVADA

## Verna R. Johnston

*Verna Ruth Johnston, born in 1918 in Berwyn, Illinois, grew up in this residential suburb of Chicago. She received her B.S. and M.A. degrees from the University of Illinois in 1939 and 1941, respectively, and taught high school biology in Illinois until 1944.*

*A course in plant taxonomy under Dr. Harry Fuller at the University of Illinois introduced Verna Johnston to the pleasures of field work in natural history and put an end to her ambition to become a journalist. She spent the next summer watching birds with the aid of Roger Tory Peterson's* Field Guide, *identifying trees with the help of a botanist, and memorizing the plates in Homer D. House's volume,* Wild Flowers. *Birds? Trees? Flowers? Birds? By September her mind was made up—a major in biology with "two nods to birds and one to plants."*

*From that time on she interspersed her winters of studying and teaching with summers devoted to natural history. In 1944 a University of Illinois Field Ecology Expedition took her for the first time across the Sierra Nevada to the West Coast. She fell in love with the mountains, found a teaching position in the Central Valley of California, and has made her home in that state ever since. Her present position, teaching biology and zoology at San Joaquin Delta College, gives her the opportunity to spend her spare time exploring the high passes of the Sierra, in any season and always*

97

with a camera. On a sabbatical leave in 1956 she lived in the Sierra at the 5,000-foot level, watching spring and summer arrive.

A skilled photographer and writer, Verna Johnston has to her credit a number of articles illustrated with her own photographs, and is the author of a pioneer booklet Natural Areas for Schools (first published in 1959 by the California State Department of Conservation and now in a revised edition) which shows schools the values and uses of outdoor classrooms.

In search of material for her writing on conservation and natural history, she visited the natural areas of schools all over California in 1960 and the natural areas, bird sanctuaries, and field study centers in Great Britain and central and northern Europe in 1962. But from all her travels to date she has returned assured "that for livable climate, birds, trees . . . the beloved Sierra is untouchable." Here, in her luminous descriptions of Sierra birds and their lofty world, she gives convincing support to her argument.

High out over the blue mountain waters a small gray form soared like a hawk with wings and tail outspread. Suddenly it plunged, erratically, steeply, and then, picking up speed, zoomed upward with a swish to land on the same high, dead limb from which it started. Here it crouched, wings partly spread showing buffy patches, tail fanned to expose the white sides. No sound came from its slender bill as the Townsend's Solitaire finished its courtship display, but moments later, the deep red fir forest of the Sierra Nevada rang with its magical melodies. From the throbbing throat of the slim thrush flowed a river of clear liquid notes—a continuous warbling full of the breathlessness of the Winter Wren, the mellowness of the Black-headed Grosbeak, the tinkling of sheep bells, the rushing of snow-fed creeks.

It was early June on the shores of Lake Tahoe, 6,500 feet up in the Sierra Nevada. Everywhere I looked birds were singing, courting, or beginning to nest. Brown Creepers spiraled up the carmine bark of the tall red firs. Olive-sided Flycatchers chipped a querulous *pip, pip, pip* or sent loud, ringing *hic three beers* echoing through the forest from their perches way up among the spires. From branches green with needle clusters shone the brilliant crimson head of a black and yellow Western Tanager as it chopped out a hoarse, lively song grouped in closely-knit phrases of three.

Nearby a Solitary Vireo's strident calls rose and fell "solitarily" with distinct pauses between. A second vireo flew in and began to sing vigorously a few feet from the first and in no time both birds were feather-deep in a chasing songfest. Without any physical attack but keeping constantly on each other's tails, they chased from branch to branch up and down every fir and pine in sight, singing madly at every pause. Sometimes their notes chimed; mostly they challenged. They came so close to me that binoculars were useless. All the features of these handsome vireos shone to combative perfection—the gray-blue head, white spectacles, clear pulsing throat and breast, yellow flanks, olive back. They had spirit enough for half a dozen warriors, yet in five minutes the musical battle was over. One vireo flew off and sang from 100 yards away, leaving the other the puffed-out king of his territory.

High above, where the red fir cones stood upright, the Ruby-crowned Kinglet sang while his mate sat on her cup of moss. Starting high with three or four bell-like notes, his rippling lyric descended the scale in a liquid half-whisper only to climb partway up again and again until it faded away. Through the heavy timber boomed the low thumping of the Blue Grouse—seven deep notes in relaxed succession in about four seconds' time, then a pause of forty seconds and another seven—like the sound of someone pounding far away, coming from many different directions. I knew where I would find him—booming from a limb well up in a conifer—calling his lady instead of going after her.

And all up and down the 400-mile length of California's great eastern backbone, the Sierra Nevada, in the shady, cool recesses of the red fir forests between 6,000 and 9,000 feet there were others like him. Below 6,000 feet, another set of birds was singing and nesting; above 9,000 feet, a different group. One of the inviting features of high western mountains is the way their slopes harbor many different plant and animal communities, each living in the altitudinal zone where temperature, moisture, and soil suit its needs. These vegetative belts or "life zones" are so obvious as you climb the Sierra that an observant eye has no difficulty in distinguishing between them, and they make a handy ecological framework to which a newcomer may tie his bird list.

From the lowest foothills to the highest peaks there are five life zones: the Upper Sonoran Zone (so-called because of its resemblance to arid Sonora, Mexico) from 500 to 2,500 feet; the Transition, from 2,500 to 6,000 feet; the Canadian, from 6,000 to 9,000 feet; the Hudsonian, from 9,000 to 11,000 feet; and the Alpine (sometimes called Arctic or Arctic-alpine), usually above 11,000 feet. These figures are, of course, not absolute, for the altitudes which mark the zones vary under different conditions of latitude, exposure, and moisture.

Some birds limit themselves to one zone; others range over several. The finches of the genus *Carpodacus* have divided the mountains among them in quite an intriguing manner. The House Finch, or Linnet, of this group is the common red-breasted, red-rumped finch of California valleys and foothills. The very similar Purple Finch is the bird of mid-mountain ponderosa pine forests. The almost identical Cassin's Finch lives in the high Sierran red fir and lodgepole pine belt.

Museum displays in Yosemite National Park group the trees, birds, and mammals in exhibits according to the life zones in which they occur. This makes Yosemite Valley an excellent place to begin a study of Sierran wildlife—to learn what is known and how very much is yet unknown.

The panorama of snow-capped peaks that give the Sierra Nevada its name—"snowy range"—shows most dramatically from the eastern side where one can look up from sagebrush-filled valleys of the Great Basin to the steep, granite escarpment and finally to the "high country"—over 14,000 feet above sea level—glittering with saw-toothed peaks of white magnificence. In wetter years snow will stay on most of the higher peaks well into July. From Bishop and from US Route 395 both north and south of Bishop, several roads lead west—up steep canyons into this high country. And from the ends of these roads there are trails to the highest peaks.

But to climb the range more slowly with a longer look at the birds of each zone, an approach up the western slope is better. Here the mountains rise gently and curvingly from the valleys to the high mountain passes. From the Central Valley, seven pass roads climb gradually into Sierran Foothills. The higher and more intimate of these passes—Carson on State Route 88, Ebbetts on State Route 4, Sonora on State Route 108, and Tioga on State Route 120—traverse subalpine country by road or put it within reach by trails leading off from little lakes and campgrounds on either side of the summits.

The western foothills, representative of the Upper Sonoran Zone, can be hot in the summer but delightful during April and May when the blue oak woodlands and silvery-green Digger pines and the chaparral are alive with birds and flowers. Lark Sparrows flit from fence to tree with white tail-spots flashing. Bullock's Orioles build hanging nests in the oaks. The Nuttall's Woodpecker, found only in California, hitches its black-and-white-striped form up telephone poles. It is a quiet feeder compared to the noisy Acorn Woodpeckers which are forever moving their endless supply of acorns in or out of freshly dug holes—all with a maximum of larruping chatter. Over the fields where carpets of California poppies and blue lupine roll between the oaks, the Plain Titmouse, which lacks the rusty flanks of the eastern Tufted, makes frequent flights to find food for its young. From the Fremont poplars comes the nasal scolding of a pair of Yellow-billed Magpies, restricted in range to California west of the Sierra. (A trip across the Sierra is almost the only way to see the two American species of magpies in one day—the Yellow-billed on the west side, the Black-billed on the east.)

The solid hillsides of woody shrubs which climb many of the south slopes of the foothills were named chaparral by the early Californians. Practically impenetrable to man except by crawling, these "elfin forests" of chamise, toyon, and *Ceanothus,* are home to one of the Pacific Coast's unique birds—the Wrentit. There is no song remotely like its loud staccato trill all on one pitch, starting slowly and getting faster, ringing out of the chaparral clumps. The singer, a dark brown wren-like bird with a white eye and long cocky tail, if it appears at all, will be quickly up and then down out of sight.

The Wrentit's companion in the chaparral and foothill woodlands, and a bird found only in California, is the California Thrasher, a large gray-brown thrasher with a sickle bill and cinnamon belly. From the scrub oaks its Mockingbird-like song floats over the foothills, thinner and less musical than the "Mocker" but a pleasant melody compared to the rasping squawks of his fellow Scrub Jay, California's crestless blue jay with a brown back. On the western slope, the foothills stretch for thirty or forty miles, chaparral alternating with woodland, ravines with brushy thickets from which the California Quail call.

Above 2,000 feet, the darker green ponderosa pines begin to mingle with lacy open Diggers, and soon incense cedars become plentiful, then the spires of white fir and the outstretched arms of sugar pines. This is the Transition Zone—heart of the Sierra—the open, sunny, fragrant forests that cover the great central mass of the range from roughly 2,500 to 6,000 feet. Here live more kinds of flora and fauna than in any of the other zones.

This is the zone of Yosemite Valley with its famed waterfalls and granite cliffs, countless summer camps where counsellors can practically bank on rainless days, *Sequoia gigantea* groves—timeless cinnamon and green marvels. This is the land where big saucy blue jays with black crests, the Steller's Jays, land on your camp table, looking for scraps, and chipmunks poke noses inquiringly round your picnic basket. Where gray squirrels with bushy tails hunt acorns under the Kellogg's black oak in which a Nashville Warbler is singing his heart out. Where the single long plume of the Mountain Quail bobs sedately as the mother leads a new brood of fuzzy chicks from the safety of one manzanita clump to another. Where the White-headed Woodpeckers nest low in tree stubs while the rose-bellied Lewis' Woodpecker prefers its holes higher up.

Although this is, I think, the most livable and in some ways my favorite of the Sierran life zones, each in its season has no rival. Certainly the next higher zone, the Canadian (6,000 to 9,000 feet), the land of lodgepole pines and red fir forests, has no rival when at sunset a Hermit Thrush voices his ethereal spirals.

Nor is there anything to equal the "flower show" of the Hudsonian Zone (9,000 to 11,000 feet). Here, in July and August, the high-mountain flowers of the subalpine forests spread over the rugged, rocky soils and boggy seeps. From the dwarf steer's head and pink *Linanthus,* that color the forest floor under the mountain hemlocks and lodgepole pines, up the boulder-strewn slopes to timberline, shine sulphur-flowers, bistorts, pink laurel, red heather, Sierran jewel-flower, the scarlet penstemon, and a host of others with the colors of the rainbow—easily 100 kinds in bloom in mid-July. On the ridges white-bark pines crouch before the blasting winds, their leaders bent back toward earth. To the white-barks, come the beautiful gray, black, and white Clark's Nutcrackers. With their dexterous bills, the extracting of a seed from the gummy resinous cones every two or three seconds seems no trick at all. Here, too, lives the Mountain Bluebird, the male's breast half the depth of a Sierran sky. It nests in holes in stumps, often where it can look out on a tiny gem of a lake fed by melting snow from the peaks above.

On these peaks, usually above 11,000 feet, lies the Alpine Zone of the Sierra, a rocky treeless region of climactic extremes, scattered like islands through the crests of the range. The birdlife in this highest mountain zone is sparse, mostly limited to Gray-crowned Rosy Finches which flit over the rocky terrain and nest in rocky crevices. Hoary-shouldered marmots like to sun themselves on the boulders. Pikas bark from their holes or come out to sniff the short-stemmed wildflowers that brighten the ground in August. This is a land of wind and snow and rocks and sky—and a hardy dwarf flora adapted to it.

From the ruggedly wild top of the world, the descent down the east side to the Great Basin is a rapid drop through aspen and mountain poplar groves, past beaver dams and rushing streams where Dippers bob and swim, into a new and still different bird world, the pinyon-juniper woodland of the Upper Sonoran Zone, that lines the eastern slopes. Here, where stretches of silvery green sagebrush contrast with compact clumps of dark green juniper and the softer pinyon pine, or one-needled pine, is the home of the Piñon Jay, Ash-throated Flycatcher, perky Green-tailed Towhee, and a host of other attractive species.

The Sierra Nevada is one of the most accessible of mountain ranges. All but the highest of its varying bird worlds lie within easy reach of the motorist. Campgrounds and lodges dot all the passes. Ranger-naturalists lead parties up the alpine slopes of Mt. Dana in upper Yosemite National Park several times each summer.

Occasionally, a service-station operator along a Sierran road can give one a bird tip. I once stopped at such a station in Tuolumne Meadows in upper Yosemite National Park and asked the woman operator if she had seen any unusual birds lately.

"Oh, yes," she replied, her face lighting up. "Fallopians—thousands of them—on Mono Lake."

I found the birds where she had said, and there were thousands of them—literally thousands of Northern Phalaropes!

To explore Sierran bird haunts fully, to tread the quiet side trails and sit in the meadows, to scan the vistas unique on each pass and to visit them in spring, summer, autumn, winter—all this would take the better part of a lifetime. And to preserve them as pristinely lovely as they are now requires the constant alertness of both individuals and conservation groups.

"The Range of Light," John Muir called the Sierra Nevada as he viewed it from across the Great Valley. And the light is still there. It bounces off the granite boulders, drops in shafts between the tall trees, shoots in silver streaks across blue lakes, and everywhere illuminates the vibrant beauty of these living mountains.

# THE CALIFORNIA CHAPARRAL

## Howard L. Cogswell

*Howard Lyman Cogswell, born in 1915 on a farm in Susquehanna County, Pennsylvania, met his first birds in Thornton W. Burgess's books for children provided by a traveling library that stopped at a one-room rural school. When he was about ten he discovered birds as a hobby in the* Handbook of Birds *by Frank M. Chapman and* The Book of Bird Life *by Arthur A. Allen.*

*At the age when boys like to travel and explore "wild country," he was living in Pasadena, California, and the nearest wild country within range of his bicycle was on the chaparral-covered slopes of the San Gabriel Mountains above the city. This was the beginning of his interest in the chaparral and its birds.*

*While a student at Whittier College and part-time warden at the Audubon Center in El Monte, he continued to watch birds in the chaparral. As a graduate student at the University of California in Berkeley, he returned to the chaparral for a more detailed and systematic study that led eventually to his thesis for a Ph.D. degree.*

*Now, on the faculty of California State College at Hayward, he says that he has deserted the chaparral for a study of why certain bird species choose the particular habitats they do. While he probably means what he says, I nevertheless hope that he will return now and then to the chaparral and its birds, as he has here, for there is nobody else who can discourse on the subject with his enthusiasm and authority. In a sense this article challenges any bird watcher worth his salt to tackle the chaparral, seek its drab-colored, timid birds, and find it fun.*

                 In California a large portion of the non-cultivated land is covered by chaparral, a type of vegetation composed of stiff-twigged shrubs that are mostly evergreen but not coniferous. Although chaparral is found nowhere else in the United States, vegetation of a similar structure does occur in other areas of the world.

Blanketing the rugged slopes of California hills and mountains in summer-dry areas, chaparral often becomes a fire hazard. Yet fires at rather long intervals, every fifteen to sixty years, tend to keep true chaparral vigorous. Some of the shrub species regrow rapidly from root-crowns of unburned stubs near or below the ground, and other species germinate abundantly from seeds that have lain dormant for years, waiting for the heat of a fire to crack the tough coats. The mild, rainy winters and the fairly hot summers with negligible rainfall from May to October give a unique aspect to chaparral and produce the "extreme fire hazard" conditions so terrifying to the mountainside dwellers.

For the bird watcher in chaparral country a minimum knowledge of the general ecology of the vegetation is a great help. The word "chaparral" comes from the Spanish *chaparro* meaning scrub oak, but the common usage today does not imply the presence of scrub oak or any other particular shrub. It refers merely to the general vegetation type. One stand of chaparral may have a dozen or more species that are widespread; another stand may have just a few or, occasionally, only one.

The various species grow from five to fifteen feet high. Their hard, waxy leaves are usually rather small and thus adapted to withstand the long dry summers. Thickets that are made up mostly of deciduous shrubs with softer leaves and grow in areas of the American West where there is more moisture, should not be called chaparral—not even "soft" chaparral—because such usage obscures the unique nature of the true or "hard" chaparral of the California foothills and southern mountains that are summer-dry, yet not desert.

The main, or foothill, chaparral region extends from the mountains of northern Baja California north, broadly through southern California west of the deserts, at about 1,000 to 4,000 or 5,000 feet elevation, and in more disjunct areas through the Coast Ranges and the western foothills of the Sierra Nevada to Shasta County in northern California.

The most widespread species of shrub in the foothill chaparral is chamise, easily recognized by its bunches of short, needle-like leaves and pyramids of tiny white flowers that bloom in June. Pure stands of chamise have relatively few birds, apparently because of the scant shade and lack of leaf litter.

In most places, additional species of shrubs are mixed with chamise: one or more species of *Ceanothus* or "mountain lilac," one or more species of manzanita, and black sage, coffeeberry, yerba santa, and others. At suitable altitudes in southern California some such combination of chamise and other shrubs covers most of the south-facing slopes. The north-facing slopes, with little or no chamise, bear an "oak chaparral." This is a great mixture of the broader-leaved species such as scrub oak, interior live oak (locally), toyon, poison oak, currants, gooseberries, holly-leaf coffeeberry, other species of *Ceanothus,* foothill ash at lower altitudes, manzanita and silk-tassel bush at higher altitudes, and birch-leaf mahogany around eroding areas. Since many of these species provide seeds or berries as well as an abundant insect population, and the leaf litter may be quite deep, both canopy and ground-foraging birds are common.

The species composition of the foothill chaparral in central and northern California differs to some extent, but the chamise and non-chamise types are still recognizable and the general picture of their relationship to birdlife is probably similar.

At lower altitudes toward the coast from the main chaparral region, a related type of vegetation, dominated mostly by shorter shrubs with softer leaves and less rigid branching, grows in a characteristic open arrangement with herbs or bare ground between them. This coastal scrub or "coastal sagebrush" harbors many of the same species of birds as the young, comparatively open stages of chaparral. Except in the fog belt of the outer coast north of San Luis Obispo County, the Rufous-crowned Sparrow is perhaps the most characteristic bird of the coastal sage scrub. White-crowned

Sparrows and Song Sparrows breed in the coastal scrub in the fog belt but are not found in this habitat farther inland.

Within the forest belts of the major mountain areas and at higher altitudes than the foothill chaparral, there are "brush patches" composed of various shrubs that "all fly back at your face with a biff," according to the song, "In the Land of the Lassen." Although made up of different species than the foothill chaparral, these are also true chaparral. Such montane chaparral areas are temporary stages in the forest succession and are often snow-covered all winter. Thus their breeding birds are for the most part different from those of the foothills. Some birds, such as the Fox Sparrow, breed in the montane chaparral and winter in the foothills; other breeding birds—the Dusky Flycatcher, Nashville Warbler, Green-tailed Towhee—may pass through the foothills to winter in Mexico.

For seven years I made a census of the breeding birds of the foothill chaparral of the San Gabriel Mountains in southern California and during three of those years concentrated on mapping territories. As a result of this study I found that few species of birds show an affinity for any one shrub species. Black-chinned Sparrows seem partial to chamise, but even they are absent when the stand becomes too dense. The habitat preference of the birds of the foothill chaparral and coastal scrub seems to be related to the density of the shrubs. The extent of openings between the crowns and the compactness of the branching within the crowns are both important. In fact, so many variations in the bird populations at different locations in the chaparral seem traceable to these features that I had best portray them by first describing the birdlife in mature chaparral in the San Gabriels above the area between Pasadena and Upland and then contrasting these populations with the birdlife in the stages of regrowth of the chaparral following a fire.

Despite tough branches which resist the entry of big bodies, one *can* get beneath a mature chaparral canopy by taking advantage of newly cleared trails through it. When seen from beneath— the birds' viewpoint—a stand of mature chaparral—either chamise or oak type—is truly the "elfin forest" described by Francis M. Fultz.

In southern California the most abundant bird in mature chaparral is the Wrentit, whose range is only slightly more extensive than that of the foothill chaparral itself. In six census plots of reasonably mature chaparral I found that Wrentits constituted about one-quarter or one-third of the bird population, averaging thirty-three territories per 100 acres with a maximum of fifty-seven territories in the densest oak chaparral and a minimum of twenty-three in the only plot near the upper altitude limit where snow remains for a considerable period in some winters. These figures suggest that about forty to fifty territories per 100 acres is normal for Wrentits in mature chaparral in the San Gabriels. Marie Mans, censusing two seasons near Oakland, California, found a like density in coastal chaparral of quite different composition. Everywhere, it seems, the Wrentit is the chaparral bird *par excellence*.

Yet Wrentits are secretive and drab, and bird watchers who are easily discouraged may despair at seeing them firsthand. However, from a single good vantage point, an acute ear can detect up to a dozen or so singing males, each on his own territory of about one-half to two acres. The female also "sings," ordinarily only a series of slow notes all on one pitch, *yip-yip-yip-yip-yip,* which is quite like the introductory part of the male's song but lacking his final speed-up to a trill. When foraging separately the mates keep in contact by singing (occasionally), and neighboring pairs often respond. After the early morning singing had subsided, I often resorted to crude imitations of the female's song—I cannot trill like a male—to induce waves of vocalization for census records.

Wrentits have other features of special interest: they mate for life and maintain territory the year round; their handsome, deep-cup nest is most often just beneath a particularly dense mass of foliage next to an open avenue through the canopy; they have been known to live for ten years; they spend much of their time scolding their arch nest-predator, the Scrub Jay, with a soft rasping *krrrrr* note (they use it to scold human beings, too); and they are strong of leg but so weak of wing that a flight of more than thirty feet is rare for them. A Wrentit can, nevertheless, hop and flit its way from twig to twig through the elfin forest as fast as a man can run with no shrubs to block his way. In my study plots a one-lane fireroad often formed a "no Wrentit land" between their territories, and two-lane roads were definite barriers to their movements.

No bird species is quite so tied to the chaparral as the Wrentit. However, a number of other birds are common. In order of decreasing densities on reasonably mature chamise and oak chaparral plots were the Brown Towhee, Rufous-sided Towhee, Black-headed Grosbeak (less common in medium densities), Bewick's Wren, California Thrasher, Common Bushtit, and Poor-will. It is noteworthy that five of these are drab brown in color. In addition there were Costa's Hummingbirds (where the sage was abundant), Scrub Jays, Orange-crowned Warblers, and Ash-throated Flycatchers.

The Brown Towhee is partial to the edges of openings, firebreaks, roadsides, and trails and may be less common in truly solid chaparral which is all but impossible to census because of the disturbance caused by the observer floundering through it. The Brown Towhee is even more abundant in the open, coastal sage scrub on the lower foothills and in the open oak woodland where grasses and shrubs are intermixed. No wonder it has become a dooryard bird in most California cities where man has provided just this combination of plant forms. The California Thrasher is more nearly restricted to chaparral, although it is also found in riparian and other deciduous thickets.

All of the species I have listed also breed in other kinds of western woodlands or in the more open coastal scrub. Some breed even in the very open desert scrub, but there are far too few bird censuses from these other habitats for comparison with the population densities in the chaparral. Serious amateurs can make a very substantial contribution to the knowledge of the habitat and population ecology of western birds by censusing any widespread type of habitat available to them over a period of years.

In my list, perhaps the Orange-crowned Warbler is the greatest surprise to an Easterner who thinks of it as a migrant en route to northern forests. The far-western races breed regularly in dense chaparral, especially the oak type, and in broadleaf evergreen woods. In the post-breeding season they spread chiefly up-slope into primarily coniferous forests.

Most of the fires that sweep through the chaparral occur in late summer and fall at which time most of the birds have finished nesting and many have moved up-mountain to cooler areas or into major canyons which the fires often jump. Some of these birds return after the fires and attempt for a year or two to nest in their old haunts, now barren with black snags of shrubs bristling from the slopes. With repeated winter rains, however, the ground may be covered with masses of wildflowers including some kinds seen only after a fire. During the first year or two after a fire, the common breeding birds in the San Gabriels include the Rock Wren, House Finch, Lesser Goldfinch, and Lark Sparrow.

Within two to four years the slopes usually bear an open growth of subshrubs and regrowing sprouts of old shrubs. The Lazuli Bunting is the most characteristic species at this stage and reaches densities nearly as great as those of the Wrentit in the mature chaparral. The Buntings persist in diminishing numbers until most of the openings are again covered by shrubs. The male Lazulis engage in much trespassing and chasing, and, though territorial, seem to shift their territories readily, a behavioral feature that is valuable for a species whose optimal habitat shifts with the regrowth of shrubs. The Rufous-crowned Sparrow is fairly common in this subshrub and grass stage, but not as common as in the coastal scrub proper. The finches continue to be abundant. Since they do not seem to be territorial, many of them probably come from distant areas to feed on seeds in the burns.

In one plot that I studied at three to five years after a fire, black sage was abundant and Costa's Hummingbirds, at their maximum with twenty males per 100 acres, were second only to the Lazuli Buntings. By the fifth post-fire year the true chaparral species—the Brown Towhees, Rufous-sided Towhees, and the Wrentits especially—began to return in force.

Of the birds breeding in greatest numbers when the chamise, *Ceanothus,* and manzanitas are in the intermediate stage of regrowth—that is to say, two to four feet tall with bare ground still showing between them—two species deserve special mention. The first, the Black-chinned Sparrow, gives its plaintive song, so like that of the Field Sparrow, from conspicuous bush-tops and the crests of minor ridges from which it can hear and be heard in all directions. This bird does not range north of about 38 degrees latitude. The second, the Sage Sparrow, is more wary and, unless approached with care, quickly leaves its inconspicuous song perch in a bush-top and scuttles along the ground between the shrubs. When the chaparral again becomes too dense for these birds, the breeding population described earlier moves in.

A visit between April and June to places of different post-fire age in the chaparral should enable any experienced bird watcher to become well acquainted with all of these species. He may see also the Golden Eagle, Mountain Quail, Great Horned Owl, White-throated Swift, and Violet-green Swallow—far-ranging birds that regularly live in, or forage over, the chaparral.

As to other seasons, only a few words need be given. In mid-winter, as new leaves are added to the old, the chaparral becomes bright green. Birdlife is abundant with Oregon Juncos and Golden-crowned and Fox Sparrows devouring seeds; Hermit Thrushes and roving bands of Robins, Cedar Waxwings, and even Band-tailed Pigeons eating berries; and Ruby-crowned Kinglets and Audubon's Warblers adding their insect-catching abilities to those of the Wrentits and Bewick's Wrens.

From late March to early May almost all species that migrate through the region are found in or over the chaparral slopes that confront their northward passage. Many a jutting ridge in the chaparral on the south side of the San Gabriels is a good "Hawk Mountain," from which in late March and early April one can watch Turkey Vultures and Swainson's Hawks passing by the hundreds and scattered individuals of other species. Only in August and September, the season of fire hazard and deer hunting, is the chaparral birdlife thin and mostly silent. Ecologically, this is the "winter," or dormant, period for many of the chaparral plants and animals.

In any other season, a walk along a trail through the chaparral, not too close to a high-speed highway, will give the bird finder an opportunity to become acquainted with the elfin forest that fire merely rejuvenates and with its birds that may have to be coaxed into view. For those who leave the trail the chief hazards are wood ticks, rattlesnakes, poison oak, and scratches from stiff shrubs or jagged rocks. If any bird watcher still wants to visit sections of chaparral in its different stages of growth, the district offices of the Forest Service will supply him with maps of trails and a list of fire dates for their areas.

# OLYMPIC NATIONAL PARK

## R. Dudley Ross

*Dudley Ross's reports on birds and bird-finding areas have given substance to my columns in* Audubon Magazine *for years. He has advised me; I have advised him. We have corresponded frequently and met in various parts of this country from east coast to west. He has birded and visited with many of my good friends. Yet, strangely enough, we had never been in the field or looked at a bird together until he and his wife joined Mrs. Pettingill and me for a stroll through Sapsucker Woods at Ithaca, New York, in 1963.*

*R. Dudley Ross, born in 1903 in Liscard, England, came to the United States at the age of seven. He grew up in New York, was educated in the public schools, and entered the paper business in which he has worked for forty years. He is now resident sales representative for the Westfield River Paper Company, a leading New England manufacturer of glassine and greaseproof papers.*

*The accidental discovery of Peterson's* Field Guide to the Birds *in the home of a friend aroused his curiosity and delighted his wife, who had watched the birds about her home and garden for years. They started bird watching together in 1942. Before long they were spending evenings at the Linnaean Society of New York and birding in the daytime with the masters—Peterson, Pough, Cruickshank, Sprunt, Eisenmann, and the late Ludlow Griscom. There was no turning back.*

*As soon as their daughters were grown and away at school, the Rosses started traveling to look for birds farther and farther afield. They have since watched birds in all the forty-eight contiguous states, recording 635 species; visited all the Canadian provinces except Newfoundland; and taken a number of trips to exciting bird islands off both the Atlantic and Pacific Coasts—Machias Seal Island, the Farallons, Bull's Island, the Coronados, and the Bahamas, just to name a few. As I write this, they are in Panama. Next year, who knows?*

*Although they have journeyed far and seen many birds, the Rosses' enthusiasm never wanes. The birds come first when they map their trips. If they can arrange to watch their birds against a backdrop of magnificent scenery, so much the better. No doubt this is why they chose Olympic and Big Bend National Parks and why they want to revisit them whenever possible. After you read what Dudley Ross says about these out-of-the-way, little-known parks, I have a hunch you too will try to include them in your next trips. Here he writes about Olympic National Park.*

My wife, Vivian, and I have visited a great many places in the forty-eight contiguous states which are either renowned for their scenic beauty or are of special interest ornithologically. Some of them happily combine both features and give us a deep desire to return. One such place is Olympic National Park on the Olympic Peninsula in northwestern Washington.

When we visited western Washington for the first time, it was mid-summer. We arrived from the parched, arid country to the south. Gone immediately were the hills and fields, browned by too much heat and too little moisture. Here instead was a landscape made lush and green by frequent rains. Rivers were filled with sparkling, clear water. When we reached the broad expanse of the Columbia River at a point where it forms the boundary between Oregon and Washington, we could not resist the temptation to drive beside it for many miles, even though this took us some distance out of our way. Here was one of man's prime needs— water, water in abundance.

Our objective was the Olympic Peninsula and especially the majestic Olympic Mountains. On our way we traveled for miles on excellent highways and through country which was rugged and exciting. The landscape looked healthy, as indeed it was. Gradually the jagged, snow-clad Olympics came into view as we approached Port Angeles, headquarters of Olympic National Park. (On our second trip to the Olympic Peninsula several years later we approached from Victoria, British Columbia, by the ferry which crosses the Strait of Juan de Fuca to its southern terminus, Port Angeles. Long before the ferry docked, the Olympics were in view. Vivian and I are agreed that this approach to the Olympics is by far the more impressive and is certain to instill in you a burning desire to explore a wilderness that still remains unspoiled.)

Olympic National Park, established in 1938, is comparatively new. Additions, made in 1953, brought the park up to its present size of 1,400 square miles. Located at a considerable distance from the centers of population, the park is not nearly as well-known as some of the older and more publicized members of the National Park System. It is, however, an important unit in this system, not only for its pristine beauty and wildlife, but also for its therapeutic value as a recreational area.

Accommodations on the peninsula are many and varied, with

cabins, motels, hotels, inns, and lodges to suit all tastes. Within the park, accommodations are limited to a few cabins and a lodge on Hurricane Ridge. Additional facilities will no doubt be available as the region becomes better known.

Although US Route 101 almost surrounds the park, it actually crosses the park boundary at only two points: skirting the south shore of Lake Crescent in the north and traversing part of the Olympic Ocean Strip just northwest of Ruby Beach on the west. The Olympic Ocean Strip, fifty miles of scenic coastline, was added to the park in 1953 and is separated from the park proper by several miles. From Route 101, spur roads lead into a number of the most attractive sections of the park; and from the ends of nearly all of these roads excellent trails penetrate the true wilderness, join others, and form a network which makes almost all of the park accessible to those with sufficient time and energy to travel on foot.

Heading north in the eastern part of the Olympic Peninsula, you have the feeling of being surrounded by a vast forest of evergreens, but closer inspection reveals that there are also many deciduous trees and shrubs. At the lower elevations—particularly along streams—willows, dogwoods, red alders, and bigleaf maples form a heavy growth.

From June to September, one of the outstanding spectacles of the Olympic Peninsula is the display of wildflowers. Wherever you go, the foxgloves are present, growing in profusion along the roadsides to a height of five feet or more. There are acres and acres of bleeding heart, delphinium, phlox, and both avalanche and glacier lilies. Although the greatest variety of flowers is found in the mountain meadows, there are flowers everywhere from the lowest valleys up to the timberline. The particular flower species differ, of course, depending upon the altitude and habitat.

Just a few miles west of Port Angeles, at the town of Elwha, we embarked on our first side trip and drove south on a steep winding road to Hurricane Ridge. Since the timberline in this section of the Olympics is between 5,000 and 5,500 feet above sea level and the ridge between 5,500 and 6,000 feet, we were soon above timberline. Some snow persists here until mid-summer, but nearly all roads and trails are clear by the begining of July.

Hurricane Ridge is outstanding for the variety and abundance of its flowers from June to October. Above the timberline are many plants usually found in more northerly regions such as Alaska, Greenland, and northern Canada. We found snow present in large patches in mid-July and the mountain meadows so covered with blooms that they resembled gigantic flower gardens. The profusion was almost overwhelming: glacier lilies by the thousands, subalpine lupine covering an entire field with a bluish-purple carpet. As one species reaches the end of its blooming period, it is succeeded by another just coming into bloom, so that there is a continuous sequence of color. We were tempted to stay the entire summer just to enjoy the gorgeous pageant.

On the ridge we noted several Gray Jays, and a few Oregon Juncos, Common Ravens, and Rufous Hummingbirds. Vaux's Swifts darted about overhead, and we had a brief glimpse of a pair of Blue Grouse.

We were more than delighted to see the elusive Blue Grouse whose booming notes, said to be a full octave lower than the "hoots" of the Great Horned Owl, are impressive because of their depth of pitch. Very often, even if one hears the "booms" and traces them to a specific tree, he may still fail to see the "boomer." The Blue Grouse has a way of sitting motionless overhead and paying no heed to the attempts of intruders to flush it. Whistles, shouts, even sticks tossed in the air seem to make no impression.

The view from the ridge was magnificent. To the north we could see, dimly through a slight mist, the Strait of Juan de Fuca. To the south, the highest peaks of the Olympics were arrayed before us in a never-to-be-forgotten splendor, with the three famous pinnacles of Mt. Olympus the focal point of the dramatic scene. Ancient Mt. Olympus of mythological fame was the home of Jupiter Pluvius, the god of rain. Our Mt. Olympus is aptly named. It is estimated to receive more than 200 inches of precipitation each year, the greater part of it in the form of snow.

The Olympics seem to defy analysis. Actually they are not really a range of mountains but rather an eccentric conglomeration of jagged peaks without definite pattern. While not as high in altitude as many other mountains, they are so precipitous and rugged and rise so very sharply from the neighboring lowlands that they are truly spectacular.

In the Olympics there are about fifty glaciers, most of which, with the exception of several on Mt. Olympus, are fairly small. Many swift rivers descend abruptly down the mountains from the glaciers and flow serenely through the valleys. Those which flow west or southwest eventually empty into the Pacific; those flowing east or southeast empty into the Hood Canal, which is in reality an arm of Puget Sound.

There is now a fine paved road, the Heart o' the Hills Highway, from Port Angeles to Hurricane Ridge. This makes it easier to visit this area and, in addition, permits a loop trip back to the highway at Elwha.

One of the finest trails, the Elwha River Trail, branches from the road to Hurricane Ridge at a point nine miles south of Elwha and follows the river of the same name through the very center of the park, past several of the higher peaks. Hardy hikers may cross the park from north to south by continuing on the Elwha River Trail to a dirt road which follows the north fork of the Quinault River to Lake Quinault on Route 101. This trip, which requires several days, is only for the experienced hiker packing adequate supplies.

Although we did not follow the Elwha River Trail far, we saw enough to realize that the valley floors with their thickets and meadows and their coniferous forests make this a most remarkable place to combine enjoyment of scenery with fine bird watching. Among the species to be seen from the Elwha River Trail are the Harlequin Duck, Blue Grouse, Rufous Hummingbird, Dipper, Winter Wren, Varied and Swainson's Thrushes, MacGillivray's Warbler, Western Tanager, Black-headed Grosbeak, and White-crowned Sparrow.

The immense conifers harbor two other interesting species, the Townsend's and Hermit Warblers, close relatives of the Black-throated Green Warbler which does not occur here. Also in the forest, but at lower elevations, are the attractive Chestnut-backed Chickadees and the handsome Band-tailed Pigeons. Actually the latter occupy a variety of habitats. We saw Band-tailed Pigeons in many different places from chaparral to mountain forests.

The haunting, whistled melody of the Varied Thrush is as much a part of the spruce forest on the Olympic Peninsula as the flute-like song of the Swainson's Thrush is of the evergreen forests in the northeast. Although closely resembling the Robin, the Varied

Thrush differs from that species in having two rusty wing-bars, a rusty eye-stripe, and a prominent black band across the breast. Its song, a long-sustained pure note of unbelievable clarity, followed by a pause and then another note on a different pitch— then by a succession of pauses and single notes—fits perfectly into the beauty and wildness of the setting. A chorus of Varied Thrushes, singing just before dusk, reflects the grandeur and solemnity of the Olympics and provides a lovely climax to a day in the great Northwest.

Having descended from Hurricane Ridge to Elwha, we drove westward again on Route 101. Very soon we encountered some crows obviously small with peculiarly abrupt, low-pitched calls, which reminded us very much of the familiar Fish Crows. These were Northwestern Crows, formerly considered a race of the Common Crow, but given specific status in the fifth edition of *The A.O.U. Check-List*. They occur along the shores of Puget Sound and the Strait of Juan de Fuca and also near the western coast of Washington.

We continued westward and then south until, about thirteen miles beyond the town of Forks, we came to the Hoh River Road, which follows the Hoh River Valley east from Route 101. It enters the park, and, at a point nineteen miles from the highway, dead-ends in a temperate rain forest—one of the most weirdly beautiful places we had ever visited.

One thinks of a rain forest as being in the tropics and the majority of them are. However, west of the Olympics the combination of an annual rainfall of 140 inches—the heaviest in our forty-eight contiguous states—and a mild climate tempered by the sea, have produced an unbelievably luxuriant forest. Its dominant trees are western hemlock and Sitka spruce, with Douglas fir and western red cedar also very common. Some of these giants exceed 200 feet in height and justify the park's boast that this rain forest contains the largest known specimens of all four species. Along the stream banks are red alder, black cottonwood, and bigleaf maple. Mosses of many different kinds form a spongy carpet underfoot and drape the tree trunks and fallen trees. Ferns are astonishingly abundant everywhere.

As we stood in this great forest with weak sunlight filtering down through the upper canopy, the area around us was pervaded by a greenish light which imparted a feeling of unreality. This and the cathedral-like stillness so took possession of us that we spoke in hushed tones. Never have I been so spellbound, so subdued, so completely dwarfed.

Available in this forest, at the beginning of a nicely marked nature trail, was an interpretive leaflet to explain the wonders on every side. While following this trail, we came suddenly upon a row of very large trees in a line so straight that they looked for all the world as if they had been planted by man. The explanation of this row of trees was intriguing. In time a great fallen tree becomes a moist rotting log, an ideal nursery for seedlings which cannot possibly hold their own on the forest floor because of the smothering, heavy cover of ground plants. After the "nurse tree," as it is termed, has completely decayed and the seedlings have developed into sizable trees, they still stand in a row along the site of the nurse tree—to the amazement of visitors. Sometimes the seedlings on the nurse tree extend their roots down both sides of the log and into the ground. After the log has crumbled away, a row of trees on "stilts" remains, mute, but convincing evidence of the manner in which they managed to survive.

Besides this rain forest there are others equally as fine in the valleys of the Queets and Quinault Rivers, and a visit to any one of them is a rich experience.

Birds, not too common in the rain forests, stayed, for the most part, high up in the trees and were difficult to identify because of distance and the subdued light. Two of the species that we found in the rain forests were the Winter Wren and the Varied Thrush, both of which nest in these places.

The diminutive and perky Winter Wren seemed strangely out of place among the giant trees. Nonetheless, this secretive bird prefers the shady places—especially the woodland floor with its lush mosses and tangled vines—and, by virtue of its vocal accomplishments, is a prominent member of the community even though it is more frequently heard than seen. This notable songster produces a series of exquisite, clear notes, interspersed with trills and warbles, and uttered so rapidly that the bird appears to be "bubbling over." One is ever amazed at such an outpouring of song from the tiny body. To capture the full magic of the music of the Winter Wren, it is necessary to listen closely because some of the notes, like the highest notes of the violin, are so high in pitch that they are barely audible.

From the Ranger Station at the end of the Hoh River Road there is a moss-covered trail which follows the north fork of the Hoh River closely. In the undisturbed areas along the Hoh River Trail the breeding birds you are likely to see are about the same as those found along the Elwha River Trail mentioned previously. After seven or eight miles the Hoh River Trail then turns south, crosses the river, and continues another four miles or more to its end just north of Mt. Olympus and close to the center of the park. From here it is possible to climb the Blue Glacier on the slopes of Mt. Olympus. However, this trip should be undertaken only by experienced climbers who have first consulted with a park ranger.

All the wildlife in the park is more easily observed while hiking along the trails than when driving along the roads. Squirrels and chipmunks are numerous, and the Olympic marmot and black-tailed deer are not at all uncommon by the roadsides or in the more frequented areas. The black bear, also fairly common, has an instinct for self-preservation which sends him scurrying off, permitting you limited views of him at best. There are many Roosevelt elk in the park. Although the majority of these animals stay at the higher altitudes during the summer months, some remain in the lower valleys where they are readily seen.

Returning to Route 101 from the rain forest, we drove a few miles farther south to the Olympic Ocean Strip, near the town of Ruby Beach. Off the coast at this point lies Destruction Island where there is a sizable nesting colony of Rhinoceros Auklets and Pigeon Guillemots. Through our telescopes we had excellent views of both species, as well as of the Marbled Murrelets and Tufted Puffins which occur there in lesser numbers.

Coastal Washington is very picturesque. The more northerly part is a varied panorama of rocky cliffs and promontories and, close to shore, an assortment of sea stacks, needles, and natural arches and caves, with many other unusual rock formations which seem to have been scattered willy-nilly by a giant hand. Some of the small rocky islands are breeding places for such birds as the Fork-tailed and Leach's Petrels, all three species of cormorants found on the Pacific Coast, and five species of alcids—Common Murre, Pigeon Guillemot, Cassin's Auklet, Rhinoceros Auklet, and

Tufted Puffin. Farther south, rows of sand dunes line many fine beaches that provide good "shorebirding" in the proper seasons.

We continued along the concrete ribbon until we reached Lake Quinault, just outside the park's southern border. Here, we reluctantly turned southward—toward home. Moments after doing so, the urge to return was already upon us.

Olympic National Park is the only national park which offers the visitor the unique combination of snow-covered peaks, subalpine meadows, rain forests, and sandy beaches. The summers are sunny and cool, which makes driving, hiking, or climbing ever pleasurable. While a few days spent in this wonderland will give you a good working knowledge of the region, a month's stay is not enough. If you are fortunate enough to spend an entire summer, you will never lack for new features to see and new places to explore. Such is the magnitude of this Olympic wonderland.

# GLACIER NATIONAL PARK

## J. Gordon Edwards

*J. Gordon Edwards, professor of entomology at San Jose State College in California, was born in Wilmington, Ohio, in 1919, graduated from Butler University, and received a doctorate from Ohio State University.*

*Beginning with an intense interest in scouting that led to the status of Diamond Eagle with fifty-two merit badges and experience as assistant scout-master, most of Gordon Edwards's activities, both recreational and professional, have been concerned with some phase of biology or natural history. While an undergraduate at Butler University in Indianapolis, he served as park naturalist in Brown County State Park. Later, as a graduate student at Ohio State, he assisted in a course in ornithology and concentrated on entomology. His thesis, "Coleoptera or Beetles East of the Great Plains," was published in 1949.*

*During nine summers spent as a ranger-naturalist in Glacier National Park, Montana, where several different life zones are of relatively easy access, he recognized a splendid opportunity to study insects in a montane habitat—and took full advantage of it. Giving special attention to alpine ecology and entomology, he climbed all the major peaks in the park. The details of his climbing routes, written up at the request of the Park Service, later became a book with fifty photographs,* Climbers' Guide to Glacier National Park, *published by the Sierra Club of California in 1960.*

*Although he is no longer a ranger-naturalist, Gordon Edwards cannot keep away from the tops of high mountains. His field researches in the past few years have centered on alpine insects, in the pursuit of which he and his wife and daughter have hiked, climbed, and camped numberless times in the lofty wildernesses of Montana and Wyoming. His excuse for holidays in these glorious parts of our country may always be the study of insects, but, as the following article so aptly demonstrates, he is ever aware of the setting and is interested in all forms of wildlife.*

Glacier National Park embraces more than a million acres of the Montana Rocky Mountains adjacent to Alberta and British Columbia. Visitors approaching from the great prairies of middle and eastern Montana will be excited by the sight of glistening snow and ice among the jagged summits rimming the western horizon and delighted with the prospects of cool breezes and plentiful ice water. Between the prairies and the peaks lie extensive forested areas that are not visible until one approaches the eastern boundary of this third largest national park. West of the Continental Divide the dense forest continues nearly unbroken for at least 150 miles, gradually yielding to open stands of ponderosa pine in the vicinity of Spokane, Washington.

Nearly all of the roads in the park are within this forested zone, as are the great hotels and the numerous motels and cabins. The famous Going-to-the-Sun Highway cuts across the center of Glacier National Park at Logan Pass, affording access to all four "life zones," namely, (1) the Transition or Prairie Zone, (2) the Canadian or Coniferous Forest Zone, (3) the Hudsonian or Scrub-forest Zone, and (4) the Arctic or Alpine Zone. Each of these great zones might easily be further subdivided into significantly different ecological regions, with characteristic plants, insects, mammals, and birds inhabiting the various ecologically different environments.

Along the eastern boundary of the Park there are numerous invasions of narrow tongues of the prairie life zone where Black-billed Magpies, Common Crows, Common Ravens, Western Meadowlarks, Mourning Doves, and several species of sparrows and hawks abound. The road from Babb to Cardston is lined with telephone poles that serve as popular reconnaissance posts for hawks—Red-tailed, Swainson's, Ferruginous, Cooper's, and Marsh. Numerous small, aspen-bordered ponds and swales, as well as several larger lakes, may be reached easily from Browning, St. Mary, Babb, or Waterton. These bodies of water surrounded by arid land harbor Red-necked, Eared, and Western Grebes, Red-breasted and Hooded Mergansers, and dozens of kinds of ducks, shorebirds, and marsh inhabitants.

Within the nearby forests there is less evidence of birdlife, but kinglets, nuthatches, and woodpeckers will always be seen or heard by alert bird finders here. The pleasant and persistent song of the diminutive Ruby-crowned Kinglet is heard almost constantly in the deep woods of the Canadian Zone, and around Lake Mc-Donald and in other low-level valleys the wonderfully melodious fluting of the Varied Thrush enchants the forest at dusk. Both the Red-breasted and White-breasted Nuthatches abound here, and the woodpecker clan is represented by the Pileated, Hairy, Downy, Black-backed Three-toed, Northern Three-toed, and Lewis' Woodpeckers as well as (Red-naped) Yellow-bellied and Williamson's Sapsuckers and the omnipresent Red-shafter Flicker. I have also seen the Red-breasted Nuthatch more than a thousand feet above treeline, creeping over the vertical cliff-faces and picking insects from the lichen-encrusted rocks. Woodpeckers also are frequently sighted far above timberline, winging strongly across the high passes far from any trees worthy of their attention.

In open glades one often encounters hummingbirds, and a Rufous Hummingbird nest was found about eight feet above ground on a western red cedar branch at Apgar. It was thickly lined with fluffy material from nearby cottonwood poplars while the outside was beautifully camouflaged with lichens. Other hummingbirds recorded from the park are the Broad-tailed, Black-chinned, and Calliope. It is amazing how frequently these tiny "whirring dervishes" are also observed at extremely high elevations, taking advantage of the tremendous masses of showy flowers in the alpine meadows, then darting across the very summits of the tallest peaks, rather than circumnavigating them via the snowy passes.

Along the icy, impatient streams at low elevations there are two ornithological *pièces de résistance*, the Harlequin Ducks and the Dippers (Water Ouzels). Harlequin Ducks are by far the most colorful birds in the park, and their behavior is possibly even more distinctive than their coloration. Occasionally a family of these rare ducks is discovered and reported, whereupon numerous bird enthusiasts follow the directions to the favored locale in hopes of observing them in action.

Certain places appear to rank high in the esteem of Harlequin Ducks, and intensive searching in these areas might produce them at any time. These localities include: Upper McDonald Creek and Mineral Creek (there is also a possibility of seeing an otter at play here); Avalanche Creek (between the gorge and Avalanche Lake); Grinnell Creek (between Grinnell Lake and Lake Josephine); and St. Mary Creek (above St. Mary Falls). Unfortunately, these places are not easy to reach, for they involve considerable threshing about in dense brush. The uncomfortable approach is followed by a long and usually fruitless wait and an attempt to remain mute while nourishing hordes of mosquitoes. This combination of difficulties prevents all but the most stoic (or fortunate) bird watchers from observing these elusive birds, but those who do find them are richly rewarded for their efforts.

In the foaming torrent the brilliant Harlequin drake and his drab-colored family perform as though they truly enjoy the challenge of icy rapids and cataracts. They bob about in the churning water, frequently disappearing from view completely as they are swept violently downstream through the maelstrom. They often go down single-file, then gather below the rapids for a flight back upstream and another joyous descent. Although these "aquanauts" prefer swift, secluded streams, they have also been seen on Iceberg Lake, Gunsight Lake, Grinnell Lake, and Lake Josephine.

The aquatic acrobat, even more proficient in mountain torrents than the Harlequin Duck but not at all spectacular in appearance, is the Dipper. The brightest part of the Dipper is its white eyelid, and when these drab, gray, wren-like birds blink suddenly, their eyelids fairly flash. Whereas the Harlequin displays an amazing buoyancy in the rapids, the Dipper appears as much at home beneath the torrent as when floating on its surface. Moving pictures are said to have proved that these birds practically "fly" under water, actually utilizing their wings for propulsion! Certainly they cannot rely upon their feet for swimming because their toes are not at all webbed or enlarged, so they probably *do* find it necessary to locomote by flapping their wings while under water.

Dippers are well named because they constantly do "deep knee-bends" while standing or walking confidently over the rocks in the frigid mountain streams. I have seen even the young Dippers adamantly engaging in this strenuous exercise on the first or second day out of the nest as they stand chattering on a rock in midstream, imploring their parents to hurry with their rations of mayfly and stonefly naiads. The older birds perform admirably, stalking intrepidly into the swiftest part of the rapids, ignoring the pounding of the spray and frequently walking right on down the rocky slopes *and out of sight under the water!* They may then be invisible for several seconds, after which they reappear in some totally unexpected location. They may simply walk back up onto a rock or may slowly surface and flutter to shore, but their most spectacular feat is to burst suddenly forth from the mountain stream and into full flight as if quite surprised to find themselves in a medium so much less dense than the water.

Most western ornithologists have probably already seen Dippers, because the range of these birds trends southward in the mountains to New Mexico and southern California (they also live in the mountains of Mexico and Panama). Wherever they dwell they are viewed with astonishment, and their bubbling, wren-like song is one of the happiest of any bird I know. They seldom have much time for singing during their busy summer, yet they occasionally do burst into song at any time of the year. Near Glacier National Park a man reported hearing one in January, when the temperature was 35 degrees below zero, and "looking out, discovered him sitting on a little rock in the middle of an icy stream. . . ."

Dippers construct their mossy ball of a nest on damp walls not far from the spray of waterfalls or cascades. More rarely they place them beneath bridges across swift mountain streams, and in Glacier Park they can often be found nesting beneath the Sprague Creek bridge, near Lake McDonald. Places where Dippers can almost always be seen include: Avalanche Gorge, Sunrift Gorge, Baring Falls, Trick Falls, Swiftcurrent Falls, Hidden Falls, Iceberg Creek, and along the largest stream on Logan Pass.

Although the feathered residents of prairie, lake, forest, and stream are all very interesting, it is the alpine avifauna that is the most unique. Birds found at lower elevations in Glacier Park also occur throughout most of the cooler parts of western United States, but there are only a few kinds that habitually live above timberline and these all have a much more limited geographical distribution. Because the timberline is less than 6,800 feet above sea level this far north and even scrub trees seldom grow above 7,000 feet, the alpine habitat is more readily accessible here than anywhere else south of the Canadian border. Going-to-the-Sun Highway passes through the Hudsonian Zone at Logan Pass, from which it is only an easy 500 feet higher to the Alpine Zone. The four most typical birds at these elevations are White-tailed Ptarmigan, Water Pipits, Gray-crowned Rosy Finches, and Clark's Nutcrackers.

Nutcrackers are commonly seen above timberline, but they nest in the trees far below and hence are not true residents of the Alpine Zone. I have often seen these black-and-white crows picking insects from lichen-covered rocks near the summits of our highest mountains, and a night at high camp will nearly always be terminated at dawn by the loud, raucous, almost vulgar calls of these pugnacious birds.

The Ptarmigan, or Alpine Grouse, occur everywhere above timberline in Glacier National Park, but the extensive meadows on Logan Pass appear to be their favorite habitat, despite considerable annoyance by people. Their nest has often been described as merely a depression on the open ground, but on Logan Pass they line the nest with dry grass and other alpine plants. Nearly every hiking party crossing the "Hanging Gardens" at Logan Pass will encounter adult Ptarmigan, and ornithologists can always find them with ease, but the nests are much more difficult to locate.

In their brown, mottled summer plumage Ptarmigan are difficult to see on dirt or rocks and they instinctively avoid walking across the snow. If chased onto snowfields they will immediately either run back onto bare ground or else take flight and flap their way noisily down the mountainside. By October the summer feathers have been replaced by a pure white garb that blends well with their snowy winter habitat. The birds then reverse their behavior, shunning bare ground or rocks and endeavoring to always remain on a snowy background.

One summer a female Ptarmigan was discovered nesting at Logan Pass and was kept under observation by several naturalists. Subsequently a July snowstorm blanketed the entire pass with a foot of fresh snow and obliterated all trace of the nest. Upon making a final search for the nest or the bird, two days later, we were amazed to see the bird's head projecting through a small opening in the snow. She had not deserted her nest at all, but had been calmly incubating her eggs even while buried beneath a foot of fresh wet snow! Her perseverance was not entirely rewarded, for two days later a mountain lion found the nest (probably by following our tracks through the snow). The story was clearly revealed by the marks on the snow, indicating two tremendous leaps the lion made in its attempt to catch the fleeing grouse and its slow return to the nest, where it crushed and ate the eggs, leaving only a few speckled shell fragments. Evidently the lion was feared much more than man, at least by that particular Ptarmigan, because it is usually possible for a person to reach out carefully and actually stroke the back of the incubating bird without having it take flight. I have often captured Ptarmigan by hand, even away from the nest, by simply approaching them quietly and distracting them with one hand while grabbing them behind the neck with the other.

The summer range of White-tailed Ptarmigan encompasses only the Hudsonian and Alpine regions, but during severe winter storms they may temporarily retreat into the valleys far below. I have seen Ptarmigan or their signs on nearly every high pass in this park, and they undoubtedly also occur on every peak of the several hundred above 7,000 feet in elevation here. No matter how often you have seen Ptarmigan, it is still a pleasant thrill to renew the acquaintance, and the glorious mountain scenery surrounding their environment always makes the occasion even more memorable.

Water Pipits also inhabit the high meadows and construct their grass-lined nests in lush alpine meadows surrounded by acres of glacier lilies, globeflowers, pasque flowers, paintbrush, blue gentian, and heather. The birds can be recognized from afar by their exaggerated tail-wagging, while their prominent white outer tail-feathers may advertise their identity if they suddenly dart from beneath your feet. Although common at much lower elevations during their winter migrations, Pipits breed only near mountain tops in the United States and in the frozen tundra regions farther to the north.

Far above the nesting sites of the Ptarmigan and Pipit, and right up to the very summits of the greatest peaks in the Rockies, the glaciers and snowfields provide natural outdoor refrigeration that preserves live insects in a frigid, paralyzed condition. For poorly understood reasons, great numbers of beetles, flies, butterflies, and other insects migrate up the mountains to the very highest point, often even flying against strong winds to get there. As they cross large expanses of snow or ice their flight muscles become numbed by the cold air and their adventuresome flight is abruptly terminated. Other insects, as well as small spiders, pollen grains, and vast quantities of non-living debris, are constantly being blown up onto the glaciers and snowfields.

Regardless of the origin, there is always a liberal sprinkling of frozen insects on these high snow surfaces. The native alpine ground bettles and spiders cannot possibly eat all of these helpless victims, so the Gray-crowned Rosy Finches have also learned to patronize this great natural automat. There are invariably a few of them walking busily over the snow at the mountaintop, snapping up the insects and frequently giving vent to their loud, high-pitched twitterings. Even on the most miserable, windy, sleety, foggy days they are present, and they almost seem to be welcoming the rare human visitors to their bleak domain. When they fly they may be readily recognized by their bright pink wing-patches and rump-spot, and the males frequently elevate their black crown and reveal even more clearly their broad gray head-patch. Females are duller in color but behave similarly and display the same fearless and friendly attitude toward human visitors. These hardy birds breed in high mountains in all of our northwestern states, as well as in Canada and Alaska.

Detailed observations of the unique behavior and biology of these feathered alpinists may well mark the highest point of any ornithologist's visit to Glacier National Park, and biologists who have also made good use of their opportunities while at lower elevations will surely leave the park with a great feeling of satisfaction and an intense desire to return again and again.

# IN COLORADO—LAND OF THE LONG SPRING

## Alfred M. Bailey

Among the elite of the all-time "natural history lecturers" is Alfred M. Bailey, museum director, world traveler, and photographer. Today, as in the past five decades, a Bailey program is always an assurance of exotic adventures, illustrated by a superlative film.

Alfred Marshall Bailey was born in Iowa City, Iowa, in 1894, graduated from the University of Iowa, and, as an undergraduate in 1912–1913, made his first expedition—to Laysan Island in the Pacific. After graduation he served as curator of birds and mammals in the Louisiana State Museum in New Orleans (1916– 1919); was the first representative in Alaska of the present Fish and Wildlife Service (1919–1921); and collected specimens in Arctic Alaska for the Denver Museum with which he was associated as curator of birds and mammals until 1926. He was a zoologist on the Chicago Natural History Museum's nine-month expedition to Abyssinia where he traveled some 2,000 miles on muleback through that rugged kingdom. From 1927 to 1936 he was director of the Chicago Academy of Sciences, and since 1936 he has guided, as director, the destiny of the Denver Museum of Natural History.

Although Alfred Bailey's insatiable desire for adventure has taken him to many faraway places, it can be said that his heart has stayed in Colorado. One senses this in his devotion to the fine

133

*museum in Denver, in his revealing films of the state, and no less so here when he writes of the Colorado spring and its birds.*

          For those who enjoy prolonged seasons I recommend our mountainous West, Colorado especially, where spring is dragged out far beyond the normal length known to Flatlanders. Colorado is often called "Mother of Rivers" because of the five great streams rising within its borders—the mighty Colorado and the San Juan, which make their way westward beyond the Continental Divide to flow eventually into the Pacific drainage, while the Platte, Arkansas, and the Rio Grande take the eastern course to the Gulf of Mexico. Three of these, the Colorado, Arkansas, and Rio Grande are among the five longest streams in the nation, their total length of 4,785 miles being only a few miles less than the combined mighty Mississippi and the Missouri Rivers.

The mountains are responsible for the prolonged seasons. King Winter rules the high places in late April when Spring brings the first tinge of green to cottonwoods and willows along prairie streams. Snows are deep in the mountains, but the first migrants of the avian world are beginning to trickle along the shallow watercourses of the plains and to congregate in sheltered spots, awaiting the time when weather conditions will be favorable for them to ascend into the hills to their preferred nesting habitats. The prairies range in elevation from 3,500 to 5,500 feet. Some of the resident birds here have started housekeeping. The male Horned Larks are carrying on their courtship activities, rising high in the air and singing as they descend, while in the sheltered draws Long-eared and Great Horned Owls have white downy young demanding attention.

Colorado has all the life zones of the west except the Lower Sonoran, which is typical of the desert to the southwest in Arizona. The Upper Sonoran is represented by the prairie and the pinyon-juniper country of the southern part of the state. The plains rise gradually toward the west and merge with the foothills at around 5,500 feet, where scrub oak and mountain mahogany are plant markers of the beginning of the Transition Zone, which ranges upward through the ponderosa pine belt to around 8,500 feet. This pine is the characteristic tree of the Transition, but Douglas fir grows on north hillsides and the Colorado blue spruce—the state tree—in the moist mountain valleys. The tall and slender lodgepole pines, growing close together, mark the start of the Canadian Zone, and above are the great coniferous forests of Engelmann spruce. These give way at altitudes between 11,000 and 11,500 feet, depending upon slope exposure and latitude, to sprawling, windblown, twisted trees which are characteristic of timberline and the rather poorly defined Hudsonian Zone. On above are the alpine savannahs of the Arctic-Alpine Zone where shrubs sprawl close to the earth, flowers of great beauty dot the landscape in midsummer, and lichens cover the rocks.

To journey from the prairies to the mountain tops is the equivalent of traveling northward through the Canadian forests to where the line of trees gradually becomes dwarfed and windblown and gives way to the arctic tundras.

Spring travels slowly up the mountain. June is the time of roses in Denver; birds are at the height of their nesting activity—and the high mountains are still locked with the winter snows. By mid-June flowers dot the open slopes and forests of the Transition; in July the moist borders of the mountain lakes of the Canadian Zone are massed with bloom; and after the middle of the month into August the alpine savannahs are colorful with the typical flowers of the high country. So spring in Colorado extends from April to past mid-July, giving the naturalist three and a half or more months for active field work. Let us start on the prairie and follow the nesting upward.

Each life zone has its varied topography and plant associations and the naturalist learns where to search for different flowers and birds. The country is so vast that not all areas of a given zone could be intensively studied in any one spring—there are too many species of interest. The principal habitats of the Upper Sonoran of the eastern part of the state differ greatly, and each has its quota of birdlife. We have separated the Upper Sonoran of eastern Colorado into the following areas: (1) pinyon- and juniper-clad hills and adjacent slopes; (2) grasslands of the southeast; (3) rolling prairies; (4) prairie escarpments; (5) wooded watercourses of the prairies; (6) marshes, and open and wooded shorelines of prairie reservoirs.

Spring comes first in the southeast, to the hot canyon walls and rocky slopes covered with pinyon and juniper, and to the grass-lands adjacent to the little town of Campo in Baca County. We often have started our season's work there, and memory takes us back to those days afield—early mornings in April on the open grasslands where from our photographic blinds we watched the male Lesser Prairie Chickens going through their strutting courtship per-formances for the benefit of their prospective mates. Nearby were little tree claims in sheltered swales, long since abandoned by discouraged homesteaders, which would, a little later in the sea-son, provide nesting places for Mockingbirds and Loggerhead Shrikes. And on adjacent rocky slopes, clad in juniper and pinyon, Scaled Quail were paired and the melodious calls of the males indicated they had staked out their territories for the coming season.

The Roadrunner is fairly numerous in that southeastern cor-ner of the state, and his small associates of the wooded hillside are the inconspicuous Bushtits, Plain Titmice, and Blue-gray Gnat-catchers. Each has been a challenge, for we have searched for and found their nests. The pendant beautiful structure of the Bushtit, in either pinyon or juniper, is fashioned from spider webs, silk from cocoons of insects or spiders, lichens, leaves or plant fibers—and when we examined one it literally exploded with eight fully-fledged young taking off in all directions. A little Titmouse refused to leave her eggs that we found in a natural cavity. When we picked her up she clung tightly to the nest lining, and after we had examined her, she promptly returned to her nest as though there had been no interference. A pair of tiny Gnatcatchers that we discovered nest-ing on a bare limb of a juniper had a problem, for the two adults were doing their utmost to satisfy the demands of a lubberly young Brown-headed Cowbird nearly twice the size of its foster parents.

Often we have anticipated the coming of spring by starting our field work in late winter, searching for the nests of birds of prey along wooded watercourses or precipitous escarpments. Eagles, hawks, and owls are among the first to nest in Colorado, and the majority dwell in the Sonoran Zone. Through the years we have enjoyed going out on the prairie to precipitous ledges in February to observe the magnificent Golden Eagles and to determine which of their several nest sites might be in use. Apparently the Golden Eagle remains mated for years, and over a period of time may have nested in different places in a given territory, on cliffs or in towering ponderosa pines. We have examined many nests from photographic blinds. A favorite spot for birds of prey of several species has been the escarpment in the northeast corner of the state near Hereford, in Weld County. Possibly more Eagles nest there than in any like area of the state while their neighbors are the fast-flying Prairie Falcons and the Ferruginous Hawks—the latter justly having been given the specific name *regalis*. One season we had four different Eagle nests along the line of cliffs and spent hours in blinds, securing motion-film footage.

Along the ledge we found an occupied Prairie Falcon eyrie. The female, to our astonishment, was a beautiful albinistic creature. Her four brown-splotched eggs were on rock debris on a little shelf, and our blind, which had been up for a couple weeks and accepted by the nesting pair, was in an unusually good location, with a clear view into the cavity in the cliff. However, after I was installed, the adults circled and dived at my hiding place. They would land on the cliff above and then, using its edge for a launching site, plummet downward, screaming as they swooped over my shelter. Something was amiss. Finally I realized there was a glare from the lens of my movie camera. To remedy this, I cut a piece of canvas off the blind, wrapped it around the barrel, and waited hopefully. All was quiet until suddenly there was a swish of wings and a plop. Looking through the camera I saw, straddling her eggs, the most beautiful falcon I have ever photographed—the almost white female.

At the same time that the ledges of Weld County are used as nesting sites, the Red-tailed and Swainson's Hawks are building in tall cottonwoods of the prairie stream beds, sometimes using the abandoned mud-and-stick homes of Black-billed Magpies and Great Horned Owls. The Red-tails have the more extensive habitat, for they range upward into the ponderosa pines of the Transition Zone, while the latter are more common on the prairies. Formerly we could find half a dozen nests of both Red-tails and Swainson's on a day's journey along the watercourses, but now we feel fortunate to locate one or two. Both take kindly to the efforts of photographers, once they have become accustomed to blinds.

The open prairies covered with virgin stands of buffalo grass, prickly pear, and yucca have their own quota of nesting species.

The most common of the song birds are the little Horned Larks, the first to start nesting. Soon the male Lark Buntings, conspicuously black-plumaged with white-patched wings, put in their appearance, to be followed very shortly by the females. (The Lark Bunting is Colorado's state bird.) During the latter part of May the prairie east of Denver seems alive with Larks and Buntings performing their aerial maneuvers, rising rapidly high above the ground, then settling on outstretched wing and singing as they drop to some prominent perch. Farther to the northward, at the base of our eagle cliffs, McCown's Longspurs have similar courtship actions and there is one little valley, just below the Wyoming line south of Cheyenne, in which always we find pairs of the handsome Chestnut-collared Longspurs.

Probably the prairie bird most desired by birders is the Mountain Plover—an inconspicuous upland shorebird about the size of a Killdeer. A misnomer, it lives on the short-grass prairie instead of in the mountains and still is to be found in numbers on the unbroken buffalo grass plains, especially in Weld County near the Hereford Cliffs. In the southern part of the state, in the Lesser Prairie Chicken country, the Long-billed Curlew is a fairly common bird on the dry prairie. A couple of seasons ago one nested east of Denver in a most unusual place—the center of a clump of prickly pear which obligingly came into bloom just at the time the eggs were hatching. My daughter, Patricia Witherspoon, photographed the birds in mid-June. Her view from the slit in the blind was all that one could ask—a long-beaked female Curlew half astraddle her downy young among the yellow-golden cactus blooms and, in the distance, the snow-topped mountains of the Front Range.

From a plane high in the air the eastern prairies seem dotted with reservoirs. Each adjacent marsh has its quota of nesting Yellow-headed and Red-winged Blackbirds, Yellowthroats, Virginia Rails, American Coots, and various species of ducks, including the strikingly colorful Cinnamon Teal; and on the shorelines many species of waders—Semipalmated and occasional Snowy Plovers, Dowitchers, Marbled Godwits, and small sandpipers—gather in migration. And nesting commonly here are the Killdeer, Wilson's Phalarope, and the long-legged Avocet.

Many of the ponds and reservoirs throughout the state are

lined with cottonwoods and willows where Double-crested Cormorants, Great Blue Herons, and Snowy Egrets nest when unmolested. Unfortunately, motor boats have become so numerous upon the large waterways that many species have had to abandon areas they have long used.

By mid-June spring has moved into the foothills clad with scrub oak and ponderosa pine. One of our favorite spots here is Daniels Park, twenty miles south of Denver. It is on a spur of the Transition Zone separated from the main foothills to the west by a valley fifteen miles wide. Along the canyon walls we regularly hear both Rock and Cañon Wrens and have found their nests tucked away in crevices. Steller's and Scrub Jays (usually elusive camera subjects because they are smarter than the photographers) build their bulky nests in scrub oak and pine; Virginia's Warblers and Rufous-sided Towhees nest under the scrub oaks; Black-headed Grosbeaks nest a few feet higher, in the oaks, and the bright-colored Western Tanagers just overhead in the ponderosas. Swift-flying Sharp-shinned and Cooper's Hawks nest regularly in the almost impenetrable draws. By the time the young are in the nest, in mid-June, the moist floor below is tinted with the blue blossoms of the columbine, Colorado's state flower. An attractive ecological niche nearby, just south of Franktown, is the Castlewood Dam area where, in the ponderosa pine, Douglas fir, and scrub oak standing against steep walls, we find regularly in mid-June the semi-hanging nests of the Warbling, Red-eyed, and Solitary Vireos—all birds unbelievably tame. Just to the southeast on the high, rolling prairie early in the spring is a courtship ground of Sharp-tailed Grouse. For forty years that we know of, these birds have performed here against the backdrop of magnificent Pikes Peak, white with snow.

Readily available to all is the highway leading to Red Rocks Park west of Denver, where male Yellow-breasted Chats, the largest of our warblers, serenade visitors from the tips of the shrubs, and White-throated Swifts nest in the crannies of the spectacularly uptilted formations which came to the surface during the mountain building of 50 million years ago. The road leads up Bear Creek Canyon in whose steep walls Dippers nest. At the little town of Evergreen a motel keeper attracts all the birds of the neighborhood to his feeding tray. Nearby in the open pine forests, some Goshawks built a nest in 1962 and we erected a blind for observations. The female was gentle while she was incubating, merely rising and with drooping wings gave her strident *yah-yah* of protest whenever we climbed to the blind. When her eggs hatched, however, she was a diving fury and promptly knocked the first would-be observer from the ladder.

Spring has left the prairie by the time flowers are at their best in the Transition. The highway turns to the right at Evergreen and passes through open pine country to Bergen Park. In the trees on the adjacent hillsides the Williamson's and Yellow-bellied Sapsuckers nest regularly—the young in the nesting holes often revealing their presence by wheezy cries as they await the return of parents with beaks filled with ants.

The road to the high country branches to the left, climbs above the ponderosas into stands of aspens and lodgepole pines, and on up into the Canadian Zone where the Engelmann spruce forests mass the mountainsides. Our favorite, easily accessible area is Echo Lake at 10,600 feet with its magnificent stretch of forest and views of mountain peaks. At the picnic spots assemble the Gray Jays—the camp robbers—and the equally tame Clark's Nutcrackers to obtain handouts from visitors. Once we photographed a nesting Northern Three-toed Woodpecker that had obligingly drilled its hole only five feet from the ground. The birds were so tame we stood just ten feet away while they fed their young without show of fear.

It is early July, and spring has just arrived at this elevation. The marshy area at the east end of Echo Lake shelters pairs of nesting White-crowned and Lincoln's Sparrows and tiny black-capped, yellow-gold Wilson's Warblers. Spotted Sandpipers bob along the bare shoreline and soon reveal their protectively colored eggs in short vegetation. Flowering bistort and elephantella dot the boggy places. Here we expect to see a flash of pink and yellowish color as pairs of elusive Pine Grosbeaks come to feed upon the half-ripened fruit of the marsh marigold. By taking a line on their upward flight into the dense forest of the mountainside, we obtain a clue to the location of their nests.

The twisting highway to the summit of Mt. Evans is usually free of snow and open to traffic in early June, and now in late July we climb rapidly through stands of picturesque, sprawling, windblown bristle-cone pines. Twisted and leaning, they testify to the fury of the winds. Along the cut banks of the road, under the exposed roots of a tree just ten feet away, is tucked a nest of rather heavy twigs. As the car stops, a Townsend's Solitaire settles lower in it and watches carefully, not budging as long as we stay put.

We are now in that indefinite area of timberline, the Hudsonian Zone, which is higher on sunny slopes and lower on the cold northern; above is the treeless Arctic-Alpine, where spring finally climbs and turns the moist tundra country into a vast flower garden. There are only three species of birds which nest regularly in this lofty world. The most conspicuous is the slender Water Pipit, which is readily identified by the flash of white of the feathers and the bobbing motion as it poses upon a worn boulder. Pairs of Brown-capped Rosy Finches, which breed only in Colorado and Wyoming, so far as we know, have their nests in crannies of the steep cliffs above. Their favorite feeding places are on the receding snow banks where insects and windblown seeds are readily available.

But the highlight of any visit to the Alpine Zone is the White-tailed Ptarmigan. It is still early spring in mid-July and the females are upon their eggs, so only a male is likely to be encountered. And usually he is a nonchalant individual, not the least interested, apparently, in any nest nearby. He feeds along, nipping the blossoms off the alpine plants and makes no effort to elude a photographer, unless too closely pressed.

We have searched for nests for forty years and have seen only two, one on Mt. Evans and the other along Trail Ridge Road at 12,000 feet in Rocky Mountain National Park. In the latter area the terrain is much the same as on Mt. Evans. There are numerous Ptarmigan, but the country is large and they are so protectively colored one could pass within a few feet without seeing them.

On one occasion when my daughter Pat and I were on Trail Ridge we followed a male around for an hour without getting a clue to the nest—although we knew from past experience in finding young year after year in that same spot that a female should be on eggs close by. Finally we gave up and started toward our car, passing a family of tourists on their upward climb. I asked them if they would like to see a Ptarmigan. Although they did not know what a Ptarmigan was, they were responsive to my approach and said "yes." I pointed out the cluster of rocks where we had left the male; I explained how concealingly marked the little grouse was, and how carefully they would have to search.

As we went on I remarked to my daughter that the only way to find a Ptarmigan's nest, in my estimation, was to have a bunch of Flatlanders on the mountainside who did not know what a Ptarmigan was—and cared less. We reached our car alongside the road and unwrapped our sandwiches. Just as we started lunch our acquaintance of a short time ago came rushing down the hillside. His breathless inquiry merely confirmed my remark to my daughter about Flatlanders. It was: "Would you like to see the nest?"

We would, and we did. There on the open alpine slope against a lichen-colored boulder—in plain sight—was the little gray, black, and brown hen. In our search we had walked within five feet—on the wrong side of the boulder.

# THE BLACK HILLS OF SOUTH DAKOTA

## Herbert Krause

*Herbert Krause was born in 1905 and raised on a farm near Fergus Falls, Minnesota. In boyhood he "came to know seed-time and harvest from the working end of a plow and pitchfork." Birds were common about his home on the bank of the Otter Tail River. He watched Purple Martins carrying green leaves to their nests and wondered why; he crawled stomach-fashion up a hillside to see a Ruffed Grouse drumming and was fascinated; but his slight interest was undirected and undeveloped. He only knew he wanted to write.*

*Herbert Krause graduated from St. Olaf College and received his master's degree and great encouragement in his chosen field from the University of Iowa. His first novel* Wind without Rain *(1939) was honored with an award from the Friends of American Writers. He became chairman of the English department of Augustana College in Sioux Falls, South Dakota, and continued to write novels—*Neighbor Boy *(1940),* The Thresher *(1946),* Oxcart Trail *(1954)—all concerned with pioneer life in the Upper Midwest.*

*In 1946, with borrowed binoculars, the Cornell Laboratory of Ornithology record, "American Bird Songs," and the suggestions of helpful friends, "birds and bird songs came together in exciting meaningfulness." He wanted to write about birds and realized that in order to do so he must know about birds—comprehensively and*

143

*accurately. Since his education had included no formal work in biology, he spent one of the hottest summers on record at the University of Minnesota grinding away at a course in zoology. After this came two summers studying ornithology at the University of Michigan Biological Station. It was here that I became closely acquainted with him. No student that I have ever had was more determined to absorb so much information and to pass every available moment in the field learning more about birds. For having spent a total of 207 hours in a blind watching the nesting habits of a pair of Canada Warblers, he has my greatest admiration. Birds have since invaded his writing: "Literature of South Dakota Birds: An Annotated Bibliography, 1794–1954" is now in manuscript form; a number of articles and notes have appeared in journals and magazines. In 1961, when he spent eleven months in South Africa as Fulbright visiting lecturer in American literature at the Universities of Witwatersrand and Natal, he was well prepared to study birds in a strange environment. The opportunity to see and take notes on 470 species of birds was to him a cherished experience.*

*Herb Krause's present position, professor of English and author-in-residence at Augustana, allows him ample time to devote to writing. I hope to see more of his poems such as "Giants in the Wooded Earth," composed for the Minnesota Centennial in 1958, more scripts such as "The Big Four," prepared for a wildlife conservation film produced by the University of Minnesota. Above all, I hope to see more of such pieces as the following one about birds in the Black Hills and the seasonal movements of geese along the Missouri River elsewhere in this book. Few people I know can match his smooth-flowing descriptive style and meaty anecdotes.*

It is a mountain upthrust, a pine-covered island outpost in a sea of rolling grass. Viewed from almost any direction across the miles of plains in South Dakota and Wyoming, it towers darkly on the skyline. *Pa-Sapa,* the Indians called it—Black Hills, the Abode of Thunders. *Côtes Noires,* the voyageur French described them; *Costa Negra,* the fur-hungry Spanish. Jean Vallé, meeting Lewis and Clark on the Missouri in 1804, told of his wintering camp "under the Black Mountains" where "roams a

kind of anamale with large circular horns . . . the size of an Elk"
and where is found "a white-booted turkey, an inhabitent," and
where frequently "a great noise is heard." Mystery, mammology,
and ornithology thus meet in this first appearance of bighorn sheep
and Sage Grouse in the record; it may be the first mention of birds
in the Black Hills.

And "Black Hills" James Clyman did call them in his narrative
of Ashley's 1823 fur-trading expedition through the southern part
of the region where a grizzly bear charged down and ripped off
Jedediah Smith's ear and where Black Harris and Bill Sublette
found a "putrified" forest with "putrified" trees on which "putrified" birds sang "putrified" songs. As late as 1876, Colonel Dodge,
commanding the 1875 Jenney Expedition, wrote that the area was
regarded as "the wildest and most mysterious of the unknown
regions" of the West. Today, ribboned with highways, a brooding
duskiness still hangs over the sweeps of blue valley and dour peak.

Older than the Rockies themselves, an isolated yet geographi-
cally distinct area, this outlier manifests a complex of often puzzling floristic and faunistic relationships. Though the ponderosa or
western yellow pine forest reaches its most eastern point here, it is
as an outpost with vast stretches of plains, grasses, and shrubs
between it and its duplicate in the Rockies. Northern white spruce,
marooned in such cool retreats as Spearfish Canyon, find their
counterparts miles to the northward in Canada. Bloodroot, downy
violet, and bunchberry—probably never dry prairie inhabitants—
grow here, though characteristic of eastern deciduous woods.
Short-tailed weasels forage here, although their nearest kin seem to
be found in the Laramie Range and the Big Horn Mountains;
mountain goats, whitely statuesque on Harney's shoulders, occupying a southern outpost in their range, seem far from their
kindred in the western Montana and northern Idaho Rockies.

Like the montane coniferous forms, many of the avian species
of the Rockies reach the eastern edge of their breeding ranges in
the hills. White-throated Swift and Lewis' Woodpecker nest here
as do Western Wood Pewee and Western Flycatcher, Violet-green
Swallow, Piñon Jay, Dipper, Cañon and Rock Wrens, Mountain
Bluebird, Townsend's Solitaire, two warblers, MacGillivray's and
Audubon's, and the spectacular Western Tanager.

Like the white spruce, two northern coniferous-forest birds

apparently are isolated here—the Black-backed and Northern Three-toed Woodpeckers. More continent-wide boreal species nesting in this montane outpost include the kinglets, Red-breasted Nuthatch, Gray Jay, Solitary Vireo (the Plumbeous form), and Red Crossbill. Eastern species present are Ovenbird, American Redstart, House Wren, and others.

One species, the White-winged Junco, is closely confined to the hills and the immediately contiguous environs. It is actually the only species endemic to the hills and, according to Dr. N. R. Whitney, Jr., is readily observed the year around. I've seen it in early and late spring in the pines back of the Whitneys' Rapid City home, generally with a raucous chorus of Piñon Jays.

Intriguing aspects of biological relationships pop up when least expected. One June day in the southern hills near Hot Springs, I was following a creek up a draw whose steep sides terminated in a craggy rim a hundred feet up. Chokecherry, plum, pin cherry, box elder, and festoons of wild grape, bushy along the water's edge, are plants usually associated with eastern woods. Their shade cooled my face. On the rock rim a hundred feet up, yucca thrust its hedge of bayonets protectively about the light-green flowering stalk; prickly-pear cactus hid its pads of needles in the sage. These were plants usually associated with semi-arid or arid western situations. No "togetherness" here; each in its xeric environment maintained an unneighborly distance from the other. Heat rolled down in waves.

What brought me shock-still, listening, however, was a House Wren in front of me, filling a thicket with domestic chatter while above me on the crag a Rock Wren bounced its wild *cher-wee, cher-wee* along the ledge rim. I have never forgotten that moment: two birds, as it were, voicing the dramatic difference between two ecological areas; a hundred feet apart in space, they were who knows how many hundred miles and years apart in ecological adaptation. Each in its favorable niche, they exchanged notes across the centuries of time and shift and change which brought their disparate perches within singing distance of each other.

The history-conscious bird observer will find legend and biological enigma side by side with the fabulous in the hills. Deadwood, for instance, symbolizing the hardy-spirited as well as the outlaw West; Rushmore, Shrine of Democracy; Custer State Park with its Sylvan Lake; Harney Peak, the Needles, and French Creek with "gold in its grass roots." Others the bird observer will discover for himself.

My first Violet-green Swallow appeared in Deadwood, perched on a wire no more than a block from No. 10 Saloon where Wild Bill Hickok was pistoled to death and not far from Old Town Hall where each summer "The Trail of Jack McCall" melodramatically re-creates the wild 1870's. On a July day I stood in Mt. Moriah Cemetery high on a ridge overlooking the city. Calamity Jane lies there; so does Wild Bill—his second burial. When disinterred in the earlier Boot Hill graveyard, the diggers found him "solid, petrified stone." So the legend runs. But over the city Violet-green Swallows wheeled; Red Crossbills "kipped" loudly in the silence and a Clark's Nutcracker unfolded the black-and-white of his flight pattern against the green of the opposite ridge. That was in 1957. In 1959 fire left the green ridges a bristle of charred and blackened spires: human carelessness and a trash fire escaping. But the Mt. Moriah overlook is still excellent; swallows and crossbills and an occasional White-throated Swift still circle over indestructible Deadwood.

A drive through Spearfish Canyon is to see geology rolled out on the tapestries of cliffs. As the road drops and the walls rise, red shades of sandstone and pink-hued limestone contrast with the changing foliage, but the green-stained shales are almost lost in the green of trees—dark pine, lighter spruce, still lighter deciduous. I have found MacGillivray's Warbler in the tangles along Spearfish Creek in June and July. The Black-headed Grosbeak haunts the thickets, his song deceptively like the Rose-breasted's. Dippers bob on the rocks or slip into the water, drawing what seems to be a white sheath of air about them. White-throated Swifts (common in almost every canyon) dash along the precipices or swoop down with thin whining sounds. On the dizzy ledges, Rock Pigeons, long departed from the domestic cotes, are feral here.

The road to Deerfield, running northwest out of Hill City, strikes through the heart of the hills. As Lenord and Clara Yarger told me on the way, the road, though unmarked, is clearly shown on maps available in any Black Hills information center. My first

Townsend's Solitaire was perched on a fence rail at Deerfield. It was a nondescript grayish bird, I thought, until in flight overhead I saw the wing patches were buffy windows to the sky.

Deerfield looks over the wide meadows bordering Castle Creek. Down this valley from the west in July, 1874, rode Custer, self-styled "General" of a thousand-man expedition. An invader of Indian land, clearly a violater of the Indian treaty of 1868, he brought with him 300 beefs for the larder, his brass band, and his bloodhounds. George Bird Grinnell was the zoologist-naturalist. Ludlow's "Report of 1875" pictures the command: riders in grass and flowers shoulder-high, picking bouquets to festoon their horses; the band at night, playing "Garry Owen" and "Artist's Life" to the echoing cliffs; Custer waxing lyrical while he participated in what was probably the first grab by vested interests of land set aside for specific purposes by federal legislation.

Somewhere in the valley or on the prairie above, Grinnell found Sandhill Cranes half-grown in late July. Today Cranes no longer nest in the hills, although, Nat Whitney tells me, they can still be seen over Rapid City in brief though spectacular flight in late September or early October. Instead of Cranes on the prairie —called Reynolds Prairie now—the Yargers and I saw Mountain Bluebirds lining a wire fence.

Custer's men noted thousands of burnt-over acres in 1874. Today no hazard is as threatening in the hills as fire. The Hill City–Deerfield road skirts McVey Burn, a slash of green second growth with blackened snags like tombstones to mark the fire of 1939. Here as elsewhere in dry clearings Lewis' Woodpecker can be found propped at an angle against a limb or stump—sometimes a fence post. Grinnell found it in the area in 1874. In flight the dark greenish body is unmistakable.

I remember a late afternoon at Rushmore. Shadows fell across the Four Faces. Near the museum, Audubon's Warblers, two males, were determining some kind of superiority in swift lunges and evasions among the pines. Crowds, quiet for the most part, gazed at the monolithic symbol, this figured past, framed by ponderosa slants and the arching sky. In a nearby ravine an Ovenbird lifted its "teacher" song. Shadows deepened on Lincoln's face. In the tall pines near the parking lot, I heard a Western Tanager, his note as burry as a Scarlet Tanager's but uttered more hurriedly, emphatically accentuated. For a moment the fiery scarlet of his head almost illuminated the green spray of needles back of him. A bird of the upper boughs, it can be found almost anywhere in the open pine woods of the middle elevations. A car roared past; a pop bottle exploded against a rock. The Tanager flew, a wondrous blur of yellow, red, and black. A day to remember—birds, the tired face of Lincoln, and a pop bottle thrown from a raucous car.

To visit Custer State Park is to encounter the past of buffalo herds roaming the virgin prairie and miles of grass. It means ranging through almost 4,000 feet of altitude. It means mountain meadows edging streams and massed bergamot in patches of pink lavender and coneflowers yellow as butter and sometimes a Red-shafted Flicker flashing in scarlet undulations across white acres of yarrow. It means Western Meadowlarks and Vesper Sparrows; Rock and Cañon Wrens where ledges overhang; White-winged Juncos, Piñon Jays, and Western Tanagers; Clark's Nutcrackers, kinglets, and Red-breasted Nuthatches on the shoulders of peaks. It means ranging from antelope and elk to mountain goat.

The Needles Highway—State Route 87—sweeps through northern Custer Park over ridges and down across valleys where the Ovenbird sings and the Veery's call is part of the shadows. As the road ascends, lifting one above valleys of pine, it worms through a maze of spires, campaniles, steeples of rock, chimneys with needle's-eye holes at the top, and stripes of blue sky seen as if hanging between split gray columns. One hardly notices a Clark's Nutcracker darting past a dark monolith or a Gray Jay diving down on crumbs left by tourists in an overlook.

A hike up Harney Peak begins at Sylvan Lake. We set off, Lenord Yarger and I. The jeep track up Harney leads through ponderosa woods where occasionally, Lenord told me, Ruffed Grouse explode from the bushes. A quarter way up we looked down on a green meadow below Harney's ramparts. Beaver had flung four dams across the lushness. From a ledge a Red-tailed Hawk shrilled his warning. Back of us in an open space of deciduous growth a Solitary Vireo chirred softly.

Midway up the three-and-a-half mile climb, a drink of cold water from a spring heartened the midriff for the final spurt. Here Golden-crowned Kinglets' faint *seet, seet* made us stop to listen in an uproar of half a dozen Red-breasted Nuthatches and a colony

of chickadees. A Western Flycatcher monotonously repeated his two-syllabled effort. Mariposa lilies with petals white inside and pale lavender outside dotted the open pine wood. In a moist place we came on deer sign, one pointed hoof track carefully laid on top of the other.

Then we were on the summit, wind in our faces. Below us, studded with blunt gray pinnacles of rock, lay mile on mile of green conifer forests rolling to the horizon; nearer, green blankets of meadows lay flung between mountains. Overhead a Violet-green Swallow drifted toward a crag.

I thought of Jean Vallé's "white-booted turkey." The Sage Grouse, which Colonel Dodge saw in Red Valley in the southern hills, no longer dance anywhere in the hills. Gone are the cranes, the grizzly bear, and the Indian's penitential dancing floor. But swallows still wheel and bank; Piñon Jays call on lower levels; and White-winged Juncos flash their white feathers like pale stars whirling through the thickets. To the initiate as to the initiated (on Harney's top assurance seems rock-rooted), neither time nor change can quite dim the bright hue of adventure in the Black Hills.

# *Alaskan Islands*

**THE ALEUTIANS**

Karl W. Kenyon

**THE PRIBILOFS**

Roger Tory Peterson

# THE ALEUTIANS

## Karl W. Kenyon

*The strange tastes of bird watchers for northern bogs, dismal swamps, and city sewer beds is even less discriminating when applied to islands. Bird watchers like islands—any island—from enchanting southern sand spits bathed in sunshine to rugged heaps of boulders shrouded in fog and mist. Karl Kenyon's experiences have made him an authority on Pacific isles, both tropical and arctic, and the birds and mammals that call them home.*

*Karl Walton Kenyon, born in La Jolla, California, in 1918, spent most of his spare time during boyhood skiff-fishing and watching marine birds off the southern California coast. He graduated from Pomona College, received his master's degree from Cornell University, and spent the years during World War II as a carrier-based fighter pilot in the southwestern Pacific.*

*After going on inactive duty in the Naval Reserve in 1946 he spent two months in a twenty-five-foot sloop, exploring coastal waters and islands off Baja California, Mexico, and a year as instructor in zoology at Mills College before joining the U.S. Fish and Wildlife Service as wildlife biologist. From 1947 to 1954 he spent part of each year on the Pribilof Islands, studying northern fur seals and, in 1952, participated for six months in the international pelagic sealing studies in waters off Japan.*

*Since 1955 Karl Kenyon has been based in Seattle with a*

155

*permanent assignment as project leader to sea otter investigations. This has given him opportunities to take part in side assignments such as the study of the Black-footed and Laysan Albatrosses in the outer Hawaiian Islands, particularly at Midway, work on the Pacific walrus on Little Diomede and Round Islands in the Bering Sea, and three extensive aerial surveys over the Bering Sea ice sheet to determine the distribution and population of walruses. His sea otter investigations on the Aleutians, for periods of three or four months at a time, add up to well over a year, mainly on the island of Amchitka. Here birds are an important and exciting part of the ecological picture.*

*Amchitka is definitely for the armchair bird watcher to read about on a cold winter evening before a roaring fire. Few bird watchers or ornithologists will ever focus their binoculars on the birds of the remote Aleutians, but many will enjoy Karl Kenyon's word picture of Amchitka.*

The marine habitat of coastal Alaska, isolated, often windblown, fog-shrouded and drizzle-swept, keeps the human bird-watching population to a minimum. A generous estimate might allocate one bird watcher to each 1,000 miles of shoreline, and, at that, the bird watcher is usually non-resident and of sporadic occurrence.

Except at widely scattered spots in coastal areas, such as Ketchikan, Juneau, Seward, Sitka, Kodiak, and St. Paul Island, accommodations for the migrant bird watcher are discouragingly sparse. In the nearly 1,200-mile-long Aleutian chain of islands only at Unalaska Village and on Umnak Island may a tourist find privately operated overnight accommodations, these obtainable through Reeve Aleutian Airways. Food and shelter from the damp and chilly climate are, for the most part, under government control.

With few exceptions the Aleutian Islands are part of the Aleutian Islands National Wildlife Refuge. The naval base at Adak is the only sizable human assemblage in the chain, and smaller military outposts are maintained on only five or six other islands. These government bases are closed to the general public; only visitors with official business are permitted to enter. Four native

Aleutian villages, Akutan, Unalaska, Nikolski, and Atka, constitute the remnant of a once large Aleut population; a fifth, Attu Village, was never reestablished after World War II when the entire Aleut population there was captured by the Japanese. Most of the captives who survived this ordeal now live at Atka.

For the hardy bird watcher, resistant to seasickness, tolerant of an unpredictable transportation schedule, and oblivious to chilly weather, the services of a monthly mailboat are available. The M/V *Expansion,* operated by the Aleutian Marine Transport Company of Seattle, offers accommodations for twelve passengers and the opportunity to enter waters along the Alaska Peninsula and the Aleutian Chain. The mailboat customarily calls at about thirty-five ports, among them Kodiak, Sand Point (in the Shumagin Islands), King Cove, Akutan, Unalaska, and Nikolski Villages, and may be boarded at either Seattle or one of its stops in Alaska that is also served by air. An *Expansion* cruise provides opportunities to go ashore while the ship unloads freight and mail, and at sea to observe an unending array of pelagic birds, predominantly alcids and procellariids. Abundant species include both Horned and Tufted Puffins; Thick-billed and Common Murres; Least, Parakeet, and Crested Auklets; Black-legged Kittiwakes; Fulmars; and Black-footed Albatrosses. A stroke of exceptional luck might provide a glimpse of a Laysan Albatross near the northern limit of its range.

A trip among the outer Aleutians is beyond the reach of most bird watchers. Accordingly, let me take you on one of my Fish and Wildlife Service expeditions to Amchitka Island. At 8:30 A.M. a DC-4 and a DC-6 bearing Reeve Aleutian Airway markings taxi from their hangars, nose in among refueling jet liners and open their doors to the early daylight of mid-February at the Anchorage International Airport. "Planes for Kodiak, Port Moller, Cold Bay, St. Paul Island, and Adak are now loading." Sailors, airmen, soldiers, construction workers, and a few civilian government employees hurry across the snowy ramp to the waiting planes. The DC-6 is destined for St. Paul Island where in summer a million and a half fur seals, thousands of Steller's sea lions, and an overwhelming multitude of seabirds participate in a season of intensive breeding-ground activity. Our DC-4, however, is bound for Adak in a more southerly latitude. With a roar of engines we are airborne and over Cook Inlet. A bleak winter sun intensifies the blinding whiteness of the Alaska range to our right and rare good luck in weather gives us an opportunity to view the smoking symmetrical 8,000-foot cone of Pavlof Volcano. Our southwesterly course takes us along the north side of the Alaska Peninsula. We may see a scattered herd of Grant's caribou and the twinkling white wings of flocks of Steller's and Common Eiders as our plane swings low over tundra, then the vast mudflats of Izembeck Bay as we descend for a landing at Cold Bay near the tip of the Alaska Peninsula.

A refueling stop permits us a brief reconnaissance of the area, treeless, littered with the rotting remains of wartime occupation, and seemingly devoid of wildlife. Our short winter list includes only a Common Raven, a Gyrfalcon, an (Aleutian) Gray-crowned Rosy Finch, and a small congregation of Snow Buntings. During spring and fall migrations the nearby mudflats are host to huge flocks of Black Brant, Emperor and Canada Geese, and an excellent representation of American duck species. Although a visitor to Cold Bay can obtain accommodations at the Reeve Airways Hotel, he will find that transportation to mudflats, where waterfowl and shorebirds forage among eel grass beds, is most difficult—if not impossible—to arrange.

As our plane wings out over the Bering Sea toward Amak Island, then turns southwest again toward Unimak Pass, we see the glistening snowy and spectacularly symmetrical 9,000-foot cone of Shishaldin and its neighbor, Isanotski, on Unimak Island. We glimpse dark patches on the glassy sea below and know from past experience in these waters that these are bird concentrations, probably Crested Auklets, perhaps Slender-billed Shearwaters. In spring and summer, shearwaters from "down under" in hundreds of thousands join other seabirds, sea lions, fur seals, and whales to feed in the plankton-rich currents and upwellings of Unimak Pass.

As we gain altitude, our aerial path carries us north of Unalaska Island's precipitous cliffs and steep slopes of tumbled boulders splotched here with a snow patch, there with a mantle of dry yellow grass. Black cliffs of volcanic rock rise to pyramidal snow-clad peaks as we pass Umnak and the Islands of Four Mountains. Here in spring millions of murres and kittiwakes will crowd each cliff ledge. Finally, nine hours out of Anchorage, the rough-hewn

4,000-foot profile of Great Sitkin takes form in the blue-white haze. Adak is only minutes ahead.

Once aground at the Adak Naval Station we plunge into a busy schedule preparing for a three-month stay on Amchitka. Our gear has arrived from Seattle aboard the Military Sea Transport Service vessel *Flying Dragon*. Two days of frantic purchasing at the commissary, sorting, repacking, and trucking, courtesy of the Navy, and we have our gear, groceries, sleeping bags, outboard motors, drums of gasoline, and fuel oil aboard a chartered plane and are heading southwest on the final 180-mile leg of our nearly 3,000-mile journey from Seattle.

Our weather has changed, we see only a fleeting glimpse of cliffs partially revealed through horizontal layers of fog as we pass around Adak, Kanaga, and Tanaga; then, relying mainly on our pilot's years of Aleutian flying experience, we dead reckon our course to Amchitka. In a light drizzle, we land on a surfaced airstrip 400 feet wide and two miles long, one of the few usable remnants of World War II. Under the inquisitive gaze of six Bald Eagles perched on nearby poles, we hurry to unload and stow our gear in a crumbling hangar. The 20-knot wind howls and loose boards bang. Green moss grows on the cement floor where water drips from the leaking hangar roof.

Two of us leave immediately on foot to wrestle with the problems of starting the jeep pick-up truck that has stood for six months in a patched-up building three miles from the airstrip. Only birds greet us at the airport, for Amchitka is now unoccupied by humans except for the occasional visits by Fish and Wildlife or military personnel. Facilities that sheltered thousands of men during wartime now survive only as wind-broken ruins, but vehicle tracks slashed across the tundra have created scars that even centuries may not erase.

As we hurry along an old crushed-rock military road, flocks of Mallards and Common Teal, and a Common Goldeneye or two, take wing from a shallow lake. A dozen Rock Ptarmigan in white winter plumage skim low over the yellow-brown tundra, then disappear on set wings over a broad knoll. The ground is nearly free of snow and the air temperature is about 35 degrees Fahrenheit, for we have now nearly reached the southern limit of the Aleutians, only a little north of the latitude of Vancouver Island in

British Columbia and almost exactly on the opposite side of the Northern Hemisphere from London.

The jeep gets a new set of points and a bit of ether to prime the carburetor, and then it hesitantly starts. We are lucky that National Wildlife Refuge Manager Bob Jones left the batteries well charged on his last visit.

Flurries of Rosy Finches and Snow Buntings burst from the roadside as we hurry back to the airstrip. The distant roar of motors, a fleeting form in the mist, and the chartered DC-4 has left us on our own.

We pile a load of gear into the truck, then bounce over four miles of road to an aging frame house, another relic of the war. Near the sandy beach at the head of Constantine Harbor we stop for a quick look at a flock of Emperor Geese busily foraging on heaps of kelp, storm-wrenched from the sea floor and cast on the beach. Glaucous-winged Gulls search nearby for mollusks attached to the uprooted kelp stems, and the derelict pilings and crazily tilted remains of a wartime pier provide perches for a group of Pelagic Cormorants, their red gular pouches barely visible through our binoculars. Thirty Common Teal, heads up and alert, cruise about near a partially exposed reef where they habitually feed in winter at low tide. The distinctive white scapular streaks on the males' backs are clearly visible.

The tar-papered house is tight and dry, and we feel relieved to discover that for once the rats failed to invade it. Bob's poison stations were successful! Invading rats in past years knocked all the canned goods from the shelves, chewed boxes to bits, and left ugly holes in cupboard doors. But this nuisance damage by the Norway rats, introduced to Amchitka during wartime military occupation, was as nothing compared to their destruction of native birds. In 1937, when Dr. Olaus J. Murie conducted a wildlife survey of Amchitka, he found the large dark-plumaged Aleutian race of the Song Sparrow and an Aleutian race of the Winter Wren nesting abundantly along grassy seaside bluffs. During nearly fifteen months that I have spent on Amchitka since 1955, I have been able to find only one Winter Wren on the island and this one was of the race *tanagensis,* never before taken on Amchitka and almost certainly carried there from another island by storm winds. The disappearance of the endemic Song Sparrow and Wren, coinciding as it does with the introduction and establishment of rats, suggests that the latter exterminated the resident population of these two birds. Like the Wren and Song Sparrow, the rat chose the slopes near beaches as its favorite habitat and today large numbers of rats occupy all such beach areas that I have visited. The rats prey on other species, too. I found rat-gnawed remains of ducklings beside a teal nesting pond, and broods of the Common Eider suffer when mothers bring their ducklings up among beach rocks to sleep at night.

Late winter and early spring winds, rushing cyclonically around tight storm centers that move eastward from Siberia, bring strange visitors to Amchitka. To find these we must look in favored but varied habitats.

Our first excursion takes us along six miles of excellent crushed rock road past hundreds of rotting Quonset huts to a knoll overlooking both the Bering Sea and Pacific Ocean. Over a waving tuft of dry rye grass we aim our 50-power telescope at five white dots on a finger-like lake, near the Bering Sea shore and called Silver Salmon Lake by our Aleut assistants. We are right in our preliminary guess that they are swans. The birds are the better part of a mile away, but even at this distance they are aware of us. Their long necks are erect and they move steadily downwind to prepare for flight into the wind. Two of the birds are snowy white with a large yellow patch at the base of the bill, while the other three are dingy as if soiled, and the bills are pinkish, rather than yellow, and black-tipped. We identify the swans as Whooper parents with young of the previous spring.

In 1941 this species was added to the North American list when a specimen was taken on St. Paul Island of the Pribilof group. Here on Amchitka this Eurasian bird appeared during each of my late winter and early spring visits. Published accounts of Whistling Swans reported by natives of the outer Aleutians undoubtedly included a number of misidentified Whoopers. Almost daily our regular work on sea otter studies will take us near Silver Salmon Lake and we will see other Whooper Swan families, some with one, others with two or three young. Individual families will stay only a day or two and sometimes two or three families will be traveling in company.

Certain less spectacular but equally unusual Asian visitors that we can expect to find may lurk among seed-bearing stalks of rye grass and *Senecio* in somewhat sheltered draws where streams and rivulets trickle over sand or cobbles to the sea near the heads of bays.

One drizzly day in such an area we sight a small yellowish warbler. It looks so nondescript that we quickly bring it down with the .410 and identify it as an Arctic Warbler (an old world warbler belonging to the family Sylviidae); but not until several months later do the biologists at the U.S. National Museum inform us that it is a first record for North America of an Asian race of this bird.

Below our sea otter blind are kelp-covered rocks left exposed by low tides, and here, during winter and until sometime in late March, we see at close range feeding groups of Harlequin Ducks and Common Eiders paddling close to the rocks to gather tiny chitons and marine snails, or diving in the shallows to search for small green sea urchins and starfish. While watching sea otters is our primary objective, we are able to steal a glance at the birds now and then.

Time passes rapidly on Amchitka. A variety of weather—sleet

and snow squalls, followed by drenching downpours, then as the season advances, drizzle and fog and almost always wind—keeps us busy maintaining our gear and quarters when we are not out on the beaches.

Before the day in April comes when we send out a call through the Navy radio at Adak to send us a plane for transportation, we have become familiar with the resident island birds. We have watched the eider and teal pair, then the males gather in flocks while the females settle down to the business of incubation, and the Emperor Geese melt imperceptibly away during April.

The day for the plane is here. The wind is blowing thirty knots from the southwest. It is a rare sunny day and we gaze back from the window at receding rocky beaches, cliffs, and grassy slopes and wonder what Asian visitor this same wind may even now be blowing to Amchitka shores.

# THE PRIBILOFS

## Roger Tory Peterson

*Most of us would be quite content if we could be top-notch in just one endeavor, whether it be in painting, writing, photographing, or lecturing. Roger Peterson excels equally well in all of these activities. That one person should be so multifariously talented seems to us ordinary mortals a rank injustice.*

*Roger Tory Peterson was born in Jamestown, New York, in 1908, and grew up in the same industrial city. While in grade school he joined an Audubon Junior Club; from that time on, birds began to receive his attention. He worked in his spare time painting designs on lacquered cabinets in one of the local factories. At the age of seventeen, having saved up enough money, Roger attended the 1925 meeting of the American Ornithologists' Union in New York City where he met and took field trips with "the ornithological great" including Ludlow Griscom and the famed artist Louis Agassiz Fuertes. His desire to be an ornithologist-artist was immediately kindled. Two years later he was back in New York City studying art—first at the Art Students League and then at the National Academy of Design—and relishing weekend jaunts in the field with such energetic young birdmen as Allan Cruickshank and Joe Hickey.*

*In the early 1930's, while a natural science and art instructor at the Rivers School in Brookline, Massachusetts, he conceived and prepared a guide to the quick identification of birds, based on*

164

*their essential field marks. A daringly new concept in a bird book, remarkable in its streamlined simplicity, the manuscript was shunned by publisher after publisher. Finally Houghton Mifflin Company in Boston risked taking it, cautiously printing 2,000 copies. That was in 1934. Now, thirty years later, there have been three editions, and* A Field Guide to the Birds *has enjoyed a sale of close to 800,000 copies.*

*Following the appearance of what is now "the bible" to countless bird watchers, Roger Peterson's life has been a crowded one. In 1934 he joined the staff of the National Audubon Society, serving as director of educational activities and art editor of* Bird-Lore *(later Audubon Magazine). After serving with the U.S. Army during World War II, he became a free lance ornithologist, artist, writer, photographer, and lecturer.*

*Besides his field guides to eastern, western, and Texas birds, Roger Tory Peterson has authored* The Junior Book of Birds *(1939),* Birds over America *(1948),* How to Know the Birds *(1949),* Wildlife in Color *(1951),* A Field Guide to the Birds of Britain and Europe *(1954), with Guy Mountfort and P. A. D. Hollom,* Wild America *(1955) with James Fisher,* The Bird Watcher's Anthology *(1957), and* The Birds *(1963). Chief among the many honors to come his way are the Brewster Medal of the American Ornithologists' Union (for his eastern field guide), the John Burroughs Medal (for excellence in nature writing as exemplified by* Birds over America*), the Geoffrey St. Hilaire Gold Medal from the French Natural History Society, the Gold Medal of the New York Zoological Society, and doctorates from Franklin and Marshall College and Ohio State University.*

*To all the continents, except Australia and Antarctica, Roger Peterson has traveled, observing and photographing birds and, on many occasions, meeting and sharing his wide knowledge and contagious enthusiasm with ornithologists and conservationists in Japan, Chile, Argentina, Kenya, France, the United Kingdom, Finland, and many other countries. One can confidently say that he is the world's best known ornithologist or, in the words of Peter Farb, the "birdman to the world."*

*Here Roger Peterson takes us to those little dots of land, the Pribilofs in the Bering Sea, that rival the Peruvian Coast in the millions of seabirds they attract in the breeding season.*

The fog-swept Pribilofs in the Bering Sea have been called the greatest bird cities in North America. In our hemisphere, only the Chinchas off the desert coast of Peru can boast greater aggregations of seabirds.

Lying 250 miles north of Dutch Harbor in the Aleutians and 2,000 miles north of Midway in the central Pacific, the Pribilofs are visited by few ornithologists other than those biologists who are assigned to the fur seal work. However, the Reeve Aleutian Airline takes tourists to the islands. Usually the scheduled tourist flights, once a week, give too little time—a day or so—for a birder to make a proper survey even of St. Paul Island where the airstrip is located. But serious ornithologists can arrange for a longer stay. They may go out with the Fish and Wildlife personnel, stay at the rooming house at headquarters, and return on a later flight as we did in early July, 1953—James Fisher of England, Finnur Gudmundsson of Iceland, William Cottrell of Cambridge, Massachusetts, and I.

Taking off from Anchorage in a DC-3 we headed southwest over the indented coast down the narrowing Alaskan peninsula. We hoped for a glimpse of Spurr, the 11,000-foot peak that had been spitting smoke and ashes. Everyone was expecting an eruption this Fourth of July, but billows of clouds hid the mountain. Dropping through the overcast we flew over bleak, treeless moors at an altitude of a few hundred feet, low enough to spot an Alaskan brown bear retreating from the water's edge. A fuel stop at Cold Bay, where the Aleutian Chain starts, and then we struck out across the Bering Sea.

Although fog may hide the Pribilofs for weeks on end we had the rare fortune of coming in on the bluest of blue days. We could see from the air every one of the seal beaches that Kipling wrote about in his story of the white seal—Novastoshnah, Lukanin, Polovina, Kitovi, Tolstoi, Zapadni—and all the other famous seal rookeries of St. Paul. The red dust of the runway below was in striking contrast to great fields of blue lupine and golden poppies, now in their glory. Although not a single tree grows on these islands, they are a botanist's paradise; more than 170 species of flowering plants have been listed.

Like other small oceanic islands the Pribilofs have had their share of wind-drifted strays—including species from Asia. The

*A.O.U. Check-List* records such waterfowl as the Whooper Swan, Smew, Falcated Teal, Pochard, and Tufted Duck, as well as a number of Old World shorebirds—the European Jacksnipe, Ruff, Polynesian Tattler, and Long-toed Stint. Among the landbirds listed are the Oriental Cuckoo, White-rumped Swift, Hawfinch, and Brambling. Few islands in the world, other than Fair Island off northern Scotland and Heligoland off the North Sea coast of Germany, can claim as many accidentals.

The Winter Wren, which has colonized many of the Aleutians, must have arrived here in much the same fashion—caught in the wind and unable to do much about it. We were to see a number of Winter Wrens, but their high-pitched tinkling songs were almost drowned by the surf, for here, in the absence of forests, they are rock nesters as they are in the Aleutians, Iceland, St. Kilda, and many other northern islands.

Aside from the Wren there are only three other songbirds during the summer, the Snow Bunting, Lapland Longspur, and Gray-crowned Rosy Finch. The Rosy Finches, like large, dark, rosy-rumped sparrows, nest about the neat frame buildings of St. Paul; but we also found them feeding their young among the rough boulders of the lava slopes. In certain other subarctic parts of the world such as Iceland and Spitzbergen where Rosy Finches do not exist, the Snow Buntings have become the village sparrows, but here on St. Paul the more aggressive Rosy Finches fill that niche.

Throughout the fields of lupines and poppies the Lapland Longspurs, in display flights, sang their brief lark-like snatches. Like the Snow Buntings they seemed to prefer the higher, more inland areas, leaving the perimeter of the island to the Rosy Finches and the Wrens. Among the rough rocks of the lava flows there were many stub-tailed youngsters just out of the nest.

One species of sandpiper nests commonly on St. Paul, the Rock Sandpiper, which some taxonomists would lump with the Purple Sandpiper of the Atlantic. Although it does look like the Purple Sandpiper in non-breeding dress, it is quite unlike it during the early summer. Rusty on the back and with a dark splotch on the underparts, it looks very much like a summer Dunlin.

The seal beaches of the Pribilofs are among the greatest wildlife spectacles of the world. More than 1,500,000 fur seals crowd, jostle, and bellow on the hauling beaches, but where cliffs rise precipitously from the water's edge the birds take over. Their great colonies are every bit as spectacular as those of the seals.

As we progressed away from the village of St. Paul each point of land with its seaward cliff seemed more exciting than the last. The bird colonies were less populous near the village, we supposed, because the Aleuts harvest some of the birds. They have "aboriginal rights," even though as seasonal employees of the sealing commission they are fed with good red beef shipped in for their consumption. Every cliff-face nook, every ledge for miles was occupied by murres, puffins, auklets, and kittiwakes.

The murres, both Common and Thick-billed, facing the rocks with their dark backs to the sea, each stood guard over a single big pyriform egg. By making sample counts of the birds that stood shoulder to shoulder we estimated that at least 1,000,000 murres were on the ledges of St. Paul at any one time. Perhaps nearly as many were off fishing. Flotillas of hundreds gathered on the sea below the cliffs and swam beneath the surface using their wings as flippers as penguins do.

Not only do two species of murres live side by side in the Pribilofs but also two puffins—the Tufted Puffin (called *tawpawkie* by the Aleuts) and the Horned Puffin (*epatka*) which looks not unlike the familiar Atlantic bird except for its yellower beak and the fleshy papillae or "horns" above each eye. Whereas we had expected the Horned Puffin to be the counterpart of the Atlantic Puffin we found that it laid its egg far back in the rocks, not in the turf; the Tufted Puffin was the turf-nester. Neither were easy to census, for whereas a few hundred puffins might be in sight at any one time, thousands or even tens of thousands could be hidden in the nesting holes.

Here and there among the others were little groups of smaller white-breasted birds with upturned red bills—Parakeet Auklets, the *baillie brushkie*. Like the Horned Puffins, they lay their eggs behind the rocks, deep in the crevices where their high musical trills give some hint of their numbers. These were the birds that guided A. C. Bent through the fog to a safe landing on St. Paul in 1911.

Similar in size to the Parakeet Auklets, but slaty-gray, are the Crested Auklets (*canooskies*)—droll birds with a ridiculously recurved crest that suggests the plume of a California Quail. During the first few days of our visit they seemed to be still prospecting the cliffs, flying in from the sea, veering, and flying out again.

Smallest of the auks, no larger than stubby-billed, stub-tailed young Starlings, are the Least Auklets or *choochkies* which sit about on the beach boulders, chirping for all the world like some sort of landbirds. Their population in the subterranean rock chambers certainly far exceeds the few hundreds visible at any one time.

It is quite likely that the auk family had its origin, or at least its main evolution, in or near the Bering Sea. All but three of the twenty-one living species are found in the north Pacific. Of these, eight nest on the Pribilofs, although we saw the Pigeon Guillemot only once, a recently fledged young bird.

Even though the ornithological literature lists the Pelagic Cormorant from the Pribilofs, we were sure of seeing only the Red-faced Cormorant. This handsome, tame, two-crested shag was found on all the four islands, but nowhere did we find more than several pairs nesting together; usually they were in single pairs, quite unlike other cormorants which almost invariably form sizable colonies.

Very often when we were stalking the birds around the rim of the island we had the uneasy feeling that we too were being watched. Glancing about we would often spot the arctic fox peering at us through the tall grass. These little foxes are bird watchers too and we frequently found their burrows, the entrances littered with the wings and feathers of murres and auklets. No real harm is done, however; this is part of the natural economy of these islands.

Two species of kittiwakes share the open cliffs with the murres and their numbers in the archipelago must certainly run into the hundreds of thousands. The ordinary Black-legged Kittiwake whose raucous *kitti-waak* can be heard on sea islands around the top of the world is by far the commonest. With them live a minority of the Red-legged Kittiwake, one of the world's scarcer gulls. We saw nests of the two species within two feet of each other. Again, we wondered, isn't there interspecific competition here? Their cries sounded much the same to our ears. Is there some subtle ecological separation or is the delicate Red-leg a relict species slowly losing out to the dominant Black-leg?

The common big gull of the islands in summer is the Glaucous-winged. Normally one sees no other, but one afternoon near the north side of the island we saw among a gathering of 1,000 Glaucous-wings a dark-backed bird, unquestionably *schistisagus,* the Slaty-backed Gull of Asia.

There are Fulmars around the islands too—the same large petrels that live in the colder parts of the north Atlantic, but the dark birds appear darker and the light birds whiter and patchier looking, almost like partial albinos. We did not see any dark birds on the cliffs of St. Paul, but we saw many when we took the boat across to St. George, perhaps birds from one of the Aleutian colonies 250 or 300 miles to the south.

The average tourist would have no opportunity to make the passage between St. Paul and St. George. Periodically, the Fish and Wildlife Service boat, the *Penguin,* makes the journey to the southeast over forty miles of some of the roughest water in the northern oceans. But on the afternoon when we made the routine trip the sea was relatively calm and we experienced no difficulty using our binoculars. We looked particularly for Slender-billed

Shearwaters which regularly wander to the Bering Sea from their nesting grounds south of Australia. It is quite possible to mistake dark Fulmars for these dusky shearwaters. I made that mistake, much to my chagrin, in the presence of James Fisher who knows a Fulmar, whatever its hue, at the limit of human vision.

As we approached St. George the number of auks on the water increased and the air soon became a swirling mass of birds. Putting our binoculars on the great 1,000-foot cliff of Staraya Artil we were awed by the traffic pouring to and from the sea. By the most conservative estimate I believe we had more than 1,000,000 birds in sight at one time.

The boat that put out to meet us when the *Penguin* dropped anchor was one of several picturesque *bidarrahs* operating in the islands, traditional long boats rowed by Aleuts who stand like gondoliers while working the oars.

St. George with its higher cliffs seemed to have far more sea-birds than St. Paul. Staraya Artil, where the Red-legged Kittiwakes have their largest colonies, is probably the greatest single bird cliff anywhere in North America. The numbers of murres alone must run to several millions.

Clouds of choochkies swarm in from the sea to pitch among the volcanic boulders high on the hillside behind the town. On St. Paul they nest under the loose beach boulders, but on St. George the largest colonies are well inland where they flush from the lupine-covered slopes like clouds of Starlings. A biologist stationed on the latter island once tried to estimate the number of Least Auklets there and concluded, after watching the morning and evening flights for several days, that there were about 36,000,000. We saw no such numbers, but Dr. Ira Gabrielson assures me that there are certainly millions.

Seldom visited is a smaller island not far from St. Paul, Otter Island, a volcanic cone with a perfect crater. Although the colonies are not large, the birds seem tamer here than on either of the big islands, probably due to lack of pressure from the two Aleut settlements.

But probably the most spectacular aggregation of all, though perhaps not as large as the cliff-face colony of Staraya Artil, is on Walrus, a flat island seven miles to the east of St. Paul. Some years no boats land on this isolated rock. Fog conceals its ragged contours and a pounding surf makes landing treacherous. However, we had the great good fortune to visit Walrus one sunny day, the first time in four years that the *Penguin* had ventured there. This colony is certainly one of the most unusual murre colonies in the world, for the birds, free of arctic foxes, are able to nest safely on a large horizontal surface, much as they do on Funk Island, the ancient home of the Great Auk, off Newfoundland. Most other murre colonies, except for a few on the flat tops of stacks, are on vertical cliffs.

The bewhiskered walrus for which the island was named has long since retreated to more northerly latitudes, and today 3,000 or 4,000 northern sea lions make the island their headquarters. The huge animals give some anxious moments as they porpoise around the dory of the landing party. But on this island the great show is really the murre colony. A solid mass of birds breaks rank as we walk through their midst and closes again behind us. The air above is a constant blizzard of wings. In the year of our visit nearly all of the murres on Walrus were Common Murres, but the ornithological literature shows an unexplained switch back and forth from one species to the other over the years.

Although there are a few Red-faced Cormorants, Tufted Puffins, and smaller auks on Walrus Island, the multitudes of murres swamp out nearly everything else. A few Glaucous-winged Gulls live high on murre omelets. Ornithologists who have landed on the island in earlier years have stated unequivocally that there were "millions." Our own appraisal, made by taking the ship's charts, plotting out the occupied acreage, and making sample counts of eggs, was that there were about 1,000,000 pairs. We all agreed that the day on Walrus was the high point of our visit to the Pribilofs.

# The North Country

ARCTIC ALASKA
Olaus J. Murie

CHURCHILL ON HUDSON BAY
John C. Schmid

ONTARIO'S ALGONQUIN PARK
Fred Bodsworth

# ARCTIC ALASKA

## Olaus J. Murie

*"In recognition of his inspired contribution to the cause of wildlife conservation, as scientist, counselor, author, artist, and leading champion of the wilderness unspoiled." Thus reads the citation in part that accompanied the Aldo Leopold Memorial Medal awarded to Olaus Murie in 1952.*

*Olaus John Murie spent his boyhood in Moorhead, Minnesota, where he was born in 1889. He went west for his undergraduate education at Pacific University, east for a master's degree from the University of Michigan.*

*He began his professional work in natural history as conservation officer for two years with the Oregon State Game Commission. After that came numerous expeditions, a list of which seems like a travelogue: Hudson Bay and the Labrador as field naturalist and curator of mammals for the Carnegie Museum; Alaska for six years of field research, mainly on caribou, but with time for a study of waterfowl in the Yukon and seabirds in the Aleutians; British Columbia for an inspection of national forests waterfowl nesting areas; Alaska again for a general biological survey of the Aleutians; New Zealand, on invitation from the government to study the introduced wapiti; and the Brooks Range in Alaska to make recommendations for its preservation as a wilderness area.*

*As an author-artist, Olaus Murie wrote and illustrated many articles for periodicals and several books, one of which,* The Elk of

175

*North America (1951), received the 1961 award from the Wildlife Society for the outstanding ecological publication. As a lecturer he toured the country, showing films and speaking on natural history, travel, conservation, and the esthetic appreciation of our wildlife heritage.*

*Although his writings and lectures covered a variety of subjects, one basic theme prevailed—the preservation of our wilderness. In 1945 he resigned from active duty with the government to become director and president of the Wilderness Society, an organization he helped found in 1935 and which he guided with quiet perseverance and skill from his headquarters in Moose, Wyoming. At his death in 1963 he was chairman of the Society's council, its governing board.*

*Many honors recognized his contribution to conservation: a doctor's degree from Pacific University, the Cornelius Amory Pugsley Bronze Medal of the American Scenic and Historic Preservation Society, the Conservation Award of the American Forestry Association, the Audubon Medal of the National Audubon Society, and the John Muir Award of the Sierra Club.*

*But probably no honor or award gave him greater personal satisfaction than having the northeast corner of Alaska, the site of his 1956 expedition, designated the Arctic Wildlife Range in 1960 by the Secretary of the Interior. And it was with great joy that the Muries—just the two of them—returned in 1961 to their old camping ground in the Sheenjek River Valley, a part of the Range. The following chapter is Olaus Murie's story, a postscript to the delightful book,* Two in the Far North *(1962) by his wife and wilderness companion, Margaret E. Murie.*

We arrived by commercial airline in the little town of Fort Yukon, Alaska, very near the Arctic Circle, on May 27, 1961. Mrs. Murie and I were going even farther north—to the Sheenjek River Valley in the southern slope of the Brooks Range. Fort Yukon was only the take-off point. From here we chartered a little bush plane, a Cessna, the only means of transportation into the Sheenjek country. Our pilot, Keith Harrington, knew the country well. He had serviced our 1956 expedition to the same valley, which was sponsored by the Conservation Foundation. Then we were a party of five; now just the two of us were going back, on our own, to be with the arctic birds and flowers again for a little while.

This was early spring in the north—before "breakup"—and Keith was using a wheel-ski combination plane. In what seemed like only a few very active moments, he and his Indian helpers loaded us and our gear for ten days into the plane and we were on our way. An hour and twenty minutes later we landed on the ice of Lobo Lake, two hundred miles north of Fort Yukon, and taxied up to the very same spot where we had camped in 1956—a strange sensation for both of us.

The ice was thawing a little along the edge of Lobo Lake, but we managed to get our bags and boxes ashore and up onto a mossy slope. Keith lifted his plane into the sky and was gone. When he came back in two weeks, he would be flying his float plane and would have to land on the ice-free Sheenjek River a few hundred feet west of the lake. Not until after June 20 would he be sure of having open water on Lobo Lake.

A strange wonderful feeling came over me. Here we were, just we two. In front of us the ice-covered lake. Behind us a wide stretch of tundra tussock, some willows, a lot of dwarf birch, a few white spruce trees, the snow-streaked mountains, west, north, and east, clouds in a blue sky. It may sound ordinary, but to us it was arctic wilderness, unoccupied. We had a feeling such as we might have, I imagine, if we should find ourselves, just we two, on the moon. It is hard to find words for this—remoteness, freedom, closeness with nature. But spring was here; we knew this land would soon come alive. Even while we were making camp, Mardy exclaimed: "There are two Bohemian Waxwings!" She next saw a Yellow-shafted Flicker, then some swallows flew by. The birds were beginning to come north again for the delectable arctic spring.

In the next few days, while we explored the country, searching out all the favorite places of five years before, we realized that a great many birds had already come. We saw a Short-eared Owl, a number of Tree and White-crowned Sparrows, and two Common Ravens. There were Northern Phalaropes in the open water along the lake shore, a Lesser Yellowlegs on the shore, and Least Sandpipers on the tundra. Across the lake we could hear a Common

Snipe "winnowing" frequently. A flock of Cliff Swallows flew by our camp several times. Where were they going to nest? The only available cliffs were in the mountains, back from the Sheenjek River. And then I saw what I thought was a Golden Eagle sailing across, high against the blue. Yes, the birds were coming. And with them the flowers! The first of these is the bright reddish purple saxifrage; with it some pussy willows and a few cotton-grass flowers. All this in the last few days of May, nearly two hundred miles north of the Arctic Circle!

As the days went by we were inspired by the voice of the Willow Ptarmigan, at all hours of the twenty-four. At this time, the latter part of May and early June, the female was already brown speckled, silent and secretive, as befitted the one which was preparing a nest full of eggs and assuming the responsibility of incubation. But the male was still showy, with his white body and brown neck of springtime. He perched prominently on knolls and in the tops of the scattered spruces, often giving out his guttural, crowing call. There was perpetual daylight now, and from our sleeping bags in the tent at night we could hear the ptarmigan calling out in the soft full light—a prominent and unforgettable feature of this part of the Arctic.

Apparently ptarmigan were numerous this year. As we know, both ptarmigan and snowshoe hare have a ten- or eleven-year population cycle, all details of which are not yet clearly understood. We saw Rock Ptarmigan in a few places too, but farther up on the mountains, and they were not nearly as noisy.

Another very vocal bird was the Oldsquaw. The ice on the edge of the lake melted rapidly and in a few days there was a wide lane of water around the shore where the waterfowl gathered. There were lots of sounds but above all others rose the high-pitched, goose-like *a-ha-we! a-ha-ha-we!* of the Oldsquaws. The call seemed to arise wherever there was open water.

And up through the Sheenjek Valley there was plenty of water —ponds and sloughs and many streams. On the flats the tundra muskeg was wet. Rubber footwear was imperative and we found that the rubber-bottomed shoe-pac, or Maine hunting shoe, was light weight and comfortable. On this 1961 trip I had a pair almost knee-high.

Each day more ducks arrived. We identified the American

Widgeon, the Green-winged Teal, White-winged and Surf Scoters, a few scaups, and a very few Shovelers. In June we found the nest of a Pintail on the top of a hill, high above a pond—not at all like the marshy environment we are accustomed to associate with nesting ducks.

In the widening water of Lobo Lake, Northern Phalaropes were numerous. They swam around, picking at insects, sometimes whirling in circles on the water as all phalaropes do. They and the muskrats appeared to monopolize the water in front of our camp, but there were many grayling trout down below!

As Lobo Lake cleared of ice and the waterfowl spread out more widely, the landscape became colorful with blooming flowers in an exciting array. Mountain avens and anemones, mats of moss campion, the ever-present saxifrage, the showy rhododendron, and many more helped to give a brilliant background to the birds we saw. One day Mardy flushed a White-crowned Sparrow from a tussock, and found its nest in the midst of a vivid display of blooms. Both the White-crowned and the Tree Sparrows nest on the ground, among the tussocks or at the base of bushes.

Not far from camp, in a small pond, we found two nests of the colorful Horned Grebe. I often chose my route to pass this place just to admire the male bird floating on the water, with his reflection sharp before him, against the background of the arctic valley.

We saw various hawks in the distance as we tramped, day after day, in all directions, and we identified the Bald and the Golden Eagles which nest there. On our previous trip some members of our party found, on a cliff ledge of the mountain across the Sheenjek River west of camp, the nest with three young of the Gyrfalcon, a truly arctic bird. This was the only Gyrfalcon nest we found. These birds are probably more numerous in suitable locations on the north slope of the Brooks Range.

For some of the other birds I should like to go back to our 1956 expedition, when we remained at Lobo Lake for a while, then moved up the Sheenjek Valley to another, smaller lake which we named Last Lake, and beside which we camped until early August. From this camp some of us made journeys afoot to the head of the Sheenjek River, into the mountains of the central part of the Brooks Range itself. That gave us a wider knowledge of the birdlife of the area. Altogether, in the summer of 1956, we identified eighty-six kinds of birds. However, we should keep in mind one thing: in this far northland no one species, with perhaps one or two exceptions, is abundant. The Willow Ptarmigan, of course, becomes abundant in its cycle. On the whole, although there may be a variety of species, the individuals of each species are widely scattered.

We saw a few Bonaparte's Gulls in spring migration, but we had no idea where they nested. We also identified some Herring Gulls, feeding on insects on the remaining overflow ice at Last Lake. But the gull most often seen was the Mew. At our camp by Last Lake we had a pair of Mew Gulls with one young as companions. The adults often made a pleasing picture, perched in the tops of little spruces near our tents, always on the lookout for offal, especially when grayling were cleaned for supper!

The most exciting thing at our camp at Last Lake was a pair of Arctic Loons. They were always there, out on the lake somewhere, and often came very close to our camp shore, giving us fine views of this beautiful bird of the Far North. It was a special occasion for us all when these birds came close to camp; before the summer was over they seemed like members of our party. One day Mardy and I watched a Red-throated Loon swim by on the river, an unforgettable sight. These are the two loons we found in arctic Alaska.

In many places in the Sheenjek Valley we came across the Upland Plover. They flew over us, uttering their ascending whistle, and perched in the tops of spruces in the muskeg, as did the Lesser Yellowlegs, scolding us as we went by. Obviously there was a nest in the immediate vicinity.

On the gravel bars of the Sheenjek River we found many Semipalmated Plovers, and, in the alpine lakes as well as at the head of the Sheenjek, there was the Wandering Tattler. It was a special treat to find these Tattlers on their nesting places far up in that wild country.

We became more and more fascinated by the country itself. Why do so many species of birds find appropriate summer homes up there? The answer, at least partly, must be in the variety in the environment itself. In the valleys are many streams, large and small, and many lakes and small ponds. It is a very wet country, with the permafrost underground, the melting patches of overflow ice here and there, lasting nearly all summer, and the accumulation of water among the tussocks. There are quite extensive areas of white spruce forest, mostly on the sides of the Sheenjek Valley, the lower slopes of the mountains. There are the willows bordering all the lakes and streams, and in many places the dwarf birch. The mountains rising on both sides of the valley have their cliffs and ledges, and, after a certain elevation, there is only the high alpine plant growth, and the lichens.

That kind of country suits so many species of birds. The tundra-loving birds find what they like. In the open country we saw the Least Sandpiper, Smith's Longspur, and other ground-nesting species. There, too, usually among dwarf birch bushes, we found nests of the Willow Ptarmigan. The numerous water places were attractive to the waterfowl, some shorebirds, and gulls—all those that choose a wet world.

Among the cliffs of the mountains we looked for the Golden Eagle, the Gyrfalcon, Say's Phoebe, Cliff Swallow, and Wheatear.

The groves of white spruce form another habitat. Mardy and I, wandering along in one of these groves one day, discovered a nesting pair of Robins. It was like a greeting from home to see the Robin so far above the Arctic Circle. And that reminds me of another time, still farther north, just beyond the limit of trees, when we came across a group of Violet-green Swallows! They were nesting in some bluffs above the Sheenjek River, far toward its head.

In the wooded areas we saw such birds as the Gray Jay, Northern Shrike, Varied Thrush, and Myrtle Warbler. The high alpine country, above the tree growth, was not devoid of life either. There we found birds of the high country—the Water Pipit, Horned Lark, Gray-crowned Rosy Finch, and Wheatear.

Birds and flowers are not the only organisms which grace this north country. Grizzly bears wander freely everywhere. Although we came across places where they had dug ground squirrels out of their burrows or had feasted on the remains of caribou left by wolves, mostly these great bears feed on vegetation. We found areas where they had dug up a lot of ground for the roots underneath.

The Indians warned us about grizzlies. At Fairbanks they persuaded us to take along a fifty-gallon steel drum with a clamp-on lid which could be fastened. In this we kept most of our food supplies, safe from bears, in a shady place at the back of the tent.

The grizzlies never came to our camp. However, we did have great respect for them and tried to be watchful and keep out of their way.

Wolves are a part of the Arctic. They were scarce, but they were there. We occasionally found the carcass of a caribou on which wolves had fed, but it was a very special day when we caught a glimpse of one. In 1956, a wolf came very close to camp, then trotted off across the ice of the lake. We named it Lobo Lake in his honor.

Of course the wolf depends on the caribou for a living. Large and small bands of these interesting arctic deer traveled back and forth through the country, always going somewhere else! We witnessed part of the big migration from west to east, at Last Lake in mid-July, 1956—an experience none of us will ever forget. As one member of our party exclaimed while he was watching that exciting scene: "This is *it!*"

There are white mountain sheep in the Brooks Range. They were farther north, up near the summit, where for some reason there was enough plant growth they like and need near the cliffs.

And of course we also saw foxes, lynx, wolverine, and many ground squirrels.

I suppose I must mention the mosquitoes! They were there, swarms of them after mid-June, and they lasted until late July. Somehow we did not have much trouble with them; we kept well smeared with "6-12" or "Off" and tried to forget them. However, I must state that the early part of the season, *before* June 15, is truly Paradise Time in the north!

About camping in this region, there is one thing I always wish to stress. Timber is so scarce in many places, especially at good camping places, that I hated to cut a single tree. I had to cut wooden poles for our cook and supply tent, but these I was careful to leave where the next campers would find them. For sleeping we had a small, light Aberlite tent, waterproof and mosquitoproof, which had a set of nesting aluminum T-top inside poles which worked very well.

We were careful about fires. We had a little folding grate and did a good deal of cooking on it, using only dead limbs and sticks for fuel. Since we did not want to burn up all the dead wood—we wanted to leave some for the next campers—we also had a two-burner Coleman stove and a supply of white gas. In the tent during rainy spells this stove kept us cosily warm. Our sleeping tent, of course, had no heat in it, but with air mattresses and down sleeping bags we were usually very warm. There were a few nights early in the season when we crawled into our bags with our clothes on. Later, the daylight nights did not cool off enough to be uncomfortable and the days were so hot we got very sunburned. Most of the time we traveled about, comfortable and sometimes a bit too warm, with ordinary heavy cotton trousers and cotton flannel shirts.

When trying to load everything needed for a ten-day or two-week period into a Cessna plane, it is important to keep the weight of the outfit down. There are some very good dried foods on the market now and we depended a great deal on these, plus a minimum amount of staples. The permafrost, right below us under eighteen inches of moss and peat, furnished refrigeration for the few types of foods which kept better if cool. I do think it is quite necessary to have two tents—both waterproof, mosquitoproof, and of light weight material—one small tent for sleeping and the other high enough to stand and sit in for storage, rainy days, and inside work. We were surprised, in 1961, that Keith was able to carry us, all our gear, and enough food for two weeks in one load of the Cessna. Incidentally, we made a list of every item which we took into that country, from the least to the greatest, just in case it might be useful to others making a similar expedition.

This whole northeast corner of Alaska about which we have been talking was, in 1960, set aside as the Arctic Wildlife Range by former Secretary of the Interior, Fred A. Seaton. It is an area of 9,000 square miles from the Canadian boundary west to the Canning River, taking in both slopes of the Brooks Range and extending to the Arctic Coast. Mr. Seaton's courageous action was opposed by certain Alaskan politicians and they still may be hoping to undo what he accomplished, but I think the *people* of Alaska are beginning to realize the value of his act.

The important point is that such an area, *if left alone,* can be an immeasurably valuable place not only for scientific research, but also for people who really care to share the freedom of the Arctic with the birds, the mammals, the plants, the mountains, and the lakes—to see how life goes on in an original environment, and to savor the arctic world untouched by man.

# CHURCHILL ON HUDSON BAY

## John C. Schmid

*It is a long way from New York's Madison Avenue to Churchill on Hudson Bay, and there is a wide difference between watching birds on the shores of Connecticut, Long Island, and New Jersey, and searching for birds in the Far North. Even in this age of jet planes and rockets, ice machines and air conditioners, the gap is still prevalent. With this statement I am sure John Schmid will agree.*

*John Conrad Schmid, born in 1905 and raised in Paris, France, graduated from the Sorbonne and came to this country in 1927. After serving for nine years as a foreign-exchange trader with a bank on Wall Street, he became associated with the Eastman Kodak Company where he has worked for the past twenty-five years. At present he is manager of the New York sales promotion advertising office for the northeastern sales division of Eastman Kodak.*

*It is a question as to which of John Schmid's interests came first: cameras or birds. Regardless of the answer, he is skilled in both photography and bird watching, happily combining the two. He is best known for lectures illustrated by his own films. In the field of bird banding he has been notably active, capturing birds with both traps and mistnets, and being a participant for the last six years in Operation Recovery (at Island Beach, New Jersey), a cooperative project for the study of the migratory birds along the Atlantic flyway under the sponsorship of the U.S. Fish and Wildlife Service.*

*He is a member of the Explorers Club and a member, director, or staunch supporter of a number of other ornithological and conservation organizations.*

*Churchill, Manitoba, is a little nearer Manhattan than it was thirty years ago. I was there with George Sutton in 1931. That year the Hudson Bay Canadian Government Railway instituted regular passenger service and we were the first ornithologists to take advantage of it, arriving in late May in advance of the spring influx of birds. Since that day many ornithologists, photographers, and museum workers have been to Churchill. Now it enjoys a tri-weekly air service. Despite its greater accessibility, comparatively few bird watchers have visited Churchill, perhaps because they are unaware of what it has to offer by way of birdlife so characteristic of the Far North.*

*John and Mary Schmid went to Churchill on their own in the summer to see and photograph birds. They waded through marshy tundra and muskeg, fought hordes of mosquitoes, put up with wretched weather, endured the weariness that comes from continuous physical effort during the long, long daylight. And they came back thrilled—indeed, absolutely enchanted—with the miracle of spring in the Far North.*

*Bird watching on Hudson Bay is for the hardy, but its rewards far outweigh the discomforts, as you will learn on reading John Schmid's story that follows.*

To many persons, Churchill brings to mind the famed statesman with a cigar. To ornithologists and botanists, Churchill is the most accessible arctic outpost in North America. Even though it is somewhat south of the Arctic Circle, its avifauna and flora are truly of the Far North.

Situated in northern Manitoba on the west side of Hudson Bay, Churchill is easily reached by train from either Winnipeg or The Pas in Manitoba, or by commercial plane from any major city in Canada. A trip to Churchill offers the bird watcher a unique opportunity to see, study, and photograph a number of arctic or subarctic species of birds, and to explore the tundra with its fantastic display of arctic flowers.

The Townsite of Churchill lies along the Churchill River just before it enters Hudson Bay. Icebound for nine and a half months of the year, the Townsite is nevertheless an important grain-shipping center and railhead. During the two and a half months when the port is open, many ships from Europe dock alongside the giant grain elevators—enormously tall, cylindrical structures that are a landmark readily spotted from thirty miles away.

North of the Townsite, jutting between the river mouth and Hudson Bay, is Cape Merry. This guards the entrance to the river's wide, treacherous estuary. Here the tide, with a rise of from twelve to eighteen feet, periodically changes the appearance of the river, submerging huge rocks that make navigation hazardous. Upstream, at low tide, the river and its rapids are dangerous to negotiate.

While still a frontier town, Churchill in recent years has felt the influence of modern commerce brought about by the railhead and airport. It has hotels which serve adequate meals and just recently one of them added a motel to its facilities.

When Mrs. Schmid and I visited Churchill to find and photograph birds, we stayed at one of the hotels. Each day we carried our lunches into the field and returned late for an evening meal. Since Churchill is a busy port during the short summer, as well as a gateway to the Arctic, there is a constant flow of travelers on their way to and from the Far North. Advance reservations at the hotels are, therefore, necessary.

A shield of rock extends south along the shore of Hudson Bay, rising at times to a 100-foot ridge. Five miles south of the Townsite and inland from the ridge is Fort Churchill, built during World War II and now part of Canada's Department of National Defense. Between the Townsite and the Fort, and south from the Fort for fifteen miles, stretches a flat, boggy tundra with numberless clear-water pools and ponds. Then comes a twenty-mile-wide belt of spruce forest and muskeg and south of this forty or more miles of tundra.

Today it is possible to drive southward from the Townsite, over rough roads built by the military, traversing tundra, forest, and muskeg. One road leads to Twin Lakes, another to Landing Lake, and still another to Goose Creek.

Taxis are available to take visitors to some ideal bird-watching locations but they are quite expensive. Having our own car, we found, was economical and a great convenience, enabling us to see and do more than we could have otherwise. Against the purchase of four round-trip, first-class tickets from Winnipeg to Churchill, the Canadian National Railway transported our automobile on a boxcar, free of extra charges. The freight train took five days from Winnipeg. In the fourteen days that we had our car we traveled 756 miles on the three roads in the area. Driving our own car saved precious time and effort when going to areas too far to reach by walking. Since we carried all our necessary equipment, driving saved our strength, too, for the strenuous walking in the wet, cushion-like tundra where we sought nesting birds.

When we arrived in Churchill on June 21, the ice had gone out of the river but the floes were still in the bay. The weather was extremely changeable. Beautiful sunny days were often replaced suddenly by cold, driving rain or thick, dense fog rolling in ahead of a raw, penetrating wind, accompanied frequently by a drop in temperature of 20 degrees or more within the hour. When the sun was out, it was comfortably warm—in the high 50's. We even had a reading of 86 degrees on July 2. Unfortunately, when the temperature rose and the wind dropped, the mosquitoes and black flies became abundant and voracious. Using an excellent spray repellent, we were seldom bitten, yet we were often irritated by swarms of insects that did not know enough to stay out of nose, mouth, and ears. A head net or any breeze brought a welcome relief.

Churchill's unpredictable weather, of course, makes warm, light, easy-to-peel-off clothing highly desirable. Footgear should be waterproof and, depending on the area covered, can be shoe-pac, knee-high boots, or waders. The prevailing cold wind makes a light sweater and a windproof parka with hood a must.

It is not absolutely necessary to have a car to enjoy Churchill, as there is much to be seen around the Townsite. Arriving early in June, one can witness the ice breakup in the river and bay. At the same time he can add to his list many migrants stopping off or passing over on their way farther north to nest. On two mornings we watched several hundred Whistling Swans in flight overhead.

In the Townsite, we noted Horned Larks, Snow Buntings, and Lapland Longspurs. Bird boxes put on houses attracted Tree Swallows. A small colony of Arctic Terns occupied the grounds of the

Esso tank farm, their nests protected by empty drums put there by kindly truck drivers. Robins, Yellow Warblers, White-crowned Sparrows, and Savannah Sparrows liked the shrubs and grassy areas bordering the Townsite slough. Oldsquaws and Greater Scaups frequented the Townsite ponds.

All along the ridge at the edge of the bay, within walking distance, is a bleak, rock-strewn wasteland, dotted with mirrored pools. As the days grow long and the sun brings its summer warmth, here suddenly, among tiny willows and vividly colored mosses and lichens, thousands of small wildflowers appear, transforming the ridge into a land of enchantment.

Overlooking the river and Hudson Bay, Cape Merry Point is a perfect spot from which to observe white whales (belugas) and seals following and feeding on schools of fish that come at the change of tide. We saw Sabine's Gulls here the first day, but never again. We watched Bonaparte's Gulls and Arctic Terns being harassed by those air-borne thieves, the Long-tailed and Parasitic Jaegers, until they were forced to drop the capelins they had just obtained from the sea. The jaegers then swooped down and caught the fish in mid-air. Red-breasted Mergansers fed with Common Eiders. Red-throated and Arctic Loons, Double-crested Cormorants, and Oldsquaws flew past us, going up the river.

With the telescope we saw Eskimos in the distance hunting for seals on the ice shelf at the edge of the open water. Others in canoes were hunting whales. Rafts of White-winged and Surf Scoters exploded in the air as the canoes of the Eskimos approached them. Around us Water Pipits flushed from their well-hidden nests among the rocks.

Birds often noted in our travels back and forth, some twenty-five miles from the Fort, were Common Ravens, Rough-legged and Marsh Hawks, Short-eared Owls, and, of course, Willow Ptarmigan. The cocks were still conspicuous with their white plumage half turned to brown and their "eyebrows" a brilliant red. They never took flight at our approach but instead sought cover under the lower branches of spruce trees, standing still until certain they had been discovered. Then they walked over to another tree and repeated the same performance. The hens were a good example of camouflage in nature. A person could walk close to an individual sitting on a nest and fail to see her. Many other birds whose nests were dispersed over the tundra we observed swimming or feeding on the lakes and ponds. The most common ducks were Oldsquaws, Greater Scaups, and Pintails with an occasional Black Duck, Mallard, or Green-winged Teal. Northern Phalaropes, the little clowns of the tundra, whirled and dunked themselves in shallow pools. Meanwhile, feeding on the gravelly edges of pools were Stilt, Semipalmated, and Least Sandpipers, Semipalmated Plovers, and Lesser Yellowlegs. In wet parts of the tundra Hudsonian Godwits, Dowitchers, Dunlins, and Rusty Blackbirds were numerous.

In one small area of tundra we found nests and eggs of the Golden and Semipalmated Plovers, Whimbrel, Semipalmated and Least Sandpipers, Horned Lark, and Lapland Longspur. Stilt Sandpipers with chicks and Smith's Longspurs were also here. Other nests that we located were those of Northern Phalaropes, Arctic Terns, Herring Gulls, and Parasitic Jaegers.

With the scope we discovered the nest of a Parasitic Jaeger on a distant hummock. We decided to wade through three-quarters of a mile of marshy tundra to try to photograph the pair at their nest. Our first attempt ended when I stepped into water deeper than my knee-high boots. Returning to the car I changed to dry socks and waders, and, after slow, cautious progress, we finally reached our goal.

At our approach the Jaegers put on an elaborate broken-wing act, flopping in opposite directions away from the nest, then one bird taking off to rejoin the other. Only when we were very close to the nest did the birds fly over our heads; but at no time, contrary to our expectations, did they attack us or even try to hit us.

As we started to wade away from the Jaeger nest, Mary told me that the single-lens reflex camera she carried had fallen out of the case and into the water. Hoping to give the camera first aid by drying it as soon as possible, we hurried back to the car. But in rushing through knee-deep water with a heavy movie camera and tripod on my left shoulder and a smaller movie camera in my right hand, my foot suddenly went down into a hole. The next thing I knew I was sitting chest-deep in ice water—with the camera in my hand under water. The moral: Never tell your wife how clumsy she is until you are on solid ground.

Upon reaching the car I peeled off my wet clothes promptly

and climbed into the car. Mary wrung the water from my clothes and was frantically fanning the air with my shorts, trying to dry them quickly when a passing military car ground to a sudden stop and out stepped two soldiers. While I took cover in the car under the bright orange top of my foul-weather suit, they inquired about the telephoto lens on the camera I had left standing in front of the car. Mary answered their questions good humoredly, still fanning my underwear behind her back. Why at that moment, when all I wanted was to get dry and warm, should two G.I.'s want to discuss my 400-millimeter lens?

This episode taught us a lesson: Now, when walking through a marsh, we use a long stick as a third leg and practice our own preaching of wrapping cameras in polyethylene bags. As for the Jaeger's nest, it took on special significance to us and we greatly regretted having to leave on July 10 before the eggs had hatched.

Some of the eggs in the nests of other birds did hatch in time, however. We banded the chicks of the Dowitcher, Least Sandpiper, Stilt Sandpiper, and Lesser Yellowlegs, and nestlings of the Horned Lark and Lapland Longspur.

We saw our first Harris' Sparrow near Landing Lake, as well as Common and Hoary Redpolls, and White-crowned, Savannah, and Tree Sparrows. Bonaparte's Gulls were nesting in small spruce trees nearby and consequently dived at anyone approaching them. Arctic Loons broke the silence of the Lake with their weird cries.

We inquired about the caribou which migrate northward every spring and were told we were too late to see any. Yet on three different occasions we saw caribou—a full-grown adult with a splendid set of antlers, a younger one in velvet, and a small female. We also saw weasels, both adult and kit foxes, and, in the mud, a large footprint of a wolf.

The most common rodent and one of the great regulators of the ecology, the lemming, was, unfortunately, never seen, nor was the polar bear which is a common habitant of Churchill from October to April. We were told we would not see polar bears, yet a friend reported one on July 17. Unbelievable adds to unbelievable in this area.

The flowers of Churchill contribute enormously to its appeal.

Every moss-covered spot, every crevice in the rocks, every patch of tundra, clearings in the woods, ditches by the roads, all are at once brilliant with miniature blooms. In the protective lee of boulders, willows and birches spread out their tiny branches two inches from the ground. Each little plant struggles bravely to survive the harsh climate and icy winds. Catkins, large in proportion to the plants on which they grow, add colorful variety while dwarf rhododendrons produce delicate blossoms, each the size of a nickel. The arctic avens follow with their lovely white petals and golden centers.

Every plant seems to feel the competition for survival. Thus in a matter of hours the bleak tundra of the week past becomes a bright carpet of lovely flowers, millions of them, that disappear as fast as they appeared. The days are long; the summer is short. All living things are working to preserve their kind for another year. What can be more memorable than a Golden Plover sitting on a nest amid a profusion of arctic flowers? That is our vision of Churchill, to which we will someday return.

# ONTARIO'S ALGONQUIN PARK

## Fred Bodsworth

*Fred Bodsworth, a Canadian novelist and nature writer, was born in Port Burwell, Ontario, in 1918. During his high school years in this Lake Erie fishing port he became intensely interested in natural history and writing.*

*Following his first jobs as reporter and editor on newspapers in St. Thomas and Toronto, he became a staff writer for* Maclean's Magazine. *In 1955 he resigned this position in order to devote full time and energy to his pen. This was a fortunate move for us all because it resulted in three skillful books that have since enjoyed wide acclaim.* The Last of the Curlews, *published in 1954, was a Reader's Digest Condensed Book Selection and has appeared in seven foreign editions. The second book, a novel titled* The Strange One *(1960), was a selection of the Literary Guild of America. A third novel,* The Atonement of Ashley Morden, *was published in 1964.*

*Magazine assignments have taken Fred Bodsworth by plane, train, boat, and car the length and breadth of Canada—from Newfoundland to British Columbia and north as far as Axel Heiberg, only 700 miles from the Pole. During these travels he has rarely lost an opportunity to study birds. He insists that the most pleasant method of bird watching is to "stock up a canoe and paddle and portage one's way back into a wilderness lake country," and that his favorite lake country is in Algonquin Park, an area readily*

*accessible from his home in Toronto and to which he has been*
*going regularly for fifteen years, "camping beside its canoe routes*
*in summer and along its snowshoe trails in winter."*

*A natural history writer balances on a tight rope. He must not*
*be maudlin or anthropomorphic or his readers will close the book*
*in disgust; he must not be text-bookish or pedantic or his readers*
*will be bored. The trick is making the subject come excitingly alive*
*in its own true fashion and in its own peculiarly fascinating envi-*
*ronment. Fred Bodsworth shows his mastery of the tight rope as he*
*introduces us to Algonquin Park.*

We had been paddling and portaging all day. A chain of eight Algonquin Park lakes now lay behind us, and since this was bear country and bears are reluctant swimmers, we had chosen an island in McIntosh Lake for our first-night camp. It was about twelve miles, as the raven flies, from the highway landing where we had started. And we could reflect with some comfort and satisfaction that the boggy, uphill portage between Blackbear and Ink Lakes was now behind us too, although that notorious mile-and-a-half carry had been made a little easier this trip because we had found wolf tracks on one of the beaver dams—thrilling evidence that our sweat and labor were already getting us into genuine wilderness country.

We were suffering the usual first-night canoe-tripping complaints. Our legs were aching, and newly sunburned shoulders were sore from the chafing of pack straps on the portages. My companion, school inspector-naturalist Donald Young, while carrying our eighty-five-pound canoe on the last leg of the Ink Lake portage that afternoon, said he was sure he must be leaving tracks an inch deep in the granite-gneiss rocks on the trail behind him.

The tent was up, sleeping bags were rolled out, and behind the jagged skyline of spruces in the west a florid sunset was waning into purple. But despite the sore muscles we were not yet ready for bed. There was still the traditional first-night ritual of listening for Common Loons. We had seen or heard a number of northern birds that day—Common Ravens at numerous points, Gray Jays at the lunch stop on Blackbear, a Boreal Chickadee as we paddled down

Ink Creek, and several Olive-sided Flycatchers keeping company with a lone Black-backed Three-toed Woodpecker in the drowned-out spruce stubs behind one of the beaver dams. But despite these, for us no Algonquin trip seemed properly and fully inaugurated until we had sat by a fire under the pines on the first night out and listened to a loon chorus. We had paddled late, making a long day of it, in order to reach McIntosh, because we knew from previous trips that McIntosh could be relied upon to provide a good evening rendezvous of loons.

We moved close to the fire as the evening chill settled in and waited silently, confident that we would not be kept waiting long. Here beneath the big pines, the shadows began darkening, but the lake beyond remained a silver mirror of light. A Winter Wren launched into its tinkling, bubbly song and we wondered, as always, how a bird so small could store up enough breath to produce so long a song. White-throats joined in with their evening serenade— the clear and whistling song that the bird books render as a prosaic *Old Sam Peabody, Peabody, Peabody,* but that to our Canadian ears here in the northern forests of the White-throat's breeding range is distinctly and unequivocally *Dear, Dear Canada, Canada, Canada,* and can never be anything else.

And then it came, as we knew it would. It started with a single tremolo, the "laughing" call, quavering and sonorous, and we heard it before we saw the loon itself peering curiously at our fire from a few hundred feet offshore. It was answered immediately by a pair down at the south end of the lake near the Ink Creek outlet and then they came in on whistling wings to join the first one off our camp. There were more answers, farther away at first from neighboring lakes, and then close by as they flew in to join our McIntosh trio. In a few minutes we had seven and with the loon chorus rising in earnest now we had a good opportunity to sort out their three basic calls. The tremolo predominated, the call that is said to resemble maniacal laughter, but it was interspersed with the three-syllabled *oh-a-lee* yodels and with the "wail" calls, mournful, drawn-out and unsyllabled, the call that is often mistaken for the howl of a wolf by newcomers to the North Country.

The three calls merged in a tremulous medley and the spruce shores threw back the echoes so that it was impossible at times to sort the echoes from the real. To my mind, no sound and region

are as intrinsically linked, as mutually complementary and interpretive, as this wild and rollicking loon laughter and the forested
lake country of the north in which the big diver summers. It is the
purest epitome of the northland's wildness. No sound I know except
possibly the howling of wolves on a subzero winter night carries an
equal measure of wild, enchanting beauty. The loons were still
calling when twilight had darkened to night and a Barred Owl
down the shore began adding its muted *Who cooks for you?* to the
weird chorus. We doused the fire and sought the warmth of our
sleeping bags.

If the wolf tracks on the Ink Lake portage had left any doubts
in our minds, the doubts were now dispelled. We were in wilderness again. The loons, Algonquin's self-appointed greeters, had put
their stamp of genuineness upon it and made it official with their
welcoming chorus.

We had not come to Algonquin solely for its birds, we had
come to unwind psychologically in its wilderness solitudes, to shed
the tensions that had built up during a desk-bound winter, to smell
again the scent of balsam fir, to hear the roar of rapids, and to feel
muscles toughening once more on the portages. But the birds were
an essential part of it, a reminder that we were in new environment, for there are many northern species here that are very rare
or only fleeting migrants in our home region 170 miles to the
south.

Algonquin is Ontario's largest provincial park. Roughly seventy
by forty miles, its 2,900-square-mile area is greater than the state
of Delaware and most of it is roadless wilderness, for the only
major, public highway entering it is a thirty-seven-mile stretch that

loops up into its southwest corner. It is 170 miles north of Toronto, 270 miles by road from Buffalo, 400 miles from Detroit. The ideal way to see it is to take off from the highway by canoe and spend a week or two following the waterways that link its labyrinth of 2,100 lakes. There are outfitters from whom canoes and camping gear can be rented, and guides who will welcome the opportunity to earn their $10 or $12 a day guiding a leisurely bird seeker instead of the fishermen who usually employ them. Your guide will be mystified to learn that you are looking for birds instead of trout, and he will not be much help with your bird finding, but he will cook, do the heavy work on the portages, catch you trout dinners, and be an essential safety factor if you are an inexperienced canoeist. And if you shy away from canoes, there is a twenty-mile hiking trail with cleared campsites at intervals along it.

But one can have good birding in Algonquin without straying far from its highway. Although the highway traverses only a small part of the park, it takes one close to examples of most of Algonquin's various types of bird habitat. Lodges and several campgrounds provide accommodation. A number of labeled nature trails lead off the highway and a museum at Mile 13 is headquarters during summer months for a park interpretation program that includes hikes led by park naturalists and evening films and lectures. For a more formal introduction to the region's plants and birds, there is a Federation of Ontario Naturalists' nature school conducted during the first two weeks of July each year at Camp Billie Bear, a few miles west of the park.

Algonquin lies near the southern rim of the four-billion-year-old Precambrian Shield that arcs in a giant horseshoe around Hudson Bay. What were once lofty, granite-gneiss mountains have been rasped down by 800 million years of erosion and glacial scouring into humping hills and ridges with cold, blue lakes and rushing rivers in the hollows between them. Only the mountain roots survive and the highest elevations have been reduced now to about 1,800 feet, but it remains a rugged landscape of sheer cliff faces and rolling skylines nevertheless.

For the bird watcher, Algonquin's main attraction is its northerners, for it is here that the bird watcher's north begins. Not all the northern forest species are breeding here, for Algonquin is still too far south for some of them, but a number of boreal birds are present. Algonquin lies in the Transition Zone between the deciduous forest biome of the south and the coniferous forest biome that stretches from here northward to the subarctic limit of trees, and its forest is a mixture of both. Here the hardwoods, like maples, beech, and yellow birch, are beginning to peter out as they approach the northern extremities of their ranges, and the boreal spruce and fir are taking over.

Algonquin offers two groups of birds that are of special interest to the bird watcher from farther south—the boreal species seen in the south only in high-mountain country or as very rare winter stragglers, and the northern breeders which the average bird watcher knows only as migrants.

In the first group are the Common Raven, Gray Jay, Spruce Grouse, Black-backed Three-toed Woodpecker, Boreal Chickadee, and Red and White-winged Crossbills.

Ravens, once almost wiped out by wolf poisoning programs, have increased conspicuously in the last twenty years since the poisoning campaigns have been discontinued. You will have no difficulty finding them along the highway which they patrol regularly for road kills.

The Gray Jay, an early nester, is secretive in early summer, possibly because it is still feeding young, but it begins to become fairly obvious after mid-July. By late summer and autumn it is unusual to stop for a roadside lunch without having this camp scavenger join you—you will not have to look for it then, it will look for you.

Spruce Grouse, Black-backed Woodpecker, and Boreal Chickadee require some hunting. The Spruce Grouse is probably relatively common but it is difficult to flush from the dark spruce tangles in which it lives and thus hard to find. The woodpecker and chickadee are regular but not common Algonquin nesters. Ask a park naturalist where they have been seen recently. The Black-backed Woodpecker will usually be in areas where beaver ponds or bogs have drowned out trees and left dead stubs standing.

The crossbills are not normally nesters this far south, but in some years flocks of them remain throughout the summer and are believed to nest. When you arrive, ask a park naturalist if it is "a crossbill summer."

Less exotic than these boreals but equally interesting to most bird seekers are the warblers that are familiar migrants in the south but can be studied here as breeders in full song. Algonquin has fifteen common or relatively common nesting warblers—Black-and-white, Nashville, Parula, Magnolia, Black-throated Blue, Myrtle, Black-throated Green, Blackburnian, Chestnut-sided, Ovenbird, Northern Waterthrush, Mourning, Yellowthroat, Canada, and American Redstart. There are three others that normally nest farther north but have nested rarely in Algonquin—Tennessee, Cape May, and Bay-breasted Warblers.

In this same category—usually migrants or winter residents farther south but nesters here—are Common Loon, Common Merganser, Broad-winged Hawk, Saw-whet Owl, Yellow-bellied Sapsucker, Yellow-bellied Flycatcher, Olive-sided Flycatcher, Winter Wren, Hermit and Swainson's Thrushes, both kinglets, Rusty Blackbird, Evening Grosbeak, Purple Finch, Slate-colored Junco, Lincoln's and White-throated Sparrows.

To leave some empty spaces on your check-list that will serve as an excuse for a more northern birding expedition another year, there are a few boreal forest nesters that Algonquin cannot provide. Five warblers that go farther north to nest are the Orange-crowned, Blackpoll, Palm, Connecticut, and Wilson's. Other boreal species that are also farther north in summer are Great Gray Owl, Northern Three-toed Woodpecker, Gray-cheeked Thrush, Pine Grosbeak, the redpolls, Pine Siskin, and two sparrows—Tree and White-crowned. These are the far-northerners, for them even Algonquin is south.

For a thorough birding coverage of Algonquin you will have to seek out its different forest types because most of its nesting species show quite apparent tree and habitat preferences. The western half of Algonquin is a highland with a forest of hardwoods, spruce, and balsam fir; the eastern half is a lowland with extensive sand plains left behind by glacial spillways and here the dominant forest is pine. The pine areas are remote, hard to reach even by canoe, and their bird populations have not been carefully studied, so I am going to have to plead ignorance and say no more about them. In the park's western half, however, readily accessible from the highway, there are five types of forest to be considered, each of which has a fairly distinct bird community associated with it. The experienced Algonquin birder can be led blindfolded into the forest and name the dominant tree species around him by the bird songs he hears. If you miss one of these classes of forest habitat, with it you are likely to miss some birds that don't occur anywhere else.

A widespread hardwood forest type in Algonquin today is aspen-white birch because these are the pioneering tree species that produced the first stage of new forest following the fires and lumbering of 50 to 100 years ago. Characteristic birds of aspen-white birch forest in Algonquin are the Ovenbird, Red-eyed Vireo, Veery, American Redstart, Chestnut-sided and Canada Warblers, and Hermit Thrush.

The other deciduous type, typical of older forest stands that were not burned or leveled during the initial lumbering era, is a hardwood association with sugar maple and yellow birch the dominant species. Characteristic birds here are again the Ovenbird, Red-eyed Vireo, Veery, and Redstart; but the Hermit Thrush, Chestnut-sided, and Canada will be less numerous, and replacing them will be Black-throated Blue Warbler, Wood Thrush, Rose-breasted Grosbeak, and Scarlet Tanager.

A third distinct forest type is represented by the pure stands of eastern hemlock which occur as scattered conifer islands amid the hardwoods. Here a very different bird community appears. Its commonest members by far will be Blackburnian and Black-throated Green Warblers. Others found more commonly in hemlock than elsewhere are Brown Creeper, Red-breasted Nuthatch, and Slate-colored Junco.

The two remaining habitats are boreal in character and harbor most frequently Algonquin's boreal species of birds. They are the white spruce-balsam fir forest, often with white or red pine intermixed, a widespread forest type in Algonquin, and finally, the open bogs with black spruce and tamarack borders. Look in these two habitats for the Spruce Grouse, Gray Jay, and Boreal Chickadee.

Dominating the white spruce-balsam fir forest will be the White-throated Sparrow. Here too will be most of the Myrtle Warblers, customarily in the treetops, and Magnolias in the middle stratum beneath.

Bogs are fascinating little worlds of their own that are treasure troves for the exploring naturalist. Although cradled by the northern forests around them, they are yet distinct and apart. They occur where undrained pockets of water are filling in with floating, spongy mats of sphagnum moss which will bob up and down beneath one's weight like rubbery ice. Tread carefully and stay away from the edges where the sphagnum mat meets open water, because the moss can be thin and you can fall through. They have their own distinctive plant and shrub communities characterized by leatherleaf, sweet gale, Labrador tea, pitcher plant, and *Pogonia* orchids. They are invariably encircled by thickets of black spruce and tamarack where the sphagnum mat is thick enough to support limited tree growth. And they have their own birds—Swamp Sparrows and Yellowthroats out in the stunted shrubs of the open bog, and Yellow-bellied and Olive-sided Flycatchers, Swainson's Thrushes, Nashville and Parula Warblers in the black spruce borders.

For the naturalist interested in mammals as well as birds, Algonquin has attractions that few remaining wilderness areas on the continent can duplicate. It is impossible to drive its thirty-seven-mile stretch of highway without seeing a number of white-tailed deer. In fact, of all the northern mammals that originially inhabited this region, only the wolverine and lynx are now missing from Algonquin. Mink and beaver are often seen as soon as canoe-trippers reach undisturbed lakes or rivers a few portages back from the highway. Moose and otter are seen more rarely. Marten and fisher are practically never seen because of their nocturnal habits but their tracks are numerous in winter indicating that they are there and worth watching for. Live-trapping surveys by biologists have revealed that some parts of the park have four or five marten per square mile.

But Algonquin's major mammal attraction is probably its timber wolves. It is one of the last readily accessible wilderness areas on the continent where one can still thrill to the sonorous and quavering howl of wolves on the hunt, that ultimate attestation of genuine wilderness country. Until a couple of years ago wolves were hunted in the park every winter by rangers, but Algonquin is now the center of a major wolf research project and the winter killing of wolves has been discontinued. Biologists carrying out the wolf research estimate that there are 300 timber wolves in approximately fifty packs within the park. The wolves are more vocal and heard more frequently in fall and winter than in summer, but summer visitors hear them commonly.

And there are black bears of course—sometimes too many.

My family and I once shared a campsite for a night on Algonquin's Burnt Island Lake with a bear that stubbornly kept returning each time we drove it away. We finally crowded food and five people into one tent, zipped it up and left the bear in possession outside. At dawn, after a night of apprehensive and rather fitful sleep, I discovered four bears rooting about the campsite for food scraps. Apparently we had been driving off not one bear, but four bears one at a time. Obviously, the bears regarded it as their domain and us as intruders who didn't belong. We shooed them back into the bush and did a rapid breakfastless breaking of camp that broke all our previous records.

I was thinking of this as Don Young and I paddled away through the morning mists and left McIntosh Lake again in possession of its loons. I hope that I and others like me will always be the intruders in Algonquin. I hope that Algonquin will remain a living museum of the primeval America that is now almost obliterated by roads and the commercial trappings that roads inevitably bring. I hope it will always be a place where one can hear loons and wolves and be forced at times to dispute a brief tenure of occupancy with an obstreperous bear or two whose rights to the land will retain precedence over my own.

# The Wetlands

NORTHERN SPRUCE BOGS
> Betty Darling Cottrille

THE DELTA MARSHES OF MANITOBA
> H. Albert Hochbaum

AN IOWA MARSH
> Paul L. Errington

MALHEUR AND KLAMATH LAKES
> Ira N. Gabrielson

THE BEAR RIVER MIGRATORY BIRD REFUGE
> William H. Behle

THE GREAT DISMAL SWAMP
> Joseph James Murray

THE EVERGLADES
> William B. Robertson, Jr.

# NORTHERN SPRUCE BOGS

## Betty Darling Cottrille

*When Betty Cottrille speaks of warblers, her eyes sparkle and her voice becomes vibrant with enthusiasm for her favorite subjects.*

*Betty Darling Cottrille was born in 1910 in De Smet, South Dakota. After graduating from the University of Minnesota, she taught physical education until she married W. Powell Cottrille, an osteopathic physician.*

*A search for outdoor recreation led this remarkable couple from a variety of sports to photography and thence to nature photography which very shortly centered on birds. Since the Cottrilles never do anything without doing it well—and one must know something about birds in order to photograph them successfully—their next step was to study birds. At first they were satisfied to study any bird, all birds, around their home in Jackson, Michigan, but a visit to Kirtland's Warbler country with the late Josselyn Van Tyne changed all that. Henceforth they would travel, study, and photograph warblers.*

*When the Cottrilles turned to the literature for information on the life histories of parulid warblers and discovered how very few solid facts were available for most species, they decided to seek some facts themselves. This meant going to the warblers' mecca— the North Country—and penetrating the spruce bogs where so many dwell in the warmer months.*

*Although the Cottrilles insist that their strenuous work in the bogs of northern Michigan and Minnesota is still only recreation, they have nonetheless assembled a wealth of valuable, hitherto unknown facts about parulids. Here Betty Cottrille shares some of her enthusiasm and knowledge while realizing full well that the number of bird watchers who will venture into the northern bogs for her elusive "little jewels" among the spruces will stay small for many a day.*

My husband and I, having become familiar with the birds nesting in the vicinity of our home in southern Michigan, decided to venture farther afield to find how other species—our north-bound migrants particularly—behave on their nesting grounds. At this stage it was fortunate for us that we knew two experienced ornithologists, Lawrence H. Walkinshaw from Battle Creek and William A. Dyer from Union City, who permitted us to join them on a field trip to the Upper Peninsula of Michigan. The region north of the village of Seney—a country of many spruce bogs—was our destination. Thus came our introduction to the nesting grounds of the Olive-sided and Yellow-bellied Flycatchers, Winter Wren, Hermit Thrush, White-throated Sparrow, and about twenty species of warblers, as well as the year-round home of such strangers to us as the Gray Jay and Boreal Chickadee.

In the years to follow we took many trips with Larry Walkinshaw and Bill Dyer to the spruce bogs in northern Michigan. Often we were joined by the late Josselyn Van Tyne and other ornithologists. More recently my husband and I explored spruce bogs farther away, in northeastern Minnesota.

With us, the exploration of spruce bogs is not work but a hobby. Our greatest enjoyment comes from finding nests—the rarer the better—and photographing the birds occupying them. If the nests are "firsts" for the states—as some of them have been—I would be dishonest if I did not admit to our receiving an enormous satisfaction in contributing in a small way to the ornithological history.

A soggy, cold, frustrating baptism marked our introduction to northern bogs. In my notes I wrote: "June 25. Here one week

today. Rain every day but one." Blackflies, mosquitoes, and other
insects were numerous beyond belief. We soon realized that this
was neither camping, shirt-sleeve, nor tennis-shoe country. One is
better off making his headquarters in a cabin as we did. And we
soon understood, too, why, despite the abundance of birds, there
are comparatively few nesting records: People simply avoid looking for nests in bogs because they consider bogs unpleasant. We
have encountered an occasional birder visiting the area, but precious few other souls. Fishermen know this country better than
birders and when we meet them and they ask "How's fishing?" we
always reply "just wonderful" and leave them to figure out what
new tackle we are hiding in binocular cases and camera boxes.

Most people fail to realize just what spruce bogs are and how
they developed. I believe that if people knew more about them,
they would find them, as we do, an alluring world for discovery.

A bog is a step in the succession of plant life from open water
to forest, the result of the filling in of a pothole or glacial lake with
vegetation—mosses, sedges, and other plant material—until sufficient soil has been formed to support trees. In the early stages the
surface is covered by a continuous mat of sphagnum moss that
shakes and quivers beneath one's feet and seems to be, and often
is, merely floating. This "quaking" bog supports a very limited
variety of small plants and shrubs. Later, when the sphagnum mat
has been anchored more or less securely to a peat base and one
need not carry a pole to guide one's rescuers in case one falls
through the mat, more plants move in. In time the sprouting seeds
of tamaracks, cedars, and spruces take root and the thick growth
of young trees cuts the sun from the small plants. The spruces
become dominant and we have what the ecologists refer to as a
"wet conifer swamp" and the laymen call a "spruce bog."

The spruce bogs in northern Michigan and Minnesota are dark
tangles of black spruce, tamarack, and cedar on a mat of sphagnum and peat. The trees, some of which are quite large, are so
close together that their branches, both dead and alive, weave
together to form walls and tangles tougher and more treacherous
than barbed wire. Dead trees have no room to fall—they can only
lean and interlace with their living neighbors. *Usnea,* a lichen
sometimes called "old man's whiskers moss," hangs in festoons

from rotting limbs turning them gray and pale green. In the deepest parts of bogs a sunlessness prevails and the air carries a faint chill and the odor of decay.

From the sunlit, quaking mat to the shadowy depths of a spruce bog are many gradations of vegetation, forming varied habitats. While a few bird species wander freely through them and a few others confine themselves to one habitat or another, the greatest number are likely to be found in those places where the quaking bog meets the spruce bog, where leatherleaf and Labrador tea grow among sapling spruces.

An important addition to field guides, in my opinion, would be advice on appropriate apparel for such habitats as spruce bogs. Since the Spartan life is not for me—nor for many birders—I want to be reasonably comfortable anywhere, even if the comfort is only relative. To enjoy myself in bogs I prepare for the worst—cold mornings, chilly days of rain, and the ever-present assortment of insects. The first rain suit my husband gave me delighted him more than a Paris original. I use waterproof boots worn over comfortable oxfords for general use and hip boots for early mornings and particularly wet places. I wear clothing that fully covers me, hot weather or not, for protection against branches as well as insects. I have insect repellent—an essential item, of course. Though its odor repels me as much as it does the insects, I have overcome my reluctance to use it, even over my face. During two of our seasons in bogs the insects were so rife that the lumbermen could not work and few fishermen wet their lines. Head nets were consequently necessary at those times.

We have always chosen to be in spruce-bog country during June because it is the month when all of the species are in full song and nesting is at its peak. In northern Michigan the season is very short and nesting comes to an abrupt end by July 4. In northern Minnesota, however, we found that the season is extended a week or two.

In searching for nests our attention soon centered on those bog species whose nests have been infrequently found. Certain species of warblers were a real challenge because few of their nests have been seen and described. But this is not to say there were certain other species any less challenging.

A Golden-crowned Kinglet nest was one of my first surprises.

The small ball of mosses hanging from the high limb of a black spruce immediately raised the question of how many young it contained. Up the tree and out on that precarious limb went one of our party to investigate. "A couple," he said casually, "and just about right to band." An amazing sight was in store for those of us on the ground when the climber, grinning mischievously, carefully lowered a binocular case containing *nine* bumble-bee-size nestlings. The banders had a field day.

In searching for nests it is not enough to recognize a singing male on his territory, for on the nesting ground his mate is more intimately associated with the nest and thus more likely to provide clues to its location. Besides observing the behavior between the males and females, you must learn to recognize the various chips, clicks, and squeaks that serve as their communication. At times the behavior of a female gives away the location of her nest so unmistakably that we say we have caught her "with jam on her face." On the other hand, we listened to Cape May Warblers sing on their territory a week and a half before we saw a female or heard a sound of communication between a pair. Several attempts to find a Connecticut Warbler nest failed because of our inability to recognize communication between the birds. When, at last, we heard the hollow *whik* from the female, we knew why they had eluded us. This was an entirely new sound—not recorded in the literature—to add to our storehouse for future use.

To crouch on a low collapsible stool in a bog is the most comfortable way I know to be inconspicuous and have a dry vantage point from which to watch birds for nesting clues. It is much easier to move the stool than to find a log or stump in just the right position. Your attention must not be distracted. When the Olive-sided Flycatcher leaves his singing perch high on a dead stub and flies to his nest on the branch of a dying black spruce, you must not be looking at the wildflowers growing about you in fascinating array. Your attention must not stray, even though a horsefly uses your head for a pylon. You must ignore this pest even when its buzzing makes it almost impossible to follow the soft *pee-wee* song of a female Yellow-bellied Flycatcher returning from a feeding excursion to her nest so well concealed in the sphagnum.

Time spent in a blind gives you an opportunity to become well acquainted with a bird and, occasionally, vice versa. I saw my first "people watcher" while photographing Canada Warblers engaged in the care of their young in a nest tucked cosily in the side of a dead stump. I was tracking the male's return by his repeated, sprightly song. As he drew close, my finger reached for the shutter release of the camera. At that moment the singing stopped; no bird appeared at the nest. Naturally I was puzzled. Then a slight movement on the ground in the blind caught my eye. There beside me was the little beauty—he had come in the back of the blind which I had left open because of the heat. Even in the semi-darkness of the blind his necklace of black beads stood out clearly against his yellow breast as he perched on tarsus tip, cocked his slate blue head, and peered at me. Apparently he found my work more interesting than his! Although I hated to be inhospitable and endure the heat by closing the blind, this I had to do in order to take his picture at the nest.

Identifying all sounds is a necessity. Acute hearing is often more important than keen eyesight because in the dense growth many living things are heard before they can be seen. Where dead leaves, sticks, and bracken formed the ground cover, I soon learned to identify an Ovenbird walking, chipmunks running, squirrels scampering, deer bounding, and—although I was always afraid to admit it—bears crashing through brush. I even learned that saw-beetles sound like rasping files. But the acid test of my hearing came the day I spent alone in a deep forest taking notes on an unusual Chimney Swift nest. The nest was in an old Pileated Woodpecker hole in a gigantic live yellow birch. Since the only reference in the literature to this sort of nest site was many years ago and indefinite, it seemed important that I spend the time to establish the credence of this record. Before long I had identified all my companions in the environs. Suddenly I was startled out of my wits by the near-human, maniacal screams of Common Ravens engaging in their high jinks nearby. Nothing had ever startled me more except possibly the whistled snort of a deer that was once almost beside me before it caught my scent. Rather comforting after this outburst from the Ravens were the guttural mutterings of a mother Ruffed Grouse escorting her young brood, and I resumed my note-taking.

Because human voices are lost in a spruce bog, we use referee whistles as our walkie-talkie. I fully expected to have trouble some day re-finding an area I had marked, but the whistle around my neck made me feel confident that I could not be lost for long. It had never occurred to me that I might panic and not be able to blow the whistle, but that was the case one day after I followed a male Black-throated Green Warbler deep into the bog. The bird eluded me and I turned to back-track. All the trees and hummocks of moss looked exactly alike! Realizing I was lost, I became so breathless with fear that it was some moments before I could produce enough decibels with my whistle to carry the "lost" signal the whole distance to my husband.

"If you learn to use your compass and use it all the time," voices of experience told me repeatedly, "you won't get lost." However, I noticed that no questions were ever asked when, once in awhile, a member of the party disappeared for a whole day and sometimes even missed dinner at night. I often suspected that it wasn't always a bird that detained him, but that he, like me, had such a good sense of direction that he didn't believe his compass.

Offsetting the cold, the rain, the torturous insects, and the fear of being lost is the elation that comes with the finding of a new nest or discovering a new behavior. With our early companions we served an enviable apprenticeship in witnessing the first nest records for Michigan of the Boreal Chickadee, the Yellow-bellied Flycatcher, and the Tennessee and Connecticut Warblers. In all probability the birds were there all the time, but we weren't. Our companions taught us that hours in the field pay off in proportion to results obtained.

In our search for nests we became increasingly aware of the constant struggle for survival among the denizens of the bog. I found it hard to enthuse over the nest of a Sharp-shinned Hawk when we felt certain that the four young had been nourished on the owners of the first and only Tennessee Warbler nest found in the state of Michigan. A violent storm destroyed the nest and eggs of a Black-throated Green Warbler so perfectly situated for photography on a low spruce branch. The agitated chipping of a pair of Magnolia Warblers attracted me to their nest in a tiny balsam just in time for me to see the last nestling devoured by a fox snake. The well-incubated eggs of a Mourning Warbler were smashed by the hoof of a deer. While we waited for the rain to stop in order to take pictures of a Veery nest so beautifully situated in a clump of grass, one nestling disappeared each day until the nest was empty. The predator was probably a chipmunk.

After our apprenticeship in northern Michigan my husband and I went to northeastern Minnesota. Here in the vast wilderness of the Quetico-Superior Country were magnificent spruce bogs where our approach was heralded by the nervous protestations of White-throated Sparrows and excited chipping of Slate-colored Juncos.

Totally unconcerned over us were the Tennessee Warblers, the nests of which we were so anxious to find. The numerous males sang on incessantly, urgently, piercingly while we parted the grasses and peered into the deep recesses on the sides and tops of sphagnum hummocks where the females were concealed on their nests. Each female sits so closely that she will leave only if the nest is touched. Even then she can be missed because she silently disappears into the leatherleaf or tiny spruces. The first nest we decided to photograph contained six young and was tended solely by a female, so tame that we needed no blind. But to get pictures of a male, and to satisfy our curiosity as to the part he takes in care of nestlings, we eventually set up blinds on three of the six nests we had under observation. We found the male to be not as attentive generally as the female, although individuals varied in their degree of attentiveness.

Finding the nest of a Cape May Warbler required drawing on all our previous field experience. For eleven days we listened while the male sang for long periods from the tops of the tallest trees. We knew of no familiar behavior patterns to follow; the literature gave us slight help. After several days during which we saw no female, the singing began to subside. We were about ready to admit defeat when I noticed an unfamiliar female warbler gathering food. She was soon joined by a male Cape May and together they flew out of sight. Our forces were reactivated. Due to the denseness of the black spruces, it took us almost two days to triangulate the area. When we at last saw the "little tiger" engage a male Tennessee Warbler in combat, we were sure we were in the right location. Soon thereafter the female Cape May flew out of the top of a spruce near me. In about twenty minutes she reappeared at the base of the same tree near the trunk and silently worked her way to the top where she remained a short while before flying away. We were ready for her on her next return. When she reached the top, we jarred the tree slightly causing her to flush. We brought ladders, climbed twenty feet, and found her nest containing eight small young.

We spent five days in blinds observing and photographing the Cape May family. During this time we noted the absence of singing and the meaningful chips as both birds worked efficiently as a team carrying countless spruce budworms to their nestlings. The female did not range as far afield as did the male, but she waited in a nearby tree for the male and together they entered the tree at a low level and began their stealthy ascent to the nest. Fortunately, the observation blind was manned on the day that a Broad-winged Hawk followed the male to the nest, and we were able to conclude our observations with the fledging of the young.

Our long days in the Quetico-Superior Country had a timelessness that are a bird watcher's dream. We found some of the finest birding we have ever enjoyed. Our trails through the bogs soon became so worn that it was impossible for me to tell at a glance whether I was tracking my husband or a stray bull moose. Nowhere else have I listened day after day to the songs of the Blackburnian, Bay-breasted, and Cape May Warblers until I could distinguish them. Having been preceded by relatively few birders, we again delighted in discovering nests in an area where only singing males had been reported during previous breeding seasons. We discovered the Connecticut Warbler nesting in a sphagnum hummock, so different from the dry, weedy ground of its Michigan home. Most exciting of all, we obtained the first nesting records for Minnesota of the Yellow-bellied Flycatcher and the Tennessee, Cape May, and Bay-breasted Warblers.

Our discoveries, such as they are, are only teasers, challenging us to search for and learn more and more about birds. Nothing could induce me to abandon the sheer pleasure derived from my "aviacation."

# THE DELTA MARSHES OF MANITOBA

## H. Albert Hochbaum

*To the North American ornithologist who is expert on matters relating to geese and ducks the word "delta" has a connotation far beyond the basic Greek. To him Delta is a marsh, a great marsh in south-central Manitoba, Canada; an incubator, a nursery, and a haven for waterfowl; and the site of a research station which Al Hochbaum has directed for over twenty-five years. Any ornithologist who hasn't been to Delta, dreams of going; any ornithologist who has worked there, plans to return. For the Delta Marsh is a very special place.*

*Hans Albert Hochbaum, born in Greeley, Colorado, in 1911, graduated from Cornell and received a master's degree from the University of Wisconsin. In 1938, after working with the National Park Service for three years, he became the first director of the Delta Waterfowl Research Station at Delta and has been there ever since.*

*When I first knew Al Hochbaum, he was a Cornell undergraduate who spent much of his time in creaky, drafty old McGraw Hall, studying and painting birds under the guidance of Arthur A. Allen and George Miksch Sutton. The promise he showed then has never let his mentors down. The researches, carried on at the Station which he has managed so skillfully, have resulted in many scientific papers and popular articles. His two books,* The Canvasback on a Prairie Marsh *(1944 and 1959) and* Travels and Tra-

214

ditions of Waterfowl (*1955*), *were both personally illustrated and received the literary award of The Wildlife Society. The former also received the Brewster Medal of the American Ornithologists' Union. His work in the province of Manitoba was recognized in 1962 when the University of Manitoba honored him with an LL.D.*

*Here Al Hochbaum colorfully pictures the changing year on the Delta Marsh and the pothole country to the northwest, and offers lucid and enticing suggestions to the ornithologist or bird watcher who would visit this waterfowl haven in the wide expanses of Manitoba.*

In spring and early summer there come fine days when fluffy fair-weather clouds dominate the sky of southern Manitoba, evidence of the earth's warming after the long winter. Lakes remain cold, however, with no rising air currents to make cloud. The traveler starting out across the prairie from Winnipeg is soon aware of open sky in the northwest where the shape of Lake Manitoba is clearly patterned in blue. Breaking away from the main road to follow gravel toward cloud edge, one is led to the great Delta Marsh, a wide span of cane and bulrush, open bays and narrow sloughs separating the wheat prairie from the wooded south shoreline of Lake Manitoba.

At the start of spring, the best wildfowling with camera and glass is on the agricultural plain south of the marsh. As snow melts, wide sheets of water are left on the black fields, and in wet years nearly every section of land is partly flooded. To these temporary lakes the waterfowl return. Canada Geese are first, usually arriving by late March. With Common Crow and Marsh Hawk, the big Canada "Grays" herald the passing of winter. Only a few days behind are Mallard and Pintail; and by the third week of April, most of the prairie waterfowl are on the fields, all but Ruddy Duck and White-winged Scoter, species that wait until May to bring up the rear.

On the fields, Canada Geese are restless, for they are close to their home ranges and breeding pairs will have eggs before April is finished. Flocks may linger for only a day or so; then they move on with the swift advance of spring. Pairs native to the Delta Marsh go directly there, settling on a central rendezvous from which the adult breeders move out to examine the marsh for suitable nesting locations, a large muskrat house away from the shoreline being a favored site. Canada Geese do not nest until their third spring, but in the yearlings there is much sexual activity; pair-formation begins on this first return to the homeland. Two-year-olds are already in firm pairs and they explore the marsh, some establishing briefly held territories even though nesting itself will not take place until the following year.

Most migrant waterfowl have passed through the Delta region by the end of the first week of May, but the annual mass passage of Blue Geese and Snow Geese is mid-month. Their wide skeins travel at elevations of two to three thousand feet, aiming toward James Bay, the next stopping place on the way to the Arctic. Whistling Swan also wait until the middle of May before moving on. And the little Richardson's Canada Geese, always to be recognized by their rapid wing-beat and tight flock formation, some years stay on the prairies until the end of May, continuing north with the very last of the shorebirds and Snow Buntings.

Nesting in Mallard and Pintail begins in April; they are incubating long before snow drifts are melted from marsh-edge willows. Their status as breeding pairs is revealed by a *three-bird-chase*. On an April evening one may see a pair of Mallard set wings to alight in a small slough, then flare suddenly to make hasty departure as a resident drake Mallard rises in swift pursuit. Away they go in dashing flight, two drakes and a hen, the pursuer quickly overtaking the intruding male and driving hard at the very tail of the female. The chase carries for half a mile or more; but on reaching the edge of his home range, the local drake turns and on set wings glides back to join his waiting mate. Apparently he is intent upon sexual conquest, hence his pursuit of the female rather than her drake. The effect, nevertheless, is to limit the number of pairs any parcel of nesting range can hold. This chase also occurs in Gadwall (and in the east it is typically territorial behavior in Black Duck); but such flights are uncommon in Shoveler and Blue-winged Teal where there is a much higher degree of male-to-male aggression in territorial behavior.

Because of sexual strife, pairs of ducks on their breeding grounds are spread far and wide. Moreover, a loafing spot is a requirement of territory, hence nesting pairs are settled along shorelines. The ratio of edge to water area is greater in small sloughs and potholes than in the big marsh itself where the large, open bays are nearly vacant of waterfowl. In May and June the little marshes are the best places to see ducks. Indeed, the finest sight of breeding ducks in the whole of the Delta region is along the "borrow" ditch that follows the gravel road to the village of Delta. Here, from early May until mid-June, pairs of most species native to the Delta Marsh may be encountered at close hand. Gadwall, Blue-winged Teal, and Shoveler are the most common ditch residents, but there are always several pairs of Mallard and Pintail, Redhead, Lesser Scaup, and Ruddy Duck. Sometimes a pair of Canvasback is established there.

Ducks in spring have a strong attachment to the home range and when a road or farmstead is nearby, breeding pairs become accustomed to human activity. This is the most favorable time of the year for the waterfowl photographer: the birds are in fine plumage, male and female sit side-by-side, settled and unafraid, allowing close approach. But one must not be misled by their disregard of the car passing within a few yards. They take little notice as long as it moves; but when it slows to a stop, with a photographer leaning from the window, they become quickly alarmed. The photographer's blind is always the first requirement for pictures of pairs at ease.

At this spring season, with ducks paired and on territory, the most rewarding view of waterfowl is to be had not at Delta or on any other big Manitoba marsh, but in the pothole country west of Neepawa. Neepawa is fifty miles northwest of Delta on No. 4 Highway. Most of the way there is across the flat bottom of glacial Lake Agassiz; but just three miles west of the little city, on the south side of the road, there is a round pothole. Thenceforward to the Saskatchewan border one is seldom beyond sight of ducks or of marshwater. Truly, this rolling farmland, spangled with small marshes, sometimes as many as 125 reedy potholes per square mile, includes some of the finest waterfowl breeding habitat in North America. In visiting this pothole range, it is best to leave the main highway for the gravel country roads where, no matter the direction one takes, there is always another little marsh just ahead, each different from any other and all, in years of strong numbers, holding breeding pairs in spring and broods during summer.

This pothole country is especially important as Canvasback breeding range, and in May Canvasback pairs or waiting drakes are seen in every square mile of farmland, their nests sometimes located only a few yards from main roads. And here the Ruddy Duck is a common breeder. This is one bird that will not shy from a stopping car. The drake, in bright russet plumage and sky-blue bill, does not take flight; instead he challenges with display, erecting his tail, puffing out his chest, bobbing head and bill, and uttering a frog-like rattle.

Northwest of Neepawa, beyond Minnedosa, the marshes are larger and there are many small lakes. In this country one finds the White-winged Scoter at home in the best of its prairie breeding range.

Pairs of ducks in bright plumage are seen through early June at Delta and in the pothole country. Even though some of the April-nesting Pintail and Mallard drakes have long since abandoned their mates, now with brood, and have molted into the eclipse, there are others of the same species remaining in bright breeding plumage. But the middle of June is the deadline. After that, all males of every species excepting the Ruddy Duck are molting into the drab eclipse plumage. Drake Mallard, Pintail, Gadwall, American Widgeon, Green-winged Teal, Redhead, and Canvasback leave their females soon after incubation starts, joining bachelor bands for this molt; they depart from the slough and pothole country, moving to the Delta Marsh and other large marshes. In Blue-winged Teal, Shoveler, Lesser Scaup, and Ruddy Duck, however, the male generally waits alone on his territory throughout incubation. Such drakes (again excepting the Ruddy Duck) are well advanced in the post-nuptial molt before they finally move on to the molting waters. The drake Ruddy Duck holds his bright colors until August.

The finest time to visit the big Delta Marsh itself is from mid-June onward. The great heart of the marsh is set in a matrix of *Phragmites,* a nearly impenetrable jungle of tall yellow cane. The outside edge of the cane is wet meadowland where Sora and Short-billed Marsh Wren are typical species and where, in the bordering willow thickets, there surely are more nesting pairs of Yellow Warblers per acre than anywhere else in the whole of North America. The *Phragmites* is almost barren of birdlife except where it surrounds a closed slough. In such a locality Yellow-headed Black-birds nest in colonies, the droning of the males background music for the visitor making his way to the open bays of the main marsh.

Outboard motors are barred from Manitoba's waterfowl breeding areas, hence travel across the bays and through the wilderness of bulrush is by canoe. One's first impression is of grebes and pelicans, gulls and terns. All five North American grebes nest at Delta, and the tinkle of the silvery Western Grebe is the voice of the marsh itself, night or day, fair weather or bad. In June the Franklin's Gulls have their nesting colonies in the islands of hardstem bulrush and with them nest the Forster's Terns. Black Terns are common, but have their own separate colonies, in the quiet edges of small bays or isolated sloughs. White Pelicans nest on islands of Lake Manitoba, making daily trips to the Delta Marsh to forage for food. When they are finished with their meal, they climb the thermals at the south edge of the marsh to play in wide wheeling circles until, specks in the sky, they turn and glide home to their stinking islands.

The rattle of the Long-billed Marsh Wren and the grunt of American Coot are the voices of the bulrush. The Coot, perhaps Delta's most widely distributed bird, is territorial in the classic pattern of territory. Pairs set up their little domains at the start of nesting in early May, defending against all intruders until the young are nearly fledged in August. The main summer function of the marsh, however, is not the breeding of Coots or gulls, terns, or blackbirds. Its most important service of the year is sanctuary for the dabbling ducks during the flightless season of the molt.

The first evidence that some ducks are nearing the flightless stage of the post-nuptial molt is seen when a drake is startled at marsh edge. He cannot rise abruptly, but takes off at a shallow angle, sometimes unable to clear the reeds. Rarely one has the good fortune of seeing a drake drop his pinions; he jumps into the air, but cannot take flight, flopping away, leaving shed feathers in his wake.

The first flightless drakes are found during the second week of June. Wary and secretive, they hold close to edge cover, sneaking to hide the moment a canoe is sighted. Through June and early July there are daily arrivals of more drakes coming from far and wide; and there is a steady increase in the number of flightless birds. In the large July aggregations, flightless drakes are bold, feeding by day in open water. But when approached by canoe there is a roar, the birds frantically churning their wings as they scramble to the cover of bulrush.

The period of flightlessness is three to four weeks. By early August large flocks of Mallard and Pintail, Blue-winged Teal and drakes of the other dabbling ducks are on the wing again. Drake Canvasback, Redhead, and Lesser Scaup rendezvous on the marsh prior to the flightless period; but before losing their wing feathers they shift to lakes where there is an abundance of aquatic food plants and sanctuary in open water far from shore. In all species, the molt of adult females (except in thwarted or non-breeding individuals) is delayed until after the mother bird has left her brood. Hens thus follow the drakes in the wing molt, some still flightless when the shooting season opens.

By late August, the waterfowl population on the Delta Marsh has grown to several hundred thousand ducks. The Mallard is the most stable element of this late-summer aggregation. Great flocks of Mallard—mostly adult males and birds-of-the-year—loaf in the marsh or on the lake shore, flighting morning and evening to feed on the grain fields. Surely one of the most stirring of all prairie experiences is to catch the dawn flight of Mallards or to lie on a grassy hummock on a warm September afternoon to watch their seemingly endless passage to the fields.

Pintails, in lesser numbers, join in this stubble flight, as well as a few adult drake Black Ducks which have strayed far from their breeding grounds. In late September and early October there comes a week or ten days when many little bands of Richardson's Geese flight regularly between marsh and stubble. But there are no large fall aggregations of Canada Geese, and the Blue and Snow Geese seldom stop in autumn passage.

The main migration of Blue-winged Teal is in late August and early September, with all the little Blue-wings gone by early October. A general build-up of Canvasback and Redhead takes place through September, mostly of young birds and adult females, for old drakes stay on their molting lakes until the journey south is made. And then regularly, year after year, there is a mid-October departure of Canvasback and Redhead, the birds moving southward even though there is food aplenty and two or three weeks more of open water.

From mid-October onward, Mallard and Lesser Scaup make up the main body of wildfowl at Delta. Mallards continue their twice-daily visits to the fields while the Bluebills trade back and forth between lake and marsh. It seems as though these hardy birds have established routines that might carry on endlessly. But then in early November comes a period of cloud, storm, and north wind followed by clearing sky. A mass departure of wildfowl takes place with the passing of the front; and the cold that comes with the first night of open sky freezes the marsh in a few hours, leaving only a few holes, temporary sanctuary for the crippled birds that must remain forever behind.

# AN IOWA MARSH

## Paul L. Errington

*Now and again we meet a scientist and teacher—a "thinking man"—who patiently, determinedly, and without fanfare leads his students and contemporaries through the maze of scientific findings to new horizons of discovery. Such a man was Paul Errington. Though he spent most of his life on the campus of one university and concentrated his research on the wildlife of relatively few acres, his views were boundless and his ideas always fresh and stimulating.*

*Paul Errington was born in 1902 on a farm along the Oakwood-Tetonkaha Lake and Marsh chain west of Bruce, South Dakota. He received his B.S. degree from South Dakota State College and Ph.D. from the University of Wisconsin. Prior to his graduate-school days he made his living by hunting and trapping. While in graduate school he was an Industrial Fellow, financed by the Sporting Arms and Ammunition Manufacturers' Institute. From Wisconsin he moved to Iowa State University where he was professor of zoology. Except for one year as Guggenheim Fellow and visiting professor at Lund University in Sweden, he served continuously at Iowa State until his untimely death in 1962.*

*Paul Errington's scientific interests were chiefly in "vertebrate ecology and population dynamics with special reference to predation and the 'cyclic' phenomena in animal populations." He published over 200 titles, mostly in technical journals, and was the*

*author of three books:* Of Men and Marshes (*1957*), Muskrats
and Marsh Management (*1961*), *and* Muskrat Populations
(*1963*). *Twice he received the Wildlife Award "for the most outstanding paper ... in the field of wildlife ecology and management" and in 1962, the Leopold Memorial Award.*

*Much of Paul Errington's research concerned marshes, an
environment that fascinated him from boyhood days. Here he
writes about a favorite marsh in Iowa, but what he offers is more
than an account of a few acres of water on a midwestern prairie.
It is the story of thousands of marshes over thousands of years—
places which, if left alone, will repeat again and again the cycle
from dry marsh to open-water lake.*

Goose Lake is a glacial marsh into which run-off
waters carry silt, windblown dust settles, and peat materials accumulate along with mollusk shells and other humble animal debris
according to patterns set long before modern birdlife belonged to
the ecology of any wetlands. Compared to the time required for
the advances and withdrawals of glacial ice that fashioned the
basin for this lake in central Iowa, the period of my familiarity
with the Goose Lake does not seem long.

Even so, since I first parked a Model-A Ford beside this marsh
thirty years ago, it has gone through several radically different
stages. Twice, during my observations, it has had lake-like open
water and a maximum surface area of about 140 acres. Several
times it has been dry or nearly dry with tracts of cracked bottom
or puddles or frost-buckled mud and ice remaining in the low spots.
At least once its dead stalks of cattail, bulrush, reed, smartweed,
cut grass, and sedge have been swept by fire. Essentially the entire
bottom has been overgrown with cattails and bulrushes. Or the
emergent vegetation has been restricted to the shallows or to the
deeper parts where the bottoms were exposed in late summer, at
exactly the right times for the germination of seeds.

I shall not say that I have always thought primarily of birds
during the thousands of hours that I have spent at Goose Lake. My
memories may be of old things—a pre-settlement beaver jaw picked
out of the side of a muskrat lodge or a bison skull cradled in the
mud of the bottom. The memories may be of rotting bullheads that

drifted to shore in windrows one spring following a winterkill; of snapping turtles crawling by the hundreds over muddy bottoms as they tried to adjust to a drought; of woodchuck dens and fox dens and mink dens and weasel tracks and a stream of ten deer mice leaving a muskrat lodge to bound away on the ice into the shore-zone vegetation. It may be of wooded islands that man had never tampered with enough to spoil their naturalness; or of volunteer cottonwood seedlings that grew into a grove near the marsh during the years I was present. I might remember the nest of a Red-tailed Hawk in the cottonwood grove, and the Great Horned Owls that frequented the nesting site of that Red-tail the next winter and spring but did not breed; or the Common Crows that pestered the Horned Owls, circling and diving and sitting around cawing; and a Virginia Rail that some students and I discovered on the ground in the middle of the cottonwood grove—a perfectly normal rail but one that didn't seem to know what it was doing there.

Birds do, in fact, have their ways of being represented in almost any scene on or about the marsh. In a sense, birds—that is, ducks—may be considered one of the principal reasons why this privately-owned marsh has continued to exist as a marsh at all, why it was not drained long ago to make another Iowa cornfield. All of the years I have known Goose Lake, it has been leased to a club for hunting rights; and, outside of the usually short, late-fall hunting season, when its ecology is right it can have a superlative abundance and variety of birdlife.

At Goose Lake the binocular season begins in March before the ice is out. The first Mallards and Pintails and Blue, Snow, and Canada Geese rest in patches of water in the rotten ice or in water-filled depressions on top of the ice, and they feed in the nearby cornfields. These birds are high flyers and are inclined to settle down on the far sides of the islands out of sight from the nearest roads. As the softening and opening up of the ice progresses, American Coots and more ducks come, more Mallards and Pintails, together with the Gadwalls, American Widgeons, and Green-winged Teal, among the dabblers; and the Ring-necked Ducks, Lesser Scaup Ducks, some Common Goldeneyes, maybe some Redheads, and possibly some Canvasbacks, among the divers. In my opinion the Canvasbacks are the most elegant ducks of all.

The first Mallards, Pintails, and geese may largely push on, but more and more of the other early species of migrating waterfowl may come in. The newcomers are dominated by Blue-winged Teal, Shovelers with bold markings on the drakes, more Widgeons, and, depending on the year, possibly by Wood Ducks as well. There may be some of the dainty, perky, dark and white Buffleheads, Ruddy Ducks with their preposterously painted males, Whistling Swans lifting their heads and tootling, Common or Red-breasted Mergansers and, if the water has food for them, a Common Loon or two or a flock of White Pelicans. The Pelicans may hang around for weeks if there are stunted populations of pan fishes for them to feed on. The mergansers, which are popularly regarded as fish eaters, do not necessarily avoid a marsh if fish are not present, but may feed upon water insects and other invertebrates.

When spring really comes, the Red-winged and Yellow-headed Blackbirds stake out their territorial claims. The Red-wings are more of the shores and fringing growths of vegetation—the weeds and brush and even trees of the adjacent land; the Yellow-heads like the deeper parts of the marsh where there is some water under their nests; but both species may fill up and quarrel over that which is not first-class habitat for either, with the Yellow-heads, by reason of their greater size and strength, generally being able to take what they really want. Dry stands of cattails and bulrushes and sedges have their marsh wrens. Soras skulk and run over floating vegetation and fly weakly if alarmed. American Bitterns poke through or stand in the wet meadow and the sedge and bulrush shallows to strike at frogs or whatever prey may come by, including meadow mice. The meadow mice, although hardly to be classed as water animals, often behave as such, whether moving down to marsh edge from higher land or actually living out in the marsh in the muskrat lodges.

Great Blue Herons may be seen standing or flying or alighting —giving the impression of being all wings and legs and necks. The fringing willows and box elders have their Green Herons which seem to have even more neck than the other herons. The small but very-much-their-own-birds-living-their-own-lives Least Bitterns frequent both the shore zones and the deeper stands of cattails and bulrushes. Belted Kingfishers rattle and fly along the edge from perch tree to perch tree. Black Terns and the graceful white Forster's Terns hover or swoop. There may be Herring or Franklin's or Bonaparte's or Ring-billed Gulls.

Shorebirds on the mudflats or on the sand include the "peeps" (Least and Semipalmated Sandpipers), Killdeers, and Lesser Yellowlegs. "Jacksnipes" (Common Snipes) are scattered along the marsh edge or on the shallow flats that may barely protrude above the water out in the marsh. There are the Dowitchers and Pectoral Sandpipers, and the phalaropes whirling in the water with their peculiarly webbed feet. And now and then, but not every year, Ruddy Turnstones, Willets, Avocets, godwits, Black-bellied or Golden Plovers. If one is lucky, he may glimpse a big King Rail before it slips out of sight, or a Common Gallinule flying up ahead of a canoe cruising through the heavy bulrushes near shore.

A Peregrine Falcon or a Pigeon Hawk may fly over, pointed wings outlined against the sky. Occasionally, yet rarely, an Osprey may hover and plunge or perhaps fly like a big gull with talons clamped on a fish. Rarer still is the sight of a Bald Eagle, almost always a juvenile, sitting on a dead stub.

Breeding-season birds are not always breeding birds. Some just loaf. I recall three Snow Geese that stayed on Goose Lake all summer, together with a White-fronted Goose and one of the smaller *Branta canadensis* (probably *hutchinsii*). In addition to the loafers there are ducks stricken with lead poisoning which leaves its victims at Goose Lake as on other Iowa waters. The ducks are unlikely to find much shot to swallow in the deep mud or peat of this lake's bottom. However, birds already carrying the potentially deadly shot in their gizzards are among those responding to the attractions of the marsh. The lead-poisoned ducks may comprise any of the gizzard-grinding species that come to Iowa, but the poisoned birds at Goose Lake run largely to divers—the Ring-necked Ducks, Lesser Scaups, Redheads, and Canvasbacks. They sit on the bases of muskrat lodges, flap along the surface of the water or dive if disturbed, and die when their turn comes. The feeding habits of the Redheads especially predispose them to lead poisoning; the gizzard of a Redhead may contain as much as a teaspoonful of shot, polished, and partly ground away in digestive processes.

By mid-summer, the medley of bird sounds is basically one of

Red-wing and Yellow-head calls cut through by the melodious whin-nying of the Soras. Super-imposed are the calls of the Coots, the harsh cries of the Black and Forster's Terns, the squawks of Black-crowned Night Herons, the pumping sounds of American Bitterns and Pied-billed Grebes—and a miscellany of whistles and chirps that I admit I have never been able to identify. And often there may be the quacks of a Mallard hen telling her ducklings what to do.

Fuzzy young Yellow-heads make short flights or climb among the stems of emergent vegetation by means of their astonishingly strong feet; Least Bitterns may flush out of the bulrushes wherever a person wades or pushes a canoe, flapping off to alight another 50 to 100 yards away; the maddened terns, watching over floating or swimming downy young, dive at the intruder's head; Pied-billed Grebes sneak off their wet nest mounds, tossing coontail or blad-

derwort streamers over the eggs as they leave; and the sound of Coots skittering over water comes from interspersed bulrushes and water up ahead.

Mallards nest on the muskrat lodges, as may Ring-necked Ducks—though Goose Lake is close to the edge-of-range for nesting Ring-necks. There may be a Ruddy nest built over the water with the tops of bulrushes woven into a canopy, or, also over water, a Redhead nest of rush stems. Both of these species are great parasitizers, laying their eggs in the nests of other birds, and the clutches in their own nests may be laid too late in the season for a successful rearing of the young. Very exceptionally, a Pintail hen may be seen with a brood of flightless young which she hatched nobody knows how far away, possibly out in a pasture or hayfield. Brilliant Wood Ducks may either nest in the vicinity or just come to pass the time. Broods of Blue-winged Teal are not at all uncommon. Young Pied-billed Grebes ride on the backs of parents or trail behind. Coot chicks stay near one or both parents or venture out by themselves, swimming and feeding in their jerky way, very independent enterprisers even when quite young.

Endless relations chain the eaters and the eaten. Maturing damsel-fly larvae crawl up on the rush stems, break out, dry their wings, and fly away, leaving the stems gray with the empty larval cases. The terns, among others, hunt the damsel-flies. Blackbirds, swallows, Yellow Warblers, Yellowthroats, and Baltimore Orioles all search the marsh for insect food. Young blackbirds, particularly during periods of abundance, often become the summer diet of minks and Marsh Hawks. Young Coots and Soras and Virginia Rails, the young Least Bitterns, and the young of the common landbirds of the marsh edge may also be staple prey while their vulnerability lasts. The larger herons and the bitterns too take what they can of vulnerable young birds. As the young marsh birds grow, they may help to feed the Great Horned Owls frequenting the cottonwood grove or the ancient trees of the island.

Fall brings a quickening of life processes and leisurely, lush times. Before any real southward movement begins, there may be a local massing of ducks on Goose Lake with birds coming in from all directions. They gather and loaf and pass on, the migration consisting of a dribbling through that continues for weeks before cold weather forces the spectacular flights. The Blue-winged Teal, particularly, may congregate by hundreds or thousands on parts of the marsh having a rich food supply of duckweeds and seeds of pondweeds, bulrushes, sedges, and smartweeds.

Shorebirds come, parades of them, the big and the little, standing, running, flying, alighting, calling, and feeding on the flats. The peeps run ahead as one walks the shore or come tamely up to feed within a few yards of a standing person. Jacksnipes may remain practically invisible on the mud and vegetable debris until an observer is almost up to them; then they are swiftly away with their scraping cry and erratic flight.

Blackbird flocks reach incredible sizes. I once calculated that a great roosting aggregate contained three-quarters of a million birds. A Marsh Hawk—usually in buffy juvenile plumage and acting hungry—sails low over the edge zone of the marsh or openings in the cattail stands, wheeling and dipping suddenly, and rather consistently not catching anything. Sometimes it succeeds, however, and Red-wing feathers, a mouse stomach, or a rush stem with dried blood on it may lie on top of a muskrat lodge where the Hawk stopped to feast.

By the opening of the hunting season in October the herons and rails are almost all gone. So are a lot of the ducks and blackbirds. Even so, Goose Lake might still have 10,000 ducks and hundreds of Coots resting and feeding. With the approach of the shooting hour as the duck boats are being rowed or poled in their midst, the nearest ducks lift their heads uneasily. In the confusion of the first few minutes after the shooting starts ducks crumple in flight; then the birds gain altitude and learn where the hunting blinds are. For awhile perhaps 5,000 Mallards (plus Pintails and other wary ducks) mill around at a height of a quarter of a mile. Finally they head for the Mississippi River on the eastern border of the state. By the next morning, the thousands of Blue-winged Teal are gone too and the Coots represent the principal waterfowl remaining, feeding and swimming placidly as long as they themselves are not the target of the gunfire.

The shooting does not terminate all opportunities to see ducks during the hunting season. Flocks of Widgeons or Ring-necked Ducks or Lesser Scaups may keep coming in from time to time, especially on a weekend when it may be assumed they have experienced hunting pressure farther north. They may come in high, glide or sideslip downward to alight in the open water, sit there ready to get up again if anything looks suspicious. Or the newcomers may be Mallards that work around and around, almost alighting on the water, rising up to circle some more, veering this way and that, over and over, and then, despite all the preliminaries, arising to fly on out of sight. Or, if they have a storm behind them, the Mallards may go through in string after string of immense flocks very high up.

After the close of the hunting season there may still be some open water, the larger patches of which may attract hundreds of Mallards. They sit around the edges or swim in the center, rising to visit the cornfields to feed or alighting on their return with bulging crops. The raised rim of mud around the lake becomes slick and discolored from splashed water and droppings, strewn with feathers and parts of corpses—an occasional head or a leg or a breastbone with wings attached. Out on the ice sit the always-opportunistic crows and maybe a visiting Snowy Owl.

As the oncoming winter shrinks the open water, the functional Mallards leave, but there may still be some cold-tolerant mergansers—usually the Red-breasted but sometimes the Hooded—and a few Goldeneyes and other birds that stay late because they want to. There may be Whistling Swans to leave white feathers and big droppings on the ice. In addition there will be the birds that cannot fly—any of the ducks and the Coots that have been gathering since fall.

After the last of the open water seals over, these luckless ones walk over the surface for a time; snow collects in tiny drifts from blowing past their bodies; crows peck, foxes sniff and eat heads and feet, and minks wrench and drag away. The bodies of blackbirds that did not leave in time to escape the first blizzards may lie in the reeds and cattails. At an open tile flow, the last Jacksnipe sits or probes hopelessly. Minks lay down their tracks in formations of twos, threes, or fours and drag dead ducks and Coots into holes. Smoky snow blows, and the sun forms new crusts, and, in the intervals between cold snaps, sometimes melt-waters swirl downward over enlarging ice cracks. Ice ridges buckle and minks drag feathery objects into the recesses and into the openings in muskrat lodges. Winter is harsh in Iowa.

In recent years, the ecological pendulum at Goose Lake has

swung all the way from a birdlife that thrived in a setting of cattails and bulrushes and muskrat lodges to a birdlife that existed in an open slough which had little to offer except a place to fly over or to sit on while feeding on the scant produce of the submerged or floating life. In lean years Goose Lake still had pondweeds, duckweeds, larvae of water insects, water fleas, crayfishes, frogs and garter snakes, some family groups of muskrats living in bank burrows, ducklings and grebe chicks on the water, hovering, swooping terns and swallows above the water, Green Herons and Kingfishers in the trees, Night Herons and Great Blues wading in the shallows. Although it was by no means birdless, the multitudes of birds dependent upon cattails and bulrushes were simply not there any more, and no one should have expected them to be.

The collapse of the emergent vegetation was all according to the rules of order governing marshes and life of marshes. Everything happened naturally; the marsh went through its natural stages and so did the marsh life with it; and, as long as man does not interfere overmuch, the story may be expected eventually to repeat itself—a lush period again following the not-so-lush. Goose Lake may still be an undrained marsh rather than just one more Iowa cornfield.

# MALHEUR AND KLAMATH LAKES

## Ira N. Gabrielson

*Ira Gabrielson cannot remember a time when he was not interested in birds. Although he began his ornithological career as an egg collector as did many a budding ornithologist before the turn of the century, he showed his conservation colors early by never taking more than one egg from a clutch and never becoming a collector of sets. I suspect that the wealth of birdlife around the little marshy potholes and shallow lakes, so common in northwestern Iowa where he grew up, fascinated him far more than mere eggs.*

*Gabe is a big man—big in stature and thought. No doubt even as a youth he did big things in preparation for later life when he was to manage big areas, plan big projects, and fight big battles. Fortunately it was all in the cause of wildlife conservation.*

*Born in 1889 in Sioux Rapids, Iowa, Ira Noel Gabrielson graduated from Morningside College, and taught biology in high school before joining the staff of the U.S. Bureau of Biological Survey. In 1918 he was assigned to Oregon and during the next seventeen years worked continuously in the field in Oregon and the other Pacific States. He became familiar with the refuges, recognized their importance, and began the fight for money and water with which to save them.*

*In 1935 he became chief of the Bureau of Biological Survey and in 1940 the first director of the U.S. Fish and Wildlife Service, a new agency which combined the Biological Survey with the Bureau of Fisheries. Six years later he resigned from federal service to assume his present position as president of the Wildlife Management Institute.*

*Oregon State College, Morningside College, and Middlebury College have all acknowledged his contribution to wildlife conservation by presenting him with honorary degrees. Awards from the Department of the Interior, the National Audubon Society, Friends of the Land, American Forestry Association, and The Wildlife Society show how highly he is regarded by his colleagues in the battle for preservation of our natural resources.*

*In addition to numerous articles, in both popular and scientific periodicals, he is the author of several books including* Birds of Oregon *(1940) with Stanley G. Jewett,* Wildlife Refuges *(1943),* The Birds of Alaska *(1959) with Frederick C. Lincoln, and* Birds: A Guide to the Most Familiar American Birds *(1949) with Herbert S. Zim.*

*Malheur and Klamath Lakes, two great refuges in southeastern Oregon where he has worked and studied and for the restoration of which he has persistently fought, mean very much to Gabe personally. In a letter to me he once wrote: "Malheur, when I first saw it, was full of water and was so vast and had so many birds that it almost stunned me. I never quite got over the feeling of vastness. . . . I saw the marsh dry up and die and I had a hand in its restoration." His article that follows presents a graphic picture of these great lakes and marshes and points out the miracles that can be brought about in wild areas properly managed.*

I first saw Malheur Lake in Oregon as a young federal biologist nearly a half-century ago, and the impression of that first visit is one of my most vivid memories. Since that time I have seen many spectacular concentrations of wildlife in various parts of the world, but nothing that I have seen since has dimmed the almost physical impact that the sight of Malheur Marsh made upon me as I stood breathless on a grassy ridge called Cole Island on a late summer morning. A sea of marsh vegetation, broken only by occasional patches of open water and a few low dunes, stretched almost endlessly from horizon to horizon. There had been more than usual precipitation that summer, and Malheur Lake was well filled with water; farther beyond, Mud Lake shimmered in the sunlight; and there even was water in Harney Lake which usually was reduced to a broad white salt flat by late summer.

In, over, and through this sea of bulrushes, arrowhead, and pondweed moved the most awe-inspiring concentration of birdlife that I had ever seen. Squadrons of White Pelicans, so densely crowded that they appeared from a distance as shifting banks of snow, fished in the open water. Fleets of Canada Geese cruised the lakes, ignoring the American Coots and the ducks of a dozen species that thronged about their flanks. Great Blue Herons and Common Egrets stalked in stately silence among the rushes. In the intervening space, the flats were covered with smaller herons, American Avocets, Willets, Black-necked Stilts, plovers, and sandpipers loafing, walking, running, or rising in flashing clouds to alight on a better hunting ground a few rods beyond. This moving, pulsing mass of life extended far beyond the range of my binoculars—and these were only the forerunners of the autumn migration!

Once the impact of the sight had subsided enough to permit detailed observation, the number of species that could be identified from a single spot was amazing. In later years, I have seen greater concentrations of birdlife in the nesting rookeries of colonial birds throughout North America, but nowhere in any one spot have I identified anything like the variety of birds that was present upon that first trip to Malheur.

Soon after my first visit, Malheur began to decline, although it remained a waterfowl paradise until the early 1920's. Malheur Lake had been set aside by Theodore Roosevelt as a national wildlife refuge in 1908, making it one of the oldest refuges in North America; but the early reservation had failed to include the water rights above the lake. Malheur and Harney Lakes form the sump for a great watershed, including the south slope of the Blue Mountains and the west slope of the Steens. When irrigation developed in the Harney Valley, the water in Silvies River, which rises in the Blue Mountains, never reached the lake in drier years. When similar developments in the Blitzen Valley diverted the flow from the Steens Mountains, the fate of Malheur Lake seemed sealed. By 1926, Malheur had become almost a desert, and a few years later, in the late summer, one could drive an automobile anywhere over the exposed lake bottom. Little remained of what, a decade before, had been one of the greatest wildlife spectacles to be seen in America since the passing of the bison migrations. Only remnants could be found of the nesting concentrations, and the waterfowl and shorebirds that had once thronged its marshlands now passed over it without stopping on their journeys north and south.

Malheur appeared to be gone, but it was not forgotten. In Oregon, a small group of dedicated conservationists and naturalists fought long and hard to obtain funds to restore it. Negotiations with the landowners who controlled the water rights along the Blitzen and the Silvies made little progress. Land prices were prohibitive, and the legal problems involved were insurmountable for any small local group.

Hope for restoration of Malheur Lake came from an unwelcome source. The great depression of the early 1930's spelled disaster for many Americans, but it was responsible for making possible the restoration of Malheur Lake. Land prices suddenly declined sharply. At the same time, Jay N. ("Ding") Darling was appointed chief of the Bureau of Biological Survey and arrived in Washington bursting with enthusiasm for saving waterfowl by extending the national wildlife refuge system. Moreover, he had wrangled from a not-too-sympathetic Administration and Congress the largest appropriation for wildlife ever made up to that time for waterfowl in America. Those of us in the Service who knew Malheur were unanimous in recommending that the water rights, controlled by the "P" Ranch in the Blitzen Valley, be given top priority in Ding's far-reaching land acquisition program. I still was in Oregon in the fall of 1934 when a telegram reached me from Darling stating in effect: "The 'P' Ranch is ours. Turn the water back into the lake." It was one of the most welcome messages I have ever received.

Restoration began as soon as the water began to flow. The eastern third of the lake was bisected by an eleven-mile dike to retain the returning water, but provisions were made to reflood the entire lake bed as more water became available. Ponds, sloughs, and channels were created in the Blitzen Valley—a long, narrow gorge hemmed in by basalt cliffs—and this area, with the Double

O Ranch on Silver Creek, acquired in a later purchase, became one of the most important waterfowl production units of the region.

I saw Malheur Lake die and saw it reborn, and it remains one of my favorite spots in an increasingly complex world. I visit it as often as opportunity permits. Many times, I have stood for hours at the site of the present headquarters, watching the birds moving about, all the while drinking in the beauty of the endless vista of marsh.

The heart of the Malheur National Wildlife Refuge was, and still is, Malheur Lake. In the fall it first becomes the feeding and concentration area for most of the waterbirds produced in the entire Harney Basin, and later it becomes a great aquatic marshaling yard for south-bound migrants.

Harney Lake, the sink for the basin, is dry much of the time, and frequently appears as a broad salt flat rimmed with sparsely vegetated dunes. It is one place in eastern Oregon where the Snowy Plover may be found with some certainty, although even there it is not a common bird. On Malheur Lake the concentrations of herons, pelicans, cormorants, grebes, ducks, geese, and shorebirds reach incredible proportions.

The Blitzen Valley and the Double O Ranch are not only the most important waterfowl nesting grounds but they also offer the greatest possibility for seeing a variety of birds within a limited area. Along the spectacular rim-rock cliffs, Great Horned Owls, Prairie Falcons, and (Western) Red-tailed Hawks nest regularly. On occasions, I have seen pairs of Canada Geese incongruously nesting far above the valley floor on the cliffs. One pair nested precariously for several years between a pair of Horned Owls and a pair of Red-tailed Hawks. The gander, standing guard above the nest, was the most conspicuous bird in the landscape.

The fact that greasewood, rabbitbrush, and sagebrush grow from the base of the rim rock to the edge of the marsh provides a fascinating variety of habitat. By turning 180 degrees, one can watch nesting cranes, geese, ducks, avocets, stilts, and other waterfowl and shorebirds on one side and Sage Thrashers, Brewer's Sparrows, and Swainson's Hawks on the other. There are relatively few places where one can see, from the same spot, Long-billed Marsh Wrens, Rock Wrens, and, less frequently, Cañon Wrens without moving a step.

With the approach of fall, northern migrants begin swelling the numbers of birds present, and within weeks the panorama of life reaches a peak. Malheur is a regular gathering spot for Snow and White-fronted Geese, and long files of Whistling Swans pitch into the open water to feed and rest before moving south. Shorebirds, ducks, and other waterfowl from the northern nesting grounds become prominent players in a spectacular autumnal show whose cast of characters and performance vary from one day to the next.

Malheur also offers a wide variety of mammalian life, especially in the Blitzen Valley. Mule deer are common and unafraid of the observer; pronghorn antelope are conspicuous residents of the more open and drier areas; coyotes are often seen; and the beavers' engineering activities are much in evidence. These industrious rodents may often be seen in the early morning and late afternoon. Black-tailed jackrabbits and cottontails are abundant in some years and are present in numbers at all times.

Many small desert rodents, including chipmunks, ground squirrels, kangaroo rats, and a number of species of mice also are to be seen. If one turns the lights of his automobile across an area laced with tracks, he is likely to see many of these nocturnal creatures. The kangaroo rat is the most interesting of all. Its comical antics often have furnished me with a more than acceptable desert substitute for a feature television show.

Malheur today holds within its boundaries every species of bird that was nesting there on my first visit. Some species may be even more abundant now than they were at that time, and a well-organized management program is increasing its value to wildlife each year.

In contrast to Malheur, Lower Klamath Lake, when I first viewed it, was a pitiful remnant of its former magnificence, and its companion, Tule Lake, was rapidly approaching that condition. The Bureau of Reclamation, by diverting the waters of the Klamath Marsh, had virtually destroyed its productivity as a wildlife area. Tule Lake, the old sump of Lost River, was being treated similarly, but enough return-flow irrigation water reached it to maintain a sizable area of permanent marsh. Later, as more land was brought under irrigation, the return flow of life-giving water increased, and Tule Lake was restored to its present size. It became a national wildlife refuge in 1928.

Eventually, so much water was flowing back into Tule Lake

that the 6,000 acres diked off by the U.S. Fish and Wildlife Service were unable to contain it. When the dike broke and several thousand acres of cropland were flooded, the surplus waters were diverted through a tunnel, built by the Bureau of Reclamation, into Lower Klamath Lake, and the Fish and Wildlife Service constructed a dike along the Oregon-California boundary to impound the water on the bottom of Lower Klamath Lake. Through this interservice cooperation, both Tule and Lower Klamath Marshes were partially restored to their original magnificence.

There are five national wildlife refuges in the Klamath Basin. All of them are worth visiting; but the Tule (37,000 acres) and Klamath (22,800 acres) areas, while small when compared to their original size, still furnish food and living space to the most spectacular duck and goose concentrations to be found on this continent. From late September until freezing weather, these two refuges play host to "millions" of birds.

One of my favorite pastimes while in Oregon was to climb well up the talus slope of the rim behind what is now the Tule Lake headquarters and watch the multitude of birds coming and going. There were similar vantage points on the present Klamath refuges, and either offers a vivid autumnal picture that is beyond my ability to describe. Once, when instructed to estimate the number of birds present on Tule Lake, I watched for hours trying vainly to find some formula with which to make even a rough estimate of the number of ducks within the range of my binoculars. My report that there was a "hell of a lot of ducks" failed to satisfy those sponsoring the estimate, and I was instructed to go back and try again. I did, only to find even more birds, if that were possible. My second effort didn't give me a more accurate estimate, but I did submit a figure that was pulled completely out of the air. Since I heard no more about it, the powers were either satisfied or gave it up as a bad job.

The Klamath Basin refuges furnish food for the migrant hordes but, equally important, they hold birds out of the ricefields in the Sacramento and San Joaquin Valleys of California until the harvest is well along. If for any reason, these areas ever cease to be available to the birds, the crop depredation problem in the valleys to the south will become disastrous.

This is not their only value, however, for all refuges in the basin contain spectacular colonies of breeding birds. On these areas in May and June are to be found colonies of White Pelicans, herons, egrets, cormorants, gulls, terns, and grebes. Avocets, stilts, Wilson's Phalaropes and a great variety of other birds are also common nesters.

Upper Klamath and the Klamath Forest Refuge are both bordered, to some extent, by coniferous forests, which attract additional arboreal species of birds to the basin refuge. Among the more interesting are the White-headed Woodpecker, Black-backed Three-toed Woodpecker, and Williamson's Sapsucker, all of which I have seen on the Upper Klamath.

All of these refuges provide nesting habitat for Canada Geese and many ducks, the most common of which are the Mallard, Gadwall, Redhead, Cinnamon Teal, and Ruddy Duck.

The refuges in the Klamath Basin and the Malheur gave me my first opportunity to see really big marshes. Looking back over the seventeen years in which these areas were within the district assigned to me by the U.S. Bureau of Biological Survey, there were so many new experiences that a mere catalogue of them would fill many pages.

My first Golden Eagle nest was on a rim close to Malheur. Incidentally, it was the only one I ever found that could be reached without strenuous effort, and it afforded a real opportunity to become acquainted with this splendid species.

As a boy, I saw each spring the movements of Sandhill Cranes through western Iowa. Their "quiver dance" in the fields and sonorous calls, as they circled slowly high overhead, were spectacular, but it remained for Malheur to give me the first sight of a crane nest and the first chance to watch the spindle-legged youngsters after they hatched.

Similarly, I found my first Western and Eared Grebe nests at Malheur, and there I first sighted a Common Egret's nest. The Klamath area likewise showed me my first Canada Goose, Redhead, and Cinnamon Teal nests. Willets, American Avocets, Black-necked Stilts, Long-billed Curlews, and Common Snipe were among the shorebirds whose nests and courtship performances I first witnessed in one of these basins.

It would be a serious omission if I failed to mention the great colonies of pelicans, California and Ring-billed Gulls, Caspian and Forster's Terns whose nests are still found here.

The opportunities for serious bird students to add to present ornithological knowledge are almost unlimited on these refuges, and while it is true that the Fish and Wildlife Service is carrying on considerable biological work, the men assigned to these studies would be the first to admit that they have not been able to avail themselves of existing opportunities. The chance to study behavior, life histories, population dynamics, and interrelationships between species, to mention only a few possibilities, are endless.

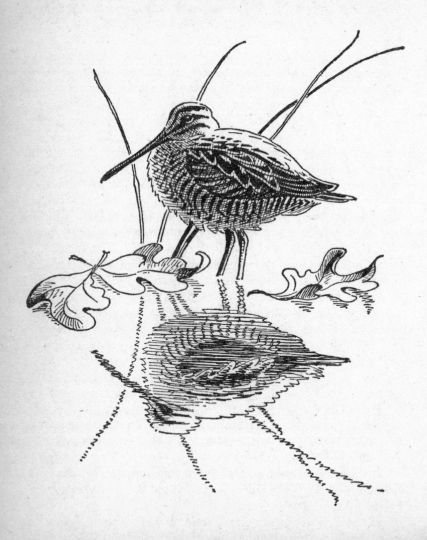

It always has been one of my regrets that these areas became refuges staffed with biologists only after I was no longer a field biologist and had become deeply entangled in administrative details.

If I were a young biologist again, nothing would suit me better than to be able to live and work with the abundant wildlife on those refuges. It would make little difference whether the assignment was to study the big and showy water birds, or some of the shy and obscure small desert birds about which so little is known; it is one opportunity that I still wish had been my lot.

Lists of the birds found on the Malheur and Klamath Basin Refuges, as well as other informative pamphlets, are available either from the U.S. Fish and Wildlife Service office in Washington, or its regional office in Portland, Oregon, in addition to refuge headquarters. For local information on roads and water conditions, address the Refuge Manager, Malheur National Wildlife Refuge, Burns, Oregon; or Refuge Manager, Route 1, Box 74, Tule Lake, California.

The personnel on the refuges always are willing to supply information to anyone interested in birds. Malheur is so vast and the available water area varies so widely, both seasonally and annually, that it is well to ask for information before starting out to look for any species or colony. For example, in my experience in some years, it was difficult to find nesting pairs of Sandhill Cranes and in others, it was difficult to miss them.

At Malheur, it is possible to see a great bird show at refuge headquarters. On my last visit, hundreds of California Quail were on the edge of the lawn or darting in and out of the sagebrush bordering it, while just beyond, Trumpeter Swans, including young-of-the-year, a variety of herons and ducks, Pied-billed and Western Grebes, and a number of White Pelicans and cormorants could be viewed in the display pool. Neither Klamath nor Tule Lakes provide such a good show that is so easily accessible.

Malheur is most easily reached from Burns (thirty-two miles to the north) where there are good hotels and motels, and there are accommodations for a limited number of persons at French Glen near the south boundary. There are numerous hotels in Klamath Falls and many motels close to that city or along the major highways.

# THE BEAR RIVER
# MIGRATORY BIRD REFUGE
## William H. Behle

*Ornithologists, like the organisms they study, stake out their territories. Utah has been Behle territory for a long time.*

*A native of Utah, William Harroun Behle was born in Salt Lake City in 1909 and was introduced as a boy to the birds in the Bear River Marshes where he went on hunting and fishing expeditions with his father, a physician and surgeon. After receiving his A.B. and M.A. degrees from the University of Utah, young Bill Behle went farther west—to the University of California at Berkeley—to work for his doctorate under the direction of the late Joseph Grinnell.*

*Four years later, in 1937, armed with his Ph.D. degree and inspired by the methods and philosophy of his great teacher, he returned to his alma mater as an instructor in zoology and director of a newly established course in general biology. He is now, twenty-five years later, professor of zoology and still director of the course.*

*Although William Behle will tell you that relatively little of his time is devoted to the study of birds, he nonetheless regularly teaches a course in ornithology and over a period of years has carried on a series of distinguished avifaunal studies throughout Utah. To his credit are about sixty-five publications on the birds of the state including a book,* The Bird Life of Great Salt Lake

*(1958). No ornithologist has more admirably justified his territorial claim.*

*In the following pages William Behle writes enticingly of his state's famed spot for bird watchers, the oldest federal refuge in America.*

         In driving north along US Route 91 through the business district of Brigham City in central northern Utah, one's attention is attracted to a large sign arched across the street, reading "Gateway to the World's Greatest Game Bird Refuge." The area referred to is, of course, the Bear River Migratory Bird Refuge. Not only is it of tremendous size—about 65,000 acres—but it bears the distinction of being the first waterfowl refuge in this country to be established by federal statute, having been created by a special Act of Congress on April 23, 1928.

    The Bear River Refuge is located at the delta of the Bear River in a broad, mountain-ringed valley on the edge of Bear River Bay of Great Salt Lake at an elevation of 4,200 feet. It is truly one of North America's most outstanding places for waterfowl, serving as

a resting and feeding area for the hordes of waterfowl that nest in Alaska and Canada and pass through Utah in migration to and from their wintering grounds, and also as an important nesting area for marshbirds, shorebirds, and waterfowl.

While the refuge is man-made and relatively young in terms of years, the Bear River Marshes have been in existence for eons of time. The first white man known to have penetrated to the mouth of the Bear River was the fur trapper and trader, Jim Bridger, who floated down the river in a bullboat in 1824. The first recorded description was that of the pathfinder, John C. Fremont, who visited the site on his second government-sponsored expedition in 1843. He recorded in his journal under date of September 3: "The whole morass was animated with multitudes of water fowl, which appeared to be very wild—rising for the space of a mile round about at the sound of a gun, with a noise like distant thunder. Several of the people waded out into the marshes, and we had to-night a delicious supper of ducks, geese, and plover."

It was the deterioration of the marsh that led to the establishment of the precedent-making sanctuary. The decline of this primeval, incredibly populous marsh was due to multiple factors such as the diversion of water from the Bear River for irrigation, a periodic backing up of brine from Great Salt Lake during high-water periods, excessive market hunting, the insidious malady known as western duck sickness that was once thought to be due to alkaline poisoning but is now known to be a type of botulism—a poisoning from a bacterial toxin.

Dikes were constructed on the refuge so as to impound the fresh water from the Bear River, to stabilize the water level for the control of botulism and, at the same time, keep out the brine. The dikes are laid out in such a manner that the refuge is arranged as five artificial lakes or units. A diversionary dam at the mouth of the river at Unit 2 and a system of canals and spillways allow manipulation of the water level. The dikes are 100 feet wide with sloping, beach-action sides and roadways on top. There are about forty miles of dikes and 30,000 acres under water. From an initial program of revegetation there are today miles of lush, stabilized marsh on the landward side with much open water beyond, and the modern visitor can see birds reminiscent of those described by Fremont more than a century ago.

Refuge headquarters is at the dam, where several attractive buildings for administration, maintenance, and research are arranged along the Bear River. An observation tower 100 feet high affords a panoramic view of the vast area. As a backdrop of the view from here, there are the towering Wasatch Mountains to the east and the lesser Promontory Range to the west, beyond which lies the inland sea, the Great Salt Lake. To the north is Little Mountain, while to the south extends the flat, glistening-white former lake bed.

There are attractions for bird watchers during virtually all phases of the annual cycle of birdlife at the marsh. The designation Bear River Migratory Bird Refuge highlights the migratory aspect of the sanctuary. Even before the area was set aside as a refuge, it was discovered that a great concentration of water, marsh, and shore-frequenting birds occurred at the Bear River Marshes in late summer and early fall at the termination of the breeding season and before the southward migration. Consequently the Bear River Refuge constitutes an important resting and feeding area at this time as well as during the migration period following. During the fall migration the visitor can literally see a million birds at one time. Indeed a closer figure at times would be two million. To give some idea of abundance: as many as 500,000 Pintails have been estimated to occur at one time on the refuge; Green-winged Teal are almost as abundant; and concentrations of 100,000 Canvasbacks have been observed.

During the bleak winter months Bald Eagles are present as winter visitants, as many as thirty having been seen by members of the Utah Audubon Society on their field trips to the area. Another astonishing phenomenon is the congregation of Whistling Swans which stop off for a few weeks in late February and early March while en route to their northern breeding grounds. As many as 15,-000 to 25,000 of these handsome birds have been estimated from year to year. They may arrive some years even before the breakup of the ice and they stand out on the expanse of dull gray ice as conspicuous white dots.

The northward spring migration of many birds starts early in February. Many of the resident species begin nesting by mid-April. Of the 200 kinds of birds known to occur on the refuge, about sixty have breeding status. The nesting season extends through

June to early July with young birds becoming increasingly numerous, often gathering in flocks to feed and socialize. Late July and early August is a slack time, as the birds start to molt and so hide away in the vegetation. By mid-August migrating shorebirds begin to arrive from the north and the waterfowl start to congregate on the marsh from the surrounding regions.

Probably the greatest interest centers on the breeding species. An abundant and conspicuous shorebird is the Avocet with its long legs, upturned bill, cinnamon head, and black and white body. The figure of 7,000 breeding pairs on the refuge is a conservative estimate. A close relative of the Avocet, the Black-necked Stilt, though less abundant, is seen frequently. Occurring in the deep water adjacent to the dikes are Western Grebes and Ruddy Ducks

which dive with alacrity as cars pass. Overhead wheel California Gulls and Forster's Terns, the former nesting in large colonies on dikes of other units not disturbed by cars. The clowns of the marsh, the American Coots or Mudhens, are everywhere. White Pelicans, conspicuous because of their great size and coloration, feed and loaf on the refuge. Their breeding grounds are on Gunnison Island to the west in Great Salt Lake. The factor of protection in choosing this nesting area outweighs that of accessibility of food. Pelicans feed mostly on carp which abound in the waters of the refuge. Thus, they must make a round trip of about 100 miles between their nesting and feeding areas. Furthermore, they must surmount the Promontory Range; thus flocks may be seen circling higher and higher to gain the necessary height. Considerable time seems to be spent by White Pelicans just resting on the refuge. At the spillways of the dam there are almost always Double-crested Cormorants, Great Blue Herons, and Snowy Egrets, all of which nest.

The Bear River Refuge is widely known as an arena of research, especially on botulism. Yet despite all the work on this problem, which appears to be largely ecological, it has not yet been entirely solved. One of the buildings at headquarters is a laboratory for research. Also, there are a pond and some retaining pens where sick ducks are treated. This is known as the duck hospital. Before release the cured ducks are banded. Over a twenty-year period, from 1929 to 1948, 35,171 birds, mainly those picked up for treatment for botulism, were banded. There have been 2,967, or 8.44 per cent, returns. The routes used by these birds in migration were mostly within the Pacific and Central Flyways.

Bird observation need not be confined to the actual sanctuary area. Indeed, some of the most interesting forms will be encountered outside the refuge boundaries. Particularly noteworthy is the Long-billed Curlew which frequents the flat, dry, grassy areas lining the approach road from Brigham City. If a nest is near, the adults will fly overhead, clacking their bills and uttering their distinctive call. This large sickle-billed bird, with characteristics fitted more for a marsh than dry land, seems out of place in such a habitat.

Since the refuge is administered by the Fish and Wildlife Service, Department of the Interior, it is managed as a multiple-use area with fishing, muskrat trapping, hunting, photography, and bird watching all allowed, but with regulations governing each activity. In the autumn, hunting is permitted on 40 per cent of the marsh, and during the hunting season cars are not allowed beyond headquarters. During the spring and summer, visitors may drive the twelve miles around Unit 2, starting at headquarters. The opportunities for bird observation are truly amazing. Just sitting in a car and driving slowly along the dikes one may see in the spring and early summer about fifty kinds of birds. Most are large, showy types which are so abundant that they are seen again and again. Indeed, just remaining at headquarters and viewing the parade of birdlife along the Bear River at the diversion dam is a satisfying experience.

The Bear River Refuge is easily accessible to the interested public, being just fifteen miles off two major US Routes, 90 and 30S, and may be reached by car over a paved road that winds along the Bear River past farms, expanses of salt grass, alkaline flats, ponds, and private duck clubs. Since public visitation of the marsh is encouraged and hunting is allowed in season, the refuge has great popularity. It is open from 9:00 A.M. to 5:00 P.M., daily. Hotel and auto-court accommodations are available at Brigham City.

The whole setting of the Bear River Migratory Bird Refuge, like the nesting area of the Long-billed Curlew, is somewhat incongruous—an animated marsh in the inhospitable region of the great American desert on the edge of Utah's dead sea. As the adage goes—one has to see it to believe it.

# THE GREAT DISMAL SWAMP

## Joseph James Murray

*Joseph James Murray was born in Summerville, South Carolina, in 1890. After graduating from Davidson College and the Union Theological Seminary in Richmond, Virginia, he studied at the United Free Church College in Glasgow, Scotland, and at Oxford. He received a D.D. degree from Washington and Lee University in 1927 and was minister of the Lexington Presbyterian Church in Lexington, Virginia, from 1924 until his retirement in 1957.*

*Dr. Murray's interest in natural history began early when his father, also a Presbyterian minister and a student of natural history, taught him to read from a nature-study book. By the time he was ten, young Jim Murray had his own museum. Although he studied all forms of natural history, insects occupied first place until, shortly after his marriage, his wife gave him a pair of Zeiss binoculars. Since then, he writes, "it has been exceedingly difficult to divide time between church and birds. At times, I fear, it has been the church that has suffered."*

*Dr. Murray is the author of a number of books. Among those related to birds are:* Wild Wings *(1947),* A Check-List of the Birds of Virginia *(1952), and* The Birds of Rockbridge County, Virginia *(1957). Since 1930, when he and two others formed the Virginia Society of Ornithology, he has edited its publication,* The Raven, *which recently graduated from mimeographed form to print.*

*Dr. Murray is in a position to know about—and does know about—almost every last bird that has dared to cross the borders into Virginia. Although he has concentrated in recent years on the altitudinal distribution of birds in the southern Appalachians, he is ever enchanted with the Great Dismal Swamp. Here he tells of its accessibility, its beauty, and its choice species, and, understandably, makes a fervent plea for its preservation.*

There has always been a hint of mystery in the very name of the Great Dismal Swamp, a region that is distressingly fearful to some and fascinatingly beautiful to others. To me, who first explored its aisles of dense shade and dark water over thirty years ago, it is an entrancing place with an appeal beyond description. Each little canal is a waterway to beauty. In April, when its lake is ringed with the gentle, springtime colors of the maples and its shallow margins are guarded by outposts of gaunt, moss-draped cypresses, the Great Dismal is an invitation to romance. In May, when the hollies whiten the ground with their tiny blossoms and the air is heavy with the fragrance of sweet bay trees, and when the northern thrushes pause in migration to add their alien but lovely voices to the chorus of nesting Prothonotary and Hooded Warblers, I feel that "the time of the singing of birds" is come. At sun-up in the spring the Great Dismal is vibrant with sounds; at twilight it is truly dismal and any of its strange legends take on credence.

The Great Dismal stretches across the Virginia–North Carolina line with its eastern edge only twenty-five miles from the salt water. Today, greatly reduced from its original size because of the inroads of civilization, it is roughly about thirty-five by fifteen miles in extent. Although more than half of this area is in North Carolina, the more interesting and accessible parts, including its largest body of water, Lake Drummond, and the small canals which are called "ditches," lie in Virginia. The Dismal is a finger of the palustrine forest of the coastal plain, extended north yet orientated to the south because of high temperatures, high humidity, and a long growing season.

The beautiful oval of Lake Drummond, nearly four miles long by three miles wide, lies near the center of the swamp. The white sand of its bottom, barely visible through the six feet of dark water, is stained the color of sherry by the juices of maples, gums, and white cedars (locally called junipers). Because the surface of this great saucer of sand and water on top of the mass of peat is the highest part of the swamp, the drainage from Lake Drummond is outward in all directions. The water, everywhere perfectly wholesome, tastes somewhat insipid from the sun-warmed lake but deliciously sweet from the shady canals.

The Dismal has had an interesting place in the history and folklore of Virginia. In the days of the sailing ships, the captains of the vessels which took on cargo at Norfolk made the hard journey inland to fill their casks with the dark waters of the swamp. They insisted that it kept sweet much longer than the water from any wells.

Not everyone appreciated the Dismal. William Byrd, who headed the Virginia party in the survey of the disputed line between Virginia and North Carolina in 1728, called it a "morass of noisome exhalations," and gave an account of the swamp as ludicrous as it was lurid: "Since the Surveyors had enter'd the Dismal they had laid Eyes on no living Creature: neither Bird nor Beast, Insect nor Reptile came in View. . . . Not even so much as a Zealand Frog cou'd endure so Aguish a Situation. . . . Not even a Turkey-Buzzard will venture to fly over it." Since travel in the swamp was difficult, one senses an excuse to give up the job.

George Washington, on the other hand, was fascinated by the Dismal and described it as a "glorious paradise." Washington Ditch commemorates the name of the great surveyor who visited the Dismal not less than six times and was responsible for a number of the canals. In 1763 he organized the company of "Adventurers of draining the Dismal Swamp," and hoped to turn it into productive farmland. His agricultural efforts bore little fruit, but, unfortunately, the canals long served for getting out logs. In his will Washington listed 4,000 acres of land in the swamp, valued at $20,000.

To the regret of some of us, access to the Great Dismal Swamp is no longer difficult. Main highways circle it. There are good motels at Suffolk on the western side and along US Route 17 on the eastern boundary. And if you must, you can drive your car from Suffolk into the heart of the Swamp toward Lake Drummond on most any of the logging roads.

It should be remembered, though, that the slowest method of

transportation in the Dismal is the quickest way into the life and beauty of the swamp. Walking is always perfectly safe, provided one sticks to the waterways and trails. However, the stranger who strikes off alone in the woods may easily become lost. April and May are the most delightful months. Unless one knows the region, he may well be warned against entering it in summer—after the first weeks in June when the thick brush on the banks of the ditches is infested with mosquitoes and ticks and the air is hot and humid.

Any police officer in Suffolk can direct you to the mouth of the Jericho Ditch or put you in touch with the local representative of the lumber company which maintains the logging roads. You can either walk on the logging roads or, better still, on the path along the north side of the ditch. At the Suffolk end of the Jericho Ditch, the dark swamp waters, coming out of the distant juniper brakes, pour over a simple dam of logs and boards. Soon you cross an open glade where the watery soil is covered with banks of cinnamon fern and beds of pale blue iris. Along the logging road the banks of sand, dug from below the peat, are filled with fossil shells, some of them as large as a man's hand. The proper time to enter the Jericho is just before sunrise when the wet woods ring with the songs of birds.

US Route 12, south from Portsmouth, follows the Dismal Swamp Canal on the eastern side. Eleven miles south of the village of Deep Creek, the Feeder Ditch from Lake Drummond enters the western bank of the canal. Here, at Crockett's Landing, you can either rent a boat and paddle up the Feeder Ditch or, better still, be rowed across the canal and walk along the north bank of the Feeder. Some use motor boats but not those who plan to look for birds. One sees too little even from a rowboat because of the high banks of the canal.

The two major ecological communities in the Dismal are the Light Swamp Community, locally known as the "Lights," and the Dark Swamp Community. Although there are marked differences in the birdlife in each of these communities, and in the several minor communities, certain species—the Yellow-billed Cuckoo, Great Crested Flycatcher, Carolina Wren, Red-eyed Vireo, Yellowthroat, Hooded Warbler, and Cardinal for example—occur throughout the swamp.

The Lights, mostly in the northern sector, are wide stretches of open-looking, but far from open, country where the original growth has been burned off and the swamp is now densely covered with ferns and shrubs, interlaced with fallen logs, and where there are bits of open water, occasional deciduous trees, and small patches of junipers.

A good view of the Lights may be had from the banks of the Feeder Ditch or the Portsmouth Ditch which will be discussed later. Characteristic of the Lights are the species common in all second-growth areas in eastern Virginia, with Prairie Warblers, Yellow-breasted Chats, and Yellowthroats of the race *typhicola* predominating. Red-eyed Vireos, Hooded Warblers, Rufous-sided Towhees, and Indigo Buntings are common.

Three miles up the Feeder Ditch from Crockett's Landing and within half a mile of Lake Drummond is the U.S. Engineer Corps Reservation, the one place in the swamp inhabited by humans. Two families live here with the wilderness so close at hand that they can watch Prothonotary Warblers feeding at the edge of their lawns and listen to the buzz song, *zee, zee, zee, zu, zee,* of Wayne's Black-throated Green Warbler in the great trees around the clearing.

In this part of the Dismal the lowering of the water level has made it possible to walk freely along fairly dry trails. From the Reservation you can follow the Feeder Ditch directly to Lake Drummond, or take a winding path for a couple of miles to the point where the Portsmouth Ditch leaves the lake.

Between the Reservation and Lake Drummond in the center of the Dismal we are in the Dark Swamp Community, which is the dominant association of the swamp. It consists of a heavy growth of large and beautiful deciduous trees—thick stands of cypress, tulip poplar, maples, white ash, and especially gums. In some places, although not near the lake, are remnants of the vast original growth of white cedar. The Dark Swamp association is the typical Dismal Swamp Community, not only because it covers so much more territory than any other, but because it is the original growth, much less disturbed by fire and by man.

In the Dark Swamp Community many species of birds are widespread. Red-eyed Vireos and Hooded Warblers are the most common. Acadian Flycatchers build over the waterways, their

nests at times within reach of a man standing in a boat. Chimney
Swifts still inhabit their ancestral hollows in the cypresses by the
lake. Pileated Woodpeckers beat their drums on the dead
branches. The nests of Parula Warblers swing in the drooping
Spanish moss. Prothonotaries, so brilliant in color and so quick in
movement, are everywhere. Even in daylight the wild laughter of
Barred Owls can be heard.

More interesting to the visiting bird watcher than any of the
large spectacular species are two small warblers, Swainson's and
Wayne's. While the Swainson's occurs regularly in small numbers,
it is so retiring and unobtrusive that it is more often heard than
seen. The occasional visitor can count himself lucky if he finds
one, for the Swainson's coloration—brownish olive back, snuff-
brown cap, and yellowish white underparts—blends perfectly with
its background and its nest which is a mass of leaves fastened to
canes or set in a web of vines on a small shrub.

Wayne's Warbler, the southern race of the Black-throated
Green, is much more common but for a long time it was missed
even by ornithologists. As late as the 4th (1931) edition of *The
A.O.U. Check-List* its range was considered to be limited to "the
coastal district of South Carolina," although by that time its occurrence in eastern North Carolina should have been recognized. In
1932 William B. McIlwaine, Jr. and I discovered that the bird
nested commonly in several areas in the Dismal and we collected
two males and a fledgling for the U.S. National Museum.

Possibly the reason that Wayne's Warbler was overlooked for
so long is that it nests early, at a time when individuals of the
northern race of Black-throated Green Warblers are just passing
through. It is very difficult to distinguish between these two races,
impossible in the field. The most dependable difference is that
Wayne's Warbler has a smaller, more slender bill.

Wayne's Warbler probably has eggs by mid-April, for by the
latter part of May there are young on the wing buzzing in and out
of the trees and sounding like large bees. In the proper season they
are very easy to find. One afternoon in mid-May we heard ten
singing males and saw two families with young out of the nest
along the trail from the Reservation to the Portsmouth Ditch. At
the present time Wayne's Warbler is known to breed not only in
the Dismal but also in the lowlands to the east, and although it

prefers conifers, it does nest in deciduous trees in places where the great pines have become scarce.

A streak of orange fire across the dark waters of a canal means a Prothonotary Warbler, one of the most beautiful birds of the Dismal. Its jet black eye and bill stand out against its brilliant plumage, all a rich orange-yellow except for the back and wings, which shade from greenish yellow to bluish gray, and the inner sides of its tail feathers which are white. One sees flashes of white as the bird spreads its tail when darting in and out of the vegetation along the canals. The Prothonotary Warbler seldom nests far from water and the cavity it chooses for its nest is rarely higher than twelve or fifteen feet and sometimes only inches above the water.

The Parula Warbler is not as common in the Dismal as it was in the days when Spanish moss festooned so many of the trees. Now very often it must use substitute materials—true mosses and plant fibers—which it gathers together to form a little hollow and lines with plant down. Like the Prothonotary, it prefers to build near water—on the edge of a canal or beside Lake Drummond— where its nest can swing in the soft breeze and the male can find a perch from which to utter his song which is merely a buzzy, ascending trill with an emphasis at the end.

The Dismal is so specialized in its habitats that, even when the Lights are included, fifty species is not a bad day's list. Nor, except in winter, would the number of individual birds be great. A list of eighty-five species would probably cover the breeding birds. To be sure, in a three-mile walk I have seen twenty Prothonotaries, by no means a poor reward. In this forest community the interest of the species makes up for the paucity of numbers. Strangely enough, there are few birds on the lake itself in summer, probably because the sandy bottom supports little food for them. As for the other seasons, there has been so little ornithological work done that any attempt to estimate the total species to be found in the Dismal would be only a guess—a guess I do not intend to hazard.

Although the warblers are for the most part silent in the summer and many of the other birds are quiet, Catbirds, Carolina Wrens, Acadian Flycatchers, Yellowthroats, and Rufous-sided Towhees are still in good song. And one hears more Bobwhites and more Carolina Chickadees than in May. However, the vegetation is so dense that what was a pleasant path in May may be choked with a rank, shoulder-high growth of shrubs and weeds in July or August. Bird watching in summer is not easy.

Due to the flocking of certain species in winter the population of individuals in the swamp is certainly higher than at any other season. The Lights entertain a huge blackbird roost. Flocks of ducks gather on Lake Drummond. Sparrows, including the White-throated, are common—even though this is not a suitable area for sparrows. The permanent residents include five species of wood-peckers—Downy, Hairy, Red-bellied, Pileated, and Yellow-shafted Flickers—with Downies and Red-bellies predominating.

The list of waterbirds and waterfowl that nest in the swamp is surprisingly small. Great Blue Herons, Little Blue Herons, Green Herons, and Black-crowned Night Herons are all found along the canals, but the Green Heron is the only one that breeds commonly. There are heron rookeries nearby. The only duck recorded as nesting is the Wood Duck which lays its eggs in old Pileated Woodpecker holes or other large cavities in old trees near water. Female Wood Ducks with flotillas of ducklings are seen frequently in the spring along the edges of Lake Drummond or on the canals. Woodcock most certainly nest in the Dismal. Spotted Sandpipers occur frequently but no nest has ever been recorded.

The only hawk that breeds fairly commonly in the swamp is the Red-shouldered and when its wild cry, *kill-yer, kill-yer, kill-yer,* rings out, one has the feeling of being in a real wilderness. Ospreys, though they do not nest, often circle overhead and groups of Turkey Vultures wheel against the sky. Occasionally a Bald Eagle is reported.

The Great Dismal Swamp is in transition. Unfortunately it is already less "dismal" in the sense that lovers of the swamp like to use the word—less isolated, less impenetrable, and consequently less alluring than it once was. Since the beginning of the century there have been increasing pressures to change the nature of the Dismal, to use it, and to tame it. Agriculture has taken a big slice of its eastern edge. Many square miles have been planted to stands of alien pine. There are persistent rumors that the Army Engineers may abandon control of the water level in Lake Drummond and thus drain a great portion of the area.

Although the future of the Great Dismal is uncertain, one thing

is certain—its present condition will not persist. Almost all of the swamp is privately owned, chiefly by lumber companies. Either a considerable part of the center of the swamp, including Lake Drummond, the Feeder Ditch which controls the lake level, and a wide zone around the lake, must be brought under permanent government protection or there will be increasing encroachments on its wild nature from all directions. This northern frontier of the great southeastern hygrophile forest, with its remarkable flora and its striking fauna, is too precious to be destroyed or denatured.

Every statement in this chapter is a plea for the preservation of the Great Dismal Swamp. Here, only a few miles from the dense population of Hampton Roads, is a country such as the Indians knew in pre-Columbian days. Here, in spite of forest fires, drainage squads, and logging crews, the wilderness still lives. Here are wild creatures that have not yet looked on the face of man.

# THE EVERGLADES

## William B. Robertson, Jr.

*"My main philosophic interest and desire is to understand more adequately the history of the biotic interplay between the mainland (of Florida) and the Antilles." These are the words of William Robertson, a true scientist and tireless researcher.*

*William Beckwith Robertson, Jr., born in 1924 and brought up in Berlin, Illinois, graduated from Carthage College and received his master's and doctoral degrees from the University of Illinois. He cannot remember a time when he did not watch birds. He identified his first birds, using a pair of field glasses "of Civil War vintage" and the Reed Guide. His next acquisitions—a pair of binoculars purchased with the proceeds of two winters of muskrat trapping, the Fuertes plates in T. Gilbert Pearson's Birds of America (1917), and a membership in the Springfield Nature League—helped widen his horizon. Peterson's first Guide and a subscription to Bird-Lore sealed his fate.*

*By 1944 Bill Robertson was already an able ornithologist. Here I speak from personal knowledge because it was the summer of that year that he came under my tutelage at the University of Michigan Biological Station. Quiet spoken and retiring by nature, Bill showed a marked talent for research and a stick-to-it-iveness that I have never ceased to admire.*

*He enrolled as a graduate student at Illinois just as someone was needed to work in south Florida and made his first extended*

258

*visit to the Everglades in 1950. That first summer, living with another graduate student in the crumbling remains of the old hotel in Royal Palm State Park, might have broken the spirit of Audubon himself. The weather was miserable; insects, birds, and rats moved freely through the moldy structure—"A Barred Owl and a large yellow rat snake shared the attic." Yet outside everything was new and exciting; every day brought a different challenge. Bill Robertson not only survived, he was wedded forever to the Everglades. He returned there to live at the first opportunity.*

*Since 1956 he has been park biologist at Everglades National Park. He is the author of a booklet, "Everglades—The Park Story," published in 1959, and numerous technical papers. He writes that "a major danger about this area for the biologist is that it offers him too much." At present he is investigating the nesting success of Bald Eagles, populations of white and blue herons of the genus* Ardea, *movement and demography of Sooty Terns at Dry Tortugas, and fire effects on vegetation.*

*Naturally Bill Robertson's subject here concerns south Florida, its birds, ecological aspects, and conservation problems, and the future of the Everglades, "the last functioning unit of the south Florida wilderness."*

The Everglades is a prisoner of its notoriety. Everyone within reach of TV, movies, and the funny papers has heard of it. A surprising number have formed very definite ideas about it based upon odd mixtures of overcolored fact, half-truth, and outright fable. Many find the real thing pale and unsatisfactory beside the synthetic Everglades they built themselves. Or, reality be hanged, they see it as they made it.

Because bird watching promotes at least a slight acquaintance with biogeography, visiting bird watchers are seldom guilty of the gaudier misconceptions of the Everglades. Almost always, however, they expect too much, too easily. Judging by the mail that comes to Everglades National Park, the Everglades means great concentrations of wading birds to veteran ornithologist and amateur the world around. Often imagination fills an out-of-focus landscape with birds in impossible profusion, exempt, somehow, from the strict biological accounting that prevails elsewhere. The bearing of many a bird student on arrival plainly says, "I am here. Astound me."

This essay will succeed, if it encourages a few to see the area whole. The Everglades is not a mere stage for witless avian extravaganzas, but a unique and highly complicated web of life. If all connections are in order, it expresses itself in a remarkable abundance of waterbirds and much else of interest besides. The visitor who looks only for the spectacular is a loser, even if he finds it. The Everglades loses, too, because it needs all the understanding friends that can be found.

For present purposes I take "Everglades" to mean all the wild lands of the southern part of peninsular Florida. This usage is correct in spirit if not quite so in strictest geographical terms. In its times of ecological prosperity few places offer the bird watcher so much. In even the best of seasons, however, success is seldom effortless. In the Everglades as anywhere else, birds have to be found and they are where you find them. The area is large, roughly 200 by 80 miles. Much of it is not easily accessible. It's also a different sort of place than most visitors have seen before, and it takes some knowing. Even those who keep to the roadsides and smoothed paths at times will meet with some of the cross-grained contrariness of the country. The Everglades bird watcher who begins by finding mostly mud, mosquitoes, and hard going should know (though it probably won't help much at the time) that his very frustration is of a classic cut.

Audubon dreamed of Florida for half his life, but when he finally got there in 1831, he at first saw little that pleased him. The insects were a constant plague, the landscape dreary, the swamp-bound St. Johns River was not the equal of his "fair Ohio." Not far from a part of Florida now known to bird watchers for its 200-species Christmas Counts, he confided a fine bit of peevishness to his journal.

Here I am in the Floridas . . . which from my childhood I have consecrated in my imagination as a garden of the United States. A garden where all that is not mud, mud, mud, is sand, sand, sand; where the fruit is so sour that it is not eatable, and where in place of singing birds and golden fishes, you have a species of ibis that you cannot get when you have shot it, and alligators, snakes, and scorpions.

Which is to say, it takes a little time to get used to wild Florida. Just as any other real wilderness, the Everglades must be met on its own terms. Nearness to the tropics does not soften this quality. From all who would know it, it claims the usual period of adjustment, during which false notions are shed and the bounds of the possible determined. Audubon thought much better of Florida when he left it six months later.

No amount of advice ahead of time can give the Everglades bird watcher complete ease and competence on his first visit. Even if it could be done, perhaps it wouldn't be fair to tell him everything. A short sketch of the area and its birds, however, may smooth the meeting without much trespass upon the right of each newcomer to find out for himself. The present south Florida scene has in it so much bizarre contrast that it must seem almost incredible when viewed from a little distance.

Perhaps the simplest useful concept is that geography has determined man's range in south Florida just as closely as it controls the distribution of other organisms. The entire area is low, flat, and wet. Nearly all of it is flooded some of the time and some of it is flooded nearly all the time. In surface profile the country resembles a soup plate, lower in the middle and a trifle higher at the edges. Modern man, a less amphibious mammal than the Seminole inhabitants, clustered his settlements on the higher ground along the coasts. The coastal strips south to Naples on the Gulf side and to Homestead on the Atlantic side have become almost continuous cities. The interior remains nearly uninhabited, a wilderness enclosed to east and west by densely settled urban belts. The Everglades and the Florida of tourist-resort ballyhoo exist side by side with only a narrow buffer of farms and ranches between. Few stranger ecological juxtapositions can be imagined.

Much of the native biota of the coastal strips has been civilized out of existence. The beaches and sandy barrier islands are, of course, prime real estate. Some birds that once nested there have disappeared from south Florida as breeding species. Others, such as the Snowy Plover, have an uncertain tenure on the few Gulf Coast beaches not yet accessible to development.

The bays that separate the outer islands from the mainland once had great waterbird rookeries. Remnant colonies persist, but the habitat that fed the multitudes is shrinking daily as dredging and filling obliterate the productive shallows and intricate mangrove-fringed shores. Often newly dredged fills are good places to find nesting Least Terns, Wilson's Plovers, and Black-necked Stilts, but any air of ecological well-being is false. Within a few years the fill is covered by houses and the birds must find a new site. Dead end, a sterile habitat of artificial islands and artificial shores, has already been reached in many places.

Pine once covered most of the coastal ridges. Any place that seldom was flooded but often burned was occupied by open piney woods. Today, clearing for agriculture and real estate has reduced the coastal pineries of south Florida to isolated shreds and tatters, and even these exist on borrowed time. Long Pine Key in Everglades National Park (lumbered just before the park was established) soon will be the only large block of pine that remains in the south Florida landscape. The birds most closely tied to pine forest—Red-cockaded and Hairy Woodpeckers, Brown-headed Nuthatches, Pine Warblers, and Eastern Bluebirds—have disappeared from much of the area.

Two coastal vegetation types that originally were limited in area have fared better than the others. "Hammocks," dense stands of tropical or semi-tropical hardwood forest, were found on upland sites that had some protection from fire. Some have survived simply because the small area to be gained wasn't worth the effort of clearing it. The hammocks left isolated in subdivisions or fields usually are in a ruinous state. Stripped of their orchids, rare ferns, and tree snails, they soon become handy neighborhood rubbish dumps. A few, however, are preserved as public parks. Most of the hammock birds are familiar species such as the Great Crested Flycatcher, Carolina Wren, and Cardinal. One of south Florida's Antillean landbirds, the Black-whiskered Vireo, occurs commonly from April to September in coastal hammocks and adjoining mangrove swamps. The "Florida scrub," a peculiar stunted vegetation of sand pine and small oaks, occupied local areas of deep sand, the dunes formed along shorelines of the geological past. Much of the scrub has become part of the Florida citrus desert, but patches that still support Scrub Jays, the special bird of this habitat, persist here and there along both coasts south about to Naples and Fort Lauderdale. Jonathan Dickinson State Park north of Palm Beach includes a representative area of scrub.

Because the civilizing of the coasts isn't quite complete, wilderness birds appear at times in incongruous urban settings. Great White Herons, Reddish Egrets, and Roseate Spoonbills still visit the few unaltered mudflats that remain in Biscayne Bay and can be seen with the Miami skyline for a backdrop. One Bald Eagle eyrie commands a distant, but adequate, view of the plush ocean-front warrens of Miami Beach. Such things are possible because south Florida is relatively new country. Few significant works of man date back as much as fifty years. Modern technology, however, makes for speedy pioneering. Some sections have developed from mangrove swamp to metropolitan senescence in little more than a generation.

The thoroughly despoiled coastal areas still offer the bird watcher many opportunities. Inevitably, some birds have prospered with change. Burrowing Owls are quick to colonize airports and golf courses. Cattle Egrets often troop behind the bulldozers of the land developers. Street and yard plantings in the older towns and the brushy tangles on abandoned farmlands provide most of the south Florida records of Western vagrants and the rarer wintering warblers and sparrows. Gray Kingbirds range the most sophisticated shores and have spread far inland in some towns relegating the Eastern Kingbird to the countryside. The Spotted-breasted Oriole is almost altogether a bird of the heavily-settled areas coastwise from Homestead to Palm Beach. Smooth-billed Anis also are seldom seen in native vegetation, mainly frequenting groves and brushy edges along the southeast coast and around the south end of Lake Okeechobee.

I have said so much about the settled coast country, because the most important thing to know about the Everglades may be the fact that it is caught in an urban embrace that tightens daily. Development in south Florida kept to the coasts until the high ground there was gone. The pressure now is inland as expanding subdivisions crowd farther out into wild lands. The ultimate confrontation of opposed needs for water and space is not far in the future.

Where not yet prettified by man, the Everglades has the same "wild and scraggy look" that Audubon found objectionable in Florida landscape. Vegetation provides the only scenery, and the pattern of vegetation is controlled by the recurring natural disturbance of flooding, fire, and hurricanes. Four main areas comprise the interior wilderness of south Florida—the prairies, the Big Cypress Swamp, the sawgrass Everglades, and the south coast mangrove belt.

The prairies lie mainly north and west of Lake Okeechobee. They are great expanses of half marsh, half grassland, with many shallow ponds, straggling stands of pine, cypress heads, and groves of cabbage palms. Parts of the prairie country are perhaps the closest approach to the conventionally scenic that Florida wilderness landscape offers. Nearly all of the area is given over to cattle ranches, and little of the native wildlife—for the bird watcher, particularly Sandhill Cranes, Caracaras, and Burrowing Owls— has been displaced. Late years, however, have brought ominous signs of change. The day of the lean, wild cow in the palmetto patch is closing. Modern ranching with better stock, better husbandry, and improved pastures is not likely to favor the survival of wilderness creatures.

Extending south from the prairies along the west edge of the sawgrass Everglades is the Big Cypress Swamp, a big area (some ninety by forty miles) of small cypress that formerly enclosed many smaller areas of gigantic cypress. Of the latter, only the National Audubon Society's Corkscrew Swamp Sanctuary remains.

There in favorable years one can also see a remnant winter rookery of Wood Ibis. The rest of the Big Cypress was cut over in the 1940's. Fire swept the country in the wake of lumbering, and it has burned so frequently since that great areas are degraded to fire-stunted tangles of willow and red maple. The story of America's plundered wilderness has few sadder pages.

We come finally to the Everglades proper, the sawgrass river that occupies the low center of Florida south of Lake Okeechobee and the mangrove swamps that form a sort of delta at the southwest coast where the Everglades river comes down to the Gulf. Everglades National Park takes up approximately the southern third of this area. Most of the upper reaches are presently held by the state of Florida as water and wildlife conservation areas.

The key to the Everglades is its annual cycle of flooding and desiccation. Most of the rain falls from May through October. The water spreads across miles of marsh, and food chains of freshwater organisms flourish in the warm shallows. The summer flood poured into brackish coastal bays feeds nutrients into other cycles. As the water recedes with the onset of the dry season, aquatic life is forced into an ever-diminishing volume of water. At various points of optimum food concentration, the summer's production of lesser creatures is translated into an increase of alligators, otters, egrets, ibis, Anhingas, Limpkins, all the rest. Near the end of the dry season, lightning storms often set fires that sweep over large areas of the marsh. Then come the summer rains and repetition.

That, in brief, is the way the system is thought to have worked before man tampered with it. In the past forty years, the Everglades has been hurt by drainage and by fire. It's a scarred and dog-eared sort of wilderness, but it has great powers of recovery. Fire and extreme variation of water levels have always been characteristic elements of its ecology and, in a sense, the man-caused disturbances have been no more than nature intensified. All its latterday trials have cost the Everglades no major species, although the Everglade Kite is not likely to survive much longer in Florida. The basic Everglades mechanism is intact. Given enough water, it still produces its annual miracle of fishes.

Within the next decade, we should know whether Everglades water can be managed to permit the peaceful coexistence of wilderness and metropolis in south Florida. Millions of dollars for water-control works and a great deal of study are focused on this problem. The problem, however, becomes more complex daily with the continuing rapid growth of human population and the inland expansion of settled areas. Even the most optimistic observer must sometimes wonder whether a mutually satisfactory solution is possible.

The history of man's association with the waterbird populations that are the main end product of wild Florida can be told in three chapters. Primeval abundance endured until the late 1870's. Then came a decade of organized plume-hunting. Revisiting the Gulf Coast in the spring of 1886, W. E. D. Scott found that the great coastal heronries were shattered, the survivors widely dispersed. The plume-hunters had already diverted their lethal attention to Brown Pelicans, shorebirds, and terns. Scott's classic paper in *The Auk* for 1887, "The present condition of some of the bird rookeries of the Gulf Coast of Florida," was a damning piece of straightforward reporting. It began the shift of sentiment toward bird protection, but nearly a quarter century was to pass before the tide had fully turned. Birds then were few, but the habitat was almost untouched. Another quarter century, this time of protection, saw the return of many species in unbelievable numbers. By the early 1930's rookeries stretched for miles along the creek banks where mangrove rivers on the southwest coast finger out into the sawgrass. In 1934 sober men estimated a round million nesting herons and ibis in the Shark River Rookery alone. Soon after, the cumulative effects of drainage and drought upon the Everglades began to be felt, and today the third act happy ending is endangered in an epilogue.

At its establishment, Everglades National Park was the climactic achievement of conservation efforts in south Florida. Now it is an excellent example of the fact that such battles do not always stay won. Changing times have brought new pressures to bear upon all wild lands and yesterday's victories have become irrelevant. Despite its size the park is not in control of its own ecological destiny. Located at the bottom of the Everglades drainage, its health depends to a large extent upon upstream flow. If forced to make do with local rainfall alone, it will have good years and bad, but the certain trend will be downhill to a predictable conclusion— loss of the last functioning unit of south Florida wilderness.

# Prairies, Deserts, Desert Mountains, and Canyons

A VIRGIN PRAIRIE IN MINNESOTA
> Walter J. Breckenridge

NORTH DAKOTA PRAIRIE
> Ann Magrete Gammell

THE NEBRASKA PINE RIDGE
> Doris B. Gates

THE BLACK MESA COUNTRY OF OKLAHOMA
> George Miksch Sutton

THE ARIZONA DESERT
> Gale Monson

THE CHIRICAHUAS AND GUADALUPE CANYON
> Dale A. Zimmerman

BIG BEND NATIONAL PARK
> R. Dudley Ross

# A VIRGIN PRAIRIE IN MINNESOTA

## Walter J. Breckenridge

*Plants, reptiles, amphibians, mammals, and birds—*
*anything alive comes within the province of Walter J. Brecken-*
*ridge, director of the Minnesota Museum of Natural History. He*
*is likely, in the morning, to make a photographic record of a pair*
*of Wood Ducks nesting along the Mississippi River outside his*
*kitchen window and, by afternoon, be tracking toads on a virgin*
*prairie northwest of Minneapolis. Evening may find him in his*
*studio, painting a watercolor of an Avocet or writing an article on*
*the mammals of Manitoba. His energy and talents are boundless.*

*Walter John Breckenridge, born in Brooklyn, Iowa, in 1903,*
*graduated from the University of Iowa, and received his Ph.D.*
*from the University of Minnesota. As curator at the Minnesota*
*Museum in the days of Dr. Thomas S. Roberts, he helped move*
*that institution from a few drab rooms in a science building to its*
*present jewel-like setting, where its growth, under his guidance*
*since 1946, has been so phenomenal that an addition—nearly as*
*large as the original—is now in progress.*

*Walter Breckenridge is one of our true conservationists—of*
*everything, but especially of the prairie which has been his particu-*
*lar love since his graduate-school days. In the article that follows*
*he describes two high points of prairie bird watching and makes an*
*eloquent plea for the protection of America's few remaining acres*
*of the virgin prairie sod. Although I asked him for an article on*

269

*bird watching, he could not resist including a few paragraphs on a red fox vixen and her eight cubs.*

The powerful pinions of the little group of Sandhill Cranes had been beating the air monotonously for hours, and for hours the irregular pattern of spruce forests, lakes, and waterways had passed steadily beneath them. Finally, here and there, a few somewhat angular openings began to appear on the landscape below. As the birds flew on and on to the south, more and larger openings, irregular squares or rectangles, dotted the surface until they made up the major part of the land. The regular spacing of the fields indicated that the land below was flat and there were no natural barriers to prevent man from blocking it off into segments with fences and roads. Yes, the prairies were moving under the migrating cranes. And the prairies appealed to these birds because they were treeless, at least in part, like the tundra they had only recently left.

Years before, these prairies had had no square patterns of cultivated fields and no bordering roads. They were vast expanses of grasslands—some parts very flat, others rolling or hilly—broken only by threading watercourses. Some areas were still unpatterned, and the cranes watched these intently for others of their kind which might be resting or feeding there. The birds watched the rectangular fields as well, for they realized that certain of these were very good, although somewhat dangerous, feeding grounds. Suddenly in an isolated cornfield, the birds recognized a mass of tiny white dots as a group of feeding cranes. They began to circle and descend, calling occasionally to announce their arrival.

It was at this point that I first heard the characteristic trumpeting high above me and I strained my eyes to distinguish the minute pepper dots in the blue. I had been installing some field equipment for the study of the Great Plain's toad (*Bufo cognatus*) at a marshy pond some distance from a cornfield in which, unknown to me, some cranes were feeding quietly. The arriving birds circled and dropped steadily until they were perhaps a hundred yards from the ground. Then, heading into the gentle breeze, they set their huge, finger-tipped wings, lowered their retractable landing gears almost to a walking position, and, dropping rapidly, finally bounced on the ground. During the next couple of hours several more flocks of Sandhill Cranes repeated this performance until the flock feeding in the field numbered between two and three hundred.

Very often an undisturbed pilot flock, such as the one I have described, will lure other cranes to the same feeding area. This trait of cranes in recognizing the safety guaranteed by other feeding birds can be helpful to bird watchers in locating migrating cranes. Once the cranes are found, one might expect that a screen of unharvested corn would make it easy to stalk these large birds. Although it is possible to find them this way, cranes can stretch their necks nearly as high as the standing corn. To outwit the alert birds requires a very careful and tiring approach.

Other species of birds may more perfectly typify the virgin prairies, but the Sandhill Crane is one of the most exciting of the prairie migrants. If you are looking for a genuine ornithological thrill, visit the Platte River Valley in western Nebraska in late March or early April when northward-moving crane flocks make this area their rendezvous. As they await the melting of the snows to the north, they feed in the surrounding fields during the day and roost on the marshy islands in the river at night. Often, as though keeping in good physical trim for the long jump to the Arctic, they take advantage of the air currents that rise on sunny days and soar in large flocks into the sky. Up and up they wheel until they actually pass beyond the range of human vision. The tiny specks appear and reappear as they circle about, now conspicuous against a white cumulous cloud, now vanishing into the dark blue sky. Sometimes the sky holds layer upon layer of soaring cranes numbering into the thousands. Their stuttering honks are heard constantly as one ascending flock replaces another moving beyond earshot. With the approach of evening the circling flocks that have not struck out for points farther north settle back to earth to feed for a while, gathering on the river flats in impressive numbers.

One March day, Florence and Lee Jaques and I were watching these swarms of cranes assembling on the flats. We decided to flush the birds for a really spectacular panoramic movie sequence. As we approached the flock, the birds started up like the end of a blanket being lifted from the ground, but, to our surprise, the flock was so extensive that the alarm was not transmitted to the far end of the multitude and we could not get them all to rise at once.

"There's a Whooper!" Lee shouted suddenly.

"Sure enough," I thought, reaching for my binoculars. "We're finally going to get a look at a Whooping Crane."

To our great disappointment the "Whooper" proved, on careful examination, to be nothing more than a Snow Goose that had chosen to travel with the cranes. However, Whooping Cranes do migrate across this area and one can always hope . . .

How often one hears that travel over the prairie is monotonous. True, the relatively flat grasslands vary less than do wooded hills, and today's touring naturalist must keep his eyes glued to the road as he whirls along the eighty-mile-an-hour turnpikes so fast that even the riders can distinguish little of the details of either wooded hills or rolling grasslands. Yes, bird watching from a car on a major highway is a thing of the past—so let us take the next exit, into the real prairies, and walk for a change. Let the prairie grasses and flowers swish against our boots as we take off across an inviting "endless meadow." Distances seem far less on the prairie and before we realize it the car is a speck on the horizon.

The prairies are made up of such widely-varying ecological units that one cannot generalize. One must be specific. So let us visit western Minnesota in the late spring and investigate a virgin tall-grass prairie the like of which is fast disappearing.

The slight swales gather moisture and here the grasses grow taller, inviting the Bobolinks to stake out their territories. Here too, but rarely, a Chestnut-collared Longspur may flush and circle upward, soon to settle back to earth on vibrating wings, appearing to forget his wing movements in the vigor of his Bobolink-like song. Farther west in the Dakotas the Bobolink is found less often and the Chestnut-collared Longspur takes over in the moist habitats. And still farther west on the even drier, dustier prairies the McCown's Longspur replaces the Chestnut-collared.

Overhead a beautiful, plaintive, long-drawn-out *quail-ee-e-e-e-e* whistling call directs our attention to an Upland Plover. This is not really a plover at all, but the name persists. The Upland Plover nests in a variety of grassland habitats, but a larger companion, the Marbled Godwit, is tied much more closely to the virgin prairie.

Where the prairie sod has been broken, the Marbled Godwit seems to find his tie to the land severed, and, as a result, his nesting range continues to shrink with the dwindling prairies. His loudly repeated *go-wit, go-wit, go-wit* is almost as positive an indication of virgin prairie as are the tiny white lady slippers *(Cypripedium candidum)* of the marsh borders and the sweet-scented showy milkweed *(Asclepias speciosa)*, prairie clover *(Petalostemum purpureum)*, the prairie potato *(Psoralea esculenta)*, and the ground plum *(Astragalus caryocarpus)*.

Many of these wild elements of the virgin prairie appear unable, or (one often wishes to think) unwilling, to withstand the heavy hand of man's disturbing use of these ancient lands. They seem to have no power or desire to fight back or to readjust their living needs to the advancing changes. Quietly they shrink away and seek out what remains of the ancestral habitat. And when it is gone, they too will be gone with no fanfare announcing their demise, leaving only the more competitive, the more flexible, the more adjustable forms to struggle on for survival.

Even on the wide-open prairies I often feel that I am intruding among these delicately balanced forms of wildlife so carefully shaped by Nature's evolving forces through eons of time. I feel I should move slowly and quietly so as not to disturb their complex lives. Strangely enough, I experience a deeply-rooted love and kinship for all of this life and strongly resent the fact that man will sooner or later move in to displace it. And still I am a man myself and my own presence is the first step in the displacement that I abhor. At these strange times I feel that I am an actual part of this marvelous natural complex—not a man at all. And in this role I love to walk mile after mile over the prairie or sit hour after hour watching and learning more about the normal, daily experiences of these wild creatures.

Walking on the prairie is usually fairly dry—a ten-inch-leather-boot type of hiking—but in early spring many only slightly lower areas may still be awash with melt-waters and one must slosh through them or detour frequently.

I recall vividly an experience in the pothole country near Waubun, Minnesota. Leaving my companion's car before dawn one morning with a heavy packsack of camera equipment, I was intent on entering a previously established blind on a Greater Prairie

Chicken booming ground. Although it was dark, I knew that the blind, several hundred yards from the road, would loom up as a dark object above the horizon which was somewhat lightened by the coming dawn. Time after time I walked head-on into one or another of the marshy swales which lay between me and the blind and which I had avoided readily in daylight. Even with hip boots pulled high, I had to back out and search again and again for the shallow places that permitted progress toward my blind.

I preferred not to use a flashlight for fear it might disturb the arriving Prairie Chickens and, with all the detours, I lost my bearings temporarily and walked more than double the distance to the blind, reaching concealment barely ahead of the earliest chickens.

Here the birds had chosen to boom, as they often do, on one of the drier, slightly-elevated ridges, but even so some of the subordinate cocks were forced to dance on ground so wet that they splashed water with their pounding feet preliminary to their boom.

Watching this strangely organized dance is one of the characteristic prairie experiences. Most modern bird students observe this performance with spotting scopes from parked cars, but it is far more thrilling to sit in a photographic blind on a booming ground and see these little prairie cocks strutting, inflating their orange neck sacs, and erecting their horn-like "pinnae" only a few feet distant. The climax comes when, occasionally, a bird alights on the top of the blind, shakes the whole structure as he stamps his feet, and booms within inches of one's head.

This is the time you are the "mouse in the corner." You can see, like Rip Van Winkle, the little people, not bowling on the green, but dancing on their own ancestral prairie—something they never in the world would do if they knew you were sitting in their midst. Many times, rather than burst out and alarm them before the dance was over, I have remained hidden in my blind longer than I intended in order to allow them to leave the dance floor of their own accord.

Once, while locating a Prairie Chicken booming ground with my spotting scope, I saw, far behind the performing birds, a figure in motion that I first took to be a jack rabbit. After careful study, however, I decided it was a red fox cub playing near the mouth of a burrow. As is so often the case, this vixen had dug her burrow just below the crest of a low rise and almost in the exact geographic center of a two-square-mile open prairie tract. In approaching the burrow later, I started a fox, probably the male, which ran across in front of me on an unnatural and conspicuous course, off at an angle, away from the den. I cannot help thinking that this was intentional on his part, luring me to take up the chase and to prevent me from discovering the family home.

I erected a low blind beside a small willow bush about seventy-five yards from the burrow and spent several hours watching the amusing play of the eight half-grown cubs. At last the vixen returned to the den, no doubt after carefully examining the blind from concealment. She was obviously disturbed and, on hearing the whir of my camera even at that distance, uttered a low, warning bark. The cubs instantly dived for the nearest of several burrows and she bounded away over the crest of the rise. Before long the cubs reappeared but not the vixen. Several hours passed and she did not return. When dwindling light finally forced me to give up, I packed up my blind. Ready to leave I glanced up at the crest of the rise. There she was silhouetted on the skyline only a few yards from her den—a triumphant fox calmly watching my departure. Her long wait had accomplished its aim.

The prairie, like most wilderness habitats, gives up its secrets slowly and grudgingly. One does not make exciting discoveries every day. An individual without a deep-seated love of natural things would doubtlessly give up in discouragement after a few of what he might consider unproductive visits. But over the years, from many days afield in rainy and sunny weather, in winter and in summer, one gradually accumulates a wealth of choice experiences. Lured by this possibility one can spend long hours tramping over the "monotonous" prairies in constant anticipation of the unfolding of another exciting episode.

# NORTH DAKOTA PRAIRIE

## Ann Magrete Gammell

*Ann Magrete, born in Bellingham, Washington, in 1909, grew up in a small town in east-central North Dakota. While a student nurse at the University of Minnesota she met Robert T. Gammell, a medical student at the University. They were married the year they graduated, lived in Minneapolis during his internship, and, in 1934, moved to Kenmare, North Dakota, where he now practices medicine.*

*The Gammells, alert and aware of everything around them, watched with interest the development of the Des Lacs National Wildlife Refuge, which was established in 1935, and became acquainted with one of its first managers, the late Seth H. Low, who introduced them to a new world—the world of birds. From that time on, birds gradually and insidiously began to invade and then take over the Gammells' leisure time. Ann gave up golf when she found herself "listening to pipits instead of watching the ball."*

*In 1948 the Gammells became regional editors of* Audubon Field Notes, *a post they held for ten years. Meanwhile Seth Low, having moved to the bird-banding office outside Washington, D.C., urged them to try banding. When they succumbed to his pleadings, their success soon so excited and astonished them that they were lost to all else. They gave up their editorship; relegated their music listening, "almost as important as birds," to winter and days when weather made banding impossible; and limited attendance at the opera, "almost a vice," to one week in mid-May.*

276

*The Gammells' banding activities are spectacular. Up to October 1964 they have banded 84,000 birds of 215 different species. One room in their home is an office for records; another holds their equipment; their station wagon is tailored to accommodate traps, nets, poles, bands, records, and, of course, lunch hampers. During the summer they "drop everything and spend every available moment in the field." Naturally a practicing physician is never overburdened with leisure time. Nevertheless, the Gammells are in this banding work together and it is hard to tell whose interest is greater, Bob's or Ann's.*

*With the same enthusiasm that they apply to the banding they welcome fellow bird watchers. Ever since the Gammells first supplied information for my* Guide to Bird Finding, *I have been mercilessly recommending Kenmare, the Des Lacs Refuge, and the Gammells to all bird finders headed west. The reports that come back to me can best be summarized by a young man who followed my directions and stated: "Everything about the Gammells and bird watching in North Dakota is the greatest."*

*There may be some doubt as to whether bird watching on the short-grass prairie of North Dakota is the greatest; but after reading what Ann Gammell has to say here, you will have to admit that it is greater than you ever expected.*

The telephone rang and I answered. The caller identified herself as a school teacher from Ohio.

"My husband and I are on our way to Glacier Park and have an hour to spare," she said. "Could you possibly tell us where to find Baird's Sparrows?"

Since it was easier to take her than to tell her, I summoned a long-suffering neighbor to greet house guests who were expected momentarily and was on my way. Within the hour Baird's Sparrows were listened to, looked at, and added to another list—and I had added to my list of "Baird's Sparrowers." The school teacher was followed in a few days by a businessman from New York. He had just five hours to spare, but he hoped to see Baird's Sparrows and several other species besides.

Run-of-the-mill tourists rarely linger within the borders of North Dakota. Those from the East hurry through as rapidly as possible on their way to the Rocky Mountains or the Pacific Coast; those from the West, having seen the Rockies, rush on, considering the Plains just something to be crossed on the way "back east." During recent years, however, bird watchers have been stopping in North Dakota in increasing numbers. They have discovered our varied habitats—our prairies, our wetlands and badlands, and our little trench-like valleys or ravines which we call coulees. Because distances mean little on the open plains, they have traveled with ease from one habitat to another, stopping along the way to watch birds from the car windows. These specialized travelers soon reject the popular impression that North Dakota is a remote, frigid land somewhere west of the Mississippi—a land devoid of vegetation and natural beauty, a barren land inhabited only by a few of the more hardy species of birds and by a solid people of predominantly Scandinavian ancestry.

The climate of North Dakota is one of extremes. During the long winter the temperature may drop to 60 degrees below zero; in summer the mercury may rise to 120 degrees. However, such recordings are unusual and the summers with their long twilights and cool evenings are pure delight. Rainfall, which North Dakotans refer to as "moisture," varies from twenty-two inches in the east to fourteen inches in the west. The wind is a constant companion. In dry years it drives the tumbleweeds like whirling dervishes and piles them in huge drifts along the fence rows and shelter belts. We feel it our privilege to speak derisively about our weather, but we take offense at slurring remarks from others.

Our small town, Kenmare, is on a hillside overlooking Middle Lake of the Riviere des Lacs, a part of the Des Lacs National Wildlife Refuge. Having a wildlife sanctuary almost in the back yard has had a profound influence on our lives. In its marshes, wooded coulees, and upland prairies our interest in birds was first stimulated. Over the years we have watched the restoration of habitats and the resulting return of birdlife which the fine management of the refuge has made possible. About sixteen miles west of Kenmare is the Lostwood National Wildlife Refuge in the Coteau du Missouri, an area of countless small potholes and large alkaline lakes where Avocets and Piping Plovers nest and other shorebirds of many species stop briefly during spring migration and return in early July to linger into late summer and fall. Sharp-tailed Grouse are abundant, with thirty dancing grounds active from April to June. Sprague's Pipits and Baird's Sparrows are common summer residents.

To the southwest of Kenmare are the Missouri River and the spectacularly beautiful Badlands where one first notes the overlapping of the Baltimore and Bullock's Orioles. The Red-shafted Flicker becomes more common in the Badlands and other western species such as Mountain Bluebirds, Black-headed Grosbeaks, and Lazuli Buntings appear. Here, also, one may find Golden Eagles and Prairie Falcons nesting.

After more than twenty-five years of birding in all these varied habitats we find that the prairie—the short-grass prairie—draws us more and more to its environment. With its many species of grasses and sedges, its low shrubs, and its profusion of wildflowers, the prairie has a subtle beauty that is indescribable. The prairie is big, wide open, free. Its grasses, uninterrupted, ripple on to meet the sky on the far horizon. We can understand why the plains dweller feels "hemmed in" when moved to another setting.

When winter reluctantly gives way to spring—and almost before the snow is gone—pasque flowers appear, covering the slopes with a delicate blue-violet cloud. With the coming of the spring rains the browns and yellows change as if by magic to greens and silver. Contrary to general belief, the prairie is not flat. Rather it rolls in huge, gently-sloping waves. Vegetation varies according to elevation with more species of plants in the depressions which retain moisture longer than the hilltops. Needle-and-thread grass, needleleaf sedge, niggerwool, little sage, patches of wolfberry and silverberry—light greens, blue greens, dark greens, gray greens—puccoon, false mallow, bedstraw, beard-tongue, harebell, wild rose—yellows, reds, whites, purples, blues, pinks—an infinite variety of color. This is the home of the Baird's Sparrow, a somberly clad bird whose most distinguishable features are a necklace of delicate black streaks and a crown-stripe of rich ocher.

It is fitting, though possibly a bit strange, that this little grasslands sparrow, discovered in North Dakota by John James Audubon more than a century ago and named in honor of his friend, Spencer Fullerton Baird, is one of our most sought-after birds.

Could Audubon have imagined, even in his most extravagant moments, that bird finders would one day travel halfway across the continent just to see his Baird's Sparrow?

Baird's Sparrows are late arrivals in the spring, seldom appearing before May 17. There is no evidence of migration. Suddenly they are on the breeding grounds, using weed stalks, low fence posts, silverberry and wolfberry shrubs as singing perches. When their musical tinkling songs are added to those of the other birds, the symphony of the prairie is complete.

Although the short-grass prairie is their home, some factor or combination of factors limits Baird's Sparrows to certain sections. We have never been able to discover the differences which make one hillside a desirable nesting ground while another hillside, quite similar to us at least, is uninhabited. The birds are usually found in colonies where each pair occupies and defends a large territory. Baird's Sparrows are amicable and get along well with their own kind as well as with their neighbors—Sprague's Pipits, Grasshopper and Savannah Sparrows, and, sometimes, Chestnut-collared Longspurs—whose territories often adjoin and frequently overlap.

Their nests, well-concealed in slight depressions on the ground, are constructed of grasses and usually contain four or five eggs. When the young hatch, both parents join in bringing food consisting for the most part of grasshoppers. By the end of August the birds have gone. Again there is no evidence of migration. For several years we have done a great deal of bird banding during September, both in our yard and by a prairie waterhole, but we have never encountered a movement of this species nor have we seen a single individual.

A prairie waterhole may be a stockpond, gravel pit, or a spring-fed depression the margins of which are relatively bare. On hot, sunny days in July and August one can always find prairie birds at such places.

One early July day we took two friends—lady birders from the East—to visit one of our favorite waterholes which we refer to as "Longspur Pasture." This is on a quarter section of prairie, fenced for grazing but not grazed that year because of the drought, so the grass, though sparse, showed some growth.

When we arrived at Longspur Pasture in our Chevrolet carryall, which is fitted out to transport banding gear, poles, nets, etc., the sun was beating down mercilessly and it was obvious that our guests, scantily clad in shorts, needed some protection to prevent sunburn. By pounding four net poles into the ground, throwing a tarp over the poles, and securing the corners with twine, we constructed a "squaw-cooler." Then, setting up a few mist nets beside the waterhole, we spread a blanket on the ground beneath the squaw-cooler, ate our lunch—and watched the birds in comfort.

A Baird's Sparrow sang from atop a weed stalk so near us that we could see his necklace without glasses. Chestnut-collared Longspurs fed young on our right. Occasionally an incredibly beautiful male, still in breeding plumage with jet black breast, bright chestnut nape, and immaculate white tail pattern, rose into the air to sing aloft before dropping to the ground. Sprague's Pipits walked along the damp shore. Horned Larks came and went constantly. All at once we realized that an antelope was drinking on the far side of the waterhole. How, we asked each other, had he avoided our nets? We sat motionless until he had drunk his fill, and held our collective breath as he walked unerringly to an opening between the nets without once glancing in our direction.

Frequently, as we walked to the nets to remove birds, a pair of noisy Marbled Godwits flew over our heads, uttering their harsh screams. Although we searched for the young that must have been nearby, we were unable to find them. Avocets, too, dropped in but did not dive-bomb us, so we were quite certain they had no young. Shorebirds were beginning to return, and among them were some Northern Phalaropes—a "first" for our delighted guests.

With the cool breeze of early evening, the flight of birds to the water dwindled and then ceased. When we tallied our records, we found we had banded 92 Horned Larks, 40 Chestnut-collared Longspurs, 10 Sprague's Pipits, 8 Baird's Sparrows, 7 Savannah Sparrows, and one McCown's Longspur—a total of 160 birds during the afternoon. As we gathered up the nets and poles, we noticed some activity near a knoll on the horizon. Looking through the glasses we discovered four fox cubs playing outside their den. Why were they so careless, we wondered. Was their mother away hunting? We left wishing her luck and hoping that the youngsters would go unnoticed by a "sportsman," eager and anxious to destroy "predators."

After a day on the prairies and marshes, the wooded coulees

invariably come as a surprise to out-of-state visitors. "Coulee" is a western term and, in our part of the country, refers to a steep-walled valley or ravine which may or may not be wooded and may or may not have a stream or spring. The reaction of one stranger on visiting Tasker's Coulee on the Des Lacs National Wildlife Refuge, where he saw American elm, green ash, box elder, trembling aspen, and several species of shrubs including wild plum, was simple: "I don't believe it."

Among the fifty or more species of birds breeding in Tasker's Coulee are Cooper's and Swainson's Hawks, Long-eared and Great Horned Owls, several woodpeckers, flycatchers, vireos, warblers, and fringillids. In wet years the Ovenbirds remain to nest. Occasionally, a pair of Lazuli Buntings can be found. In the evening the unearthly voice of the Veery can be heard from one end of the coulee to the other. How many picnickers, one wonders, stop to listen or are aware of how different these songs are from those of the prairie lieder singers. During July and August when the coulee creek beds are dry, mammals and birds can be seen at the springs.

Modern farming methods and the high cost of machinery have all but eliminated the small farm. As a result there are, in our vicinity, a number of abandoned farmsteads with buildings in various stages of disrepair—sagging, unpainted houses with boarded-up or broken windows, and yawning gaps where doors once hung; weedy overgrown yards and groves choked with dead wood and underbrush—lonely, abandoned, forgotten. These places have a unique picturesqueness that invite the passer-by to stop. Vesper and Clay-colored Sparrows sing in the dooryards; Black-billed Cuckoos, Catbirds, and Brown Thrashers call in the groves; Barn Swallows fly in and out of the buildings and the plaintive note of the Say's Phoebe is heard. Nearly all these deserted farms have a pair of Phoebes which prefer indoor nesting sites. Nests may be found snug on a closet shelf, on a ledge, in an open cupboard, or over a door. Say's Phoebes arrive early—about April 17, often when the snow is still on the ground—and yet rarely nest until June.

Whenever we drive past a cow pasture where there are Richardson's ground squirrels, we stop and fully expect to find Burrowing Owls. These comedians of the prairie prefer places with a plentiful supply of dry cow chips for lining their tunnels and nests.

How well I remember showing some professional ornithologists their first Burrowing Owls. When we arrived at the pasture, the young were standing atop the burrow and staring. They jerked their heads, they bobbed, and they stared. Nearby were a number of ground squirrel burrows—"gopher holes." One ground squirrel popped out of its hole and assumed an upright position, then another and another and another. Everybody—humans, birds, mammals—stared at everybody else until our visitors broke down with laughter.

Late the following morning I was surprised to meet my new friends in town, for I knew they had planned an early departure. The Burrowing Owls had detained them, they explained. They had gone to the pasture early for just one more look and had spent the morning there.

If winter doesn't come too early, October is often one of the most delightful months of the year. The goldenrod still blooms, and the air is full of the sounds of migrating longspurs—Lapland Longspurs and Smith's Longspurs (the Chestnut-collared Longspurs have long since gone). We had always been curious about Smith's Longspurs and our banding gave us some information. During the drought years of 1960 and 1961 when there were only a few waterholes, we banded beside them as long as the weather permitted. In the fall of 1960 we banded 2,441 Lapland Longspurs and 9 Smith's Longspurs; in 1961 we banded 3,529 Laplands and 4 Smith's. On two occasions in late September, 1960, we had the good fortune to band all four species of longspurs—the three mentioned above and the McCown's as well.

Winter passes into spring and reports of birds begin to come in. A friend calling to tell me about the first Baird's Sparrow may also comment on the Lark Buntings. We always hope for a "Lark Bunting year" when all along the roads these striking black and white birds perch on fence posts or flutter skyward and descend in butterfly flight.

And close behind (and as sure as) the returning birds are the birders who are on the scene by mid-June. Their cars bristle with cameras, binoculars, telescopes, waders, field clothes, and eastern and western "Petes" and "Pets." I welcome them warmly, for all of these itinerant birders have enriched our lives and many have become our warm friends.

# THE NEBRASKA PINE RIDGE

## Doris B. Gates

*Doris Berta Gates, born in 1915 in Lincoln, Nebraska, spent her first nine years on a farm near Chadron in the Pine Ridge Country. A subsequent move to Lincoln, her years at the University of Nebraska from which she received both the B.S. and M.S. degrees and where she later did some research work in entomology, even summer school farther afield—in Wyoming, Colorado, and New York—did not dull her memory of the Pine Ridge. After several years of teaching biology in high school, she assumed her present position as assistant professor of biology at Chadron State College in Chadron. This last move, made in 1955, was the fulfillment of a wish generated in early childhood—to return to the Pine Ridge to live.*

*Although her scientific studies have been for the most part in entomology, she has always enjoyed every aspect of natural history and had more than a casual interest in birds. And this interest quickened in 1947 when she accepted the first of a continuous series of offices in the Nebraska Ornithologists' Union. Currently she holds the most arduous and time-consuming job of all—editor of* The Nebraska Bird Review.

*Doris Gates has traveled in most of the forty-eight contiguous states and across Canada to Alaska, and she has enjoyed looking for birds along the way, but she insists that she would not live anywhere—anywhere at all—except in the Pine Ridge of northwestern Nebraska. In this chapter she indicates why.*

Much of north-central Nebraska consists of the Sandhills—a region of the Great Plains whose terrain is a succession of grass-covered dunes with intermittent marshes, wet meadows, and shallow lakes. But in extreme northwestern Nebraska the scenery is suddenly and strangely varied—and rugged. There are oddly flat-topped hills or "buttes" and steep-walled valleys and canyons, stretches of weirdly eroded, generally plantless "badlands" and stands of pines and junipers on lofty slopes. This is the Pine Ridge Country. To the overland traveler it seems to be a conglomeration of scenic features totally lacking in pattern.

If one could see Pine Ridge Country from the air he would readily discover that there is no ridge at all, that what we call the Pine Ridge is a north-facing escarpment where the Great Plains drop down to the Missouri Plateau (a northern division of the Great Plains). He would see also that the escarpment cuts a semicircular pattern across the northwestern corner of the state, disappearing into Wyoming on west and South Dakota on the north. In South Dakota it soon takes an easterly direction nearly across the state.

South or outside of the semi-circle is a rather flat area which we speak of as "the table." This is somewhat cut into valleys many of which have steep, clay banks. Some of these valleys have permanent streams such as the Niobrara River; others have drainage systems which are dry most of the year. In general, grasses are the predominant cover of the table, except in a few valleys where there are deciduous trees—mostly cottonwoods—and shrubs, and, in low, moist places, cattails and sedges.

Underlying the surface of the table is a thick stratum of hard sandstone. This becomes exposed at the Pine Ridge as the "rim rock" or "cap rock" and accounts for much of its ruggedness.

The Pine Ridge itself varies in width from one to ten miles. It is not only dissected by canyons but has many northward extensions that have been cut off by erosion, forming isolated hills. Flat-topped and called buttes, they are in reality no higher than the table of which they were once a part.

Nearly all the slopes—those of the Pine Ridge and its canyons as well as those of the buttes—are quite precipitous with bold outcroppings of the rim rock, sometimes many feet thick. Often the outcroppings on the buttes give them fantastic shapes, with the result that they are known by such colorfully descriptive names as "Saddle Butte," "Giant's Coffin," and "Pants Butte." (Unfortunately, Pants Butte recently lost a leg!)

Since the distance from the top of a butte to its base may be a sudden drop of over 300 feet, the niches and shelves in the rocky walls of these formations frequently provide suitably inaccessible nesting sites for Prairie Falcons, Golden Eagles, White-throated Swifts, and Rock Wrens. The Rock Wren generally chooses a cavity under a flat rock or in a split rock—a recess that is difficult to follow. The entrance is usually high enough to provide a wide view of the country below, although I have found a nest in the hole of a clay bank only four feet above the edge of a country road. Once, too, I found a family of six well-developed young, one with down still on its head, on a ledge under a large rounded rock with a deep cleft. When the nestlings became alarmed at my approach, they left one by one, each bobbing in a rhythmic manner before diving into the safety of a cavity under the root of an old pine tree.

The trees which give the Pine Ridge its name are the western yellow (ponderosa) pine and the junipers, including the recumbent type. For the most part, they are confined to the higher slopes. Among the birds which find the pines excellent habitat are the Piñon Jays (sometimes in flocks of thirty to forty), Red-breasted and White-breasted Nuthatches, Audubon's Warblers, and Western Tanagers. Pygmy Nuthatches have been attracted to the pines recently, while Red Crossbills, as erratic here as elsewhere, are numerous in some years.

North or inside the semi-circular Pine Ridge are lower hills, badlands, and flatlands. The badlands flank the escarpment and toward the west broaden into arid stretches where the ground is baked into small geometric designs, interrupted here and there by hardy plants or peculiar rock formations. Toadstool Park north of Crawford embraces a typical stretch—and it's truly an extraordinary place. The flatlands are used mostly for pasture, but in some spots for crops, especially wheat. Grasses of several varieties, sedges, prickly-pear cacti, yuccas, and sagebrush make up much of the natural cover except along streams. Here deciduous trees and shrubs—cottonwood, ash, elm, box elder, willow, chokecherry, plum, buffalo berry, skunkbrush, and buckbrush—thrive, sometimes forming a dense growth. In its low bushy edges both Indigo and Lazuli Buntings nest and, indeed, hybridize, and Bell's Vireos occasionally occur. Nearby, in isolated clumps of plums and chokecherry, or thickets of buffalo berry, one may expect to find Loggerhead Shrikes nesting.

The climate of the Pine Ridge is extreme, with temperatures very high—over 100 in the summer—and very low in winter. However, the high altitude, from about 3,600 to over 4,000 feet above sea level, the low relative humidity, and the annual rainfall of only sixteen to eighteen inches make the summer nights cool and reduce the expected discomfort.

The Pine Ridge is rich in history of Indians and fur traders. Chief Crazy Horse was killed near Fort Robinson, an outpost so well described by Mari Sandoz in her books on Indian conflicts. Many canyons and gullies bear self-explanatory names, such as Sowbelly Canyon where a group of marooned soldiers subsisted for one long winter on the above commodity.

To me the Pine Ridge is a particularly interesting place to

study birds because it attracts species of the prairie grasslands, arid lands, and wooded streamsides, together with occasional species from the Black Hills of South Dakota, not far to the north, and sometimes such rarities as Gray-crowned Rosy Finches from the Rocky Mountains far to the west. My greatest number of species recorded for a period from January 1 to July 1 is 124.

The most conspicuous bird along the roads in the Pine Ridge is the Lark Sparrow with the Lark Bunting a close second in particularly favored spots. Other grassland birds include Horned Larks and Chestnut-collared Longspurs. Very likely the latter breed in this area though I have never found a nest. Western Meadowlarks are everywhere and Eastern Meadowlarks can be found particularly in moist lowlands. Sharp-tailed Grouse occur, especially around the Walgren Refuge south of Hay Springs. Grasshopper Sparrows sing from the tops of dried yucca stems, and Upland Plovers and Long-billed Curlews can be found in dry, grassy places.

For a wide variety of birds characteristic of the Pine Ridge, one should go nine miles south of Chadron to Chadron State Park whose 1,500 acres encompass suitable habitats from escarpments to tree-bordered streams and a pond. Accustomed to the presence of people, many birds are easily seen. I once observed Black-headed Grosbeaks, apparently a family, so tame they hopped about my feet, and I have frequently watched them come for crumbs to a picnic table only a short distance from people.

Always conspicuous in the park during the summer are both Eastern and Western Kingbirds—the Western Kingbirds especially so—on fences, poles, or tree stubs. No less conspicuous are the Mountain Bluebirds, with the common habit of hovering just above the ground, then dropping suddenly to pick up an insect or two. Eastern Bluebirds also occur. In seeking insects, they show a greater tendency to watch for them from a perch rather than from on the wing as the Mountain Bluebirds do. Eastern Phoebes nest under almost every bridge and Say's Phoebes show up in many places near water and about escarpments where they usually nest under overhanging ledges.

The most abundant summer birds in the park are Common Grackles, American Redstarts, and Red-eyed Vireos (their voices monotonous on long summer days), but Western Wood Pewees,

Warbling Vireos, Yellow Warblers, and Chipping Sparrows almost rival them in numbers. Handsome Bullock's Orioles, in trees and shrubbery, call attention to themselves with their loud chatter and clear, piping whistles. Yellow-breasted Chats and Rufous-sided Towhees are numerous in shrubby areas. Violet-green and Rough-winged Swallows frequent the boating pond where they skim its surface for insect food. In the evening Common Nighthawks pursuing insects over the pond are so numerous and come so close to boaters that people are sometimes afraid to go out on the water. Later in the evening the Nighthawks' "zooming," given high in the sky at the end of a long dive, becomes a familiar sound. Another familiar sound during the twilight is the call of the Poor-will from the high, conifer-studded slopes. Among other birds which one may count on observing regularly in the park at the same time of year are flickers—usually hybrid forms of the Yellow-shafted and Red-shafted—Red-headed Woodpeckers, Black-billed Magpies, American Goldfinches, and Pine Siskins.

On calm sunny days in the summer the thermals rising from the valleys provide ideal updrafts for sailing birds. One day I counted nine Turkey Vultures circling above a little valley. Another day, I watched a Red-tailed Hawk making lazy passes at a Golden Eagle, which gracefully dodged it, while both birds gradually soared higher and higher.

Recently I found the nest of a Prairie Falcon in Chadron State Park right above a road and very close to a horseback trail which was used several times each day. When I first saw it, the young had already left, but I was able to locate four of them. Three were roosting quite close together on the side of a butte a short distance from the nest. As I watched, one began to feed on something it held in its talons. Then it flew to another station, not far from the first, carrying the food. When it alighted, it extended both feet—one holding the food—and landed, apparently, with the same weight on both feet. Then it began feeding again. I was unable to determine what the food was other than that it was some kind of a bird. Later, I circled below this steep butte to hunt for remains of former meals. I found one immature Lark Sparrow, mostly eaten; a meadowlark with little more than a feather or two left on the bones; and several blackish feathers, which could have been those of a Common Grackle.

When fall comes to the Pine Ridge Country, Mourning Doves congregate in flocks of from around 50 to 300, causing me to wonder if the Pine Ridge is not an ideal nursery for this species. Merriam's Turkeys, reintroduced not long ago in the area, were numerous enough in the fall of 1962 to be hunted.

Almost every year winter brings Evening Grosbeaks and, in some years, flocks of Bohemian and Cedar Waxwings, but usually more flocks of Bohemians than Cedars. Townsend's Solitaires come, too, as well as Slate-colored, Oregon, and White-winged Juncos. A few White-winged Juncos nest in the Pine Ridge during the summer.

The Pine Ridge Country is not an outstanding area for marshbirds, waterbirds, or shorebirds, although there are many farm ponds which have water in wet years. Whitney Lake, part of an irrigation project between Chadron and Crawford, is large enough to support ducks and geese and attract a few Double-crested Cormorants during migration. Great Blue Herons stalk fish along its edges during the summer.

There are, however, places for marshbirds, waterbirds, and shorebirds not too far distant. From Chadron one has only to travel south on US Route 385 or east on US Route 20 to enter the rolling pasture lands of the Nebraska Sandhills. Among these treeless hills are many shallow lakes, thick with cattails and other marsh vegetation. Here in the summer the chatter of Long-billed Marsh Wrens is almost continuous, and there are many Yellowthroats and Red-winged and Yellow-headed Blackbirds. Black and Forster's Terns are quite common, as are Pied-billed Grebes and a number of species of ducks. Some of these lakes have broad mudflats where large numbers of shorebirds gather during migration and near which Avocets, Wilson's Phalaropes, and Killdeers regularly nest.

Nebraska's Pine Ridge Country has much to offer the bird watcher. Just come and see for yourself!

# THE BLACK MESA
# COUNTRY OF OKLAHOMA
## George Miksch Sutton

*In the fall of 1930 I began graduate studies at Cornell University, taking up my abode on the third floor of McGraw Hall. A dismal building, it could have been deadening had it not been for the warm friendship and infectious vitality of several fellow occupants including one George Sutton, just recently returned from a year in the Arctic. Here was a person at once painting birds, writing a book, preparing specimens, discussing profound taxonomic problems, and—in less industrious moments outside McGraw—playing the piano, attending concerts, and thoroughly enjoying innumerable social functions. Little did I know then that this wonderfully versatile, outgoing person, nine years my senior, would play such an immeasurably influential role in my personal philosophy, attitudes, and concepts in all the years that were to come.*

*George Miksch Sutton was born in Bethany, Nebraska, in 1898. The son of a minister-teacher who moved often, George passed his childhood and early youth in widely scattered places— in Nebraska, Minnesota, Oregon, Illinois, Texas, and finally West Virginia where he was to graduate from Bethany College. Birds, he remembers, were a constant source of fascination and he saw many different ones with each move. His parents, ever sympathetic with this interest, once gave him a mounted bird that became his pride and joy. He was sketching birds early. His idea of a tolerable*

291

*church service was being near enough to a lady's hat adorned with
a bird that he could draw somewhere in his hymn book. He prepared his first birdskin in Oregon at the age of seven. In Texas, at
the age of thirteen, he was a confirmed ornithologist, keeping profuse notes, building up a skin collection, and drawing pictures
galore. He was already an admiring disciple of Fuertes whom he
would meet and study under at intervals a few years later.*

*After college days he served on the staff of the Carnegie Mu-
seum, 1919–1925, and as state ornithologist on the Pennsylvania
Game Commission, 1925–1929; then he was off for a year's adventure in the Far North. On his return he went to Cornell University where he earned his doctorate and was curator of birds until
World War II when he was called to serve as a technical officer in
the U.S. Army. From 1945 until his departure for Oklahoma in
1952 he was on the staff of the University of Michigan's Museum
of Zoology. He is now research professor of zoology at the University of Oklahoma. Here, as at all his previous institutional posts,
his influence in shaping the ornithological careers and personal
objectives of many young men has been truly immense.*

*The books from George Sutton's skilled pen are* An Introduction to the Birds of Pennsylvania *(1928),* The Exploration of
Southampton Island, Hudson Bay *(1932),* Eskimo Year *(1934),*
Birds in the Wilderness *(1936),* Mexican Birds: First Impressions
*(1951), and* Iceland Summer *(1961). For his superior craftsman-
ship in nature writing, as in* Iceland Summer, *he was awarded the
John Burroughs Medal. Among the many books, besides his own,
which he has illustrated are* Birds of Western Pennsylvania *(1940),
the two volumes of my* Guide to Bird Finding *(1951 and 1953),
and* Georgia Birds *(1958).*

*I know of no ornithologist who has more thoroughly explored
the North American continent than George Sutton. A few times I
have been with him, to Hudson Bay, to Nebraska, Colorado, and
South Dakota, and to Mexico. Once I prevailed upon him to ac-
company me and my wife outside the continent, to Iceland. He finds
every place he visits exciting, challenging, rewarding—I have no
way of knowing whether he really likes one better than the other.
But this I do know: when he speaks about the Black Mesa Country
in the extreme northwestern part of the Oklahoma Panhandle, his*

*face lights up with a very special expression. This place, the very one he writes about here, could be his favorite.*

       The Black Mesa is a dark, lava-capped spur of the great Rocky Mountain cordillera. It extends southeastward beyond the confines of Colorado and New Mexico into the northwestern-most corner of Oklahoma. For the people of Oklahoma it is of considerable note, for on it is the highest point in the state. A 10-foot-high marker, situated not far east of the New Mexico line and a few miles south of the Colorado line designates this spot, whose "true altitude" as stated on the marker, is 4,972.97 feet. An earlier marker at the very same spot gave the elevation as 4,978 feet.

      What annoys me about markers of this sort is that they fail so miserably to call attention to anything truly vital. They mention statistics, nothing more—the highest point above sea level within certain artificial, man-made limits; the position of some of these limits. Not a hint as to what is there because the place *is* high, or as to what is there despite the highness. Not a word about the lava. Not a hint of the fact that some of the little wind-ravaged junipers are one-seed junipers (*Juniperus monosperma*), a Rocky Mountain species. Not a hint as to the possibility that the arborescent cholla cactus, scattered clumps of which grow in the immediate vicinity, might not survive at a slightly greater elevation. Not a hint of the fact that the Indians, who loved this high ground, watched bands of antelopes from the mesa's rim. Not a hint of the fact that even today, when September mornings have a frosty sharpness, great bows of Sandhill Cranes sweep southward just above the mesa's top, bugling happily as they circle in reconnaissance and descend to the broad bed of the Cimarron. Not a hint of the fact that in the slightly lower country off to the south and east, among canyons that cut through sandstone and shale topped with cap rock or caliche, are cliffs on which Golden Eagles nest, cool springs so tucked away that they have about them an air of virginal innocence, and scattered ponderosa pines that tower majestically above the pinyons and cedars and scrubby oaks.

      No, those markers designate very little. And they are unlovely. They remind me that the white man, with his surveying instruments and cement and mania for conquering, has been here. They remind me that when the white man conquers he nearly always destroys. In their silent, formal, dreadfully eloquent way they explain the absence of so very much.

If I can manage to forget the markers I enjoy tremendously the sweep of sky and vastness of plateau. Part of this enjoyment is the realization that I have climbed up. I chuckle as I tell myself that there must be a road or trail somewhere but that I've never looked for it or even asked about it. I have always followed my own personal route up a not-very-steep southeastern slope from the road that skirts the base of the mesa's easternmost tip.

It is early spring. Nowhere has the grass become really green, but all over the plateau, even where the dark lava is exposed, white-and-pink evening primroses have opened. It is a bit early for the blossoms of the prickly pear and yucca and much too early for the slender-petaled, satin-white *Mentzelia,* which all the cattlemen call the "prairie lily." The chollas, which at a distance look as harmless and as soft as kittens, but which are covered with the sharpest of spines, are bright yellow in spots, especially at the tips of the stems. This is not the yellow of flowers or buds; indeed, it may be a result of malnutrition or frost-bite, but I have noted that it can be very pretty in spring.

In the distance I hear the louder parts of a Lark Sparrow's song. In another direction, a full quarter of a mile away, a Mockingbird is laying claim to a nest-territory with phrases occasionally his own but mostly borrowed from Sparrow Hawks, Killdeers, Greater Yellowlegs and heaven knows what pups, pigs, and squeaky barndoors. I cannot help wondering where he built up his repertory—not here, surely; not on this all but silent mesa-top! Two House Finches fly past at little more than eye level, one of them a rosy-chested male. Far overhead sounds a faint tinkle of Horned Lark music. Downslope, below the lava cap, a Rock Wren calls *tee-keer, tee-keer,* and sings briefly. I listen in vain for the *pee-yee* of a Common Nighthawk and for the plaintive *dleeee, diddilit, diddilit* flight-song of the Cassin's Sparrow. Both of these species are known to nest here. The former has not, I decide, yet returned from the south; as for the latter, one guess is as good as another: perhaps, for reasons best known to itself, it is not singing just now; perhaps it is simply not to be here this year. Nowhere, either near or far, do I hear a bird chorus. Nowhere do I hear a Western Meadowlark. The solemn, rather hard-to-accept fact is that there are very few birds here.

I do not forget, of course, the hawks and eagles, one of which may appear at any moment. All the nesting falconiform birds of the region are likely to fly over or around the mesa from time to time and the wintering species may still be on hand since in this high northwestern part of the state the advance of spring is slow. Among the diurnal birds of prey to be looked for are the Turkey Vulture, Sharp-shinned, Cooper's, Red-tailed, Swainson's, Rough-legged, and Ferruginous Hawks, Golden Eagle, Bald Eagle, Marsh Hawk, Osprey, Prairie Falcon, and Pigeon and Sparrow Hawks. The Red-tails of this country nest on cliffs, the Swainson's and Ferruginous Hawks invariably in trees. The Mississippi Kite breeds along the Cimarron River about twenty miles east of the Black Mesa. The Goshawk has been seen in the rough country southeast of Kenton. The Peregrine Falcon must surely visit the Black Mesa country occasionally, but I know of no valid record. I can't help giving special thought to these fine species partly because I've always loved them, partly because there is something about the mesa-top that keeps calling them to mind. Is this something merely the highness, the feeling of being in the sky, or is it the soul-comforting experience of looking down at things that we know are big but that appear to be little?

Is it this same something that accounts for the peculiar exhilaration I feel when I look *down* on a flying Golden Eagle? I recall observing one of the great birds thus, almost from this very spot. The eagle was carrying a prairie dog that it had caught in the low country. It moved gracefully, as always when in flight, but it was working hard; the load was heavy; there was no fancy maneuvering; the task of the moment was gaining altitude enough to make possible straight-away horizontal flight to the nest-cliff five miles away.

Another very special mesa bird crosses the mind, a bird that has not, so far as I know, been seen anywhere in this region except close to the mesa—the White-throated Swift. The species nests in the mountains of Colorado and New Mexico. Flying is so easy for it that whipping across into Oklahoma of a spring morning is no task at all; but it would no more dream of leaving the mesa than a trout would dream of leaving its brook. The mesa is part of the mountains and the mountains are the White-throated Swift's home.

Among the owls of the region the best known is certainly the Great Horned, a species which holds its own no matter how many roads and fences are built. Hereabouts it nests on ledges or in holes in the rock almost as frequently as in trees, and it is astonishingly common. A Long-eared Owl's nest that I found in 1937 was in a cottonwood along the Cimarron. How the Screech Owl manages to survive the fierce appetite of the Great Horn I do not know; I suspect that were it not for the abundance of kangaroo rats and other small mammals the Great Horns would have exterminated the Screech Owls long ago. The Burrowing Owl lives where there are prairie dogs as a rule. The Barred Owl, which is common in eastern Oklahoma, does not range westward quite to the eastern end of the panhandle. The Short-eared Owl and Barn Owl I have never seen in the Black Mesa country.

One further fact of a general nature enters my mind. Although the Cimarron flows all year it is only at times of high water that it becomes much of a river. The new impoundment in Black Mesa State Park, southeast of Kenton, is sizable. There are scattered farm ponds here and there, not to mention the springs. But this is not a region of water or of waterbirds. The list of ducks, geese, herons, and shorebirds that have been seen is a long one, but only a few of these, notably the Killdeer, are at all common or widely distributed.

I walked to the mesa's edge. Off to the southwest, a mile or so beyond the cottonwood-fringed Cimarron and several hundred feet below me, is Kenton, almost a ghost town really, a town laid out in 1892, long before statehood, and known in the wild early days as the Cowboy Capital. For thirty years Kenton has been one of my favorite towns. Not because of its restaurants or movie theaters or mineral springs. Heaven forbid! It has none of these. Not because of its elegant houses, gardens, and lawns. It has none of these. But because it has a quality not very closely related to fame or money or worldly success, a quality that must, for want of exactly the right word, be called spirit or character—a lingering of the force that put it there. A lingering spelled out by the faded but still legible letters CIMARRON COUNTY BANK on the front of a small frame building that totters at the west edge of town. A lingering that declares itself each spring when ragged old peach trees burst into bloom.

Just east of what remains of the bank building—I can see the details if I use my binoculars—is the slightly larger, two-story building that in the fall of 1932, the time of my first visit to Kenton, was called the Collins Hotel. I recall the pleasant hours my friend "JB" Semple and I spent there—afternoon hours of drawing, note-writing, and preparation of specimens in an up-stairs room; hours of good sleep; middle-of-the-night hours when, wakened by the brightness of the moon, I listened to the far-carrying *who, who-too, whoo, whoo* of a Great Horned Owl or to that most enchanting of wild music, the coyote chorus. I admit that I might not have this feeling of affection for Kenton had I not been well treated there. The lonely little filling station always provided us with gas. Mrs. Collins served excellent meals. Jimmy Springer, a spaniel we had with us, had a grand time playing with a goat whose abode was the ruins of an adobe house across the street. All this, for me, is Kenton—my Kenton.

I cannot look at the cottonwoods that almost hide the Cimarron without thinking of the Black-billed Magpies that live among them. Fifty years ago, if we are to believe those who studied the birdlife of this area in those days, there were no magpies here. In 1919 a few of them appeared. By the fall of 1932 they had become fairly common, but they were very local. John Semple and I may have shot the first specimens ever to be taken in the state. Today the species is common not only in the vicinity of Kenton but eastward at least as far as Boise City. Its home is the big cottonwoods. Rarely does it stray far from them. This means that it lives almost exclusively along the Cimarron, for it is near this river that the big cottonwoods grow. The cattlemen do not like the magpies; but I thrill every time I see one of the handsome birds flying from the grazing land toward the woods, and I get a special charge out of climbing to their huge, domed-over nests and counting the seven or eight or nine speckled eggs.

Thinking of magpies takes me back to the fall of 1952 when several graduate students and I made our annual 400-mile Thanksgiving pilgrimage from Norman to the Black Mesa. To our surprise we found the highway in the eastern part of the panhandle almost impassable because of snow. By the time we reached Kenton, we were ready to hole-up anywhere. No one in Kenton had room for us. Someone suggested that we try the Wiggins Ranch, north of town beyond the Cimarron, almost at the Black Mesa's foot. By dint of sincere pleading and a display of bacon and eggs we had with us, we prevailed upon Charlie Wiggins and his good wife to take us in. We spread our sleeping bags all over the floor. We skinned specimens on tables, chairs, even windowsills. We had the time of our lives. Especially delightful were the hundreds of Scaled Quail that poured down the slopes to feed about the sheds. They had a way of gathering under the farm machinery precisely as we had seen them gathering under cedars out in the "wild" places. A young Prairie Falcon did its best to catch one of them. The falcon must have been hungry; but try as it did, and it tried over and over, it could not catch one of the fleet-footed "cottontops." We could almost hear the quail laughing. They were so hearty and healthy that they looked positively jubilant as they raced from one shelter to another.

From where I now stand I can tell exactly where the Wiggins ranch house is, for the dirt road leading in from the gravel highway is easy to see. I change position a bit, hoping that the house will come into view, but it stays hidden behind the rocky hill down which the quail moved in such incredible numbers. My eye travels back to a small thicket east of the rocky hill. Yes, it was at that very spot that the two Roadrunners crossed the road just in front of the station wagon. All six of us saw the birds clearly, and all six of us had exactly the same idea: if we could surround the thicket quickly enough we might catch the birds in our hands! We jolted to a stop, piled out, and spent a full half-hour combing the haven of refuge, which could not have been more than forty yards long and twenty yards across. The wind had blown that particular spot free of snow so there was no whiteness against which we could see the birds. As things stood, we could not find them to save our souls. Had I not "lost" Roadrunners in just this way many a time, I might have continued to believe that we had trampled the poor birds to death. Poor birds, indeed; they probably observed the goings-on from a cozy spot halfway up the mesa-side!

Every road, every rock-topped hill, every patch of trees below me rouses memories. I feel like gloating over this wonderful land which has, in a very real sense, become my own, so I find a flat rock and sit down. Two miles west of Kenton is New Mexico. Not far from the road, among small hills just east of the state line, Poorwills nest. About a mile east of my rock is the confluence of the Cimarron and the North Carrizzo, a good-sized stream that flows down from Colorado. Among the big cottonwoods at the junction Red-shafted Flickers, Western Kingbirds, and Bullock's Orioles nest. Far to the southeast, off beyond the rough country, roll shortgrass plains on which Long-billed Curlews have survived in spite of grazing. The curlews are wonderful birds whatever they happen to be doing, but they are downright spectacular when, agitated because their eggs or young are in danger, they fly swiftly at one, squawking fiercely. The old Santa Fe Trail crosses the curlew breeding grounds. There is a trail-marker about halfway between Kenton and Boise City, the county seat of Cimarron County. The marker says not a word about curlews.

The road leading through Kenton is a thin, thin line—as seen from my rock. About three miles east of town it rises to a low pass and disappears among dark green cedars and pinyons. Here, even without leaving the car, I have seen some of this country's finest birds—Scrub Jays that are visible enough as they fly across the road but that disappear so completely when they dive into the thicket that the image of their vivid blueness mocks one; Brown Towhees that "squeak up" readily, perch atop a rock long enough to satisfy their curiosity, then flounce off; bustling companies of Common Bushtits whose insistence on staying together whatever the cost reminds one of a "cloud" of baby catfish moving along beneath their mother as if the whole lot of them were a single organism. Here may be seen at any season the Ladder-backed Woodpecker and Bewick's Wren, at migration time the Green-tailed Towhee and Townsend's Warbler, in winter the Golden-crowned Kinglet and an assortment of juncos.

The little pass has no name. It is a place I shall never forget, for on a quiet evening there in May, 1937, while I was north of the road watching a Cañon Wren, a black dust storm caught me and I was obliged to make my way back to the car under circumstances indescribably terrifying.

Beyond the pass the pale thread of road becomes visible again as it dips into and crosses the valley of the Texakeet (spelled variously: Tesesquite or Tequesquite may be correct) a northward-

flowing tributary of the Cimarron. This valley, and the brush-lined canyons that lead up from it into the cedar- and pinyon-studded high country, are a wonderful birding ground. In the valley itself lives the Curve-billed Thrasher, a fine singer which nests exclusively in the cholla and which moves into the oak scrub in severe winter weather, and the Black-throated Sparrow which, like the Cassin's Sparrow, has fluctuated greatly in numbers during the period of my observations. Other species that regularly nest in the cholla are the Brown Towhee, House Finch, and Mockingbird. Among the pinyons and cedars on the higher lands are to be found Piñon Jays, Plain Titmice, and, in winter, Mountain Chickadees. The flocks of Piñon Jays are sometimes so dense that while feeding on the ground they look like grayish blue carpets. Anywhere in this valley, and at any time of year, one may hear the croak of a Common Raven, but the species is not common. Neither the White-necked Raven nor the Common Crow is an inhabitant of this country; the former breeds in the flat farming land east of the curlew breeding ground, and I have heard Common Crows cawing among the cottonwoods along the Cimarron River north of Boise City, but neither species is at all common near Kenton.

There is a surprising eastern element in the Texakeet Valley's birdlife—such species as the Red-bellied Woodpecker, Blue-gray

Gnatcatcher, Eastern Bluebird, and Eastern Phoebe. None of these is common. Whenever a thoughtful bird student sees one of them he is sure to wonder whether it is the Cimarron, with its narrow fringe of trees, that manages to tie this essentially western land to the east.

Several miles up the Texakeet, and reachable by an all-weather road, is the Laurance Regnier ranch-house. This, from the ornithologist's standpoint, is a sort of wonder spot. The stone dwelling, which is sheltered by trees and surrounded in summer by lawn-grass of extraordinary delicacy, seems to me to have changed not at all since the first time I saw it thirty years ago. Here, near the barns, I have seen great flocks of Evening Grosbeaks and Cassin's Finches feeding on the ground; here, in 1960-1961, a considerable population of Steller's Jays wintered; here I have seen in the snow the tracks of real wild Turkeys, birds that must have wandered in from the New Mexico mountains; here I have observed Lazuli Buntings, Western Tanagers, Black-headed Grosbeaks, and the only hummingbird I have ever seen in the whole region, a dull-colored individual, probably a Broad-tail.

A little canyon not far from the ranch house has a good spring at its head. On a cliff above this spring Golden Eagles recently nested; across from the eyrie, on an overhanging rock-face, a colony of Cliff Swallows nests. Below the eyrie live Cañon Wrens and Say's Phoebes. The spring attracts Piñon Jays and Scrub Jays at all seasons and in winter juncos, Townsend's Solitaires, Robins, occasionally a Hermit Thrush, Sage Thrasher, or flock of Bohemian Waxwings. I have noticed that all the birds which regularly eat cedar berries or hackberries seem to need quantities of water. When the big flocks of Piñon Jays whirl down for a drink or bath the little pools are ringed with blue.

Some of the juncos of this region are exceedingly difficult to identify as to species, even in the hand. Most of them seem to be the black-headed, brown-backed Oregon Juncos, but every large flock has in it a few Slate-colored Juncos and one always looks expectantly for the big, slightly paler-than-slate-gray White-winged Juncos whose tails flash a conspicuously large amount of white. For me, the prettiest of all of them is the Pink-sided Junco, a bird I continue to regard as a full species. Rarest of them here is the Gray-headed Junco. In large mixed flocks that I have studied carefully I have often seen all five of the forms just mentioned; but many adult female birds, as well as immature birds of both sexes, are hard to place—except as "juncos."

The part of the Texakeet Valley about which I have just written is not readily discernible from my rock at the Black Mesa's rim; all I can see clearly is the lower part, the part surrounding the Labrier ranch house. But how easily is the picture filled in by memories! Of the cave in which the students and I so often camped; of the big, soft-furred woodrats, whose rummaging amongst our belongings wakened us in the middle of the night; of the badger, whose acknowledgment of our presence between him and his den was so utterly arrogant; of the porcupine that groaned and whined loudly each time we spoke but that contented itself with small, plaintive sounds when we whispered; of the big, beautifully marked rattler, resting comfortably in the dapple of sun and shade beneath the cholla; of the pretty race-runner lizards; especially of the big, bushy-tailed squirrel that I saw on one occasion along a canyon rim above the Texakeet, at another time on the Black Mesa itself, but have never properly identified.

Suddenly my consciousness is flooded with realization that it is this element of the unexplained, the unexpected, the unknown, that gives this country so much of its charm. I never come here without feeling that something remarkable is about to happen. Every bird worthy of a second glance has me wondering. Every hole in the ground, every crevice in the rocks, every cavity in a tree may have in it a mammal that I have never seen. I recall a moment when, obliged to slip quickly around a rock to check identification of a bird, I had an unforgettable look at a bushy-tail woodrat (*Neotoma cinerea*), a species that may never, for all I know, have collected in Oklahoma. I saw it clearly and noticed especially the bushy tail, which seemed to fluff out for my special benefit just as the rat disappeared.

From my high rock I look for certain big cottonwoods that I know are near the low-water bridge eight miles east of Kenton. This time I have in mind the Cassin's Kingbirds, Yellow Warblers, and Blue Grosbeaks that have bred thereabouts regularly; the Western Wood Pewees, whose presence in early June has continued to baffle me, for I have never found a nest; the Bobwhites, whose habitat touches and perhaps even overlaps that of the

Scaled Quail in this particular spot; the Audubon's, Wilson's, and Virginia's Warblers, Clay-colored Sparrows, and Brewer's Blackbirds that I have seen here at migration time; and that unwanted by-product of the white man's civilization, the Starling, which has established itself firmly wherever there are woodpecker holes in the big trees.

Woodpeckers! Can I ever forget the Lewis' Woodpecker which the whole membership of the Oklahoma Ornithological Society observed among these very cottonwoods on May 13, 1961? Can I ever forget the glossy elegance, the quiet demeanor of the bird? This is another species whose status has changed. From 1920 to 1931 that veteran observer, R. C. Tate, saw it repeatedly in the vicinity of Kenton; but within recent years, perhaps because of the drought, it has been exceedingly rare.

The other woodpeckers of the Black Mesa country, aside from the already mentioned species, are the Hairy, Downy, Red-head, Yellow-shafted Flicker, and Yellow-bellied Sapsucker. The Hairy is of a montane race which has a very black "look" because the white spots on its wings are few and small. The Hairy is an especially interesting species in that it so clearly exemplifies the way in which the western element dominates the avifauna of this part of Oklahoma. The Hairy Woodpeckers which inhabit the cottonwoods along the Cimarron thirteen miles north of Boise City do not belong to the "black" race; they are of a much-spotted eastern race which has, in my opinion, moved westward by way of the tree-lined Cimarron. The Black Mesa bird is a montane form which, like the White-throated Swift, refuses to leave the mountains that are its home.

The vast panhandle plain separates the east from the west. So unacceptable is this treeless area as a habitat for most birds, whether they be eastern or western species, that it is a barrier between two great avian populations even as an ocean is a barrier between continents. The comparison is peculiarly apt. On a hot mid-summer day between Guymon and Boise City the mirage can be so convincing that the traveler must keep reminding himself that what lies ahead is land, land, ever more land—rather than an expanse of shining water.

# THE ARIZONA DESERT

## Gale Monson

*Gale Monson, born in 1912 in Munich, North Da-
kota, was brought up on a wheat farm in the Red River Valley of
the North. He graduated from North Dakota State University in
1934, moved to the Southwest that same year and, except for
service in Asia during World War II, remained there until 1962.*

*His various positions with the federal government took him to
all parts of the desert country and gave him unlimited opportunities to look for birds, a long-standing interest. He worked for the
Indian Service on the Papago Indian Reservation for one year; for
the Soil Conservation Service at Safford, Lowell, and Tucson, Arizona, and Gallup, New Mexico, for the next five; and since 1940
for the Fish and Wildlife Service.*

*As manager of the Havasu Lake National Wildlife Refuge
from 1946 to 1954 and the Kofa and Cabeza Prieta Game Refuges and Imperial National Wildlife Refuge from 1954 to 1962,
Gale Monson has introduced many an Easterner to the delights of
bird watching in the Southwest and helped many a bird finder add
new species to his life list.*

*I could not hold back a feeling of deep regret when Gale
Monson wrote me that he had been transferred to headquarters of
the Fish and Wildlife Service in Washington, D.C., even though
"still with the Branch of Refuges" as he hopefully stated. In my
mind he will always be associated with Arizona. With Allan R.*
304

*Phillips he authored the* Checklist of Arizona Birds *(1964). He prepared the chapter on that state for my* Guide to Bird Finding *(1953) and it was he to whom I immediately turned for something in this book about opportunities for bird watching in the Arizona desert. That this country and its birds mean much to him is clearly demonstrated here by the movingly intimate manner in which he writes.*

My bird-watching country is along the Mexican border of southwestern Arizona.

It is a big country, stretching from the Baboquivari Mountains to Yuma, from Casa Grande and Gila Bend to the boundary of Sonora. It encompasses the Papago Indian Reservation, the Organ Pipe Cactus National Monument, and the Cabeza Prieta Game Range. It is a land of creosote bush and giant cactus, ironwood and palo verde, mesquite and catclaw, mile upon mile of boundless desert vegetation. It is plain and mountain, sand and rock and lava. It is summer heat, always blue skies, dust devils and mirages, and above all it is space and time.

It is September, a morning in the San Cristobal Valley. Dawn is breaking over a cool desert. A full moon hangs in the west, Venus is blazing in the east, Canopus shines just over the southern horizon. It is still, not a bit of wind, not even an insect chirping. But far away the silence is broken by the musical call of a Le Conte's Thrasher, perched on the dead stub of a low mesquite. It is quickly answered by another, in the opposite direction. The two birds whistle to each other for a time; one even sings a little burst of nesting-season song. Suddenly sunlight floods the plain, and the thrashers drop to the ground to begin their day's feeding. Only a single bird species has been heard, none has been seen, but the desert setting of space and morning light has created unforgettable drama.

October. The summer rains have left desert vegetation along Sinita Wash in the Sierra Arida in excellent condition. Limoncillo decks the ground, lycium is in flower, brandegea and climbing milkweed run riotous over palo verdes and catclaws. In one clump of lycium I see three kinds of hummingbirds—Costa's, Rufous, and Anna's. In an adjacent ironwood are four Black-throated Gray Warblers and a bright male Townsend's Warbler.

November has come. It is a cool, breezy, sunny day, with wisps of icy cirrus far, far over the desert. I am birding in the forenoon along Santa Rosa Wash on the Papago Indian Reservation. What a pleasure to find a large mixed gathering of Brewer's and White-crowned Sparrows singing dreamily, lazily in the sun! Nearby, a pair of Cardinals whistle, and a Green-tailed Towhee mews.

December, and the desert today is a rare scene. Large white snowflakes are scudding in the wind, sticking wetly to creosote bushes and the ground. I'm approaching Redtail Tank, a charco waterhole dug by the Fish and Wildlife Service in the Growler Valley. The water is gray and windwhipped. On it ride five Common Goldeneyes, a fine drake and four hens. They fly off and up, circle the charco twice with whistling wings, then disappear into the snow. Am I in Arizona, or Alaska?

It is early January, a beautiful sun-drenched day on the west side of the Sierra Pinta. Birding up a white-sanded wash toward Heart Tank, a wash bordered with chuparosa, elephant tree, and jumping bean, I hear an astonishingly loud, ground squirrel-like call. It turns out to be the unique winter song of a Gray Vireo. Two Ash-throated Flycatchers leave the top of a tall ironwood. A little farther on I experience the matchless thrill of seeing a large desert bighorn ram run out of the wash, and I mark where he has browsed on brittle bush-flower buds.

Now it is February. Beneficent winter rains have transformed the Pinta Sands into a sea of flowers—white dune primroses, sand verbena, and spectacle pod. Feeding industriously under an open stand of jumping cholla cactus are at least half a thousand Brewer's Sparrows, dozens of Black-throated Sparrows and House Finches, and a small covey of Gambel's Quail. A superb Prairie Falcon appears from nowhere, scattering the bewildered birds in all directions without trying to catch any.

Late March, and I am in the lower part of Moristo Canyon at the west foot of Baboquivari Peak, well above the desert floor. I watch several Broad-billed Hummingbirds—those with the blue throats and red bills—feeding at the profuse flowers of desert-honeysuckle. A short distance away, in a group of live oaks, I see a Beardless Flycatcher and a couple of Bridled Titmice. Up a distant slope, Mexican Jays are noisily calling.

The season has advanced to April, late April. Fifteen-foot high green wands of ocotillo tipped with foot-long panicles of showy red decorate the slopes of a rocky hill near Monument 179 on the Mexican border. From the direction of Las Playas comes a low-flying flock of about fifty Lark Buntings, many of them males in full black-and-white breeding plumage, singing as they sweep up the hill to alight on the ocotillos. Can any picture be more charming? The birds seem unmindful of their forthcoming journey to the Great Plains.

May. The freshest southeast breeze imaginable is soughing through the giant palo verdes and mesquites at Monreal Oasis, just off the break between the Mohawk and Bryan Mountains. White-winged Doves are cooing in the early morning. My attention is drawn to a loud, round whistle, then a burst of rich song. My squeakings call up a pair of Pyrrhuloxias, the male especially handsome and literally quivering with excitement at my presence. This is the first time Pyrrhuloxias have been seen west of the edge of the Papago Indian Reservation, some forty miles eastward. Can the birds be extending their range? Time will tell.

Then it is early June, and I am at Menager's Dam near the Mexican line in the southwestern corner of the Papago Indian Reservation. Mesquites, many of them dead, border the five-acre pond back of the dam. A number of coal-bright Vermilion Flycatcher males are using the mesquites as sallying perches. Migration is not over by any means, for a Yellow-billed Cuckoo is heard and several Traill's and Western Flycatchers are found wherever there is much shade.

It is July, the time of year when organ pipe cactus fruits are ripe. Summer rains have not yet fallen, and plants are dry and leafless, even the pod-laden ironwoods. I am at Agua Dulce Spring, the only spring on the 880,000 acres of the Cabeza Prieta Game Range. White-winged Doves arrive at water after a spectacular, loud swoop from over the top of the Sierra Agua Dulce. Scanning the ridges for desert bighorns, I make out a flock of white birds flying over the mountains. My binoculars reveal them to be ten Wood Ibises, probably on a flight from Quitobaquito to the distant Colorado River.

In late August, I have made camp in evening with my compadres after a day of seeing no less than forty kinds of bird migrants on the desert. It is warm and muggy, but a full moon shines cool and clear in the twilight. More than fifty Lesser Nighthawks come past, one by one. Cactus Wrens chortle as they go to rest. A Poor-will calls distinctly and close at hand as we are falling asleep on our cots, and off in Davis Canyon, just audible, sounds the hooting of a Great Horned Owl. Later in the night, if we awaken, we can expect to hear Elf and Screech Owls as they forage in the desert trees along the wash.

Of such vignettes is birding in southwestern Arizona made, each a separately memorable experience, yet at the same time most certainly a thread in the fabric of the seasons and the years. To a stranger these bird-watching impressions are retained because the birds are new and therefore exciting. To the resident naturalist they are recalled time after time because they form the pieces of an entrancing mosaic continually falling into place yet never becoming fixed. To both tenderfoot and veteran they are called to retrospection out of the inimitable desert environment.

The desert of the Mexican border west from the Baboquivaris is so dry and thorny and lonely, so populated by forms like tarantula and scorpion and sidewinder, that it hardly presents a pleaseing prospect to the hopeful bird finder. But everywhere at all seasons there is much to be seen, and the first good look at such omnipresent birds as Gila Woodpecker, Verdin, or Phainopepla foreshadows much bird watching of unusual quality.

Good birding in southwestern Arizona is ofttimes associated with water. A well or charco or rock tank is a magnet that draws birds from all directions, be they migrants or residents. If a rarity is in the area, chances are it will be seen near water. Many of my most cherished records come from waters on the Cabeza Prieta Game Range: the Redtail and Jose Juan charcos, Papago and Charlie Bell Wells, Tule Well, Cabeza Prieta Tanks, and Heart and Eagle Tanks. On the Organ Pipe Cactus National Monument, Quitobaquito and Bates Well are well-known waters that have an unusual affinity for birds. And there are charcos (which are earthen dam tanks) scattered all over the entire Papago Indian Reservation, where the considerable body of water, known as Menager's Dam, is also found.

These are the places where waterbirds especially can be found, even such unlikely birds as Common Loons, Green Herons, Snowy Egrets, Canada Geese, Virginia Rails, and Ring-billed Gulls. Ducks and shorebirds are well-represented at the charcos and intermittent playas. But even away from water, these birds can sometimes be found. Once I saw three Cinnamon Teal along a wash at the north side of the Cabeza Prieta Mountains, in late August, miles from any water; when flushed, they flew off and disappeared without showing any disability. On another occasion, I found a tired and sleepy Willet out in the center of the Tule Desert, and more than once I have seen Spotted Sandpipers along dry washes. And I will not soon forget a Belted Kingfisher that Luther Goldman and I discovered along a wash bright with flowering palo verdes east of Tule Well in April.

The proximity of the area to the Gulf of California may sometimes be responsible for strange records. One morning in April, I saw an Osprey perched on the top of a dead palo verde along the east side of the Cabeza Prieta Mountains. And once in late September, on a fine afternoon with southerly breezes, some shiny specks high in the sky over Heart Tank turned out to be a flock of fifty-one White Pelicans milling slowly southward.

If you like to sit all day in the heat and watch for birds, no experience can be more choice than that of staying at a desert mountain waterhole from sunrise to sunset. Then your bird watching is lent unusual expectancy by the chances of seeing a rare bighorn sheep, or a coyote or gray fox or bobcat. The premier spectacle is that of doves—mainly White-wings with a few Mournings—that come in to drink. Generally they appear one by one, often in a single zooming swoop from over the mountain ridge above. They do not go in to drink directly, but instead perch on nearby bushes or cacti, or ocotillos and rocks, until it seems that every available perch is loaded with White-wings. Drinking water seems to be their least concern. Then one bird flies in to water. This triggers off all the rest, and they swarm in en masse, landing on one another's backs and even in the water in their frenzy. A swallow or two, and off they fly, leaving the waterhole deserted until new doves arrive.

In addition to the doves, there is a procession of other birds also coming to drink, or perhaps attracted by the general animation and noise at the waterhole. These include such residents as Turkey Vultures, Golden Eagles, Prairie Falcons, Sparrow Hawks, Gambel's Quail, Roadrunners, Costa's Hummingbirds, Gila and Ladder-backed Woodpeckers, Ash-throated Flycatchers, Say's Phoebes, Phainopeplas, Scott's and Bullock's Orioles, House Finches, and Black-throated Sparrows. If any migrants are in the area, they will show up—even in June and July, one is apt to see Western Kingbirds, Western Tanagers, Black-headed Grosbeaks, and Lesser Goldfinches.

A memorable feature of any waterhole vigil is the noontime. Then, with the sun beating relentlessly down and an up-canyon breeze coming off the desert flats below, bird activity has almost ceased. But now and then a White-wing will call, the heat and breeze and light imparting to the sound a peculiarly haunting and nostalgic quality.

One of the unexpected distinctions of bird watching in southwestern Arizona is that of the migrants that literally swarm in the desert trees and shrubbery along the washes and canyons, from late March to early June in the spring, and from August to early November in the fall. Many species of birds are included, mainly hummingbirds, Empidonax flycatchers, Western Wood Pewees, thrushes, vireos, wood warblers, Western Tanagers, Black-headed Grosbeaks, Lazuli Buntings, Green-tailed Towhees, and sparrows. Some warblers are especially common—Nashville, Orange-crowned, Yellow, Audubon's, Townsend's, Hermit, Black-throated Gray, MacGillivray's, and Wilson's. Every now and then there will be some rarity, or some bird that has arrived unusually early or is staying unusually late, yielding records of great interest to the serious bird student.

As with any wild area esteemed for its birding possibilities, one is inevitably drawn to wondering what this border area will be like in the future. Much of this southwestern Arizona country is essentially as it was before the advent of the white man, and it is so wild that it is still possible to camp in the realization that the nearest fellow human is thirty to forty miles away—something it is likely impossible to do anywhere else in these United States.

Undoubtedly there are going to be changes. But let us hope that for all forthcoming bird watchers and their fellow naturalists —for all American citizens—that they will be few and of such nature that the essential feeling of space and time and distance will always be there to savor, with all the interesting plants and insects and mammals—and birds.

# THE CHIRICAHUAS AND
# GUADALUPE CANYON

## Dale A. Zimmerman

*Some men live here and there, wherever their work takes them; others choose where they want to live and find a job there. Dale Zimmerman is in the latter category. Since his chief interest is in tropical birds, he decided to live in the Southwest, to be near Mexico. He now makes his home in Silver City, New Mexico, where he is professor of biology at Western New Mexico University.*

*Dale Allen Zimmerman was born in 1928 in Imlay City, Michigan. He spent his childhood in southeastern Michigan, graduated and received his master's and doctoral degrees from the University of Michigan. As far back as he can remember he has been interested in animals, particularly birds, and nature in general. Understanding parents, who encouraged him in his pursuits, became so involved themselves that today they are both active amateur ornithologists and conservationists. They continue the bird banding projects that Dale started in Michigan and his father is an enthusiastic bird photographer.*

*During his high school days Dale visited the Museum of Zoology at the University of Michigan where he became acquainted with George Sutton and the late Josselyn Van Tyne. Both had a profound influence on his work. As an undergraduate he spent all his spare time in the museum. Later, as a graduate student in the botany department, he had an office in the museum where he wrote*

312

his thesis. He believes that it is the only doctoral dissertation in botany ever written in the bird division of the museum.

After a winter of intensive study of Mexican birds with George Sutton, he made his first expedition to Mexico in the summer of 1949. This was his introduction to tropical birds. He has made many subsequent trips to that country including one 10,000-mile journey during which he studied and collected birds in nearly every state. He also spent two summers in East Africa, the only area he considers superior to our own Southwest as a place in which to live and study animal life.

His wife Marian, also a naturalist, has accompanied him on several expeditions including the recent one to Kenya in 1963. They both hope to return there to continue Dale's work on the distribution and ecology of East African birds.

This fortunate man says: "It is difficult for me to distinguish between my work and my hobbies . . . all deal directly with birds or other animals." They "are a way of life with me." Here he tells of his two favorite spots for birds in the Southwest, the Chiricahua Mountains and Guadalupe Canyon in southeastern Arizona.

To an ornithologist there always is something special about encountering rare birds in the field. Even though he may have seen them many times before, he looks forward to finding them again. This explains part of my attachment to southwestern New Mexico and southeastern Arizona, for here we have a greater share of rare and localized landbirds than most other sections of North America. Our overgrazed desert plains and sunbaked brown hills seem to support few bird species, but the desert mountain ranges with their cool, tree-lined canyons and moisture-retaining ravines are spots of bird concentration that are choice indeed.

There are many such places in the Santa Catalinas, the Santa Ritas, in the Animas and Peloncillos, and the Huachucas, all of which justly deserve their fame as birding localities. But of all our desert mountain ranges one surpasses all others in variety, accessibility of diverse habitats, and magnificence of scenery—the isolated Chiricahua Range, "Big Mountain" of the Apaches who not very long ago ruled these mountains and the surrounding country. Anyone who has lived here close to nature will readily understand why these early inhabitants were reluctant to relinquish their land to the invading white man and why they fought so fiercely to retain it. With its abundant wildlife, the ever-changing quality of the light, the often harsh but always picturesque scenery, there is no doubting the enchanting character of this country.

Looming abruptly upward, the Chiricahuas rise like a jagged island from a desert plateau, itself averaging 4,000 feet in elevation, to extremes just below the 10,000-foot mark on Fly and Chiricahua Peaks. Some forty miles from north to south and half that distance across, the range is not large, but by the virtue of its geographical position and its many distinct habitats, it harbors species characteristic of country much farther south.

Wholly isolated from their relatives in other mountain ranges, some unique forms have evolved here. From the Chiricahua area have been recorded 75 species of mammals, nearly as many reptiles and amphibians, and well over 200 birds, including a remarkable assemblage of rare avian forms comparable to that of the Lower Rio Grande Valley in Texas. Probably nowhere else in the Southwest can one so readily find so many rare birds with Mexican affinities. Still, some visitors return home disappointed, having come too early for the arrival of the enticing Mexican species. The best birding in our borderland canyons is not before late May. In a "late year" some summer residents do not appear until well into June.

Approaching the Chiricahuas from the east is always impressive—as much on one's second or third journey as on his first. From afar, with numerous lesser ranges in the foreground, the observer becomes aware of the bigness and blueness of the mountains—capped sometimes in winter by brilliant white. On days of summer storms, first one part, then another, of the upper reaches may be obscured by angry dark clouds and pelted by sheets of rain or hail, while down on the desert short-lived dust devils whirl violently through the hot creosote-bush and mesquite flats.

Not long after leaving the main highway north of Rodeo, the motorist will notice dark patches of juniper and pine on the still-distant mountain slopes. The biotic communities up there are vastly different from that just outside the car. The road climbs steadily, easily, alongside low hills clothed with weird ocotillos, sotols, and picturesque agaves. Nearer the road, thickets of mesquite and acacia alternate with open areas supporting scattered desert annuals. But the plants may receive scant attention as one nears the settlement of Portal with its backdrop of spectacular towering cliffs which flank the entrance to Cave Creek Canyon, one of the most inviting places in the Chiricahuas. Continuing up the canyon, the road winds between stands of large sycamores and Arizona walnuts, past a guest ranch or two, and into the Coronado National Forest with its secluded wooded campgrounds where all visitors seeking birds should spend a night or two if they can. Camping is pleasant but often cool (and bitter cold, with a record of 11 degrees below zero, in winter) as cold air drains into the steep-walled canyon from above.

With insufficient time to fully explore the mountains, or with but a day or so to devote to bird finding in the entire region, the visitor would do well to give top priority to Cave Creek Canyon. Likely as not, Painted Redstarts or a Sulphur-bellied Flycatcher will welcome him to the campgrounds. There, amid the pleasing aromas of juniper, pine, and sycamore—and perhaps of wood smoke and a pot of coffee—the camper can dine and retire with the chirping of Elf Owls above him, and hear from nearby slopes the pleasantly monotonous notes of Poor-wills, Whip-poor-wills, and Whiskered Owls. He may awake, as I have, to the drumming of Arizona Woodpeckers or the penetrating, throaty calls of a Coppery-tailed Trogon right in camp—a sound as exhilarating to me now as the voice of my first trogon in southwestern Mexico a dozen years ago. By breakfast time the ubiquitous Mexican Jays steal silently through the cypresses toward your table, awaiting opportunity to procure some tasty morsel. If discovered or startled they retreat temporarily amid great corvine pandemonium, followed by an odd stillness as their alarm notes quiet the other species.

By late May, families of Bridled Titmice will be foraging among the sycamores and oaks, and the plaintive *peeur* of nesting Olivaceous Flycatchers will be heard all around. Any bright red article hung in the sunlight will sooner or later lure an inquisitive Blue-throated or Black-chinned Hummingbird to your campsite. These birds, the beautiful Rivoli's Hummingbird and even the rare Violet-crown, may often be studied at close range about the feeders maintained by the American Museum's Southwestern Research Station farther up the road.

By arising early and driving to the country below Portal, the visitor can enjoy the desert at its best in the pre-dawn hours when terrestrial creatures are about and, a bit later, during the birds' singing period which here is largely restricted to the hours before the sun rises. If one heard nothing more than the Roadrunner's odd cooing song, or the more melodious one of Bendire's Thrasher, it would nevertheless be worth the trip.

Morning comes early on the desert, but it takes a long time for the sun's warmth to penetrate deeply into Cave Creek Canyon. Thus, by the time desert activity is waning, one can still enjoy the morning flurry of activity in the riparian growth between Portal and the campgrounds, up the South Fork Trail, or along the road to the Research Station. If he wishes, he can by noon drive beyond this point through stands of juniper, pinyon, and oak, through forests of ponderosa pine with wild Turkeys and Coues' Flycatchers, to the conifers and aspen groves near the summit of the trail, having encountered with ordinary luck Mexican Chickadees, Mexican Juncos, Olive and Red-faced Warblers, Hutton's Vireos, and many more. He will have ascended through a fascinating, almost bewildering, array of floristic and faunistic zones from desert grassland with Black-throated and Cassin's Sparrows to Douglas firs, white firs, Evening Grosbeaks, and crossbills.

A luxury to be enjoyed in the Chiricahuas on hot, drowsy afternoons is a long, refreshing nap. One is easily lulled into slumber by the humming of cicadas and the melancholy calls of Olivaceous Flycatchers, symbols, to me, of many a hot Mexican afternoon. One does well to rest when the temperature rises and avian activity reaches a low ebb. This leaves him refreshed rather than exhausted at nightfall, and no naturalist visiting the Chiricahuas should miss spending at least one night afield. The nocturnal work carries with it both fascination and frustration; we know so very little about the lives of the many creatures that spend their daylight hours hidden away in dense foliage, in caves and crevices, or below the ground.

My favorite time of day in Cave Creek Canyon is dusk. Darkness comes with astonishing speed deep in the canyon. Hardly have the last reflections of sunlight disappeared from the cave-studded upper cliffs when the Whip-poor-wills begin calling and the flycatchers quiet down for the night. While it is still light a Spotted Owl may stir in some dark side canyon and become vocal, hesitantly at first as if half afraid of attracting a flock of pestiferous jays. Well before darkness sets in, the evening's first bats appear— dainty western pipistrels with their slow, almost butterfly-like flight. If you stand close by a streambed waterhole about 7:15 on any June evening you can watch these lovely, soft-furred creatures skim low over the water and thirstily drink—little more than an arm's length away. Later, you may even glimpse the large hoary bats which are fairly common here. By nine o'clock bats of nineteen species will be winging overhead in the darkness. Without a mist net to capture them as they swoop in to drink you'll not identify many, but you may be certain that flying somewhere about will be several rare Mexican forms which, like many birds, here are at their northern limits. There are strange, long-nosed bats with incredibly elongated, brush-tipped tongues for probing flower corollas. Their heads, like the crowns and throats of hummingbirds in this area, may be yellow with the sticky pollen of the century plants. There is the huge mastif bat, *Eumops,* whose high-pitched,

pulsating chipping—accelerating rapidly as the animal nears water
—may be heard by the wondering listener straining for owl voices.
The bat's presence may be revealed by its audible flight. When
*Eumops* streaks by, it sounds like the rush of air through a falcon's
pinions. Fortunate indeed is the person who actually sees this giant
bat of our southwestern border country.

There is no shortage of terrestrial mammals either. By driving
slowly along the trails, mule deer and porcupines should be seen
nightly. Skunks and raccoons are rather common, and the lucky
visitor may see a coati-mundi or catch a glimpse of a bobcat
pursuing a desert cottontail across the road. At lower elevations
one readily finds the tiny silky pocket mouse, three kinds of kangaroo rats, and various other rodents, all deserving of more attention
than most amateur naturalists pay them.

Reptiles are about at night too. With great luck you may encounter a Gila monster, interesting and perfectly harmless unless
you molest him, which is contrary to Arizona law. Normally you'll
see few snakes, and most of those will be harmless. Just don't
forget that there are rattlesnakes about, that some are as thick as
your arm, and that they may not always buzz before striking.
Remember too that you can encounter rattlers in Rustler Park as
easily as on the desert. They are not easy to spot in the dense
vegetation. In this country it is foolhardy to venture off the trails at
night without proper footgear, and anyone exploring at night without a good light is taking an unnecessary risk.

If night birds call at all one will surely hear Whiskered Owls,
more common than Screech Owls along Cave Creek. The strange
chatter of Elf Owls can be heard almost anywhere along the road
or streambed where hollow sycamores and oaks provide nest sites.
In the higher country, the low mellow hoots of Flammulated Owls
can be heard by the patient listener, though viewing the vocalist
may be another matter entirely. Rarely, the notes of these tiny
owls drift down from some high, pine-covered slope into the South
Fork of Cave Creek Canyon—a good place for Spotted Owls. Do
not feel discouraged if you cannot satisfactorily identify all the owl
voices you hear, and do not be surprised if the calls coming from
the darkness around you fail to resemble those on your phonograph records. All of the southwestern owls are more versatile
vocalists than the books would have you believe.

Should one linger in the Chiricahuas for several weeks, he is likely to uncover one or more of the unpredictable, yet irregularly-occurring, birds. Some species occur so rarely in certain years as to be all but impossible to find. One may visit these mountains half a dozen times without finding the elusive Buff-breasted Flycatcher, perhaps a dozen times before encountering Harlequin Quail. In some years trogons are found readily but in others they seem to be absent. And there always is a chance of turning up some exciting accidental or casual species such as the White-eared Hummingbird.

Part of the enjoyment in repeatedly visiting the isolated Chiricahuas is the uncertainty of what to expect. One week's work, one entire season's work, can be misleading. In another year things may be quite different, but seldom is a visit to these mountains disappointing.

Of the many fine southwestern birding localities a place astride the Mexican border called Guadalupe Canyon has attracted more attention in recent years than any other. In all our low, arid country Guadalupe Canyon is ornithologically unique. It is the only place north of Mexico where that mystery bird, Ridgway's Whip-poor-will, is known to occur; it is one of the two United States localities with breeding Thick-billed Kingbirds, and it remains the only area north of the border where the Violet-crowned Hummingbird is known to nest (although this species almost certainly breeds in the Chiricahuas where it has been seen regularly for several years).

Hidden away at the end of a dusty, partly one-lane road that in places coincides with a boulder-strewn streambed, more than thirty long miles from the nearest town—Douglas, Arizona—Guadalupe Canyon has received little publicity until the past decade. It is not a scenic canyon; it is not even deep. Remote, uncomfortable, and sometimes dangerous, it is not a place for the casual, binocular-toting visitor driving a late-model car. It is so narrow that avoiding a flash flood would be difficult. There are no campgrounds, picnic areas, or other facilities (the canyon is privately owned), and usually there is no water. In summer, the best time for birds, the heat can be overpowering. The breeze that blows up the canyon is hot and desiccating, and after mid-morning the rocky, juniper- and mesquite-dotted canyon walls seem to lack substance behind the curtain of shimmering heat waves. The grotesque xeric plants—sotols, ocotillos, and agaves—that spill over the canyon rim from the extensive desert above reflect the severe environment. But along the dry streambed in the canyon bottom is a narrow fringe of hackberry, oak, and sycamore, flanked by a broader, bright-green band of mesquite. Down there, in the only such oasis for miles, nesting birds congregate in surprising numbers. Not only are there many individuals; there is an astonishing number of species. During June, 1962, Russell Mumford and I found no fewer than seventy-two species in the New Mexican portion of the canyon below the Johnson Ranch, a strip only two miles long.

Even during the warmest hours one can usually hear an occasional Lucy's Warbler song, *tsips* from innumerable Verdins, and the chatter of Bridled Titmice. One is not in the canyon long before encountering hummingbirds, of which female Black-chins and male Broad-bills are most numerous. Both Broad-billed and Violet-crowned Hummers are more likely to be seen perched conspicuously on a dead branch than feeding among flowers. The Violet-crown, at least in some years, does not arrive in the canyon until the second week of June. We don't yet know if it is with us every year. Certainly its numbers fluctuate greatly.

Phainopeplas probably are the most abundant birds in the canyon. Early in the morning I have counted as many as thirty of these handsome silky flycatchers in the air at one time. Almost as conspicuous, though far less numerous, are the Hooded Orioles that share their nest trees with the abundant White-winged Doves. The calling of these birds and the various tyrant flycatchers imparts a decided Mexican ring to the canyon.

As in Mexico, flycatchers are common here in summer. Ten species are known to nest—probaby a record for such a small area. Here the limited habitat forces them to live very near one another, permitting helpful comparison of the "difficult" species. There are, for example, three breeding species of *Myiarchus*—the Olivaceous, Ash-throated, and Wied's Crested Flycatchers, all of which nest in hollow sycamore branches, sometimes in adjacent trees. The tiny Beardless Flycatcher occurs here regularly, and in some years we have found three kinds of kingbirds nesting practically side by side. Of these, Cassin's is most common, the Western

is rare, and the Thick-billed varies from fairly common to rare depending upon the year. Possibly the Tropical Kingbird occurs here at times, too, for non-breeding tyrannids like the Sulphur-bellied Flycatcher occasionally visit Guadalupe Canyon. However, the nearest place where I have found Tropical Kingbirds on our side of the border is near Patagonia, a delightful little place northeast of Nogales where giant cottonwoods and sycamores annually provide nest-sites for a few pairs of Rose-throated Becards, Black Hawks, and Gray Hawks, species not likely to be seen in Guadalupe Canyon or the Chiricahuas.

Patagonia is worth a visit for other unusual birds. Occasionally a Green Kingfisher or Varied Bunting may be seen there. It is the only Arizona locality other than Guadalupe Canyon that can claim the Thick-billed Kingbird as a breeding species; since 1961 one or more pairs have nested in trees by the highway south of town.

If Thick-bills are present in Guadalupe Canyon they are not likely to be overlooked. Although they feed to some extent up among the mesquites and junipers, they spend most of their time flycatching from dead branches atop the sycamores. They bicker noisily among themselves, thus attracting one's attention. Their notes are so distinct from those of the other kingbirds (with which they behave amicably) that there is no mistaking them.

Vermilion Flycatchers, Western Wood Pewees, Summer Tanagers, and Bell's Vireos are among the common birds of the canyon. Every good-sized thicket has its pair of the little vireos, but unless you know the song or are good at "squeaking" you won't see one. Occasionally, by exploring side canyons where there is more juniper growth, one can find the much rarer Gray Vireo.

Another interesting summer resident is the handsome Bronzed Cowbird. The males with their cherry-red eyes are a delight to see near at hand, especially when they display their extended neck ruffs and their iridescent plumage shines in the sunlight. Endeavoring to attract the females' attention, they repeatedly hop up and down on the ground, executing some surprisingly high jumps.

The evening hours in the canyon, as anywhere in our desert mountains, are among the most enjoyable. The temperature moderates, the colors deepen, and birds again become active. Nothing is more soul-satisfying than to sit alone on some ridge overlooking the green canyon, watching the progression of nearly indescribable colors on the cliffs and in the sky, and listening as the diurnal birds, one by one, become still.

About the time that the flycatchers noisily terminate their day, Common Nighthawks *peent* in the distance, and Poor-wills begin calling from rocky slopes on all sides. A Lesser Nighthawk may glide silently by, close to the ground, and quickly disappear into the canyon heading for a waterhole. This is the time when we remain most alert, carefully listening for the peculiar waterthrush-like song of Ridgway's Whip-poor-will. About Poor-will time, and erratically throughout the night, this rare bird sings from high up on the juniper-clad canyon sides or in brushy arroyos. Only the most painstaking, determined searching will yield a glimpse of a calling bird. He usually sings from just beyond reach of your head-lamp beam, and ceases altogether as you take another step or two, only to resume from another perch in another ravine in another part of the canyon. Customarily, on the infrequent occasions when it is found, the birds call for a few minutes at dusk, not resuming until late at night. Ridgway's Whip-poor-wills that I have heard in Mexico are not so finicky about their hours; sometimes they sing almost incessantly from sundown until far into the night. Perhaps as with so many other birds, individuals at the extreme edge of the species' range behave atypically.

Several things can sound like Ridgway's Whip-poor-wills to the eager listener—some crepuscular notes of Wied's Crested Fly-catcher, for example, and certain calls of the Elf Owl. Guadalupe's Mockingbirds are not above mimicking the nightjar. This, together with the Mocker's habit of night singing, can mislead a careless listener. More people have left Guadalupe Canyon thinking they have heard Ridgway's Whip-poor-will than have actually done so. To add the bird to your list on this side of the border takes a bit of climbing, sharp ears, watchful eyes, perseverance—and luck.

Elf Owls and Screech Owls are common in Guadalupe Canyon, but the Whiskered Owl does not occur. There are no large owls other than the Great Horned. Yet a night's owling is not without excitement when one's "squeaking"—a popular owl lure —is as likely to bring up a bobcat or gray fox as an owl. If the wind is right, they may come to within fifteen feet of an observer with a sufficiently enticing squeak. It is satisfying to visit a place like this, outside a refuge or national park, where one can be almost assured of seeing a fox or bobcat, where the dust of the trail may still reveal the tracks of a mountain lion, where on nearly any night you can approach a band of collared peccaries on foot and watch the animals continue feeding, unafraid, or merely walk slowly away. In this remote canyon a wandering *lobo* wolf or a jaguar is still a possibility. We wonder, though, how long it will remain so.

We think of Guadalupe Canyon first in terms of its rare birds. We know that an old Rose-throated Becard nest has been found there, but no ornithologist has yet seen a Becard in the canyon. We anticipate seeing the Thick-billed Kingbirds and Violet-crowned Hummers, and we wonder if our next trip might reveal an Aplomado Falcon, for one was seen near the canyon not long ago. We think of all the accidental Mexican birds that have appeared on our side of the border in Arizona and New Mexico and know that in time others will occur. It is great fun looking for them, and this little canyon is one of the most likely places.

But even aside from its rarities, Guadalupe Canyon is stimulating. Small birds are abundant and relatively fearless, thanks to little association with man. Here we can often see a Golden Eagle flapping heavily overhead, perhaps to alight on some rock jutting out from the canyon wall. In too many places the sight of even a distant soaring eagle is now almost a thing of the past. Here in Guadalupe coyotes howl lustily at night, and bobcats and gray foxes still hunt by day. We have far too few such places. Let all those who seek birds in Guadalupe Canyon treat it with respect. It is a limited area whose vegetation, already damaged by careless burning and misguided grazing, and unique wildlife values could be destroyed almost overnight. Once gone these things cannot be replaced during our, or our children's, lifetimes.

# BIG BEND NATIONAL PARK

## R. Dudley Ross *

Texas. The very name is synonymous with bigness. It conjures up visions of cactus and rattlesnakes, cowboys and cattle, enormous expanses of flat country, and a breed of giant supermen. In truth, Texas has all these—nearly all—and to the bird watcher much more. It has a list of birds larger than that of any other state. This is due partly to its immense area and partly to its fortuitous location: Texas is on a major flyway where east meets west ornithologically, and it has a southern border across which Mexican birds, unhampered by political boundaries, cross into the United States.

As if all this were not enough, Texas has Big Bend National Park, one of the loneliest and most remote of all our national parks. With an area of slightly over 1,100 square miles, Big Bend ranks sixth in size among the twenty-six national parks in continental United States. In spite of its enormous size—only slightly smaller than Yosemite—Big Bend is among the least known of all the parks, even to Texans. Comparatively few Texans are aware of Big Bend and fewer still have ever visited it.

To those who think of Texas as a vast plain, Big Bend is a revelation. Its landscape is a combination of desert and mountains with several peaks ranging up to between 7,000 and 8,000 feet. The Chisos Mountains, near the center of the park, although not

* For a biographical sketch, see his chapter, "Olympic National Park."

high as our western mountains go, rise sharply from the plains and stand out in bold relief against the sky—a rugged profile completely in harmony with this strange wild region. It is easy in the Big Bend to imagine yourself in a foreign land. Indeed, if the Rio Grande had followed a straight eastward course instead of looping south and forming the "big bend" from which the park receives its name, this entire region might still be a part of Mexico.

Two roads lead southward from US Route 90 to the park, one from the town of Alpine and the other from Marathon. There is little choice between them except that the one from Marathon traverses more of the park area. People approaching from the east usually take the road from Marathon. The road from Alpine is slightly more direct for people arriving from the west.

Heading south from Marathon on US Route 385 you travel through semi-arid plains with distant mountains on both the east and west. Bird watching is always good on these plains. The cardinal-like Pyrrhuloxia with its parrot bill is not uncommon, nor is the White-necked Raven. Black-throated Sparrows are abundant and Scaled Quail are frequently seen as they scoot along, looking for all the world like little mechanical toys. Bell's Vireos and Cactus Wrens can be both heard and seen. The Bell's Vireo's staccato song is distinctive, if not particularly musical, and the *chug-chug* of the wren is arresting because it is so "unbird-like." Other species usually to be noted along this road are the Swainson's Hawk, Loggerhead Shrike, and that "personality plus" bird, the Roadrunner.

Some forty miles south of Marathon, you pass through Persimmon Gap, cross the park boundary, and have, for the first time, a view of the Chisos Mountains which is certain to stir your blood and is a compelling invitation to explore the mysterious land beyond.

As you cross Dagger Flat, you will see the typical desert vegetation—mesquite, cholla cactus, lechuguilla, sotol, and various kinds of yuccas. If the trip is in March or April, the Spanish dagger and other yuccas will be in bloom. In June the agave, or century plant, will be at its best. Even a half dozen drops of rain will fill the air with the easily recognized fragrance of the ever-present creosote bush which bears a profusion of yellow blossoms amid tiny green leaves that are waxy in appearance.

About twenty-nine miles from Persimmon Gap, you arrive at Panther Junction and park headquarters where it is possible to obtain literature and information concerning park activities. A turn to the west at this point brings you, in three miles, to Basin Junction and the beginning of the spectacular, seven-mile drive to the Basin.

From Basin Junction a twisting road ascends steadily for nearly six miles, leaving the desert behind and boring its way into the mountains, with their cover of oaks, alligator juniper, pinyon pine, Arizona cypress, and, at the higher elevations, ponderosa pine and Douglas fir—two evergreens usually associated with more northerly climes. The road goes up through Green Gulch to Panther Pass (elevation nearly 6,000 feet) and then descends into the Basin.

Suddenly, at the pass, the Basin is before you, a natural amphitheater surrounded by towering peaks with the highest, the massive Casa Grande, dominating them all. The Basin is the heart of the Chisos and the real center of activity in the park, with wooden cabins, stone cottages, and new motel units as well as a grocery store, dining room, post office, telephones, and saddle horses.

From May to September, night temperatures in the Basin are pleasant, perhaps as low as 60 degrees; in the daytime the temperature is usually in the mid-80's. In the lower areas of the park, especially near the Rio Grande, daytime temperatures are in the middle and upper 90's, sometimes higher. During the winter, the range is from the mid-60's down to about 40 with occasional nights when the temperature is at or below freezing. Once in awhile there is snow in the Basin.

Plantlife in the park is remarkably varied and certain to attract your attention in the flowering season. From mid-March until late August or early September comes a succession of blooms, starting with the cacti and yuccas and ending with the plants of the semi-arid areas which, depending on the rainfall, will flower from July through August and into September. The Spanish dagger usually blossoms late in April and the century plants in June. Over 1,100 plants have thus far been identified in the park.

When we first visited Big Bend, we didn't know quite what to expect. There were three of us, my wife Vivian, our very good friend, Ruth Emery, of the staff of the Massachusetts Audubon

Society, and myself. Naturally, we had Roger Peterson's *Field Guide to Western Birds* and, as is invariably our custom when birding in new regions, Sewall Pettingill's *Bird Finding West of the Mississippi*. We knew the important birds to look for, we knew what they looked like, and we knew where to go to see them, but neither book told us how to ride horseback!

First of all, we wanted to see Big Bend's own bird, the rare Colima Warbler, which is known to nest in the United States in only one place—at Boot Spring on the side of Mt. Emory above the Basin. Before leaving home I had blithely arranged for horses for the three of us and a guide to show us the way to Boot Spring. I knew that none of us had ever been on a horse before, but Boot Spring was, after all, only a twelve-mile round trip. There should be no problem.

On our first morning in the park the horses and guide were waiting. We started off gaily. It was late May and the day was fairly warm; the trail was steep and dusty; and the horses which may not have been fed that morning stopped to nibble every few minutes and were very reluctant to get moving again. Then came the switchbacks—many of them. At one moment the mountain sloped sharply away to the left of the trail; instants later it dropped abruptly from the other side. Our main problem was not how to stay on the horse but rather to try to decide from which side it would be safer to fall off.

After about two miles our guide considerately stopped at Juniper Flat where we dismounted and walked about so that our blood could circulate again. When we were able to look for birds, we found Rufous-crowned Sparrows, Cañon and Rock Wrens, Brown (Canyon) Towhees, and our first Black-crested Titmice. This last was a new bird for all of us. We also saw the alligator juniper with its peculiar cross-hatched bark and the rare drooping juniper (sometimes called "weeping juniper") flourishing here in the extreme northern part of its range.

With renewed courage we pressed on, ever upward, crossed the saddle of Mt. Emory at the highest point in the Chisos—nearly 8,000 feet—and proceeded down the other side. This, we learned, was worse than going uphill. We struggled desperately to keep from falling forward, right over the front end of the horse. To our relief, we soon came in sight of the "boot"—a large rock formation resembling a riding boot upside down. In a few minutes, we were at Boot Spring.

Before we were off the horses, we heard a Colima Warbler singing, but it took us some time and a bit of chasing before we saw it. Resembling an oversized Virginia's Warbler, the Colima is not really striking. Later we had satisfactory views of a pair of Colimas and heard several others singing. We had found what we had come so far—and so painfully—to see. There have been people, luckier than ourselves, who have found the species only a mile or two after leaving the Basin.

At Boot Spring we also saw more Black-crested Titmice, the Mexican Jay, Black-chinned Hummingbird, Rufous-sided Towhee, Brown (Canyon) Towhee, and Lesser Goldfinch. Overhead the White-throated Swifts dashed wildly about, calling incessantly and excitedly, and giving the impression of urgent and frantic haste.

All too soon we were "back in the saddle again" to face the return trip. As we passed our cottages on the way to the corral, Vivian and Ruth dismounted. Our guide thereupon dismissed the two riderless horses with encouraging whacks on their respective rumps and they were off, like the proverbial bat, for home and oats. My horse, determined not to be left behind, followed full-speed, and there was nothing I could do to stop him. To say that my horse and I went back together would be sheer fabrication. There were times when we were close together and too close, and there were moments when I was positive we would never meet again. I haven't the slightest idea how I managed, but by some miracle the horse and I stayed together for the last 200 yards to the corral. In retrospect, I believe it would have been easier had we hiked to Boot Spring.

From the Basin there are two trips on paved roads to the lowlands bordering the Rio Grande. Probably the more popular is the forty-mile drive to Santa Elena Canyon in the southwestern part of the park. This is easily the most awesome of the three canyons in the Big Bend. Its sheer walls rise for more than 1,500 feet above the river. Though the Rio Grande is usually a placid, muddy stream at this point, one has only to see the rushing waters at flood times to understand how, through the centuries, the river has cut this imposing chasm out of the limestone bed. You should make this trip in the early morning because at mid-day, at an elevation of only 1,500 feet, it is likely to be quite warm—except, of course, in winter. Anyone wishing to use a camera should also visit Santa Elena in the morning when the sun from the east floods the mouth of the canyon with flattering light.

In the low areas, near the Rio Grande, mesquite and cottonwood are the principal trees, plus willow, tree tobacco, and buttonbush. While birds are rather scarce, you can probably find the Black Phoebe, White-throated Swift, Verdin, Cañon Wren, Bell's Vireo, Yellow-breasted Chat, and House Finch.

In the southeastern part of the park, about thirty miles from the Basin, the Rio Grande has carved a beautiful gorge, Boquillas Canyon, for twenty-five miles through the Sierra del Carmen. In the late afternoon the last rays of the sun accentuate the vivid red of these mountains.

In this area there are several places of interest to the bird watcher—the thickets along Tornillo Creek, especially where it flows into the Rio Grande; the trails along the Rio's edge in both directions from the mouth of the creek; and the region around Rio Grande Village.

By exploring these places, preferably in the cool of the morning, you should turn up a fine variety of birds including the Zone-tailed Hawk, Black Hawk, Scaled Quail, White-winged Dove, Inca Dove, Roadrunner, Black-chinned, Blue-throated, and Broad-billed Hummingbirds, Ladder-backed Woodpecker, Ash-throated Flycatcher, Black Phoebe, Say's Phoebe, Vermilion Flycatcher, Verdin, Cañon and Rock Wrens, Curve-billed and Crissal Thrashers, Black-tailed Gnatcatcher, Bell's Vireo, Orchard and Scott's Orioles, Summer Tanager, Cardinal, Pyrrhuloxia, Blue Grosbeak, Painted Bunting, and Black-throated Sparrow. The Varied Bunting, rather rare and local in this country, has been seen several times in the vicinity of Rio Grande Village and Hot Springs but we have never been fortunate enough to find it here.

The Rio Grande at Boquillas Canyon, as at Santa Elena Canyon, is edged with mesquite, willow, cottonwood, and tree tobacco. Along Tornillo Creek, in addition to both honey and screwbean mesquite, desert willow and buckthorn occur. The nearby slopes have many desert plants such as prickly-pear cactus, catclaw, agave, and creosote bush.

From the Basin there are three worthwhile trips—to Lost Mine Ridge, the "Window," and the South Rim. Lost Mine Trail is a self-guiding foot trail to Lost Mine Ridge, a round trip of four miles requiring about three hours. The magnificent view from the top of the Ridge is unforgettable. You can hike or ride horseback to the Window—a gap in the mountains in one side of the Basin— that affords a fine vista of the plains below. The trip to the South Rim takes all day, on foot or horseback, through some of the most spectacular scenery in the park. From the South Rim there is a broad panorama of Texas and Mexico with the Rio Grande marking the boundary between.

In addition to the Colima Warbler there are two other bird species in the Big Bend that are rarely seen elsewhere in the United States. One is the Aplomado Falcon, between the Peregrine Falcon and Sparrow Hawk in size but distinctively marked. Though never common in this country and now extremely rare, it is still seen occasionally along the South Rim. The other, and a more likely possibility, is the diminutive Lucifer Hummingbird whose preferred food plant is the June-blooming agave.

During our most recent visit to Big Bend my wife and I made a special effort to find this mite of a bird. We consulted with the park superintendent, Henry Schmidt, who was familiar with it. He welcomed us warmly and invited us to inspect his garden where he had seen the Lucifer on several occasions as early as mid-May and where he was sure it had once nested. We spent some time in his garden that afternoon and two hours the following morning. The only hummingbird we saw was the Black-chinned.

Then we headed for a nearby trailer camp occupied by park personnel where, Mrs. Schmidt told us, the bird was sometimes seen. As we approached the trailers, we noticed a thriving growth of tree tobacco (*Nicotiana glauca*) covered with its tubular yellow flowers. This shrub, native to South America, is now found in suitable situations in this country from Texas to California. Always, wherever it grows, it draws hummingbirds like a magnet. Aware of this we tarried awhile. Sure enough, after about ten minutes, a hummer flew in and commenced to feed. We noted its decurved bill, its rusty flanks, and purple throat. It was a perfectly-plumaged male Lucifer. After methodically probing the flowers for a time, he left. Moments later a female appeared and then a male again.

In spite of the fact that the latest *A.O.U. Check-List* states that Lucifer Hummingbirds range "casually north in summer to Chisos Mountains, Texas (several records)," there is the very interesting possibility that it may nest fairly regularly in Big Bend although probably in very small numbers. This may well be the explanation of its appearance in the Basin in May. To verify its nesting beyond any doubt would be a great achievement for someone because it is not every year that a new breeding species can be added to our North American bird roster. (While I was writing this article, my friend, Warren Pulich of Irving, Texas, found a nest of the Lucifer Hummingbird in Big Bend National Park and the first ever recorded in the United States. The news of this discovery was announced in *The Auk* for July, 1963.)

For some reason we have never seen many mammals in Big Bend. It may be because there is plenty of space in this wilderness for them to avoid man. We had no trouble seeing the black-tailed jackrabbit with its enormous ears, and the white-tailed and mule deer. We also watched the attractive little white-tailed antelope squirrel, the grayish rock squirrel, and the spotted ground squirrel. However, we never caught as much as a glimpse of a ring-tailed cat or the kit fox, both of which are most likely to be seen in the early morning or at dusk. Pronghorns, reintroduced in Big Bend recently, are on the increase. The collared peccary, or javelina, and the coyote are often seen. Mountain lions still occur but they are largely nocturnal.

Mountains, desert, mammals, birds, plants, solitude, vastness, mystery. Big Bend has them all—an amazing mixture which is at once both appealing and challenging. There is history too, lots of it, of Indians and border disputes, of wars and smuggling. No Texas "brags" are necessary to advertise the multiple attractions of Big Bend. The simple truth is sufficient.

# The Lower
# Rio Grande Valley

THE VALLEY

Luther C. Goldman

# THE VALLEY

## Luther C. Goldman

Whenever bird watchers get together to compare notes on the best areas for birds in the United States, the conversation is quite likely to turn to "The Valley" and then to Luther Goldman. Everybody knows immediately that The Valley is the Rio Grande Valley in South Texas and everyone fortunate enough to have visited this superb bird-finding area before 1959 knows Luther Goldman, the ever gracious and helpful, former manager of the Laguna Atascosa and Santa Ana National Wildlife Refuges in The Valley.

Luther Chase Goldman was born in Washington, D.C., in 1909. He graduated from the University of Maryland and spent four years doing extensive field work in biological research in Arizona and Mexico with his father, Major E. A. Goldman, and in Florida with Arthur H. Howell.

He first became associated with the U.S. Bureau of Biological Survey, now the Fish and Wildlife Service, in 1939, and, except for the war years, has served that organization ever since. He was manager of the Salton Sea National Wildlife Refuge in California, studied avian botulism and waterfowl nesting at Tule Lake National Wildlife Refuge (also in California), did reconnaissance work in the early days of the Havasu and Imperial National Wildlife Refuges on the Colorado River, and was manager of the Bitter Lake National Wildlife Refuge in New Mexico.

*His most exciting assignment came at the close of World War II when he was sent to Texas to manage two new National Wildlife Refuges—the large Laguna Atascosa, a haven for migrating and wintering waterfowl and shorebirds on the Gulf of Mexico, and the tiny Santa Ana, a bit of exotic wilderness inland on the Rio Grande. During his ten years in The Valley he probably showed more people more birds than any other refuge manager in the Fish and Wildlife Service and in so doing aroused in the public an enthusiasm for, and an appreciation of, our federal system of wildlife refuges.*

*This chapter was written far from The Valley in Washington, D.C., where Luther Goldman went in 1959 to be assistant chief of the Section of Wildlife Management. He has since been transferred to his present position as photographic specialist in the Branch of Interpretation of the Division of Wildlife Refuges. I suspect that there are numerous times when he misses The Valley as much as many of us miss his hospitality and guidance when we return there for more bird finding.*

After World War II was over and I returned to duty with the U.S. Fish and Wildlife Service, a choice of three National Wildlife Refuges was generously offered me. One of these, in the Lower Rio Grande Valley of Texas, was immediately more exciting and challenging than the other two. The manager of this new refuge area was to have two units under his administration —the Laguna Atascosa National Wildlife Refuge, mainly for wintering waterfowl and shorebirds, and the Santa Ana National Wildlife Refuge, an oasis for perching birds and small migrant species.

When I discussed the Texas area with my long-time friend, Dr. Ira N. Gabrielson, he became enthusiastic about the birds—the great quantities of waterfowl and shorebirds, the landbirds of which some did not occur in other parts of the United States, and the Mexican birds whose northern limit of distribution lay just across the International Boundary in South Texas. He also spoke of the opportunities of establishing new Texas records of birds extending their ranges to the north or wandering casually from the west. In all this I have not been disappointed, and Dr. Gabrielson has since referred to Santa Ana—a small refuge of 2,000 acres where one can observe a cross section of the native flora and fauna of this unique region—as "the gem of the Federal Refuge System." It is, indeed, a region different in many aspects from any other part of the United States.

In the past several years, the rich wildlife area of the Lower Rio Grande Valley of Texas has suffered mightily from the bull-dozer and the plow. Many thousands of acres of brushland, once literally teeming with birds and mammals, have been removed to make room for King Cotton and farm crops. The brushland that is best for wildlife is also the most sought-after for farmland because the soil, which will support a thick brush composed of many different species of plants, contains great stores of nutrients that are valuable for domestic crops as well. Fortunately and just in time, the Laguna Atascosa and Santa Ana Refuges and Bentsen Rio Grande Valley State Park were saved from the "dozer" blade. These sanctuaries are almost like islands in a sea of cultivated land.

"The Valley," as Texans call it, beckons to bird watchers from all over the United States. In recent years its reputation as a wonderfully attractive bird-finding spot has reached foreign countries as well, and it is not unusual now to meet an international bird watcher on a Valley road or along a refuge trail.

The Santa Ana National Wildlife Refuge, near the western end of The Valley, is one of the principal bird-finding spots. It lies southeast of Alamo, Texas, flanking a big bend of the Rio Grande which is for several hundred miles the International Boundary between Mexico and the United States. The Rio Grande, or, as the Mexicans sometimes call it, the Rio Bravo del Norte, furnishes fresh water and sand bars for birds. Within the refuge several natural depressions that formerly were flooded only when the river overflowed its banks are now filled to a constant level with water pumped from wells. These potholes are bird-rich spots attracting both waterbirds, notably the Black-bellied Tree Duck, and woodland species as well.

The refuge supports the original flora of the Rio Grande bottomland, and the names of many of the trees sound and are jungle-like and tropical—the tepeguaje, guayucan, colima, Mexican ebony, anaqua, huisache, and retama. Other trees of the wooded area are elm, ash, and hackberry. Spanish moss hangs from some of the branches, and in this moss the Olive-backed Warbler, a close relative of the Parula Warbler, makes its nest.

The black center fiber of Spanish moss, though thin and hairlike, is tough and furnishes nesting material for a number of other birds—orioles particularly, which use it in weaving their nests and securing them to limbs of trees and palm leaves. Six species of orioles have been recorded for this area and five of these—the Orchard, Black-headed, Hooded, Lichtenstein's, and Bullock's— breed here. The Baltimore Oriole is the only one that does not stay to nest. The largest—the Lichtenstein's Oriole—is also the rarest and most sought-after by visiting bird finders. It hangs its long, pendant nest on the end of a hackberry, elm, or ebony tree, or even on the electric wire that furnishes current to the manager's house, where it swings with every slight breeze right out in the open for everyone to see.

Perhaps, because of its large size and its watchfulness, the Lichtenstein's Oriole is less parasitized by the Bronzed Cowbird than the Black-headed and Hooded Orioles. The Cowbird's nuptial antics in May are worthy of special attention. The ruby-eyed male may be observed at this time, feeding in the shade of a tree or clump of trees with one or more females. Suddenly, in view of the opposite sex, it leaps into the air and, with feathers puffed out and wings vibrating, moves straight up and down as if on a yo-yo string. After this performance, it lands and struts about with raised cape while as often as not the female goes on feeding, showing little or no interest in his behavior.

The Bronzed Cowbirds have increased in numbers during the last ten years and have so parasitized the Black-headed Orioles that these birds have become extremely rare in The Valley. Other species are victims of this parasitism as well. One cannot help but resent the sight of a great hulk of a young Bronzed Cowbird being fed by a mite of a foster parent such as the Olive-backed Warbler.

Another blackbird in evidence the year round is the Greattailed Grackle, the largest of the "boat-tails" in the United States and a damaging bird, at least when colonizing with White-winged Doves. It commonly raids the uncovered eggs of the White-wings and even on occasion feeds its own youngsters on young doves.

The Rio Grande Valley is the spring and summer home of thousands of White-winged Doves that begin crossing the border from Mexico in April. The Santa Ana Refuge in particular is host to nesting and roosting White-wings and is one of the important production areas. Following a somewhat prolonged nesting season in The Valley, they return to Mexico during September and early October. Large feeding flights to milo-maize fields and to brushland roosting areas develop in late summer and are truly a spectacle. When the voice of an individual bird is heard, the call, *who-cooks-for-you*, can be singled out, but the combined sounds coming from many birds in a large brushland colony is more like a roar and can be heard some distance away. The problem of the marauding Great-tailed Grackles is serious because the large White-wing is much sought after as a game bird and, when production is good, a short hunting season on them is open to sportsmen. Unfortunately, the Grackles will sometimes cause a loss of from 70 to 75 per cent of the expected production of a White-winged Dove colony.

The Lower Rio Grande Valley is a remarkable place for doves and pigeons. Indeed, nowhere else in the United States can one find so many different species. Besides the White-winged Dove, there are the Red-billed Pigeon, Mourning Dove, Ground Dove, Inca Dove, and White-fronted Dove. Another, the Ruddy Ground Dove, was first found in the United States near San Benito in December, 1950, and is one of the extremely rare casuals, or wanderers, from Mexico.

Perhaps the most striking of all the doves is the White-fronted, a large, clean-cut bird which prefers to walk instead of fly and seldom gets far from its woodland habitat in the thickest of the brush. Its very low call has been described as sounding as if someone were blowing air into a gallon jug. When it is forced to fly, its quick wing-beat or "slap" is loud and easily recognized.

The uncommon Red-billed Pigeon, the largest of the group, is found in the southern tip of Texas and is one of the earliest of the migrants to arrive from Mexico, showing up in February or March. In good light its color appears to be maroon, and at fairly close range, with binoculars, one can make out the pink or reddish bill for which it is named. Its large size and uniformly dark appearance help distinguish it in flight.

One of the real prizes for the bird list is the White-collared Seedeater. This small finch, about four inches long from the tip of its stumpy bill to the end of its tail, takes up such a tiny space in the world that it is most readily located by its loud song. Look for this little fellow with the big voice in southern Cameron and Hidalgo Counties in the weeds beside the country roads or along weedy irrigation canal banks. Its feeding habits are similar to those of a goldfinch, and in late summer one often finds these miniatures among the seed heads in patches of wild sunflowers.

The Santa Ana Refuge and Bentsen State Park are the best places to find the Green Jay, one of the most colorful of Valley birds. This handsome woodland species with black throat-patch, blue head, green body, and yellow on the sides of its tail has the same habits as other jays—occasionally getting into henhouses and pecking the eggs, poking holes in ripened fruit, traveling with its fellow jays in noisy bands, and fussing to high heaven upon discovering an owl. Some farmers dislike the Green Jay, but bird watchers love him.

Another of the handsome birds on the "must" list of visiting bird watchers is the Kiskadee Flycatcher, the largest of all the flycatchers and well named for its call. This big fellow haunts the edges of the fresh-water potholes in the woodland where, in the manner of a kingfisher, it fishes for minnows. Also included in its diet are small lizards and baby snakes. Its frequent calls, either of its own name *kiskadee* or a loud *wheep,* are helpful in locating it.

Bird watching at the Santa Ana Refuge on any early morning from late May to early June is an unforgettable experience. From its jungle-like forest come the calls and clamor of the occupants of one of the most varied and concentrated landbird areas on the continent. This cacophony, referred to as the "morning chorus" by local bird watchers, is best enjoyed when one arrives on the scene before dawn. The first chips and chirps of the awakening birds begin while the light is still poor and, as the light increases, soon develop into a multivoiced crescendo. The background of dove notes is punctuated by the raucous calls of the Chachalaca, a small pheasant-like bird. And the others—Golden-fronted and Ladderbacked Woodpeckers, Tropical Kingbirds, Kiskadee Flycatchers, Wied's Crested Flycatchers, Green Jays, Black-crested Titmice, the ubiquitous Mockingbirds, Long-billed Thrashers, Hooded Orioles, Summer Tanagers, Cardinals, Olive Sparrows, just to mention a few—all join in singing and calling. When the sun gets higher and it becomes hotter, the birds gradually quiet down.

Along the lower Gulf Coast, about sixty miles east of the Santa

Ana-Rio Grande River area, lies the Laguna Atascosa National Wildlife Refuge, another varied habitat for birds—yet differing greatly from Santa Ana. Its 42,000 acres include coastal prairies, salt flats, low vegetated ridges that support thick, thorny shrubs, and brushlands of mesquite, huisache, and granjeno with scattered clumps of cacti and yucca in the more open spots. There are fresh-water potholes and lakes and salt-water lagoons, all popular with shorebirds and wading birds. The tour routes, designed for visitors to the refuge, are made to order for bird watchers. By following these one can see many of the birds without once leaving his car.

The Laguna Atascosa Refuge, located as it is at the southern extremity of the Central Flyway in the United States, serves primarily as a wintering area for waterfowl and many thousands of ducks and geese may be observed here. The first duck to migrate, the Blue-winged Teal, begins to show up in mid-August, but the big push of waterfowl is not under way until after mid-October. During October and November spectacular numbers of ducks and geese build up on the water areas and on the farmlands of the refuge. Lakes and potholes, impounded for wintering waterfowl, become feeding and resting places for hundreds of shorebirds and wading birds such as the White-faced and White Ibises, Roseate Spoonbill, Black-bellied Plover, Long-billed Curlew, Dowitcher, Semipalmated and Western Sandpipers. Sandhill Cranes are on hand in the fall to get a share of the sprouting grain, planted in September for the wild geese.

The mild winters of South Texas make this area attractive to birds and bird watchers alike. One look at the Christmas Bird Counts in *Audubon Field Notes* will show the great numbers of species found on both Santa Ana and Laguna Atascosa Refuges at that time of year. However, the most exciting period of all is during the spring migration in March, April, and May.

By January, the exodus of the great numbers of wintering Pintails has already started. February and March are good months in which to observe large flocks of shorebirds and wading birds arriving from the south. Many of these stop off to feed and rest for a while on the shores of the coastal lagoons and on the inland lakes and pastures moistened by early spring rains.

April and May are the important months for migrant land-birds, with the normal peak from the last week in April through

the second week in May. A cold front from the north will sometimes cause the migrants coming from the south to "stack up" so
that the trees and shrubs are literally alive with warblers, orioles,
and buntings. Lucky is the bird watcher who is afield on such a
day. It is amazing, during one of these "northers," to find such
species as the Yellow-billed Cuckoo, Whip-poor-will, Chuck-will's-
widow, Catbird, Yellow Warbler, Yellowthroat, and Baltimore
Oriole in the thorny patches of prickly-pear cactus and yucca that
grow on a low ridge paralleling the Texas Coast. Large, tight flocks
of hundreds, even thousands, of migrating Dickcissels sometimes
distress the local milo-maize growers, and one often sees the children of tenant farmers walking through the fields and waving
pieces of white cloth to frighten away the seed-hungry birds.

While the Laguna Atascosa area is a good place for adding to
your list of shorebirds, wading birds, gulls, and terns, it is also an
excellent spot in which to look for such upland rarities as the
White-tailed Kite, White-tailed Hawk, Aplomado Falcon, Groove-
billed Ani, Sprague's Pipit, Varied Bunting, and Botteri's Sparrow.
The Harris' Hawk is common, as are the Caracara, Pauraque,
Verdin, Bewick's and Cactus Wrens, and the Curve-billed
Thrasher.

No bird watcher should ever plan to limit his visit to The
Valley to one day. My suggestion is to allow, at the very least,
three days: one for the Laguna Atascosa, one for the Santa Ana,
and one at large. On the extra day take a trip east to the Laguna
Madre shore, cross the causeway from Port Isabel to Padre Island,
and look over the beach on the Gulf of Mexico for shorebirds,
gulls, and terns. Then drive to Brownsville. In winter watch for
White-necked Ravens along the way. Or, drive west up The Valley
to Bentsen State Park, which is just beyond Mission, for the local
and rare Mexican species such as the Rose-throated Becard, and
from the park continue west and explore the country roads in the
vicinity of Sullivan City for Scaled Quail, Curved-billed Thrashers,
Pyrrhuloxias, and other desert-type birds.

These, and a wealth of other species not even mentioned here,
occur in The Valley. While a person cannot possibly see them all
in a single visit, one thing is certain: Whatever the time of year,
there are always rare and exotic birds to be found. For bird watchers, there is no place quite like this southernmost tip of Texas!

# *Migration Spectacles*

AT POINT PELEE IN THE SPRING
    John Allen Livingston

AT BLOCK ISLAND IN THE FALL
    Alfred L. Hawkes

GEESE ALONG THE MISSOURI
    Herbert Krause

THE CRANES AT LAST MOUNTAIN LAKE
    John Allen Livingston

HAWKS ABOVE DULUTH
    Pershing B. Hofslund

AT HAWK MOUNTAIN SANCTUARY
        Maurice Broun

# AT POINT PELEE IN THE SPRING

## John Allen Livingston

        *John Allen Livingston was born in Hamilton, Ontario, in 1923 and graduated from the University of Toronto with majors in English, history, and languages. After serving in the Royal Canadian Navy during World War II, he took up a career in business—until 1955. That year he joined the Audubon Society of Canada as full-time director and later president.*

    *Why this change of profession in mid-stream? In Jack Livingston we have yet another case of a man's hobby taking over his life. From his earliest years Jack had an exceptional interest in bird watching, nature books, nature photography, and travel. Altogether too exciting and challenging, it was an interest that would not be suppressed, would not let him settle into the confinements of the business world.*

    *When the Audubon Society of Canada was reorganized as the Canadian Audubon Society, Jack Livingston became its managing director. His duties with the Society included editing* Canadian Audubon *magazine and writing and narrating a weekly natural science and conservation program on radio for the Canadian Broadcasting Corporation. This program, heard in all parts of Canada, was so well received that, in 1962, he resigned from the Canadian Audubon Society to be the science program organizer for the CBC network on both radio and television.*

    *Like many modern naturalists, Jack Livingston has taken an*

*increasingly active role in conservation. His efforts have been cen-*
*tered on the protection of birds of prey and the larger mammals—*
*particularly predators, the international control of oil pollution of*
*the sea, and the regulation of the use of chemical pesticides. In the*
*pursuit of these interests he has watched birds—literally—around*
*the world.*

*His undergraduate training in English has served him well, as*
*his many magazine articles and countless scripts for radio and*
*television will testify. In the following pages he has written about*
*the astonishing concentrations of birds during the migration sea-*
*sons at Point Pelee in Lake Erie. Elsewhere in this book he tells*
*about another concentration—the thousands of Sandhill Cranes*
*that gather at Last Mountain Lake with the waning of summer—*
*and points up an urgent conservation problem occasioned by the*
*effect of so many birds on local crops.*

Each spring, in the western corner of Lake Erie,
a slim finger of land beckons the concentrated onrush of countless
numbers of north-bound birds. When conditions are right, wave
upon wave, swell after swell, the urgent throng of migrants surges
up its narrow nine-mile length to fan out through much of eastern
Canada. In the fall, the finger becomes an attenuated funnel
that gently pours the more leisurely drifting masses toward the
Mississippi flyway. At either season, Point Pelee is Canada's
most extraordinary and rewarding situation for the watcher of
bird migration.

Point Pelee, much of which is a National Park, is the southernmost part of the Canadian mainland. With a latitude of 42 degrees,
the same as that of the northern boundary of California, it enjoys
an average July mean temperature of 75 degrees, highest in the
country. It is thus the nucleus of a limited intrusion into Canada of
a typically southern plant-animal association. Patches of prickly-
pear cactus, stands of tulip tree, and spicebush bespeak this southern affinity, as do gnatcatchers wheezing overhead and Yellow-
breasted Chats tooting and rasping from the thickets.

The Point's happy location at an important breach in the giant
barrier of the Great Lakes is reflected in both numbers of birds
and numbers of species in the second and third weeks of May, and

again in September. Variety has always been the keynote. Where else, I ask in some measure of confidence, can you see a Gyrfalcon and a Summer Tanager on the same day? This was my experience exactly once, and it isn't likely to happen again, but it is a fair and reasonable indication of the potential.

The Point is a post-glacial sand spit dangling into Lake Erie from Wheatley and Leamington on the lake's North shore. Typical of such formations, one side is fortified by a sandy beach; the other is chiefly marsh. (More correctly, it *was* chiefly marsh. Much of it has been drained for agricultural purposes, but those portions within the National Park are secure.) A spinal ridge supports an open forest of red cedar and hackberry which, depending upon the water level, ends about one-third mile from the tip. Dense willow scrub then takes over briefly, with the apex of the Point being a curving tentative antenna of shifting sand.

It is this ultimate tip of the Point which attracts the pre-dawn birder in mid-May. A frosty spearhead of gulls and terns faces into the wind, tight knots of Ruddy Turnstones ignore a Bald Eagle breakfasting on a beached walleye, while rafts of mergansers bob in the eddying surf offshore and herons and cormorants perch hopefully on fishermen's pound-nets in the sheltered bay.

When the sun rises, the birds begin to come. Ones and twos, then small flocks—seemingly from nowhere the great flight is on! Blackbirds, thrushes and warblers, hummingbirds and jays. Finches, falcons, swallows, flycatchers. On a good morning, immediately after dawn, the willows and cedars at the tip seethe with birds. Many were grounded the night before; others may be just now arriving from Pelee Island eight miles to the southwest, or Sandusky twenty-four miles beyond.

William Gunn, who has studied the matter exhaustively, is of the opinion that the greatest massing of birds occurs when a pronounced warm front has moved in from the south, carrying the birds with it, and coming to a stop at roughly the line of the mainland. Then the flocks channeled in by the shape of the Point, and restrained by the leading wall of the front, come to rest on the only land available to them. An additional number of birds may have overshot the mark somewhat, and in the early morning make their way back, concentrating at or near the tip.

It is sometimes possible to list seventy species before breakfast. Daily lists in the 120's, though not the rule, are not uncommon. Given a reasonable degree of luck, anyone should be able to log 100 per day during the migration peak.

If the morning is cold—and it often is—you will see exhausted Eastern Kingbirds and Barn Swallows standing on the sand, undoubtedly forced to look for beach insects because of the lack of an early hatch of midges. American Redstarts may flutter in the short grass, or Red-headed Woodpeckers and Baltimore Orioles search among the flotsam for small invertebrates.

As the warming sun gradually takes effect, the exhilarating sound, thin and hesitant at first, begins to swell in volume and intensity. Soon the length and breadth of the Point is filled with the massed voices of a variety of birds. It is claimed that nowhere—certainly nowhere in Canada—is there such a memorable morning chorus. On a good day, better than 100 species of songbirds may be compressed in this small peninsula, many of them in great numbers, all of them to some extent vocal. (All, that is, save the Gray-cheeked Thrush, which I have never heard sing in migration.) Point Pelee offers the bird listener a rare opportunity to learn the voices of the many northern-nesting warblers, some of which may not be in full song as they pass through farther south. The chorus is over, usually, by 10:00 in the morning.

At the peak of the tumult, when the pell-mell multitude fills every tree and shrub with quick, bewildering movement, an accurate ear pays off. Most of the best finds are made when someone, usually Jim Baillie, picks up some unexpected sound, something "not quite right." It's impossible to check every individual with the glasses, so before you advance to confront a songbird wave at Point Pelee, I strongly urge a home refresher course with Gunn and Borror's superb "Finches" and "Warblers" phonograph records, and Peterson's comprehensive "Field Guide to Bird Songs."

Though it is always satisfactory to turn up rarities, and Point Pelee has recently produced such Canadian improbabilities as Virginia's Warbler, Yellow-throated Warbler, and Bachman's Sparrow, these are merely the icing on the cake. The full and nutritious feast for eye and ear is in the high-key excitement of uncountable birds, the fantastic intermingling of Hudsonian, Canadian, and Carolinian species, the rich polyglot cacophony of their songs.

The Point seems to be world headquarters for the Orchard Oriole. I have never seen this bird so abundant anywhere else. Many times I have watched these impeccable birds going through their stiff, ritualized display behavior right in the middle of the tree-lined road. On some days the Orchard and Baltimore Orioles seem to contribute a very large part of the total sound as one walks along. Not so apparent are the phlegmatic, sluggish companies of Rose-breasted Grosbeaks and Scarlet Tanagers. They sing from time to time, but generally there are a great many more on the Point than one would realize from the sound.

North from the tip about a mile, there is an abrupt transition from the red cedar-hackberry association. From the east side of the road, a well-marked nature trail leads for about one and a quarter miles through a mature hardwood forest round the edge of an old apple orchard, now overgrown with vines and a deciduous succession partly natural, partly planted. In this climax woodland, virtually unique in Canada (except for Rondeau Provincial Park, about fifty miles to the east), one can imagine for a time that he is deep in the moist forests of Virginia or Kentucky.

Tall sycamores, hickories, walnuts, maples, and cottonwoods keep in nearly perpetual shade a dense understory interrupted here and there by dark, silent pools. In season, the ground is decorated with violets, spring beauties, nettles, trilliums, bellwort, and sweet cicely. A woody form of poison ivy, as thick as your arm, swarms up the trees in company with Virginia creeper.

Often the still forest rings with the staccato declamations of waterthrushes, and the exuberant shouts of Great Crested Fly-catchers. The candle-like flare of a Prothonotary Warbler gleams —and is gone in an instant. Occasionally a Cerulean Warbler will offer its gentle, teasing buzz, or a Wood Duck will thinly plaint at being disturbed. Sometimes you will hear the rhythmic, rollicking call of the Carolina Wren. But at once, the *quirt* of a Swainson's Thrush reminds us that migration still persists, even as the more southern species are beginning to establish territories.

Outside this woodland, circling the former orchard, are deep brushy tangles with their full complement of Cardinals, Rufous-sided Towhees, Catbirds, Brown Thrashers, and the occasional Bewick's Wren or Blue-winged Warbler. In the more open, grassy spots, there are still opportunities to find Grasshopper Sparrows and the infrequent Henslow's and Le Conte's Sparrows. But the most abundant bird here—as it seems to be everywhere on Point Pelee—is the ubiquitous Yellow Warbler.

It is always wise, in this clearing, to keep glancing skyward, for many and interesting have been the larger birds of passage we have glimpsed from this spot. It was here that, several years ago, Buffalo's redoubtable Bernie Nathan brought off one of his fabled ploys, to the crashing consternation of all present. A group of birders were walking across the orchard when Bernie, without apparently looking upward, backward, or to the side, jerked his thumb back over his shoulder and firmly announced, "Common Egret." Sure enough, there behind us a fine egret flew slowly across the Point. Upon immediate question, the always imperturbable Bernie, unlit cigar still firmly clenched in his teeth, stated, "I heard the flutter of its wings." There are times when I almost believe it.

To the north of the hardwood forest and its nature trail, on the east side of the Point, is the great Pelee marsh. This area is most productive in March and April, when Fox Sparrows are singing round its sides, and flights of Whistling Swans, assorted ducks, and Canada Geese (from the Jack Miner Sanctuary at nearby Kingsville) make their appearance. In May, when most birders visit the area, the marsh provides best results at night.

When the night is perfectly dark and still, the marsh throbs with life. It never fails to grip me with the indefinable enchantment I knew there as a boy and happily experience yet when there is an opportunity to sit quietly alone by its edge. The sharp clicking of cricket frogs, the screams of Fowler's toads cutting into the warm darkness, the soft dove-like notes of Least Bitterns, the whinnies and clucks of Soras and Virginia Rails, the sudden burst of sound from a Swamp Sparrow or a Long-billed Marsh Wren. Listen by this marsh a hundred times, and the hundred and first you'll be *certain* there's something new out there, something different, something mysterious you haven't yet identified. I'm sure there always will be.

Farther to the north, above the park boundary, lies that part of the former wetland which has been drained. Flat onion fields stretching interminably into the distance may seem poor substitution for a cattail marsh, but they do manage to produce, each year, flocks of Black-bellied and Golden Plovers, innumerable Horned Larks, and an infrequent Western Meadowlark.

This, then, is something of Point Pelee in the month of May. A helter-skelter, frantic welter of migrating birds, a priceless living library of natural sounds. But it is even more than all these things. For years, ornithologists have been puzzled by, and have attempted to explain, the paradoxical "reverse migration" that occurs from time to time. George M. Stirrett, chief parks naturalist of the Canadian National Parks Service, has described it this way:

> "A few individuals of some species after having arrived at Point Pelee reverse their direction of flight and fly again southward. Even on warm sunny spring days they may be seen taking off from the Point and disappearing over the lake. There are several theories to account for this behavior, but that it actually takes place has now been proven by the banding activities of the members of the Federation of Ontario Naturalists and their successors, the Ontario Bird Banders Association. ... Reverse migration is not an uncommon behavior, as birds have also been seen migrating southward in spring from the southern tip of Pelee Island and from stations in Europe.
>
> "The best birds to watch to see reverse migration are the various Swallows, Red-headed Woodpeckers, Cedar Waxwings, Goldfinches and Myrtle Warblers, but other kinds have also been observed. The best place to see it is at or near the tip of the Point where the vegetation is low and one can follow the birds as they fly back and forth and then finally leave."

Careful study of this phenomenon was conducted for some years by William Gunn, since which time an increasing force of bird banders have been adding to our store of knowledge about it. Though numbers of people are now involved in trying to unravel the mystery (not the least of the questions being, where do these "reversed" birds end up, and by what route?), there is scope here for much more intensified research—through regular banding, possibly through color-marking of some kind, and through observation.

In June, the migration is over. Summer at Point Pelee, from

the bird watcher's point of view, merits one short paragraph. The great industrial complex of Detroit-Windsor is only thirty-five miles away, and the park is amply supplied with all the appropriate amenities. I have never been there between June and September.

From the latter part of August through September, Point Pelee again comes into its own so far as the naturalist is concerned. One of the more noteworthy events in the early fall is the migration of monarch butterflies. During the heat of the day, lone individuals and small, loose groups will be seen fluttering along the shore, to the tip and out over the water, in the general direction of Pelee Island. As evening comes and the temperature falls, the insects stop for the night, gathering in clusters on the red cedars and willows near the tip. In the morning, before their torpidity is relieved, splendid orange clumps of "King Billys" are sufficient to distract even the most single-minded bird lister. Less colorful, but equally interesting, is a concurrent flight of dragonflies.

Then, the second great climax of the Point Pelee year, the September flight of the birds of prey. Usually, Sharp-shinned Hawks predominate. One day, when Jim Baillie and I cautiously listed 1,000 Sharp-shins, the trees at the end of the Point happened to contain an unusual number of fall songbirds. One Sharp-shin, in hot pursuit of a Yellow Warbler, careened around a red cedar with such momentum that even the accipiter's famed maneuverability failed to keep it from actually striking Jim's sleeve.

At that season, the majority of the buteos pass by to the north of Point Pelee, carrying on round the western end of the lake, avoiding the water mass to the south. It is unusual to see more than a handful of the soaring species, yet only a few miles away, on the mainland, Broad-winged Hawks are sometimes counted in the tens of thousands. The accipiters and falcons, however, and the Marsh Hawks, have few qualms about venturing over the water, nor do Ospreys. Eagles appear regularly, and once there was a Prairie Falcon. (Where did *he* come from? No one knows.) It would be valuable to know the source of this flow of accipiters and falcons, and indeed to know the precise route taken by all species in the autumnal flight.

There has been insufficient observation at Point Pelee in the autumn. Admittedly, a number of people do go there at that season, but the overwhelming majority of bird watchers visit it only in the spring. This is regrettable, for the ornithologist is dependent to a very great extent on the notes of experienced amateurs. If September bird watching at Point Pelee were stepped up, many clues to migration puzzles would be forthcoming more quickly than they are at present.

In winter, though interesting, Point Pelee is by no means dramatic. It is pleasant to watch Evening Grosbeaks in a tree where a few months before one watched a White-eyed Vireo, but in general the birdlife is thin. There may be immense flocks of Common Mergansers sometimes, and there is always the chance of some unexpected over-wintering waif, but, in my experience, winter is comparatively unrewarding.

In spring and fall, however, it is difficult to avoid overstatement of Point Pelee's productivity both in terms of personal bird lists and in terms of more general ornithological investigation. Its variety of habitat, its strange overlapping of northern, central, and southern forms (on Pelee Island there is a population of Traill's Flycatchers that sing like Acadians), but above all its fascinating potentialities for the study of migration offer limitless challenges to the bird watcher, whatever his level of experience.

# AT BLOCK ISLAND IN THE FALL

## Alfred L. Hawkes

*Alfred L. Hawkes, born in Medford, Massachusetts, in 1927, graduated from Cushing Academy and the University of Massachusetts. His interest in natural history developed early—on hunting and fishing expeditions with his father.*

*A series of positions—high school biology teacher in Maryland, demonstration teacher of natural science and conservation for the Massachusetts Audubon Society, instructor in biology at Rhode Island State College, and education specialist for the Audubon Society of Rhode Island—all led in one direction, namely, to a career in conservation and natural history. Summers spent as park naturalist for the National Park Service in Washington, D.C., and Virginia, as itinerant naturalist for the Massachusetts Conservation Council, and as natural history camp and workshop director for the Massachusetts Audubon Society led in the same direction.*

*His present position as executive director of the Audubon Society of Rhode Island carries many responsibilities. Besides managing the Society's extensive program in public relations, he oversees conservation education in the public schools, deals with many public and private conservation problems throughout the state, and finds time to edit the* Narragansett Naturalist. *In an effort to arouse public sentiment for the preservation of our natural resources, he has used just about all the media of communication— publications, lectures, motion pictures, radio, and television. Sev-*

*eral awards and citations from various organizations in Rhode Island mark his success in the field of conservation, and he was especially honored in 1962 when he received the American Motors Professional Conservation Award.*

*Alfred Hawkes did not "discover" Block Island, that tiny piece of sea-girt land belonging to our smallest state, until he first visited it in 1955. But islands have a strong hold and such is the pull of Block Island that he has been returning every year since. Reading what he has to say here about its unspoiled charm, friendly people, and extraordinary fall flights of landbirds, no person will wonder why.*

The approach to Block Island whether by ferry or by plane is delightful. The ferry leaves from Galilee in Narragansett, Rhode Island, and as soon as it passes the sheltering breakwaters of Point Judith, one has the sensation of being well out to sea. Only Block Island, visible on the horizon some twelve miles to the southwest, stands between the small boat and Europe, nearly 3,000 miles away.

The best time to visit Block Island to see birds is in the fall, from the middle of September to the last of October. At that time a few commercial fishing boats will be plying Block Island Sound, between the mainland and the island, and there will be numerous pleasure boats trolling for tuna and striped bass or looking for a

late-in-the-season swordfish loafing at the surface, exposing itself
to the harpoon—the only means by which it is commonly taken in
these waters. Occasionally jet planes from the Quonset Point Naval Air Station will make their presence known by muffled rum-
blings and crisscross chalk lines in the sky.

Regardless of the number of previous crossings, the chance or
the anticipation of seeing some new birds always makes the ferry
trip inviting. If fishermen happen to be cleaning or culling a day's
catch, gulls by the hundred will be hovering around the stern of the
boat, looking from a distance like wisps of paper caught in a
whirlwind. In calm weather the ferry will flush groups of gulls and
ducks and an occasional Common Loon. On rough, windy days
one may be fortunate enough, during the seventy-five-minute trip,
to spot shearwaters, or petrels and, on rare occasions, a phalarope.
When the migration is in full swing, it is not uncommon to observe
birds flying parallel to the ferry and only a few yards out, giving
one a side view usually reserved for other birds of the flock.

The alternative to the ferry trip, an inexpensive, ten-minute
flight by charter plane from Westerly, Rhode Island, changes the
perspective. While the sea fills the eastern half of the horizon, it
seems remote and lifeless and one is much more aware that Block
Island, though nonetheless an island, belongs to the mainland geo-
graphically and geologically. From the air the island looks like a
chunk of mainland that was somehow broken off, floated out, and
anchored.

As the plane climbs from the runway and heads seaward,
Block Island gradually changes from a nondescript target, small
enough to cause apprehension on the part of the novice, to an area
of green farmland with relatively few farmhouses, all carelessly
tied down by a winding system of paved and unpaved roads that
weave here and there and everywhere and always end near the
sea.

The business section of the town of New Shoreham, the formal
name of the island, seems to occupy a very small space, hardly
larger than the snug harbor beside which it lies. As the plane
circles and loses altitude, the mainland fades to an inconspicuous
line on the horizon and never, during the brief period of landing,
does one lose sight of the sea. Even when the plane stops at the
small terminal the sensation of coming down to a bit of land

completely surrounded by water persists because the airport is on the highest section of the nearly treeless island. One stands on land and sees the ocean in every direction—an appropriate welcome to a spot where the sea, land, and birds are so closely allied.

Three factors make Block Island remarkable for birds—its location, its shape, and its treeless terrain. Because of its location it is a place for unusual records. Six by three and a half miles in maximum length and breadth, Block Island is frequently the first land encountered by lost or exhausted birds coming from the sea. It is also a place where the bodies of birds which died at sea wash ashore. The finding of a Ruddy Sheld-Duck on October 8, 1951, the Magnificent Frigate-bird on November 16, 1932, the European Lapwing on November 20, 1932, the Bridled Tern on September 14, 1960, and others, most of which were victims of hurricanes or severe storms, is evidence of what may be expected.

But the appearance of rare and unusual species is of minor importance beside the location of Block Island in relation to weather and the migration of birds through New England. In the fall, frequent cold fronts pass across this area. These are invariably followed by two or three days of strong northwest winds. The New England coast, south from Cape Cod, trends south and then west for some distance. Many small birds migrating southward at night through eastern Massachusetts and Rhode Island either fail to turn west along the coast or are blown off course by the northwest wind and suddenly find themselves over the sea. Sometimes the wind is so strong that even birds migrating southwesterly are forced toward the south and those near the coast are carried out to sea. All are in trouble. And at such a time Block Island attracts like a magnet a veritable "shower" of birds pouring outward from the southern New England shore.

Many simply head for Block Island and alight here. Others pass it and continue out to sea. Some fly to ultimate exhaustion and death; some recognize their error in time to turn back to the proffered haven. Like flakes of snow, small birds of all types flutter down upon the island during the night.

With the first light of dawn all these birds, aware of the mainland lying to the north, rapidly make their way to Block Island's pointed northerly tip. Early on any morning, following the conditions described, it is possible to stand on the north end of the island and watch these small creatures struggle to take off from the beaches in an attempt to return to the mainland. Invariably they are blown back by the same north wind that brought them there. Before noon most of them have ceased trying to recross and have scattered over the entire island. Thus, in a matter of hours, the bird population on Block Island, particularly on the north end, may reach fantastic proportions. By rough estimate, the island may have as many as several hundred thousand birds on it for two or three days at a time. Just where these birds go when they finally leave Block Island is not known for a certainty.

Another factor making Block Island remarkable for bird finding is its fairly level terrain almost totally lacking in trees. This means simply that birds reaching the island are easily seen. There are many scattered open fields. Except for a few tree plantations, the woody vegetation elsewhere is a mixture—sometimes an impenetrable matrix—of bayberry, blackberry, wild rose, shadbush, and a variety of other low-growing shrubs which are only head high.

Block Island, originally forested, was cleared and converted into farmland by the first settlers over 300 years ago. Farming, combined with fishing and other pursuits connected with the sea, supported the economy of the island for many years. Gradually the farming declined and the farmlands were abandoned. Many of the houses are now used only in the summer. Fishing followed farming; both have now been replaced by catering to summer visitors— at least for eight or ten weeks of the year. At the present time most of the 400 or so permanent residents of Block Island are partially or entirely dependent on visitors for their livelihood. The natural forests have not come back to any significant degree much to the delight of the bird watchers who now make annual pilgrimages.

The general lack of trees seems to have no serious effect on the migrants that flood the island following a cold front in the fall, and it is difficult to convey a true picture of just how concentrated the numbers of small birds can become at certain times. Driving on Corn Neck Road to the north end of the island early in the morning, after a flight, is somewhat like driving through flock after flock of House Sparrows in the city. The difference is that on Block Island one drives through flock after flock of Myrtle Warblers, Brown Creepers, Golden-crowned Kinglets, or of some other spe-

cies that one would never expect to find, darting along and crossing roads which border neglected farmland and pass through a
small village.

On a recent weekend in October it was possible to pick up
exhausted Brown Creepers and Golden-crowned Kinglets from almost any front porch on the lee side of any house in the center of
New Shoreham. One Brown Creeper became so confused that it lit
on the pants leg of a lady bird watcher who was leaning over the
rail of a hotel porch, watching birds feeding in the seaweed on the
beach below. After investigating the pants leg for half a minute or
so, the bird left and its hostess was none the wiser until informed
by friends who had observed the incident. In other years Myrtle
Warblers and Slate-colored Juncos have also been present by the
tens of thousands. The reason for the fluctuation in the populations of species in different years has not been explained.

On a morning after a good flight, a mowed lawn may be covered
with warblers. A walk down any side road means stop, raise
the binoculars, look, take another step, and then repeat the entire
ritual. Everywhere there is activity. Birds moving from bush to
bush, through tangles of branches, up and down the trunks of
scattered, dwarfed trees, searching the ground, soaring overhead,
resting, or calling from a perch. Marsh Hawks are almost constantly in sight, gliding gracefully back and forth—low over the
salt marshes and brush. On occasion as many as three or four Peregrine Falcons may be seen at one time, picking up a breakfast of
exhausted birds along the island's cliffs.

Whimbrels on front lawns, Red-headed Woodpeckers on fence
posts and telephone poles, Western Kingbirds on electric wires,
Blue Grosbeaks in apple trees, warblers of all kinds in ornamental
shrubs near buildings. All these contribute to the general excitement or create confusion for the beginner who likes to check each
find in "the book" before making a final decision. On the other
hand, opportunity for practice seldom comes any faster; even the
unusual and difficult species may occur so frequently and in such
numbers that they become easy to remember.

While the numbers of individual birds on Block Island in the
fall are at times almost unbelievable, the number of different species can be high too—at least for New England. Groups of people
keeping records of all their observations over a three-day weekend

in September or October have compiled lists of as many as 140 to 150 species. A figure of 130 is low for a reasonably active weekend. Even so, a "slow" weekend usually provides better bird finding on Block Island than during the same period on the mainland. It should be emphasized, of course, that good flights require a weather factor, namely, the passage of a cold front which forces the descent and temporary stay of south-bound landbirds. When there are good flights of these migrants on the mainland following a cold front, it is safe to assume that Block Island is having good flights too, if not better.

Aside from being one of the most productive bird-finding places in the northeast, Block Island is one of the pleasantest and least expensive. Bird watchers, accustomed to being regarded with some degree of suspicion or amusement by the public, will be agreeably surprised by the signs on front lawns saying, "Birders Welcome," or flags with "Audubon" lettered on them. Much of this is due to the influence of one woman, Miss Elizabeth Dickens who died on June 17, 1963.

Born on Block Island in 1877 and raised in a family with an interest in birds, Miss Dickens kept a daily record of birds on the island for over fifty years and taught bird study to three generations of islanders in the public schools. Almost everyone on Block Island has some knowledge of birds. Even the most reserved residents are friendly and tolerant and willing to pass the time of day, describing the birds in their back yards yesterday or the day before. Occasionally a householder will go so far as to invite a shivering bird watcher in for a cup of coffee. Indeed, one soon feels that bird watchers mean more to Block Islanders than just another economic asset.

Miss Dickens, with little formal training as a teacher, communicated her own deep and well-informed interest and enthusiasm to several generations of Block Island school children. She was the first to contribute data on migration to the U.S. Bureau of Biological Survey. On August 13, 1912, she recorded in a diary the birds seen on the island that day: "2 Bartram's Tattlers, 4 Black-billed Cuckoos, 1 Yellowlegs, 5 Least Sandpipers, 2 Spotted Sandpipers, 1 Semipalmated Plover, 150 Wilson's Terns, 1 Ruddy Turnstone, 25 White-rumped Sandpipers," and thus began a day-to-day record which was one of the longest continuous records of bird observation in North America.

Through the years Miss Dickens insisted that all dead and injured birds be brought to her. All were recorded and many of the skins were mounted. Her collection, representing 148 species, is now on display at the Block Island school.

In recent years until her death she lived alone in a small cottage at the end of a dirt road only a few hundred feet from the ocean and over a quarter of a mile from her nearest neighbors on the north and east. Her nearest neighbors on the south lived on Montauk Point, Long Island, which was just visible from her front door in good weather. The cottage, weatherbeaten with blue trim, was built before her birth and had remained practically unchanged for most of her life. A call at this cottage was one of the first pleasures for visiting ornithologists. Alert and observing, Miss Dickens enjoyed discussing the currrent trends in bird study, reminiscing about how Robins nested on stone walls when the island was completely devoid of trees and shrubs, or describing how the island farms used to be kept "before work went out of style."

The rejuvenation of interest in encouraging tourists to come to Block Island in the last few years has been an advantage to bird watchers. For a long time the Audubon Society of Rhode Island has had annual fall weekends there just for members. In 1961, when asked to participate in the tercentenary celebration of the settlement of Block Island, the Society opened this trip to anyone who wished to come. An island hotel cooperated by remaining in operation after the regular season. As a result nearly 200 bird watchers from all over eastern United States gathered there on the weekend of September 15. This venture was so successful that it was repeated in 1962, and again in 1963. It will no doubt be an annual affair.

In spite of its increasing dependence on visitors, Block Island remains one of the least commercialized resort areas on the east coast. Most of the island's low, shrubby hills and 200 or so ponds, the results of its geological birth as a glacial moraine, remain unblemished by the less desirable signs of man's "progress." Its beaches provide mile after mile of sand, rocks, and towering earthen cliffs bearing no evidence of civilization other than the scattered bits of flotsam washed up on the shore. During stormy weather one can stand alone on the edge of the 10,000-year-old Mohegan Cliffs, look out to the sea with binoculars or telescope, and watch shearwaters and gulls repeatedly rising on invisible air currents and dipping out of sight between the waves below. At such a time one can truly appreciate the unspoiled beauty and charm of Block Island.

# GEESE ALONG THE MISSOURI

### Herbert Krause *

From the edge of sleep I heard them—the call of the wild geese in the hour before midnight, bringing me to sudden wakefulness. The lights of Sioux Falls were pale on my half-opened window. The last snow scattered on the lawns in this South Dakota city reminded me that the retreat of winter was recent and by no means final.

For a week I had been lifting my eyes expectantly to the southeast and the Missouri River, sixty miles away at its nearest point, sharpening my ears for a sound that never failed to send a curious stir along my spine. Now, this evening in the last days of March, it came, the clamor of the first migrants, Canada Geese probably, northward bound for their summer breeding grounds.

While winter locked with icy blasts the northern streams and potholes from Baffin Island southward across the Prairie Provinces in Canada to the middle reaches of Nebraska, Illinois, and Iowa in the United States, the congregations of the geese, especially those of the Mississippi Flyway—Blues, Snows, White-fronts, Canadas —were concentrated generally along the gulf coasts of Louisiana, Texas, and northeastern Mexico. Excepting notable populations of Blues and Snows (which are largely coastal), they also sojourn inland from Arkansas to Illinois and northward, though sparingly,

---

* For a biographical sketch, see his chapter, "The Black Hills of South Dakota."

as far as South Dakota's southern marshes. Much less restricted to certain areas than the other species, Canada Geese winter up the Mississippi and Missouri Rivers in a wide band. Huge flocks remain at Big Lake in Arkansas and in the Squaw Creek environs in Missouri. One of the largest concentrations of transient and wintering Canadas in North America, writes Olin Sewall Pettingill in *Bird Finding West of the Mississippi,* is to be found at Horseshoe Lake in the extreme southwest tip of Illinois. At all of these localities national or state wildlife refuges contain the bulk of the migrants. Sobering is the reflection that, in order to save these waterfowl numbers from their most dangerous predator, man himself, the greater share of the wintering flocks must find safety within these protected outposts—reserves pitifully small when compared with the land area of the nation.

Clear and resonant the honking rang in the night. Horseshoe Lake, Squaw Creek—the one more than 700, the other less than 400 miles from Sioux Falls. I wondered whether the flock beating its way over the city this night was an early splinter breaking from the aggregations in Arkansas or Illinois.

Standing at the window, shivering with a touch of something that was not entirely the late March chill, I thought that there is a moment when the loitering thews of winter become an irritation and the yearning for a season's change is overwhelming with the expectancy of a sign to say the ancient gods have not forgotten and the vernal quarter of the year is come again.

Since their arrival in the autumn, the flocks ranged over the wintering grounds. But now comes a day in late February or early March when the gabble and the outcry sharpen, when restlessness apparently becomes an insistent prod. As the sun mounts the zenith and the edge of winter creeps backward, this disturbance grows until, responding to stimuli that may be partly physiological, partly psychological, and partly meteorological, the geese clamor skyward. Those farthest south seem to be the first to respond. The excitement spreads like a contagion.

Northward they go, their twists and turns catching up, flock after flock rising to meet them. Threads become ropes, ropes become webs flung at the sky. At some point in their route, the flights destined to travel the Mississippi Flyway, disengaging themselves from the other flights, begin to converge. One such meeting place seems to be the Yazoo-Mississippi Delta strip, 190 miles of bottomland north of Vicksburg. Here the webs in the sky thicken to skeins as they surge northward, either following the Mississippi proper or paralleling the river in wide pathways overland.

The thousands become tens of thousands as the transients in Arkansas on the White River east of Stuttgart and the populations at Big Lake, northwest of Blytheville, are caught up in the whirl and surge of this contagious movement. They head straight into the broad flow of the Missouri River cutting across their paths eastward from Kansas City to St. Louis. Here the advancing contingents diverge. The greater portion of the Blue, Snow, and White-fronted Geese and lesser numbers of Canadas bend to the west to follow the winding Missouri, while the greater share of the Canada Geese with smaller numbers of Blues and Snows continue up the Mississippi.

Once along the Missouri the flocks become clouds drifting up the meanderings of the brushy bottomlands and over the unpredictable sand bars. By early March the circling thousands descend to the shallows of Sugar Lake near Kansas City and the Squaw Creek waters northwest of St. Joseph to mingle with the transients tarrying there. In dark billows flecked with white, about March 10, they enter Iowa in the Forney Lake environs near Thurman. By mid-March the peak of the flight sometimes reaches Kellogg and Green Bottom Sloughs near Glenwood and the river bottoms south of Council Bluffs. Adverse winds arrowed with icy rain may impede but do not stop their progress; dawns become vociferous with shrill cries as they swing out over the rich Iowa farms to feed in the cornrows. Daily the hills and bluffs, the "towers and castles and sheer cliff faces" farther upstream along the river (which delighted the Lewis and Clark chroniclers and the early travelers), the meander lakes and sloughs, re-echo with the late afternoon forays of the geese.

Not many days later they arrive in the cornfields in the Hornick, Owego, and Luton neighborhoods southeast of Sioux City, white patches of geese among the stalks along with occasional late-fallen snow.

Such wheeling legions must be seen to be believed. The highway paralleling the Missouri—US Routes 275 and 75 across Iowa from Hamburg to Sioux City—offers hundreds of vantage points—

ringside seats at one of the continent's great spectacles. Short drives on state and county roads often bring the observer "spitting close" to a cloud of Blue and Snow Geese slanting down like rain upon a cornfield or a wheel of Canadas circling in wary indecision before settling down and almost vanishing into the camouflage of an autumn-plowed field.

By the first week in April the tens of thousands come swarming into South Dakota. Previous to the 1940's, Sioux City apparently was a forking place, a fairish number following up the Big Sioux River to the Red River into Canada. More recently, apparently since the development of a buzzy airport in Sioux Falls, few migrants seem to use this route. Now the flocks continue up the Missouri until they reach the Vermillion and the James Rivers. Usually they rest on what seems to have been traditional stopping places along the bottomlands between Elk Point and Yankton. The sand bars and cornfields here are no doubt safely out of reach of the airport's distraction. From this area they leave the river on a wide front as they point the way northward again.

Northward, as the flock now passing over the city was pointing. Tomorrow or the next day the sky would echo with the big flocks; not over these city streets, to be sure, as once they had, but farther west, twenty, thirty miles. And I would be there as for ten springs now, season after season, I had been, watching the passing of the geese.

Usually, the first sights were excitingly the same. I'd be in the Grass Lake area, west of Sioux Falls and near US Route 16, or at Beaver Lake almost on the edge of the village of Humboldt on State Route 38, or down on the Missouri bottoms. Sometimes I'd see the vanguards already stationed in a cornfield or resting, a mottled island, on the water. Often glancing afar, I had to squint and look again to see whether I was looking at a smudge of cloud or a drift of geese against the sky.

I remember a hill on a prairie with the sunset burning the skyline. From the zenith to the western horizon, the sky was marked with the black pencilings of the flights. As far as I could see, north was linked with south by the uncoiling tangles, the interlacing strings of the flocks; and the evening sang with a myriad of voices.

And I remember a Sunday in early April. On the banks of the

Missouri near Elk Point I watched the geese drive in, rank on crescent rank. Sand bars and islands were a patchwork of gray and white concentrations. Above them more flights came in. As I looked across the river, I saw steps of geese slanting from the skyline of the hills down to the sand bars. Against the green of dwarf cedars on the Nebraska "breaks" opposite, they were clearly etched. Above them a crescent was beginning to break into segments of descending geese. Above these were strings and V's, their flight appearing slower with the deceptiveness of distance; higher above, moving even more slowly, tangles and broken curls of birds; higher still, imperfect M's and N's, broken letters moving across the sky; and black against a popcorn cloud, rows and chevrons in motion, orderly, precise, tiny at that great height; layer on layer they came in, each layer maintaining its direction. As I looked up, I was almost dizzied by the tracery of geese in motion, line moving against line, a flowing crisscross of birds. The highest often floated past and circled back before they began to break order, sideslipping, zigzagging, plummeting with rigid wings until they reached the lower flights when they seemed to check momentum and joined the sedately descending thousands.

Sometimes, as I remembered, winter in a backlash of fury hurled snow and sleet in a cold front upon the migration, grounding the flocks or pelting them into temporary retreat. I've seen them head south in a rain of snowflakes, but not often.

While on the river the flocks take to the country frequently before daybreak and settle to feed on waste grain in the fields, on new grasses, and such cereals as are sprouting. Sometimes the concentrations are so huge that, when disturbed, a whole cornfield seems to rise in a burst of wing-beats and wild clamor. By midmorning the main groups are back at the river to rest and preen, to gather gravel and probe for aquatic organisms in the soil of the sand bars and mud flats, to maintain the mating ties, and, among the laggards, to complete the courtship rituals. By late afternoon they are in the fields again. Often the flocks, hidden in the cornstalks, are betrayed to the observer by the restless movements of small numbers passing from group to group. At dusk they rise to circle and wheel, some to return to the river, others to break off for more distant water. Hopping from lake to lake, they cross the state in a fairly wide belt to enter North Dakota. One morning the flocks are gray and white edges on marsh and shore and island; the next evening they are threads and skeins vanishing down the skyline's slant. Cornfield and shoreline are strangely empty.

It is disturbing to remember that even here in the Missouri Valley the traditional stopping places are threatened by man's egomaniac advances. Drainage programs now have the audacity of federal sanction. Despite twisty assurances of officialdom in 1949 that the Missouri impoundments in South Dakota would provide more shorelines and sand bars for more feeding geese, more shallows for greater concentrations of transient birds, a paradise for waterfowl, time and the records, on the contrary, dramatize the fact that each year fewer and fewer geese are counted along the impounded portions of the river and that the completed Eden for waterfowl is, as far as the geese are concerned apparently, a Hades of fluctuating, almost infertile mud-reaches.

By now the flock over the city this night was only a faint disturbance. I leaned to listen. Tomorrow perhaps I would stand once more on a prairie hill or a Missouri bluff, enthralled by the crescent thousands passing. For a week or ten days I'd be aware of a queer sort of response to a stimulus—a stimulus common to those still sensitive to wild grape smell in autumn or bloodroots at the edge of snow: a strange sort of inner compulsion hard to describe in ordinary syllables and, in the gadgetry of our technological civilization, harder to explain. After that, with the last chevron fading like a wisp on the horizon, there would be quiet on the stopping places. Another year's migration would be over. But I'd remember this night and the silence after the flock's departure. Silence is a lonely sound—lonesome as the cry of the wild goose itself.

# THE CRANES AT LAST MOUNTAIN LAKE

## John Allen Livingston *

One fine August day in central Saskatchewan, when prairie horizons were limitless and anvil-shaped cumulus clouds gleamed startling white against a deep blue western sky, James Fisher lay on his back in the golden stubble, binoculars trained skyward, and murmured, "This alone was worth coming 4,500 miles to see." Above him, slowly and grandly ascending the invisible spiral staircase beneath each puffy cloud, were hundreds of Sandhill Cranes, great wings set as they soared higher and higher toward the altitude they sought for migration southward.

James had plenty of company. The occasion was a special field outing of the 1959 meeting of the American Ornithologists' Union at Regina. The cranes had been advertised as the feature attraction, and their performance surpassed every advance notice. Afterward, you heard in every corner of the continent the expression made famous at the Audubon Camp of Maine: "You should've been there!"

Each year from late August to mid-October, thousands of Sandhill Cranes and other larger birds congregate at the northern end of Last Mountain Lake to provide a wildlife spectacle that is unique in Canada. Though the focus of all the excitement is somewhat off the beaten track, and less well known than some of the

---

* For a biographical sketch, see his chapter, "At Point Pelee in the Spring."

other ornithologically interesting spots in the country, it takes second place to none, ranking with Bonaventure Island and Point Pelee among Canada's three top (accessible) bird attractions.

Last Mountain is a skinny, fifty-mile-long lake running roughly north and south, the lower end of which is about twenty-five miles north of Regina, in south-central Saskatchewan. The northern end, part of which is a bird sanctuary and game preserve, is some ten miles southwest of the little farming community of Nokomis and about twenty miles southeast of the railroad town of Watrous. At this northern tip, topped by a vestigial remnant of unbroken original prairie, a series of three or four "fingers" of water lie between gently undulating ridges.

Surrounding the lake is farmland which in some places extends right to the edge of the water. This is wheat country, and each fall the stubble fields attract thousands upon thousands of ducks, geese, and Sandhill Cranes. That the occasional Whooping Crane passes through here in spring and fall has little or nothing to do with the grain fields; the lake lies on the relatively narrow Whooper migration route between Wood Buffalo Park in the Northwest Territory and Aransas Refuge on the Gulf Coast of Texas.

Unlike Whooping Cranes, which depend in the main upon aquatic animal food, Sandhill Cranes are highly vegetarian, particularly in the autumn. Though they do take many more grasshoppers than most agriculturalists seem to give them credit for, they are extremely fond of grain. This liking for cereal crops concentrates the cranes in fall migration, when they join with equally great numbers of geese and very much greater numbers of ducks (mostly Mallards). Since it is in the heart of an intensively farmed

wheat belt, the resulting wildlife management issue is a thorny one.

Resting on muddy peninsulas between the "fingers" by night, the birds disperse during the day to feed on neighboring fields. The best time to see them in numbers is at dawn or dusk.

Well before daybreak, when the frosty chill of prairie night is still upon the land, you drive to the sanctuary area at the northern tip of the lake, making sure to arrive in darkness. There are any number of good vantage points, but my favorite is on the west side, so that the birds will be silhouetted against the dawn. Understanding farmers in the area have repeatedly allowed us to use their roads, to park our vehicle behind a tall haystack, and await the rising curtain.

At this stage, hot coffee is absolutely essential. It is cold, it is dark, and you do your best to keep silent as you hold the searing thermos lid between chattering jaws. (I have speculated, sometimes, whether this chattering is wholly attributable to the temperature.) As suspense and anticipation build, you silently watch —and listen.

While you wait so impatiently for the darkness to dissolve, you begin to be aware of a continuous undercurrent of background sound, like the distant heavy rumble of a great waterfall. It rises in volume and becomes the rough throaty voices, intermingled and strangely harmonic, of thousands of yet invisible birds.

When the first yellow, peach, and pale green flares of dawn thrust upward to pierce the prairie night, the clamor of myriad birds fragments into the individual voices of a dozen species. Cranes, geese, ducks, swans, shorebirds—all join the welling chorus in growing agitation, stimulated by their hunger and the arrival of the day.

The full vermilion majesty of sunrise fills the eastern sky as the birds take to the air. Family units, then small flocks, then great skeins, wedges, and brigades of glorious birds begin to stream past in striking silhouette. Cranes are shy birds, and will veer off course at the first sight of you, so it is wise to keep still, and well hidden. The rolling resonant calls of the cranes and the ridiculous thin peeps of their young-of-the-year predominate, punctuated by the stirring honks of big gray Canada Geese and the high-pitched giggles of White-fronted Geese (better known locally as "Specklebellies"). Throughout, Mallards quack sturdily, American Widgeon whistle, and the first pipits of the day lisp faintly overhead.

As every bird watcher knows, it is difficult and dangerous to try to estimate even roughly the numbers of birds in large flocks. The tendency seems to be to overestimate big birds and underestimate small ones. Nevertheless, by deploying our party in strategic spots and taking every care not to overlap, Harold Peters and I have counted up to 10,000 Sandhill Cranes coming out of the marsh in one morning. Another time, George Ledingham, Fred Lahrman, and Bob Nero joined me in estimating 6,000 in the air at once. The 1959 A.O.U. trip on that memorable afternoon reckoned about 7,500.

It has been calculated that there may be as many as 25,000 Sandhill Cranes at the Last Mountain Lake sanctuary at the height of migration, and there are perhaps 100,000 in the province of Saskatchewan at any one time between mid-September and mid-October. These figures are difficult to arrive at and even more difficult to prove, but they provide an approximation of the numbers to be found there. No matter what the precise figure, there are a very great many birds—big birds—and this is an experience that will rank high on the list of the most experienced and widely traveled birder.

The Last Mountain Lake bird sanctuary is said to be the oldest in Canada, and indeed in North America, having been founded in 1887. This is somewhat remarkable in view of the fact that at that time the area had not yet been settled. It reflects a foresighted wisdom and an appreciation of wild birds somewhat at variance with the prevailing temper of a period that saw the last massive onslaughts on Passenger Pigeon, Eskimo Curlew, and bison.

The fortunes of the sanctuary have been somewhat uneven in succeeding years, but at least part is still under protection and plans are afoot to expand it. At the moment there is little or no restriction upon entrance by water from the south, to the disadvantage of breeding birds, and it is vital that more land be acquired adjacent to the water, for reasons that will be immediately evident to the autumn visitor.

As the years went by and agriculture succeeded homesteading in central Saskatchewan, pressure on the sanctuary and the birds intensified. Some permissiveness on the part of local officialdom during the depression of the 1930's and through World War II led to the practices, now established, of haying and grazing right to the edge of the water, though these were expressly prohibited in the original terms of the refuge. It has since been difficult to reclaim and maintain the adjacent land as feeding areas required by the birds for whose benefit the sanctuary was created in the first place.

From late August onward the birds begin to converge upon Last Mountain Lake. Depending as it does upon the season, the harvest may or may not be well advanced by the time of the largest congregation of birds. If the wheat has been taken up, there is little or no crop depredation problem, as the birds then feed upon waste in the stubble. When rain or other factors delay harvesting, however, sharp words are sometimes exchanged between the grain farmers and the spokesmen for the birds.

There is a wry note of irony in this question. Much of the soil now under cultivation around Last Mountain Lake is marginal at best. In some places it is little better than "blow-dirt." It will support only sparse, thin stands of wheat, and is obviously land that should never have been broken. The result is relatively open stands of grain—just the sort of situation the cranes like best. They will not as a rule land in thick, dense crops, though they will occasionally walk into them from the side. In thinner crops they can easily settle in the standing grain, and commonly do. Yet year after year this poor soil is cultivated, mediocre crops are grown, and in some years the birds inflict serious damage as the result. Sometimes damage has been inflicted upon the birds as a counter-measure.

Agricultural practice in the area may be one of the farmers' worst enemies. For varying reasons having to do with the weather and other factors, farmers often leave cut grain lying on the ground for extended periods. This is an open invitation to cereal-eating species. Field studies by the Canadian Wildlife Service, the Saskatchewan Natural History Society, the National Audubon Society, and the Canadian Audubon Society have all disclosed that minor changes in harvesting procedure—wherever possible taking grain up as it is cut—would greatly alleviate the bird depredations.

Since the scattering of birds into better crops must be discouraged, exploding devices are being used to scare them, and special crops are being planted next to the sanctuary on land bought or leased for the purpose. A famous and valiant attempt to herd Sandhill Cranes by means of a small airplane was abandoned when even David Munro and Bernie Gollop of the Canadian Wildlife Service, at considerable risk to aircraft, limb, and life, had to admit it couldn't be done.

There is no doubt that the grain-depredation problem will be solved. For several years the Saskatchewan government has operated an imaginative crop-insurance scheme against losses to birds. As more land is acquired on the sanctuary and planted with distraction crops so that the birds are held in these areas, and if minor adjustments in farming technique are made, the problem should lessen. That there is a problem, no one denies. At the height of the harvest season, Harold Peters and I once estimated a minimum of 100,000 large grain-eating birds, ranging from Mallards to cranes, feeding out of the sanctuary at the same time.

In due course it is hoped provision will be made for visitors who wish to see the fall concentration of birds. An observation tower would be a great advantage and would eliminate disturbance of the sanctuary. At present there is somewhat limited accommodation in nearby Nokomis and Watrous, or one can take a sleeping bag in his own car, but these minor inconveniences pale into insignificance at the newcomer's first glimpse of the massed birds of the sanctuary area. It is possible, of course, to drive north from Regina early in the morning, spend the day and stay for the evening flight, which is every bit the equal of dawn so far as visibility and numbers of birds are concerned.

During the day, there is no difficulty in finding good flocks of Sandhill Cranes feeding in fields as much as twenty miles from the lake. Geese are also very much in evidence. The occasional flock of Blue Geese with one or two Snow Geese mixed in, viewed from a distance, can prompt a heart-stopping moment of speculation about Whooping Cranes, one or two of which *may* be in the area during migration.

Since this is typical prairie country, Sharp-tailed Grouse are relatively common in brushy areas (though Roger Peterson and I once spent two wholly unsuccessful days trying to show one to James Fisher). Nearly every sizable aspen "bluff" has its pale gray Great Horned Owl. Swainson's Hawks perch on fence posts and telephone poles.

If you walk through the stubble, short grass, and brilliant golden asters, Sprague's Pipits bound and tower in front of you; Chestnut-collared Longspurs chatter in passing. There is always the possibility of seeing the breath-taking aerial performance of a Prairie Falcon. Early in the fall there will still be flocks of Yellow-headed Blackbirds around infrequent ponds and marshes. Both Bald and Golden Eagles are occasionally seen, and White Pelicans, Whistling Swans, and a wide assortment of shorebirds can usually be depended upon.

The local crop-depredation question has been dealt with in some detail in this chapter because an understanding of what is happening to Last Mountain Lake sanctuary and its ecology is essential to a full appreciation of the birds and their environment. Though we have had a good deal to say about Sandhill Cranes, this information does not come from any vast fund of knowledge about the cranes in Saskatchewan. Information is relatively scanty. There are any number of areas of investigation for the interested bird watcher, all of which would produce results of value to the birds.

Where are the cranes coming from? What races are involved? What are their patterns of feeding? How long does the individual bird or family group rest here? Where do they go from here, when, and by what route? What in fact is their economic effect upon the area? Since cranes are vastly outnumbered by waterfowl, are they being charged with an excessive portion of the blame for crop damage? And so on. There are all sorts of questions yet to be answered. Field studies have begun to provide some useful information, but there is a vast amount of work yet to be done.

For the bird watcher, Last Mountain Lake offers new vistas of knowledge as well as those autumn vistas of unparalleled prairie beauty that make each sunrise and each sunset more memorable and stimulating than the last. I have a feeling that in the years to come we will see this still relatively little-known sanctuary high on the list of ornithological meccas in North America.

# HAWKS ABOVE DULUTH

## Pershing B. Hofslund

*While many authors of this book have had an interest in birds for as long as they can remember, only in the case of a few has the interest been acquired on their own early in life and self-sustained through their youth without encouragement from others, without any instruction, and even without proper tools such as binoculars, identification guides, and elementary texts.*

*Pershing Benard Hofslund, born in Jeffers, Minnesota, in 1918, identified his first birds with the Arm and Hammer Baking Soda cards and pictures that he clipped from magazines and pasted in a pocket notebook. These, plus a copy of* Two Little Savages *by Ernest Thompson Seton, were all he had until, as a senior in high school, he borrowed* The Birds of Minnesota *by Thomas S. Roberts from the public library and, he insists, read both volumes from cover to cover in the allotted ten days.*

*I first knew Jack Hofslund when he was a student of mine in 1944 at the University of Michigan Biological Station. He had already had one formal course in ornithology at Mankato State College from which he graduated in 1940. It was at the Biological Station that Jack decided to be an ornithologist. Consequently, after serving in the Navy during World War II, he enrolled for graduate studies in ornithology at the University of Michigan, receiving his Ph.D. degree in 1954. His doctoral thesis, "A Life History Study of the Yellowthroat," marked the start of his special*

378

*interest in the life histories and ecological relationships of all the parulid warblers.*

*In his present position as professor of biology at the University of Minnesota in Duluth, Pershing Hofslund is perfectly situated for his continued work on warblers. But he has since found a second interest—hawk flights. And this is no wonder when, in the early fall, vast numbers of south-bound raptors pass right over his home. Of the hawk flights he says: "Despite eleven years of observing them, I still find no diminishing thrills when I see these birds in passage." In writing here of this great ornithological spectacle at Duluth he shows us that there is much still to be learned about the phenomenon and leads us to believe that he will be watching hawks for many years to come.*

Duluth, on the Minnesota shore of our largest inland body of water, is an unusual city. It stretches out along the foot and slopes of a high bluff overlooking Lake Superior and is so dominated by the physiography that it has been described as "26 miles long, one mile wide, and one mile high." The physiography is responsible for an unusual climate too. At any season a change in the wind from offland to offshore may change the temperature 30 degrees in a matter of minutes. In summer an individual suffering from the heat in the highlands may move to the shore and curse himself for not bringing a jacket. This situation is reversed in winter. The tempering of the climate by Lake Superior means that Duluth, when compared to most of Minnesota, has relatively mild winters, cool summers, short springs, and long, delightful autumns.

The U.S. Census Bureau considers Duluth, nearby Superior in Wisconsin, and the surrounding suburbs a metropolitan area. There are more than 104,000 people in Duluth alone, and yet brown bears sometimes invade the city limits, moose now and again roam the city streets, and the wilderness is so close that even timber wolves may occur in the outskirts. As far as bird finding is concerned I doubt that many cities can offer much competition— and I doubt that many cities have more avid bird watchers.

Duluth lies within easy reach of coniferous forests and bogs in which two dozen or more species of wood warblers, as well as other species of northern affinities, thrive in the summer, while its suburban environs regularly attract such visitors in the winter as Hawk Owls, Bohemian Waxwings, Evening Grosbeaks, and Pine Grosbeaks. Duluth is also in the path of hordes of migrants and there are at least two fine vantage points from which to observe them. One is Minnesota Point, a long sand spit extending seven miles from the center of the city toward the Wisconsin shore. Here bird watchers in the spring and autumn can observe vast numbers of transient shorebirds and a wide variety of other birds ranging from Surf Scoters to Burrowing Owls. The other vantage point is the high bluff above the city and overlooking Lake Superior. Along this are many places—the "hawk passes"—where throngs of autumn-migrating raptors may be seen flying low, sometimes close by and at eye level or below, as they move southward over the city—or "the valley" as we sometimes call it. At the time of their flights most Duluth bird watchers become hawk watchers, for the raptor migration is truly Duluth's primary attraction of the ornithological year.

Lewis Carroll could have had the hawk flights at Duluth in mind when he penned, "And thick and fast they came at last, and more, and more, and more." Certainly this was the case on September 15, 1962.

It was a beautiful Indian Summer day. A few clouds kept the sky from being monotonous and the light west-northwest winds made the 70-degree temperature ideal for finishing my yard work before duty called me back to the university. My ambition to attend to the lawn was further stirred by the knowledge that on the morrow I would be occupied with the annual "hawk watch."

At 9:20 A.M., filled with good intentions, I stepped into the yard. A small "kettle" (spiraling) of hawks caught my eye, and, reasoning that an hour spent watching hawks would delay my work very little, I sat down in a lawn chair and began to count. This was unfortunate—for the lawn—because I did not stop counting until some seven hours and 10,526 hawks later.

The day was an extraordinary one even for me, seasoned hawk watcher that I am. Yellow-shafted Flickers came in a constant stream; flocks of small birds passed overhead, some pausing in the trees and bushes of the yard to feed. But I hardly concerned myself with them. Sharp-shinned Hawks, Sparrow Hawks, Peregrine Falcons, and Goshawks seemed to be everywhere, and overhead, like swarms of bees, Broad-winged and Red-tailed Hawks made the sky alive. I really have no idea how many hawks passed over the city that day. Dr. and Mrs. J. C. Green counted 10,000 or more from a lookout about two miles north of where I was sitting. Using the rather arbitrary figure of 50 per cent duplication, we arrived at a rather conservative total of 15,600 hawks seen in the eastern section of Duluth between 9:00 A.M. and 4:00 P.M. True, this was unusual, and yet I have little doubt that Duluth has at least one such hawk day every fall.

The falconers and hunters discovered the hawk passes first—the usual story. Falconers are still with us, but their activities are confined largely to banding. The hunters, however, no longer line the bluff, and hawk shooting, once an organized activity, now seems to be limited to an occasional nimrod with "trigger-itch" and a youngster with a new rifle. This happier state of affairs came about quickly, within six years to be exact, after the Duluth Bird Club began its campaign against organized shooting of migrating hawks from the passes. No doubt the campaign owed some of its rapid success to the fact that the better passes lie within the city limits of Duluth where people who cared little for hawks cared much less for shooting close to their homes.

Since 1951, when the first hawk census was taken, 657 hours of "official" observation have been devoted to the hawk flight. These hours were distributed over 123 days, and at the end of the 1961 season the official count stood at 124,836 hawks of fifteen species. Unofficially, other species, such as Harlan's Hawks and Gyrfalcons, have also been reported.

Our chief vantage point is on the bluff—along the Skyline Parkway above 47th Avenue East—which gives a commanding view of the northeastern section of the city from its eastern boundary to Minnesota Point near the central business area. The observation point is about 1,130 feet above sea level and nearly 530 feet above Lake Superior. This lookout has produced hawks every day of the season—from late August to early November—even on the few occasions when the fog was so thick it was difficult to see hawk watchers, to say nothing of hawks. Unfortunately it has been impossible to keep a team of experienced observers at the lookout throughout the entire season, but for the past eleven years it has been manned without fail on the second and third weekends of

September. Interestingly, each of these weekends, with one exception, has produced at least one day with a count that averaged over 100 hawks an hour.

Every year when these weekends approach, the hawk watcher scans the weather maps and listens assiduously to the weather reports. If a cold front has passed within a day or two and a wind from a westerly direction is indicated, his fever runs high, for he knows that under these conditions a good flight has never failed to materialize.

The morning of the watch arrives. For those of us who have had a great deal of experience on the hill, the watch does not start much before 8:00 A.M. One reason is that large concentrations of hawks seldom occur before 9:30 or 10:00 A.M. Another reason is that eight hours of steady watching and recording is about all one can endure in a day.

As we start the climb on the unsurfaced road leading to the lookout, we see our first hawks. Nine times out of ten they will be either Sharp-shins or Cooper's Hawks. At the top of the hill we stop the car. If other persons have preceded us, the chances are they will be friends from out of town—the Boyd Liens from Minneapolis or Russ Hayes from Waterloo. After the initial greeting and the inevitable "What have you seen?" we spread out the record sheets, set up the Balscope binocular, and get down to business. All attention is directed to the east, for it is here, across a large open field, that our first sightings are generally made.

"Sharpy in the valley!" A cry rings out and all eyes automatically scan the valley below for the telltale "flap, flap, flap, sail" of an accipiter, in this case a Sharp-shinned Hawk.

"Marsh Hawk," somebody else calls as a large hawk moves in unsteady, gliding flight across the ridge. Its rich golden-brown plumage marks it as a bird of the year. And this it should be because the young birds of this species usually migrate in early September, well in advance of the adults.

And so it goes for much of the early morning: Sharpies and Marsh Hawks with just a smattering of other species and newly arriving hawk watchers to keep it interesting. About 9:00 A.M., if the day is sunny, Broad-wings, which probably spent the night in the woods, seem to appear out of nowhere. They flap a few times until they reach the lower level of a thermal and then begin their effortless ride up on the rising current of air. Their widely barred tails gleam in the sunlight as they pass directly above our heads.

"There's a kettle over the ore boat," someone shouts. The count starts slowly—one, two, three, four, five—and then, "Look! Look at them!" Ten, twenty—the numbers roll out as fast as the observer can give them. There may be as many as 200 in one spiral. Meanwhile somebody spots another group over Moose Mountain. Once all this has started it can continue for several hours. By 3:00 in the afternoon the pace usually slackens, providing a chance to relax one's aching neck and tired eyes. Sharp-shins still move over the ridge along with a few Sparrow Hawks and an occasional Pigeon Hawk, but the main flight of the day is over. We pack up our gear and head down the hill to our homes.

On such a day there is very little time to enjoy other birds. Lapland Longspurs may be feeding at our feet; warblers may be in every bush; and flock after flock of Cedar Waxwings, Robins, Blue Jays, and blackbirds may use the same flyway as the hawks. But, with the exception of Common Ravens circling in the valley, these bird are largely ignored when a big hawk flight is on.

Of course, not all days are like the one I have described. Sometimes the hawk watchers come close to outnumbering the hawks. When this happens, Joel Bronoel, a leading figure in the establishment and development of the Duluth hawk survey, and I feel a personal responsibility. We make profound statements on the effect of the weather—which we know very little about—and we use the old fisherman's dodge, "You should have been here yesterday." Then we hasten to explain that very little is known about diurnal migration, particularly of hawks. Where from the north do the hawks come? From the northeast or northwest? Why is the concentration not noticed more than about thirty miles up the north shore of Lake Superior from Duluth? Why do the concentrations seem to disappear after they leave the city? Why do the hawks use a different flyway in the fall than they do in the spring? How do the thermals affect the concentration? We tell our disappointed friends that these are just some of the questions we hope to answer or to help answer in the future.

Actually no apologies are necessary. No person has ever spent a day at the lookout without seeing some hawks and there have been only ten official observation days when the average was less than 100. Besides, the scenery is magnificent at the lookout. Lake Superior with its ore boats and ocean-going vessels takes on the mood of the sky, and the woods below, blending into the residential and business sections, give a rural peace to an urban scene. And if the hawking is too slow, a fifteen-minute drive will take the bird watcher to Minnesota Point where the shorebird migration is probably in full swing.

The season progresses. October comes and the hills are covered with yellow and red. The Broad-wing is seldom seen; Redtails and Rough-legged Hawks take its place. Marsh Hawks still "climb" the ridges, but the immatures have given way to adults. Overhead, the small birds are replaced by flocks of geese. A Goshawk perches in a nearby tree and a Bald Eagle moves majestically down the valley.

By November the scene is left pretty much to the occasional Gyrfalcon and the Rough-legs. It is time to "tote up" the figures and to speculate on the whys and wherefores of the flyway. It is time also to look forward to the next season when, according to Miss Amy Chambers, one of the best of our local hawk watchers,

> "Sharpie" in the Valley
> "Marsh" over the hill.
> You name the hawk
> And Duluth can fill the bill!

# AT HAWK MOUNTAIN SANCTUARY

Maurice Broun

*It is heartwarming to note how many authors in this book point with pride to the men who guided their first work in ornithology. Maurice Broun is one such author.*

*Born in New York City in 1906 and brought up in Boston, young Maurice learned about ornithology the hard way—by doing. His career actually began in 1927 when he "learned by doing" under the expert direction of Edward Howe Forbush, and in due course was able to help the great Bay State ornithologist by writing several life histories for the third and last volume of his classic* Birds of Massachusetts and Other New England States.

*Following this invaluable training and experience, Maurice Broun pioneered the development of the Pleasant Valley Sanctuary at Lenox, Massachusetts; spent three years with the Austin Ornithological Research Station on Cape Cod; and nine memorable summers establishing nature trails and a trailside museum at Long Trail Lodge, the home of the Green Mountain Club near Rutland, Vermont. Since 1934 he has been director of the Hawk Mountain Sanctuary in Pennsylvania. The unique story of his years spent at this post is told movingly in his autobiographical book* Hawks Aloft *(1949).*

*Probably no man living has seen more "hawks aloft" than Maurice Broun and certainly no one in this country has worked harder to reverse the public sentiment against these maligned rap-*

tors. *Here he tempts even the most sophisticated bird watcher by describing with verve and authority the sanctuary at Hawk Mountain and the awaiting autumn spectacle of hawks, eagles, and falcons in silent passage.*

It is the season when caravans of cars converge upon a mountaintop in the heart of the Pennsylvania Dutch country; it is the time when hawks, large and small, and hosts of other birds come together along a highway in the sky. The mountaintop becomes vibrant with birds and human visitors.

We are eager to see for ourselves. So we pack a lunch, don rubber-soled shoes and warm clothes, gather up cameras and binoculars, and we are off for Hawk Mountain, the crossroads of naturalists. We come over a broad highway—Route 61, north of Reading—turn off on Route 895 and presently at Drehersville we cross a little river and continue a couple miles farther over a steep, black-top mountain road. The journey ends at a simple sign: HAWK MOUNTAIN SANCTUARY: VISITORS WELCOME.

We now pass through the sanctuary entrance after paying a nominal admission charge. Let's pause a moment at the bulletin board. Here the hawking highlights are posted. We also learn about the Common Ravens and Pileated Woodpeckers, and about the flights of Canada Geese and Common Loons that have been sighted along with the hawks. And we read about the red-letter day in September, when a few lucky observers chalked up more than 3,500 Broad-winged Hawks.

Before we move along we are irresistibly attracted to a trailside exhibit, a colorful collection of rocks. In one easy lesson we learn about the local geology, how the mountain was formed and how the local scenery took shape; at the same time—and most important—we get an interpretation of our own relationship to this dynamic world of landscape and living things.

We now pass briskly over the pleasant, gently-ascending footpath. This is a delightful experience in itself, for we move through a typical Alleghanian forest of birches and oaks, pines and hemlocks, and great tangles of mountain laurel and rhododendron. Taking it easy, we discover twenty species of the commoner trees labeled and interpreted. Warblers, kinglets, other birds flit furtively beside the trail. And then, having come a half-mile, we emerge from the woods and, at an elevation of 1,540 feet above sea level, there spreads a breath-taking, seventy-mile panorama—and not a billboard in sight!

So this is it! We have made our entry on a massive, sun-drenched promontory of tumbled rocks, and we are fascinated, exhilarated. On our left, the sheer wall of the mountain drops a thousand feet to what looks for all the world like a toy railroad and a gleaming little river (a tributary of the famed Schuylkill), both threading their ways out of the coal regions to the north. Beyond are canoe-shaped valleys and parallel ridges which fade into a sea of blue mist. Stretching before us is the Kittatinny Ridge upon whose sharp backbone we stand. The broad belt of the mountain, mantled in mellow hues of gold and russet, drops sharply and merges into gently rolling, varicolored farmland.

It is a sparkling October day. The morning air is sharp, a fresh northwesterly wind spills over the mountain. What luck, to have such ideal conditions! We have come early in the morning; all to the good. We find ourselves among kindred spirits; there is an air of camaraderie among the observers.

Eager eyes strain over the sharp crest of the ridge toward a series of numbered humps on the ridge. "Hawk over 3!" someone shouts. It's a Sharp-shinned Hawk. We learn that Sharp-shins have been coming steadily for an hour or so—"at the rate of one a minute," somebody remarks, adding "three flaps and a sail, and a long, square-tipped tail. . . ." The birds twist and turn and flutter in erratic flight just over the treetops below us. Less frequently the Cooper's Hawk comes along, and we note that it differs from its close relative the Sharp-shin by its consistently larger size, more sustained flight, and particularly by the rounded tail.

A Peregrine Falcon zooms by, a feathered torpedo, its flight so rapid we hold our breath. There is a sprinkling of Sparrow Hawks; some dart just over our heads and disappear in a flash. An Osprey materializes out of nowhere and sails past on motionless wings, in effortless flight. Several Marsh Hawks and Red-shouldered Hawks take up the procession. On they come! It is early forenoon, and the flight is steady. All morning the Sharp-shins have predominated. And then, quite suddenly, typically, the flight slackens. This is the noon-day lull. The observers relax, compare notes and haul out box lunches and thermos bottles. There is no snack bar on Hawk Mountain.

Soon the flight is on again. Now the magnificent Red-tailed Hawks take the lead and they come floating over the crest of the ridge in steady numbers. We marvel at their graceful, buoyant flight, their perfect mastery of the air currents. What a superb creature is the Red-tail! See that fellow poised out there, motionless on outstretched vans, intercepting a column of uprushing air. Suddenly he drops, plummet-like, fifty feet or so. He "jams on the brakes" just above the treetops and, scrutinizing the woods for the last time, sails on.

Meanwhile more human visitors have joined us. They ask anxiously "What luck?" Before we have time to answer, a Goshawk sweeps boldly into view, a pulse-quickening event that leaves us gasping with astonishment. The bird, an adult, long-tailed and pale gray below, came so close we were able to see the white stripe over the eye.

But what's this? A great, dark bird brings up its vans out over the ridge. All binoculars are brought into action and for the nonce nothing else in the world matters but this big bird. Obligingly it veers in the sunlight, revealing a crown and hind-neck suffused with golden brown. As the bird moves out of sight in majestic splendor a ripple of animated chatter breaks out among the elated observers; somebody announces that he may at last include the Golden Eagle in his life list. Yet before the day is spent, four more Golden Eagles pass the lookout. Nor are they one and the same bird, for we note that each individual has distinct plumage markings. All too quickly the shadows have lengthened along the mountain, and the day's aerial pageant of the hawks and eagles is over. It has been a grand show. We gather up our gear and leave reluctantly.

Thousands of people have discovered Hawk Mountain. They make the trip to the sanctuary the year round. But in the fall it becomes a mecca for nature-enthusiasts eager to watch the dramatic migration of hawks and eagles coasting on the winds to their southern wintering grounds. Why this interest in the birds of prey? Once introduced to these birds, among the most exciting in nature, one cannot help but become enthralled because their beauty is striking, their courage is inspiring and, in the words of Elizabeth Coatsworth, "Hawks stir the blood like fiercely ringing bells or far-off bugles."

And where else could one find such a spectacular backdrop to observe the hawk migrations: a ringside seat overlooking what appears to be half of Pennsylvania? Observers at the lookout see the hawks, like leaves in the wind, sometimes high and sometimes low, almost under their noses. And so we may ask: why all these hawks and eagles over Hawk Mountain?

Hawk Mountain is but a spur of the Kittatinny Ridge—the "Endless Mountain" of the Indians—easternmost of the Appalachian system. The ridge, with its crest averaging 1,500 feet above sea level, sprawls across five states from southeastern New York into Virginia. Jutting in bold relief above the surrounding country, the ridge has been from time immemorial a super highway of nature's own making for the migration of all manner of birds, from hummingbirds to hawks.

The autumn winds, striking against the steep flanks of the ridge, create an ascending stream of air on which, as though on an invisible roller-coaster, the hawks make their way with a minimum of effort, eventually riding into the southern Appalachian region and beyond. For the most part, the Kittatinny Ridge is broad, like the shoulders of a giant, so that the hawk flights are difficult to follow; but at Hawk Mountain the giant raises a shin, and the line of flight is narrowed. Hawk Mountain is a bottleneck for the fall migrating birds because of the extreme narrowness of the ridge. Beyond the sanctuary, to the southwest, the ridge zigzags and broadens and the flight again spreads out.

New York, New England, and the eastern Canadian Provinces form a vast reservoir of summering and breeding birds. At the appointed season, the flood-gates stand ajar, and together with other species, many birds of prey move down our coasts; others wander haphazardly between the coast and the mountains; and still others, a very considerable proportion, depending on weather conditions, make up the hawk flights along the Kittatinny Ridge.

Late August and early September bring the vanguard—Bald Eagles and their lesser cousins the Ospreys, in majestic flight on their way to the Gulf Coast. In mid-September there is an immense and often sudden exodus of Broad-wings from the north, and we may see 400 or even 4,000, in a day. Our record Broad-wing flight was 11,392 on September 16, 1948. Broad-wings make the longest journey of any of the hawks, their winter territory extending from southern Mexico to Peru. Many Sharp-shins and a smaller number of Cooper's Hawks, alternately flapping and sailing, appear from late September through October. From the mellow days of mid-October to late November when bleak winds and snow sweep out of the north, Red-tails and a surprising number of Golden Eagles hold the stage in the drama of migration at the sanctuary. We have observed a few movements of hawks in the spring, but nothing notable or comparable to the autumn flights.

Golden Eagles at the sanctuary, occurring quite regularly late in the season, are a great attraction. The Golden Eagles that are seen in the East are the remnant of an eastern North American population. The birds that pass over Hawk Mountain and adjacent ridges derive from the vast wilderness areas of eastern Canada; they winter mainly in the southern Appalachian region.

During a span of twenty-five seasons we have seen 1,277 Golden Eagles as against 1,686 Bald Eagles. Most of these birds were observed prior to 1950, however. The serious decline in the numbers of eagles of both species throughout the continent is reflected in our data: a 33 per cent decline in the numbers of Golden Eagles, and a 30 per cent decline in the Bald Eagles, during the seven-year period from 1954 to 1960, as against a similar period, 1935 to 1941. Even more alarming, the decline of immature birds during this same period has been over 50 per cent. Unless both species receive prompt and rigid protection everywhere, they face certain extinction.

The total number of hawks seen during a season has varied from as few as 9,291 during the mild and *windless* season of 1946, to as many as 22,704 birds during the far more favorable, *windy* season of 1939. The figures for any given season are never final by any means, for it is a physical impossibility to tally every hawk which migrates down the ridge. Yet these numbers give us a fair idea of the extent of the migrations and the relative frequency of the various species.

Before the sanctuary was created, Hawk Mountain was the favorite hunting grounds of local gunners who boasted in the newspapers that they killed 300 or more hawks in a day. Year after year, for perhaps fifty fall seasons, shotguns roared from the mountain summit and birds of all kinds were blasted from the sky; hundreds of thousands of hawks were killed. The wholesale carnage ended in 1934, when the Emergency Conservation Committee of New York City took over 1,400 acres of the mountain and converted the area into the world's first sanctuary for birds of prey.

The sanctuary has been a potent force in promoting an intelligent attitude toward these much misunderstood and maligned

| SPECIES | TOTALS | Percent of totals | August | September | October | November |
|---|---|---|---|---|---|---|
| Broad-winged hawk | 75,207 | 41.86 | | | | |
| Red-tailed hawk | 44,851 | 24.96 | | | | |
| Sharp-shinned hawk | 42,419 | 23.61 | | | | |
| Cooper's hawk | 4,066 | 2.26 | | | | |
| Red-shouldered hawk | 2,272 | 1.26 | | | | |
| Marsh hawk | 2,084 | 1.16 | | | | |
| Osprey | 2,067 | 1.15 | | | | |
| Turkey vulture | 1,924 | 1.07 | | | | |
| Sparrow hawk | 1,380 | 0.77 | | | | |
| Goshawk | 770 | 0.42 | | | | |
| Bald eagle | 709 | 0.38 | | | | |
| Golden eagle | 651 | 0.36 | | | | |
| Peregrine falcon | 354 | 0.19 | | | | |
| Pigeon hawk | 250 | 0.13 | | | | |
| Rough-legged hawk | 66 | 0.03 | | | | |

The general pattern of the hawk migrations at Hawk Mountain, showing the flight duration and abundance of each of the 15 species of hawks, based on the observations of twelve seasons: 1934–1942, 1946–1948.

raptors. Locally, there has been a tremendous change in sentiment. Hunters, who formerly slaughtered the hawks at the lookout, forgather there to hobnob with the bird watchers and to enjoy the flights. In 1937, reacting favorably to our pioneering in hawk protection, the Pennsylvania Game Commission extended protection to all hawks except the Goshawk, the Sharp-shinned Hawk, and the Cooper's Hawk. In 1957 the Commission went a step further, with legislation to protect *all* hawks in the northeastern part of Pennsylvania during the fall. Not enough, but progress nonetheless. Meanwhile, the sanctuary has been an inspiration for better protective measures for these birds throughout the country. All but six states are now making an effort to protect them.

Interest in the sanctuary was formerly limited to the fall months. In recent years it has become popular the year round, with the development of recreational facilities and educational programs. The project is supported by the Hawk Mountain Sanctuary Association, which embraces a far-flung membership of nearly 3,000 persons and forty-one affiliated organizations.

On the occasion of the twentieth anniversary of the Hawk Mountain Sanctuary, in 1954, Ludlow Griscom, then Chairman of the Board of the National Audubon Society, summarized the Hawk Mountain story: "Not only has the protection afforded our rapidly decreasing hawks by Hawk Mountain Sanctuary been of definite use and value in conservation, but the stimulus and love of outdoors and nature study to the crowds of visitors have been, it seems to me, an even more important social contribution."

# Some Avian Specialities

THE TRUMPETERS OF RED ROCK LAKES
Winston E. Banko

IN KIRTLAND'S WARBLER COUNTRY
Harold Mayfield

GOLDEN-CHEEKS OF THE EDWARDS PLATEAU
Edgar Bryan Kincaid, Jr.

ROSY FINCHES OF THE HIGH ROCKIES
Norman R. French and Jean B. French

# THE TRUMPETERS OF RED ROCK LAKES

## Winston E. Banko

*Winston Edgar Banko is chief of the Section of Wildlife Management, Branch of Wildlife Refuges, United States Fish and Wildlife Service. He was born on May 22, 1920, in Spokane, Washington, and grew up in the Yakima Valley surrounded by the eastern foothills of the Cascade Mountains.*

*With an interest in wildlife, especially birds, which began before he can remember, it was only natural for him to prepare for a career in wildlife management. In 1943 he graduated from Oregon State College with a degree in that field.*

*His employment began with the National Park Service at Mt. Rainier where he served as fire lookout and smoke chaser during the summers of 1941 and 1942. After World War II he worked for two years (1946 and 1947) for the South Dakota Department of Game, Fish, and Parks as a small game biologist concerned chiefly with pheasants. In 1948 he became assistant manager of the Red Rock Lakes National Wildlife Refuge in Montana and in 1950 was promoted to manager, a post he held until 1957.*

*It was the Trumpeter Swan which led Win Banko to accept the position at Red Rock Lakes just as they have lured many of us to visit that rugged, high, remote country in which these lakes are sequestered. How easily I recall my impressions in the late summer: Mountain Bluebirds on yellowed stalks of mullen; pronghorns grazing on grassy slopes below pink-tinted escarpments; and*

397

*the scores of great white forms, the Trumpeters, floating serenely on the sky-blue lakes. From his ten years of experience studying these largest of our waterfowl, Win Banko writes of them here with the authority of no other person. The full report of his investigations has been published under the title,* The Trumpeter Swan (*North American Fauna No. 63, 1960*).

If there is a Shangri-la in the bird world, it must be in the Centennial Valley of southeastern Montana. Cupping the vast shallow marshes of Red Rock Lakes in its higher eastern end and draining the deeper waters of Lima Reservoir through its western terminus, this high mountain valley belongs more to yesterday than today. Isolated by lofty mountain ranges, sparsely inhabited, and in the grasp of winter most of the year, the patterns of birdlife in Centennial Valley have probably changed little since bands of wandering Shoshone Indians camped and hunted in its lush meadows a hundred years ago.

In the early 1930's George Wright, a dedicated volunteer wildlife conservationist, working out of Yellowstone National Park for the National Park Service, "discovered" the last nucleus of the Trumpeter Swans in the United States breeding at Red Rock Lakes. In 1935, after preliminary surveys by the U.S. Bureau of Biological Survey, the Red Rock Lakes National Wildlife Refuge was established, encompassing over sixty square miles of virtually pristine marsh, meadow, and mountain habitat.

It is a pleasure to write of the fauna of this wonderful area, particularly of the Trumpeter Swans, which I enjoyed from the late 1940's until 1957. First a general description of the Centennial Valley and the Red Rock Lakes is necessary.

Not far from the western boundary of Yellowstone National Park, the Continental Divide turns westward and follows the 10,000-foot backbone of the Centennial Mountains which seals off the arid Snake River Plains of Idaho from the cooler and greener valleys of southwestern Montana. North of this escarpment, the Centennial Valley lies as a broad, flat trough, nearly 7,000 feet above sea level, bounded on all sides by mountain ranges and isolated from the normal travel routes of man. The modest gradient of the valley floor releases the waters of the Red Rock Lakes marshes reluctantly, as if to begrudge their long journey to the Gulf of Mexico, for the resulting stream is the longest tributary in the entire Missouri-Mississippi River system.

The cool, moist, north-facing slopes of the Centennial Valley are mantled with Douglas fir and lodgepole pine forests, bordered with aspen groves along the valley floor and watercourses. This is the home of the raucous but hardy Clark's Nutcracker that nests and rears its young in the teeth of late winter blizzards; the Blue Grouse, which, curiously enough, is found more often at the higher, stormier, and colder elevations in winter rather than summer; and the rare Goshawk, which is peculiarly adapted to hunt its prey in the forests.

The south-facing slopes of the Centennial Valley are more arid and therefore lightly clad with grass and sage instead of fir and pine. Timber is wholly absent except along the ridges and in the higher pockets and basins. This is the grand, open, foothill country of the Rockies, stretching on for mile on lonely mile, into which the few roads and buildings of man pale into insignificance. Here, cock Sage Grouse still display on ancestral booming grounds as if to proclaim the rising sun; Broad-winged Hawks suspend themselves in summer thermals, descending occasionally, to pick off a tardy Richardson's ground squirrel; and Lark Sparrows flit ahead of the solitary rancher's truck that runs along one of the winding foothill roads.

Big-game populations are abundant in this part of the Old West and may be seen in their appropriate ecological niches by the careful observer. Pronghorns range in small bands on the grassy sagebrush flats on the north side of the valley. Closer to the Red Rock Lakes, and along their tributary willow-ribboned streams, moose browse quietly morning and evening, usually out of sight at mid-day when they bed down in luxurious sedge meadows. Mule deer steal out of the aspen groves at twilight to nibble succulent forbs and timothy in the wild hay meadows bordering the lakes, and an occasional black bear may be seen "working" the talus slopes for food at the edge of the timber.

But it is the shallow Upper and Lower Red Rock Lakes and the vast encircling expanse of sedge marsh in the eastern end of the valley which hold the real attraction for naturalists. Nothing approaching these lakes and marshes can be found in all the Rocky

Mountain region, and an adequate description cannot be given in a few words.

Comprising about 13,000 acres of open water, productive bulrush and cattail marsh, but typified more by semi-floating meadows and bog mats of beaked sedge than anything else, the lakes are a biotic complex not duplicated elsewhere in the United States on such a grand scale. Lying at an elevation of 6,600 feet, a relatively stable water supply flows into the lakes from numerous springs and creeks which are, in turn, sustained by the melting of dependable snows high on the Centennial Mountains. The exceptionally gradual gradient of the lakes and their outlet, plus the short growing season found at this high elevation, are features which have produced a "climax" marsh of unusual stability.

Exceptionally productive, both of vegetative and animal life, the lakes attract birdlife in great variety and abundance. Five species of grebes frequent the open waters. Almost all of the twenty-odd species of western ducks are present at some time or other during the open-water season, but the Lesser Scaup is by far the most abundant nester. A great variety of shorebirds, gulls, terns, herons, and other marsh birds representative of the West are also seasonally abundant. But summer or winter, the Trumpeter Swan is king.

It was the thought of seeing Trumpeter Swans and perhaps studying their habits that compelled me to accept a position with the U.S. Fish and Wildlife Service at Red Rock Lakes in spite of the isolated and somewhat rigorous life it offered. The few but growing numbers of bird watchers who travel to these off-the-beaten-track marsh lakes are similarly attracted.

Trumpeter Swans—I came to know them well during my tour of duty at Red Rock Lakes. The foothills of the Centennial Mountains provided a convenient pedestal from which I could overlook the bulrush marsh of Lower Red Rock Lake and, without disturbing the swans, watch them feeding, nesting, defending their territories, and raising their young. From a higher lookout post on the crest of Sheep Mountain, some 3,000 feet above the floor of the valley, I could note the behavior of swans on all of Upper Red Rock Lake, Swan Lake, and much of the marsh system as well. From this latter perch, gained at the expense of several hours of arduous climbing, the interaction of pairs and the unorganized activity of the non-breeders could be observed through binoculars and carefully studied. At these distances of two or three miles a 20x spotting scope was useful for watching nest construction, censusing the incubating females, and checking on the numbers and fates of the cygnets from hatching in June until they were ready to fly in September.

Annual aerial counts of all Trumpeters in the Red Rock Lakes–Yellowstone Park region were conducted during the summer months when the adults were flightless due to molted wing feathers. It was exciting to tote up the census figures year after year and note the gradual but steady increase of these rare birds from under 400 to over 600 in seven years. A leveling off of the population became evident. This was puzzling until an analysis of the cygnet production, compiled carefully over the years, revealed that during low levels of population the young were produced at a rate progressively greater than during periods of high population. This phenomenon was found to coincide with observations made by other natural scientists on altogether different forms of life in limited environments.

In the winter, when all of the migratory birds of the marsh had departed, the Trumpeters restricted their activity on the refuge largely to two impounded pools of warm spring water. Here they were fed a ration of grain twice weekly to supplement their diet of aquatic plants which became scarcer as the season wore on. Always independent about their feeding, the swans often departed over the Divide for Henry's Fork of the Snake River some twenty-five or thirty miles away in Idaho where more open water and a greater quantity of aquatic plant food were available.

The long winter at Red Rock Lakes afforded time for reading and searching for historical notes in the literature. From obscure journals of early day naturalists, fur-ledger accounts and records left by Hudson's Bay Company factors, brief notes by explorers and frontiersmen, and the writings of eminent ornithologists, the history of Trumpeter Swans on the continent from early colonial times was gradually pieced together.

As a result of the research it became apparent that these great birds, the largest waterfowl in the world, were once well distributed over the breadth of the continent. One significant remark, made nearly a century and a half before Trumpeter Swans were separated on a scientific basis from their close relatives, the Whistling Swans, told of large populations of "trompeter" swans which wintered along the eastern seaboard in the early 1700's. Later, as the observations became more definitive and shifted westward, creditable notes of other naturalists told of great numbers of Trumpeters migrating and wintering in the Ohio, Mississippi, and the lower Columbia River valleys.

Such facts, fitting together like jigsaw pieces, documented what is now known about the original breeding range of the Trumpeter Swan. This range was found to extend from the Arctic Ocean south to the permanent lakes and sloughs of Iowa and northern Missouri, east to Indiana's Kankakee marshes, and west as far as the Pacific Ocean—much farther than was previously believed.

Records of actual museum specimens of Trumpeter Swans, resulting from early-day killing, were found to be relatively scarce however. Considering the once great abundance and wide range of these conspicuous birds, the paucity of museum specimens was puzzling until a study of the Hudson's Bay Company's records showed that thousands of swan skins were taken in the eighteenth and nineteenth centuries from the vast fur country of interior Canada west of Hudson Bay to satisfy the down and feather trade of Europe. Whistling Swans bred along the rim of the Arctic almost exclusively and, as a result, apparently escaped the worst of the slaughter. Thus, it is a fact that this early-day killing—for the fur trade in Canada and for food and feathers in the United States— was responsible for the Trumpeters' near-extinction and not, as mentioned in some accounts, the settlement of the country and loss of habitat. By the twentieth century, only isolated Trumpeters in Canada and the United States, which had not been as directly exposed to shooting, were extant. Among the populations that survived were the small numbers which were resident the year round in the Yellowstone Park–Red Rock Lakes region.

Whistling Swans, superficially similiar to the Trumpeters except that they are usually smaller and have a yellow spot on the bill and a distinctively different call, enrich the scene at Red Rock Lakes by stopping off during fall migration by the hundreds and staying until freeze-up. Whistling Swans traverse the watercourses at greater altitudes than Trumpeters, hence they are less vulnerable to illegal killing. Consequently the continental population of Whistling Swans has in recent years numbered about 80,000.

As the years went by and I became more aware of Whistling Swans and their characteristics, I discovered that a small flock or two were wintering regularly with the Trumpeters on Henry's Fork of the Snake River. About this time biologists elsewhere became interested in our native swans and their specific identity. A sharp-eyed fisheries biologist of the Fish and Wildlife Service in Alaska, Mel Monson, pointed out that the swans on the lower Copper River were Trumpeters, not Whistlers as previously believed. This observation kindled interest in swans by field biologists in Alaska, and a number of other substantial breeding populations of Trumpeter Swans were discovered in that state. A number were found breeding on the Kenai National Moose Range.

Because of the difficulty of making a positive identification of Trumpeters in the field, confusion has always plagued the occurrence records of the two species. I have often wondered if Trumpeters do not occur more often than suspected among the large flocks of Whistlers which winter in the United States. Here is a nice problem in practical field identification for the serious bird student. Someone, who assumes nothing and does not yield to discouragement, may be able to make a significant contribution to what is now known about the occurrence and number of Trumpeter Swans on the continent. No one, to my knowledge, has ever attempted to examine systematically the large flocks of wintering Whistling Swans for the presence of Trumpeters. Since the ancestral breeding and wintering grounds of both species overlap, it seems possible to me that even today a few Trumpeters at least may nest with the Whistlers along the rim of the Arctic, with both species making their long, semi-annual migrations to common wintering grounds. Thus, both the Whistlers and Trumpeters might still be found wintering together where only the identity of the Whistlers is now assumed.

I learned much about Trumpeter Swans before I left Red Rock Lakes. I read accounts of the Trumpeter in captivity and of the role that the swans at Red Rock Lakes played in supplying the live-bird trade abroad before the Migratory Bird Treaty Act. In the field I studied the territorial traits of the adults and many other facets of their life history. All this information I gathered together in my published report. However, I did not include the opportunities available to bird watchers who may wish to observe wild Trumpeters at Red Rock Lakes, so I shall describe them here.

The headquarters of the Red Rock Lakes National Wildlife Refuge in Beaverhead County, Montana, may be reached from US Route 91 by driving twenty-eight miles east from Monida, Montana, on a "country" road, or from US Route 191 by driving about the same distance west over a road of similar character from Henry's Lake, Idaho. Because of the undependable nature of the roads when wet or snow-covered, travel by passenger car should be limited to dry-weather periods, usually from June through October. There are no accommodations on the refuge. Food and lodgings may be secured at the Monida Hotel on Route 91, the 7L Ranch near the west refuge boundary, or the Elk Lake Resort northeast of the refuge. Those planning to visit the refuge would do well to write in advance to Refuge Manager, Red Rock Lakes National Wildlife Refuge, Monida, Montana.

Most waterfowl are, by nature, wary of man, and the Trumpeter is no exception. But if the visitor comes equipped with binoculars and a spotting scope, the slopes of the Centennial Mountains provide a wide range of places from which the Trumpeters can be watched for hours at a distance of a mile or more, without disturbing or interfering with their natural habits. Lower Red Rock Lake can be viewed in its entirety from the top of an old glacial moraine that has pushed out a short distance onto the flat valley floor. A favorable view of the larger Upper Red Rock Lake is gained by a more strenuous climb—a steep, thirty-minute hike up the slopes of Sheep Mountain from the refuge's picnic grounds about four miles east of headquarters.

Understandably, visitors are prohibited from boating on the lakes or traveling in the marsh during the Trumpeter's nesting and brooding season—from May to September. But this is no disadvantage because, due to shallow water, abysmal mud, and heavy vegetation, boating within view of the swans is most difficult. In any case, the wary nature of the Trumpeters during this season usually prevents a close approach.

Yellowstone and Grand Teton National Parks and the National Elk Refuge, Jackson, Wyoming, often offer the visitor an opportunity to see Trumpeter Swans in their native habitat much closer at hand—some, in fact, in waters near main thoroughfares. On these areas as well, a too-close approach during the nesting season is not recommended. Park rangers often know which lakes are occupied by Trumpeters in the summer; refuge managers are always pleased to direct people to the best places to see the birds on their respective areas.

Wherever you see your Trumpeter Swans you will be well rewarded and will appreciate the passage below, written by John James Audubon in 1838.

> To form a perfect conception of the beauty and elegance of these Swans, you must observe them when they are not aware of your proximity, and as they glide over the waters of some secluded inland pond. On such occasions, the neck, which at other times is held stiffly upright, moves in graceful curves, now bent forward, now inclined backwards over the body. Now with an extended scooping movement the head becomes immersed for a moment, and with a sudden effort a flood of water is thrown over the back and wings, when it is seen rolling off in sparkling globules, like so many large pearls. . . . Imagine, Reader, that a flock of fifty Swans are thus sporting before you, as they have more than once been in my sight, and you will feel, as I have felt, more happy and void of care than I can describe.

# IN KIRTLAND'S WARBLER COUNTRY

## Harold Mayfield

*Knowing full well that time to participate in his favorite sports—basketball and tennis—would become increasingly limited with the passing years, Harold Mayfield, while still a young man, considered with the logic of a trained mathematician just what recreation would best fulfill his need and be the most rewarding in the future. His choice was birds in which he had always had a minor interest, having identified his first bird from a book at the age of six.*

*Harold Ford Mayfield, born in Minneapolis, Minnesota, in 1911, grew up in small towns in Iowa and Illinois, graduated from Shurtleff College (now part of Southern Illinois University), and received a master's degree in mathematics from the University of Illinois. After one semester of teaching English and science in high school, he joined the Owens-Illinois Glass Company as editor of a company magazine. Over the years ever since he has been responsible for some phase of the company's personnel program. At present he is director of personnel relations at the home office in Toledo, Ohio.*

*Harold Mayfield's selection of birds was fortunate for ornithology. His administrative talents have been enormously helpful to two national ornithological organizations in which he has held offices, and his published articles on birds, numbering nearly 100, have widened our knowledge of avian biology. His most important contribution to ornithology is a book-length monograph,* The Kirtland's Warbler, *published in 1960 and for which he received the highest award in American ornithology—the Brewster Medal of the American Ornithologists' Union.*

*"My interest in the Kirtland's Warbler," he explains, "grew out of my friendship with the late Josselyn Van Tyne ... who started a study of this species in 1930. I assisted him in his work, beginning early in the 1940's, and eventually after his death took over the project and completed it. I have spent periods of time studying this bird in the field during eighteen years."*

*To the bird finder who has watched this large handsome warbler on its breeding ground, Harold Mayfield's comments will be nostalgic: for anyone planning a visit to the "jack-pine country" of Michigan, what he tells us here should be required reading.*

To those of us living in the cities and farms of the East and South, the Northwoods beckon to us with a promise of an escape to a different kind of world. Here is the wilderness and all it means—the solitude of the forest, deer standing in the shadows, trout on the bottom of clear streams, a canoe drifting beneath overarching boughs. Here too are the nesting grounds of colorful birds we see otherwise only as migrants in spring and fall.

To the experienced bird student no part of the northern forests holds more allure than the jack-pine plains of Michigan, for this highly distinctive region includes the entire nesting ground of one of America's rarest songbirds, the Kirtland's Warbler.

This is unique country but to the casual visitor it is not prepossessing. The Indians did not live in it, and the early white men sometimes referred to it as the "jack-pine barrens." It is not productive nor scenic in the usual sense. Yet, for the naturalist it gains a certain charm thereby. Man has passed it by, and it has retained much of its original flavor. Even today the human population is sparse, fences are few, and a walker will seldom encounter anyone in a day in the field. Here, as is often true elsewhere, the poorest of lands is rich in interest to the naturalist. Some forms of life are being tested at the limit of their endurance and others find here needed sanctuary from predators and competitors.

These jack-pine plains are a product of fire—not just one fire,

but a parade of fires that have marched across the land for thousands of years. The basic conditions were laid down by the Wisconsin Glacier, which retreated northward across this land about 6,000 years ago, leaving expanses of sandy outwash plains. Water filters rapidly through the upper layers of these light soils, and pine can hold its own against deciduous trees for a very long time—indeed, forever, if fires sweep through periodically to destroy the humus layer and return the land to its original state. In pinelands on a surface that is tinder dry, fire is certain sooner or later.

Forest fire is one of the most terrifying forces of nature. In the wake of it, we see desolation. So we are prone to think of it just as a force of destruction, an enemy of all living things. Yet, deeper understanding has brought us to realize that forest fire is a creative force too. Many forms of life are dependent upon it. Just as the ruthless blade of the glacier has ploughed and freshened our soil, the sterilizing touch of fire prepares the way for new life.

The jack pine is one of the plants benefited by fire. The cones of the jack pine tend to hold their seeds in tight resinous jackets, perhaps for years, until popped open by heat. Then, even on soil where it seems nothing could grow, the young trees sprout in profusion, sometimes forming nearly pure stands. Thus, a stand of jack pines all of one age dates the last fire, whether the growth consists of seedlings less than waist high or closely packed trunks of mature trees.

The jack pine grows from Nova Scotia westward to British Columbia and from the Great Lakes northward to the Arctic. But nowhere does it flourish in such abundance as near the southern limit of its range, in northern Lower Michigan. Here the relief is gentle and there are few lakes, swamps, or blocks of hardwoods to bar the sweep of fire. Consequently, up until modern times, fires once started could burn almost the width of the state. As a result we have great stretches that are nearly uniform in character and are clothed predominantly with jack pine.

This process was at work with greatest violence in the 70's, 80's, and 90's of the last century as the lumberman stripped away the white pine and red pine in this region. His slashings lay where they fell, and the jack pine, which was accounted worthless, stood untouched. Under these circumstances, fire was inevitable. It came from lightning, from carelessness, and from deliberate intent. Fires were started to clear the land for farming and to open the forest for blueberries. In this period there were weeks in late summer and early fall when the air was never free of the pungent smell of smoke.

We see a connection between these events and the fact that Kirtland's Warblers were found on their wintering grounds in the Bahama Islands in numbers not matched before or since that period. At the same time specimens were taken in migration at widely scattered locations in mid-western and southeastern states. In contrast, no specimen has been taken in the Bahamas since 1913, and in spite of the vast increase in watchers the bird is rarely seen today in winter or in migration.

In fact, there are some grounds for fear that better means of fighting forest fires may reduce the areas burned to such small dimensions that this bird may be squeezed ultimately to extinction. Consequently, some Michigan State Forest lands and National Forest lands have been designated as preserves for this bird, to be cut or burned if necessary to provide some of the needed habitat perpetually.

The jack-pine plains of Michigan are most extensive in Crawford and Oscoda Counties. This country is traversed by the Au Sable River (appropriately, "The Sandy"). In its drainage have been found 90 per cent of all the Kirtland's Warblers ever seen in summer. The first nesting of the bird was discovered in 1903 near the boundary between these two counties, and all of the nests found subsequently have been found in these counties or those closely adjacent—twelve counties in all. The entire present nesting range of the bird lies in an area less than 100 miles long, east to west, and less than 60 miles wide, north to south. But they are not at all evenly distributed in this area, and many miles sometimes intervene between suitable habitat locations. Censuses of the species in 1951 and 1961 showed a population of about 500 singing males on about ninety square miles (surveyor's sections).

Since it is peculiarly the bird of this one state, its name has been taken for the journal of the Michigan Audubon Society— *The Jack-Pine Warbler.*

Many parts of the jack-pine plains are not suitable for the Kirtland's Warbler at any one time. After fire, some of the tracts remain in grasslands for years. In some, deciduous scrub predominates, where the pines were killed by fire but the roots of other trees survived, particularly scrub oaks, which put up their foliage in clumps from burned stumps. In other parts, the forest has become mature, and the dark trunks stand close and straight, splotched with lichens and invariably untidy because of short dead limbs in the lower tiers.

It is just a small part of the jack-pine plains that provides the unique habitat of the Kirtland's Warbler. It is the part where the trees are growing most thickly but are still in their youth. People trying to find this habitat for the first time seldom realize how small the trees must be. If they are too large to serve as a Christmas tree in your house, they are probably too big for the Kirtland's Warbler. The stand must be dense in places and must be nearly pure over a wide area (at least eighty acres). The ground cover must be low but ample to conceal the nest, which is on the ground.

If these conditions exist, islands of large pines missed by the last fire and occasional deciduous clumps are not detrimental. But if the deciduous shrubs and trees dilute the jack pines much or if the stand of pines is sparse everywhere, the warblers will not accept it. Frequent openings clothed with grass, blueberry, bearberry, and bracken do not detract and may even add to an area's attractiveness. Seen from an airplane, many of these areas look almost like grasslands, and the abundance of the Vesper Sparrow shows that they are regarded so by the birds also.

It is not possible to state in a book precisely where the nesting sites will be in some future year. All of these situations are temporary. The Kirtland's Warbler does not appear until the young trees are big enough to touch one another and form continuous thickets. By this time, perhaps eight years after fire, the tallest of the trees will be about head high, but most of them will be shorter. The same area will become even more attractive to the warblers three or four years later when the trees are just tall enough to conceal a person walking among them but still have green limbs close to the ground. Then a few years later, when the trees are perhaps twenty years old and most of them are ten feet tall or more, the shadowed lower limbs begin to die, and the foliage in the thickets lifts off the ground. Now the warblers no longer return.

Thus, an area remains suitable only a decade or so. The exact length of time will depend on many variables, including the fertility of the soil and the density of the stand.

The best areas are those in which the jack pines have sprung up naturally. But similar conditions are sometimes approximated by forestry plantings. When the configuration is right, Kirtland's Warblers do not insist on one species of pine and have shown a willingness to nest in groves of the red pine, which have been planted widely in Michigan. However, in the natural state, the only pine that grows in thick solid stands in this region is the jack pine.

The Kirtland's Warbler is easy to find in nesting season, once the right habitat has been located. The male sings loudly and persistently. The song is short (less than two seconds), but it is emphatic, and it is usually repeated several times a minute. It can be heard a quarter of a mile. There is nothing else like it in the region. Even more helpful is the fact that where one bird is found, there are usually several; so there is seldom any prolonged period of silence in a "colony." The bird sings sometimes at length from elevated perches and sometimes as it moves about, feeding. It is tame and unsuspicious, ignoring a human observer unless he is very close.

The best time to visit the jack-pine plains is in June. The nesting season for most birds of the region, including the Kirtland's Warbler, coincides closely with the month of June. Although all the nesting birds have almost certainly arrived before the first of June, the weather in late May is quite uncertain, and a cold spell can bring snow flurries and a complete suspension of song and nesting for days at a time. Then in July, birdsong tapers off rapidly, and after the middle of the month the sandy plains bake in the sun and often seem almost birdless.

There are other birds of the region only a little less exciting than the Kirtland's Warbler. To a visitor from the South and East, one of these is the Clay-colored Sparrow, here at the southeastern-most limit of its nesting range. It is found only in burned-over land but is not limited to pure stands of jack pine. In fact, it is probably found in greatest numbers where there is an ample amount of deciduous scrub. This shy little sparrow would escape the attention of most of us except for its unbirdlike song, which sounds to me like the slow ripping of cloth a bit at a time—*buzz, buzz, buzz.*

The Prairie Warbler, here at the northern limit of its range, has a habitat preference much like the Clay-colored Sparrow's. It too has a distinctive song, a train of sweet, sibilant, evenly spaced notes that climb the musical scale toward the limit of audibility.

Where there are large pines nearby, and particularly red pines, the simple trill of the Pine Warbler is usually to be heard from high in the trees. In this region it presents a challenge to the ear of the expert who thinks he can distinguish this song unfailingly from those of the Chipping Sparrow and Slate-colored Junco, which are to be heard on every hand.

One of the rewards of a visit to the jack-pine plains in the early morning or at dusk is the song of the Hermit Thrush. This unparalleled songster nests everywhere in the region, whether the pines are large or small.

Otherwise the birds of this country are those to be expected in grasslands, scrub, and pinelands of this latitude. A list of birds seen on at least three out of ten Kirtland's Warbler areas are as follows (those found on eight out of ten areas are marked with an asterisk):

| | |
|---|---|
| Red-tailed Hawk | Black-and-white Warbler |
| Marsh Hawk | Nashville Warbler |
| Upland Plover | Myrtle Warbler |
| Mourning Dove | Black-throated Green Warbler |
| Black-billed Cuckoo | Pine Warbler |
| *Common Nighthawk | Prairie Warbler |
| *Yellow-shafted Flicker | Ovenbird |
| *Eastern Kingbird | *Brown-headed Cowbird |
| Eastern Wood Pewee | Rose-breasted Grosbeak |
| Tree Swallow | Indigo Bunting |
| *Blue Jay | Purple Finch |
| *Common Crow | American Goldfinch |
| *Black-capped Chickadee | Rufous-sided Towhee |
| House Wren | *Vesper Sparrow |
| *Brown Thrasher | *Slate-colored Junco |
| *Robin | *Chipping Sparrow |
| *Hermit Thrush | Clay-colored Sparrow |
| *Eastern Bluebird | Field Sparrow |
| Cedar Waxwing | Song Sparrow |
| Red-eyed Vireo | |

These are birds that you can expect to find. But there are other exciting discoveries possible. One rarity that has been found nesting in the jack-pine plains and nowhere else in Lower Michigan is the Black-backed Three-toed Woodpecker. The standing dead trees left by fire become infested with insects, and this woodpecker gets them by stripping away the bark.

Yes, this is a barren land but a thrilling one for the naturalist. It is not lush, but it has an austere beauty of its own. The air often has the clarity of the desert. The early mornings are frequently brilliant. In June the dawn is astonishingly chilly, and you should not be surprised if your boots collect ice crystals from the leaves of the blueberries as you walk through the low places. Yet by mid-morning you will shed your jacket and be grateful for the drink of cool water you have brought along.

At this time of year the white masses of the shadbush accent the green landscape, and the ground is jeweled with the flowers of the birds-foot violet, puccoon, harebell, and wood lily. At no other time of year is the country so beautifully displayed unless it be October, when the dark pines stand out sharply against the scarlet carpet of blueberry and the brown backdrop of the oaks.

It is a pleasant country for the field worker in more ways than one. There are few places where bird study presents fewer problems. The walking is easy. Mosquitoes and blackflies are scarcely noticeable on clear days, although they are sometimes moderately bothersome on still cloudy days or at dusk. And not least, nearly every part of the region is readily accessible. Nearly all of it is cut up into mile squares by fire lanes, along most of which one can drive by car. In addition, there are winding sand trails—remnants of former lumbering roads—that penetrate into the center of the squares.

With a constant succession of fire and regrowth, the jack-pine plains are always changing. Information from former years is already out of date. Drive the back roads and make your own discoveries. Each year brings new conditions and new opportunities.

# GOLDEN–CHEEKS OF
# THE EDWARDS PLATEAU
## Edgar Bryan Kincaid, Jr.

*A current magazine hails as a new discovery the importance of packaging products with an appeal to children who may be depended upon to push their parents into buying. Knowing this long ago, Little, Brown and Company, publishers, decorated the cover of* The Burgess Bird Book for Children *with a color plate of an Eastern Meadowlark. When Edgar Kincaid, age six, saw that picture of a bird with a breast of brilliant yellow, his favorite color, he wanted the book and he wanted it badly. There is no record of a scene in Joske's Department Store in San Antonio, but we do know that Edgar's mother bought the book and that it marked the beginning of an intense interest in birds—"in the appearance, distribution, habitat, and conservation of birds of the world."*

*Edgar Bryan Kincaid, Jr. was born in San Antonio, Texas, in 1921 and grew up on a ranch near Sabinal. He graduated from the University of Texas, and, since 1944, has divided his time, unequally I suspect, between birds and a ranching enterprise.*

*His favorite ornithological exploits to date are seeing 500 species in fifty days in Mexico and persuading Roger Tory Peterson to include Hawaii in the second edition of* A Field Guide to Western Birds *(1961).*

*Like other bird addicts, Kincaid spends much time in talking and writing about birds. His first literary effort, which was published in* Nature Magazine *between the first two world wars, urged restraint on the then-popular boys' pastime of slaughtering song-birds with slingshots, airguns, and .22 rifles. The result was one fan letter; it came from a man who boasted that he had always shot as many birds as possible and was going to continue doing so.*

*Undeterred, Edgar continued to write about birds and conservation, to draw birds, and to edit manuscripts about birds. He reviews books on birds and natural history for* The Dallas Morning News, *he contributes material to scientific journals, he gives illustrated lectures, he leads field trips. . . . This could go on indefinitely!*

*In summary, Edgar Kincaid likes birds, and he likes especially the Golden-cheeked Warbler and other birds of the Edwards Plateau which he discusses here with characteristic Kincaidian zest.*

Each March, so far, Golden-cheeked Warblers have returned to the Edwards Plateau of central Texas from Guatemala and adjacent Central American countries.

In recent years an increasing number of Austin, Texas, birders have vied with each other to find the first Golden-cheeks of the season. Contestants go out early and late to cedar-clad hills along the southeastern edge of the plateau, which begins in the western outskirts of the city. Many a distant Bewick's Wren song causes a momentary false alarm. Excitement leaps when at last the genuine, buzzing song or the soft cardinal-like *tick* of the warbler comes from the cedars. Spring and the season have arrived! Persons who hear "spring" before March 10 are subject to polite questioning; those who claim success before March 3 must show their bird to at least one dozen Golden-cheek specialists.

During the season local bird watchers, even those with unlisted telephones, can expect calls at any time of the day or night. "We have just arrived in town and we were wondering whether you could show us the Golden-cheeked Warbler, the Black-capped Vireo, and the Cave Swallow," say the callers. Some of them add the Green Kingfisher and the Zone-tailed Hawk to the standard three.

For many years the late Roy Bedichek, author of the delightful *Adventures with a Texas Naturalist* (1947), received most of the Golden-cheek calls. Mr. Bedichek was careful. Before he would agree to show off Texas's only endemic nester among the 540 species on the state list, he would make careful inquiry concerning the caller's intentions. To specimen collectors he would mention previous collecting raids and cite unrelenting reduction of habitat by ranchers. In conclusion, he would let it be known in tones dusty with discouragement that the few survivors were not worth the time and trouble it would take to find them. With non-collectors his reply was rather different. "Sure I know where there are Golden-cheeks. Meet me at daybreak and I'll take you out there!"

Bedichek took me out there. We drove out into the hills west of Austin to a large cedar brake. Thin clouds from the Gulf of Mexico, 163 airline miles distant, raced by so that the sun appeared a great ball rolling along the eastern horizon. In memory, it seems that almost every other cedar was crowned by a sunlit male, each with his pure black, white, and rich yellow plumage in the perfection of early morning and early spring.

As is to be expected, the place where Mr. Bedichek showed me the warblers has long since been burnt on the altar of "progress," but there are still spots where the bird lives.

The ideal Golden-cheek habitat consists of a dense overstory of mature "cedar" (*Juniperus*) and "Spanish" oak (*Quercus tex-*

*ana*) on unlevel ground. An understory of native bushes appears to
be important. The bird does much feeding among, and it occasionally nests in, deciduous trees, but at least some cedar must be
within the breeding territory. In woodlands of the eastern Edwards
Plateau, the Golden-cheeked Warbler, a tree nester, occurs with
the Black-and-white Warbler, a ground nester, almost as closely as
waffles with syrup. The nester on the dangerous ground breeds in
many states; the nester in the comparatively safe tree breeds in a
very few counties in one state. Why?

Nowadays good habitat remains chiefly along streams or near
large towns and cities where land is being held until the price
becomes high enough to sell for building lots.

Most of the Golden-cheek's breeding range was on private
ranches from which cedar has been removed partially or completely by ranchers with the aid of a U.S. Government subsidy.
According to government theory, livestock-nourishing grasses will
spring up when this juniper is eradicated.

When cedar is first axed, bulldozed, or burned off hills on the
plateau, little remains but alternating layers of hard and soft creta-
ceous limestone. These bare hills then resemble low desert mountains of the Southwest. Appropriately enough, that bird of the
American desert, the Poor-will, moves in. Purists who, with Kipling, believe that "East is East and West is West and ne'er the
twain shall meet," are surprised to hear calling on warm spring
nights both the western Poor-will and the eastern Chuck-will's-
widow. At present these representatives of east and west call at
various spots on the eastern half of the plateau. Unfortunately for
the future, however, Chuck-will's-widows, like the two warblers
aforementioned, require woodlands.

After a hill is burned over, there often springs up a thick cover
of lance-leafed sumac (*Rhus lanceolata*). When these shrubs reach
a height between four and eight feet, they may be occupied by
Black-capped Vireos. Even better habitat for this vireo is provided
without benefit of earthly fire by the bushy white oak shinnery
(*Quercus breviloba*) which covers sun-baked tops and sides of
limestone hills in the "hottest imaginable places," as George Fin-
lay Simmons wrote in his *Birds of the Austin Region* (1925).

The Black-capped is the most striking vireo that enters the
American Ornithologists' Union Check-List area. Blazing red eyes
stare out from wide-framed white "spectacles" set on his black

head. Bright olive-green upperparts, pale yellow wing-bars, clear yellow-olive sides, and snowy white underparts enhance his bizarre pattern.

This bird is a boon to late-arriving bird finders. Mid-day heat, so depressing to many birds, seems to have a stimulating effect. Apparently the hotter the day the faster Black-caps move and the louder they sing. Males continue singing late in the season, too. The Black-capped Vireo song in *A Field Guide to Western Bird Songs* (1962) was recorded in mid-August, at a time when Golden-cheeked Warblers had been silent for a month and a half.

The Black-cap is usually scarcer in its scrubby-bush habitat than is the Golden-cheek in its habitat. Goats seem to be partly responsible. These animals swarm over most of the Edwards Plateau, which is often billed as the greatest producer of Angora goats in the world. Goats thin out dense bushes, leaving the vireos exposed and their nests in plain sight of cowbirds. I have never seen Black-capped Vireos raise anything but Brown-headed Cowbirds.

The Devil's Sinkhole, located nine miles northeast of Rocksprings in Edwards County and 168 miles via road west of Austin, is probably the easiest place in the United States to see Cave Swallows. The species nests in fifteen other caves on the southern Edwards Plateau and in six small caves in Carlsbad Caverns National Park, New Mexico. The other Texas caves are on extremely private property, and the New Mexico nesting sites are in out-of-the-way parts of the park. Cave Swallows are seldom seen more than two miles from their nesting place. Permission and keys to enter the property embracing the Devil's Sinkhole must be obtained from the owner, Mr. Clarence Whitworth, Rocksprings, Texas.

I confess to a fondness for the old Devil's Sinkhole, which drops from flush with the ground to hidden depths containing clear pools in which live white isopods 407 feet below. On most days in spring and summer Cave Swallows fly in and out of the hole all day long. He who does not enjoy watching their flight is an impervious clod indeed. On ascending from the twilight part of the cave, where most of their nests are located, the swallows wind themselves out as if they were flying along an invisible spiral staircase. Their usual note while climbing out is a *weet,* which sounds very much like the voice of the Blue-rumped Parrotlet (*Forpus cyanopygius*) on the Pacific slope of Jalisco in western Mexico. The return to the cave is even more dramatic; it also can recall far places. A few feet above the brink the swallows close their wings and plunge down head first. About two-thirds of the way down they half-spread their wings and zigzag from side to side, rather like sailing paper "airplanes" that grade-school children used to throw. Just above the deepest rock overhang that is visible to the topside observer, the swallows straighten out, spread their wings a little more, and glide with wonderful smoothness into the depths. Not until I saw the Black-footed Albatross sailing over the blue Pacific did I see this beautiful gliding equaled.

The stony ground near the Devil's Sinkhole usually supports a few Brown Towhees, which are more gray than brown. This species occurs on the western half of the plateau. Except in the dead of winter, a flaming Vermilion Flycatcher can usually be seen hovering butterfly-like in the air or perched on top of a nearby low oak motte. In these drouth-stunted trees I have also seen in various years the Scott's Oriole, a "far westerner" that is not allowed by bird books to come into this near west area.

The Green Kingfisher is a rather selective creature. It likes to fish in clear streams in the tropics and subtropics. Clear fresh water in its old home in the Lower Rio Grande Valley of Texas is mighty hard to find these days. In recent years the clear Devil's River and its tributaries which flow down from the southwestern Edwards Plateau just west of Del Rio seem to be its center of abundance in the state.

The closest place to Austin where the Green Kingfisher seems fairly regular is at Prade Ranch, a guest ranch located just east of Ranch Road 336, sixteen miles north of Leakey (pronounced Lake-ie) in Real (pronounced Ree-all or Re-al) County. The Frio River here flows only a few inches deep over smooth rock bottom. Despite generations of travel in the actual river bed, the scenery remains refreshingly natural. The first white settlers found great numbers of Cliff Swallows plastering their mud pellet nests to rocky bluffs arising at each side of the river. Eons of swallow-time later, individuals still plaster each spring. The Green Kingfisher is often not immediately apparent, but if it appears, it is usually flying over or perched beside one of the deeper fern- and moss-lined river pools.

West-east fans like Prade Ranch. In spring, migrating MacGillivray's Warblers and various eastern species flit past breeding

Golden-cheeks. Nesting Black Phoebes often perch only a few feet from Eastern Phoebes. Cañon and Carolina Wrens sometimes sing at the same time. In winter, Audubon's and Myrtle Warblers may perch in a tree above pink-sided Oregon and Slate-colored Juncos. Bald cypress of the Old South grows at the water's edge, while scattered among the cedars at the top of the river canyon are a few of the Southwest's pinyon pines. Each species mentioned in this paragraph is near its normal eastern or western limit in Texas.

One of the highest and most scenic areas on the plateau lies between Leakey and Camp Wood. Ranch Road 337 between the two towns crosses some near-mountains in the Frio and Nueces River watersheds. This is Zone-tailed Hawk country. The procedure is to drive slowly along and examine carefully all soaring Turkey Vultures. If one shows a white band on its tail, it is suspect. If in addition the bird has a large, rounded hawk head, it is the rare Zone-tailed Hawk. In museums and in books this species shows a number of white bands on the underside of its tail. In the field, an individual often exposes only one white band, and is misidentified as a Black Hawk.

In winter Zone-tails migrate to Mexico, but Mountain Bluebirds move down from the Rockies. They have something of a preference for areas where the trees—pinyons, junipers, and oaks —have been removed. This is the second known instance of the government's clearing program helping a colorful western bird. The other is the Vermilion Flycatcher.

In the nineteenth century, Roy Bedichek grew up on a plain, where he seldom saw a tree except in yards and along creek bottoms. When he and his parents visited the well-wooded and watered plateau it was "a new world opening up like a veritable miracle."

The Edwards Plateau is no longer so beautiful as it was then. Trees, grass, and water are scarcer now. Still, in mid-August when most Golden-cheeks are in Mexico's Sierra Madre Oriental on their way to Guatemala and when most Golden-cheek listers have retreated to cooler climes, it is pleasant to go out on the plateau at dusk. Moonlight shows range after range of hills, but not the remains of dead trees on them. It is easy to believe that this is natural desert. *Poor-will, poor-will,* sounding on the night breeze, confirms the impression.

# ROSY FINCHES OF THE HIGH ROCKIES

## Norman R. French and Jean B. French

At the University of Michigan Biological Station in the summer of 1949 two of my stellar students in ornithology were Norman French and Jean Bachrach. I was never certain whether their interest in birds was first or second to their interest in each other. I knew only that I did not play cupid—they had met the previous summer at the Science Camp of the University of Wyoming.

Norman Roger French was born in Kankakee, Illinois, in 1927, and spent his boyhood in Springfield. He had his first exposure to nature study and biology at the Illinois State Museum where, during his high school years, he served as a voluntary assistant specializing in reptiles. Jean French was born in Chicago in 1929 and grew up in that city where her interest in biology was inspired by two enthusiastic high school teachers. Her goal was to be a high school teacher as fine as they were. She attended Knox College, completing her work for an A.B. degree in three years. That was 1949, the same year Norman graduated from the University of Illinois.

After their summer with me in Michigan, Norman and Jean attended the University of Colorado, receiving M.S. degrees and getting married in June, 1951. Following stints of teaching (his first ornithology course) at the University of Nebraska and graduate work at the University of Utah, Norman worked for the

*Atomic Energy Commission in Idaho. In 1959 he joined the Laboratory of Nuclear Medicine and Radiation Biology at the University of California at Los Angeles. Here he has continued his work in radiation biology (mostly at the Nevada Test Site) making special effort to measure the radiation tolerance of natural populations of desert animals. Jean, following Norman to his various positions, has achieved her ambition to teach biology and twice has had the pleasure and honor of taking students to the National Science Fair.*

*The Frenches' studies of Rosy Finches began in the high country of Colorado and have since taken them to many ranges in Wyoming, Idaho, Montana, Utah, and Nevada. Jean says that she appreciates her "retirement" in the coastal scrubland of southern California, but the reader of this chapter will know full well that, "come the holidays," she and Norman—the "Rosy Frenches" as their friends call them—will roll up their sleeping bags, fill their knapsacks, and be off for another climb to study their favorite alpinists.*

The uppermost reaches of our western mountains provide a distinct habitat called the Alpine Zone because of its resemblance to similar regions in the European Alps. In the Alpine Zone the tundra—level areas between rocky outcrops—is dominated by dwarf vegetation which contrasts sharply with the tall evergreen trees that dominate the zone just below. The short plants of the tundra, as though compensating for their lack of stature, often have large showy flowers or, if the blossoms are not unusually large, are matted with a profusion of small brightly-colored flowers.

The Alpine Zone is essentially a high, cold desert where environmental conditions are severe. During much of the year, moisture is either locked in the frozen snow, carried off by strong winds, or drained rapidly to lower elevations. Prevailing low temperatures slow the production and decomposition of organic matter that is so important in building a fertile soil.

Being confined to the high elevations in temperate latitudes, this zone seldom forms expanses that are continuous for long distances. It appears rather as a series of high islands which are remarkable for the similarity of their species composition. Many plants not only occur on widely separated mountain tops, but are circumpolar in their distribution, and are, according to the most satisfactory explanation, the remains of a vegetation that was more continuous and extensive in the colder climate of Pleistocene times.

One trait that characterizes the Alpine Zone is the wind which is memorable for its presence or equally impressive for its absence. The stillness on a windless tundra is so quiet that one can actually hear the blood coursing through one's head. More frequently the wind is so strong that it impedes one's progress and so gusty that it is difficult to keep one's footing even on level ground. The wind which shapes the vegetation may be an important molding force in the development of diminutive and matted species. Certainly the trees that venture beyond their native zone show the result of wind action in their thickened trunks and asymmetrical branching and in their small size which conceals their relatively ancient age.

Even the heavy snows of the long winter are secondary in importance to the wind. High mountain ridges are seldom buried in snow. They remain bare because of the persistent wind which carries all but a small amount of snow to the more sheltered areas below. Frequently, a hardened cornice like the frozen curl of an ocean breaker hangs at the edge of a ridge. The nature of the winter at high elevations was aptly summarized by an old timer we met in Wyoming:

"I guess a lot of snow falls here in winter," Norman said, trying to make conversation.

"Well, no-o-o," he drawled thoughtfully. "We don't have much snow, but a hell of a lot passes through."

Briefly, the Alpine Zone is one of the most inaccessible, inhospitable, and yet most fascinating areas available to naturalists in this country. The question of how some animals live and thrive in such an environment has led us repeatedly to the high elevations over a period of ten years, sometimes for extended stays. Although we found the answers to some of these questions, we raised many new ones. Our familiarity with this environment has generated, above all, a great respect for a region that can be, on the one hand, inspiring and beautiful and, on the other, threatening to one's very existence. Life is fragile in this environment. To succeed and survive, a species must have specializations that are honed to perfection. This very perfection often makes a species unsuited to other environments and hence a captive of these severe alpine islands.

There are not many locations where the Alpine Zone is accessible by road. In Colorado there are two: in Rocky Mountain National Park where several miles of highway extend over 10,000 feet elevation, and the road to Mt. Evans which attains an elevation of over 14,000 feet. In Wyoming there are also two: State Route 130 through the Medicine Bow Mountains, and US Route 212 across the Beartooth Range at the northeast entrance to Yellowstone National Park. In Montana, the main road across Glacier National Park traverses Logan Pass which, although less than 7,000 feet elevation, is sufficiently high at that latitude to provide an alpine environment. In Idaho there are no roads to the tundra. In Utah, State Route 150 from Kamas passes within a short distance of good alpine environment near Mirror Lake at Bald Mountain in the Uinta Mountains; and another road, to Alta in the Wasatch Mountains near Salt Lake City, leads to within a couple of miles of the tundra. In California, the highway over Tioga Pass in Yosemite National Park provides accessibility to the alpine habitat in the Sierra Nevada, and an unimproved, but satisfactory, road from Westgard Pass near Big Pine leads to well over 12,000 feet in the White Mountains. Undoubtedly there are others. We have found, however, that the most satisfactory and interesting areas can be reached only by trail.

The characteristic bird of the tundra and mountain peaks is the Rosy Finch which is out of place in any situation where there is no snow near at hand. Summer and winter, the "snow finches" may be found in numbers, salvaging the seeds that cling to the dried stems of plants protruding through the snowdrifts, or chasing over the surface of a snowfield, collecting insects numbed from the cold. Rosy Finches were aptly called "gleaners of the glaciers" by W. L. Dawson in his inspired account in *The Birds of California*.

Being very social birds throughout most of the year, they normally occur in large flocks. As a result, one may see them by the hundreds or one may see none. Often we have searched for hours, where we knew the birds occurred, before finding them. Then a flock would appear swooping down on a snowfield and running and hopping across it, seeming to take only the choicest of insects and leaving many behind. The Rosy Finches at the rear of such a group repeatedly hasten to the front, by flying over the heads of the others, where they in turn are bypassed by their scurrying comrades. Suddenly one of the birds gives two sharp, throaty chirps and flies up. Immediately the whole flock bursts into flight and is off around the mountain. And we, like two snails, trudge after.

The surest way to find the birds is to aim for the highest peak in the range. If the birds are present, you will almost certainly see them before the summit is reached, but frequently they may be very near the top. There seems to be no upper limit, at least in the mountains of our western states, to the elevations at which they will live.

Rosy Finches, with their rather long, pointed wings, are strong fliers, well adapted to coping with strong winds. In flight, they resemble the Mountain Bluebird more than other members of their own family. A Rosy Finch may appear to be tossed mercilessly by a gale, but on arriving at its destination the bird is in perfect control. A quick turn into the wind, an instant's hesitation with wings, tail, and body twitching, and the bird darts to a sheltered spot among the rocks. The normal flight is strongly undulating and, when viewed from below, the flashing light gray undersurfaces of the wings contrast sharply with the blue sky.

Although three species of North American Rosy Finches—the Gray-crowned, Brown-capped, and Black—are recognized in the most recent edition of *The A.O.U. Check-List,* we call all three of them here simply the Rosy Finch, for we believe them to be a single species. This is because they show extensive intergradation. For instance, during our investigation of the breeding range of the Black Rosy Finch in the Bitterroot Mountains of the Montana–Idaho border and in the Seven Devils Mountains of western Idaho, we found extensive intergradation with the Gray-crowned Rosy Finch. These intergrade populations contained individuals of every shade between black and brown, indicating several generations of interbreeding between the two types and breeding between the resultant intermediate types.

Our first search for the nest of the Rosy Finch was most frustrating. We camped between two snowbanks a couple of miles north of Togwotee Pass in Wyoming and observed the birds almost daily from June 18 on, scrutinizing every likely nesting place. One dull day after observing a cliff for two hours from different vantage points, we saw a female bird quietly perched on a rock on the talus slope below. She flew across the slope, then back to the base of the cliff and disappeared into a shallow cave. In two minutes she flew out and away to the southwest and—she was carrying something in her bill. We hurried to the cave, a hollow about ten feet high and six feet deep. Peering in we saw a small hole in the roof near the back. There was grass protruding from the hole and, as we watched, it moved! On July 27, after five weeks of searching, we had our first nest—full of young birds.

Our study of this nest was brief. One week later, while Norman watched from the top of the cliff, he saw a Clark's Nutcracker, pursued by a Rosy Finch, dart into the cave and come out, carrying a large dark object in its bill. The Nutcracker flew to a tree, dropped the object—a young Rosy Finch—which fluttered to the ground only to be retrieved and devoured by the predator. Only one young bird in our first nest escaped the Nutcracker.

Clark's Nutcrackers are very conspicuous above timberline where they occur in small groups, foraging on the face of the cliff and examining every ledge and hole. Since the Nutcracker is actually a bird of the coniferous forest, perhaps the nests of Rosy Finches in the lower portions of the alpine are the most vulnerable to attack. In the ensuing seasons we had greater success finding nests in the Teton Range of Wyoming and the Uinta Mountains of Utah, but our first nest was not the only one ruined by Nutcrackers. One nest with eggs was destroyed the day after we discovered it.

Young Rosy Finches leave the nest before they can fly well and remain among the tumbled rocks where they are inconspicuous in their slaty-gray plumage. We sometimes had difficulty spotting a young bird even when it was chirping regularly within thirty feet of us.

The long-tailed weasel searches for them in the rocks and we once observed the outcome—a brown weasel running, the limp form of a small gray bird in his mouth, and Rosy Finches fluttering and protesting overhead until the weasel and his prey disappeared into a hole. The weasel's hunting, like that of the Nutcracker's, is simply a persistent search through a jumbled pile of rocks. The weasel vanishes for a time, pops up in another location, hops to the top of a boulder, extends his long neck, glares left and right, and disappears again under the rocks. His success depends upon his speed. On one occasion we saw a weasel leap into the air in a last attempt to catch a Water Pipit that had flown just out of reach.

The Rosy Finches are adapted to life in the high country in several ways. Their aerial abilities enable them to travel considerable distances between the cliffs where they nest and the snowfields where they forage. During the breeding season they develop a pair of pockets in the floor of the mouth, a unique specialization which enables them to carry large quantities of food on each trip back to the nest to feed the young. These pockets, sometimes more than a centimeter in diameter when filled, make a conspicuous bulge on the throat of the bird. The Pine Grosbeak is the only other species of bird known to have similar pouches. In both cases the pouches are present in the two sexes and only when the birds are feeding young.

Rosy Finch territoriality—if it can be called that—is modified to suit the situation. The nesting area is not defended by the male, nor is the feeding area defended unless the female is present. Even if the nest contains eggs or young, when the female, which alone does the incubating and brooding, sails off around the mountain, the male follows her close behind, leaving the nest unattended. But he makes up for his lack of consideration for his brood by his attention to his mate. He defends her, particularly during courtship and nest-building, with a vigor that is unexcelled in the avian world. This is necessary because of the ever-present bachelor males—the result of a peculiar unbalance in the sex ratio where males outnumber females by about six to one.

We have seen a defending male do battle with an intruding bachelor on the average of every three minutes, a rate that might continue for hours. No sooner would one stranger be driven off when another would appear. These battles are furious encounters as the two birds twist and spiral and dive, sometimes becoming indistinguishable in a ball of feathers tumbling into the rocks below. It always seemed remarkable to us that they escaped crashing headlong into the face of the cliff.

As the Rosy Finch dominates the crags, the Water Pipit typi-
fies the tundra. Quiet and inconspicuous, it is actually a prairie
bird of the high elevations and occurs on the rolling fields where it
may be recognized by its two-syllable call note and bobbing stance.
In the early summer the Water Pipit has a delightful flight song
and display. The bird flies upward at a steep angle, chirping continuously until thirty to fifty feet above the tundra. Then it turns
downward abruptly, uttering a gurgling song while descending in a
fluttering flight with wings half folded and tail cocked slightly
upward.

The nest of the Water Pipit is built on the ground, usually
under the protection of an overhanging rock. One nest in the Teton
Range had two newly-hatched young and two eggs. The eggs disappeared first. Then the young, when about ten days old, were
found dead in the nest. One had a single wound on the breast; the
other a single wound on the back of the head. Although this appeared to be the work of the Clark's Nutcracker, it was strange that
the first predator took the eggs without injuring the young.

Two other bird species, characteristic of the tundra but not
uniformly distributed in our western mountains, are the Horned
Lark and the White-tailed Ptarmigan. The Horned Lark, ubiquitous on lowland prairies, is not abundant except in specific localities. It occurs commonly, for example, in the high Cascades and we
have observed a dense population above timberline in the White
Mountains of California.

The White-tailed Ptarmigan, in the early summer season extending into July, are often in a transitional stage between the
white winter plumage and the predominantly brown summer plumage. Their sedentary habits and cautious movements make them
very difficult to locate but easy to observe once they have been
found. They occur in the Rocky Mountains southward into Colorado and even New Mexico, but they are not found in the more
western mountain ranges of California, Utah, Nevada, and western
Wyoming.

Timberline is seldom distinct; more often it is a zone of the
thinning out and dwarfing of trees between the dense coniferous
forest and the open tundra. In this intermediate zone, tundra species
meet and mingle with species typical of the forest. Pine Grosbeaks
are often seen at timberline. These large, quiet birds are amus-

ingly deliberate in their activities, even when feeding young in the
nest. Like the Rosy Finches, they have an undulating flight and
they walk instead of hopping on the ground. Pine Grosbeaks are
perhaps the only birds that feed on the needles of conifers. We
have seen individuals and family groups consuming the new
growth at the tips of the branches of spruce and fir trees.

Other birds of the timberline include the Red Crossbills, sometimes mistaken for Rosy Finches because of their undulating flight
and throaty "flock call." However, Red Crossbills, erratic in behavior and movements, are not often encountered. The only place
where we found them common was near Bald Mountain at the
western end of the Uinta Range in Utah where they had reared
their young by the middle of June when the snow was still a
uniform three feet in depth.

One of the larger members of the grouse family, the Blue
Grouse, is not uncommon near timberline. We once photographed
a pair which refused to be disturbed. The male strutted and displayed before the female as though we were not there. Finally, when
Jean walked across the top of a snowdrift behind the female
to edge the bird closer to the camera, her foot slipped and she slid
down the snow, landing almost on top of the bird which, head raised
in a haughty manner, slowly paced away.

Perhaps the most abundant of all birds near the timberline are
Audubon's Warblers and Ruby-crowned Kinglets, both conspicuous because of their incessant singing rather than their appearance.
Pine Siskins fly about the tops of the tall firs and spruces and,
in the evenings, White-crowned Sparrows sing from willow
thickets along the streams or from the clumps of dwarfed conifers.

At any time in the season, birds of prey wander among the
mountain tops. The Golden Eagle seems to delight in the vast
openness. We saw one making awesome dives with wings half-
folded, gradually accelerating and steepening its fall until, with
wings spread widely, it leveled off and swooped upward, regaining
its elevation to go into another plunge.

Of the mammals the pikas are the most characteristic and
widely distributed in the alpine environment. Since they require
only a pile of rocks for shelter, pikas also range below timberline
where conditions are equally suitable. The first indication of their
presence is a short bleating call emanating from a talus slope. Then,
concealed by their grizzled color and immobility, they remain

watching. The jumbled rock pile they claim as home appears to be an endless complex of holes and passageways that would confuse an ordinary creature, but each pika seems to know its routes perfectly and travels through the cracks and crevices as though they were marked trails. In late summer, pikas busily cut and collect grasses and other vegetation to make a haystack under some protecting rock. This implies that they are active under the snow in winter, using the haystack as a food supply, but no observations have been made on their winter activities.

The yellow-bellied marmot is another animal of the rock piles from which it calls with a shrill whistle and stares in tense apprehension. One summer we established a camp at timberline in the magnificent basin at the western base of Grand Teton and Middle Teton Peaks in Wyoming. Our camp, consisting of a small two-man tent and a light-weight tarpaulin stretched as a wind-break between two small trees, was nine miles by trail from the valley of Jackson Hole. Once a week we rolled our gear and spare clothing in the tarpaulin, tied it tightly with nylon cord, and left it while we hiked to the valley for supplies. Upon returning from one trip we saw bits of red scattered about our campsite; as we drew nearer, we spotted the culprit—a marmot with a strip of red cloth dangling from one side of his mouth. At that same moment he saw us. We all stood absolutely still and stared. Then the marmot, clearly caught in the act, ambled away. One of our unanswered questions is: Why should the marmot have selected, in preference to all other items including food, Jean's long red underwear?

In the more northern mountains one may have a glimpse of a water vole, a curious rodent with a body length of seven inches or more, which lives in the small streams that drain the tundra. A glimpse is all you will get because one is never aware of a water vole until he hears the "plop" as the animal dives into the water, swims a short distance, and disappears in a burrow on the bank.

Rare is a view of the lithe, little long-tailed weasel and much rarer still is a view of a marten. One evening in the Tetons we crawled into our tent before dark as we often did when the sun went down and the temperature dropped. Outside we heard the rattle of a can. We knew what it was—an empty meat tin set aside for disposal in the morning. Cautiously we folded back the opening of the tent and peeked out. Less than ten feet from us a marten was pushing the can with his snout and licking the inside. So intent was he on the can that he failed to notice our faces in the opening. When he finished, he pushed about in the snow with forelegs hanging limp, rubbing his chin, his stomach, then his sides and back in the cold snow. He paused once briefly to raise his head and look around. Finally he rolled, slid, squirmed again and—with one more glance about—he bounded off. I think we had scarcely breathed during this whole performance.

Probing the Alpine Zone is rigorous, with considerable time and effort devoted to mere existence. Supplies and equipment must be transported to the mountains; we took ours on our backs. An assortment of specialized items makes this possible: Packs, tents, and tarps of nylon; equipment of aluminum or plastic; dehydrated foods, in such a variety now that a few pounds is enough to last two people for a week; and light, warm woolen clothing with an outer layer of windproof material. We are firm believers in layers of clothing so that one can add or subtract easily. It is as important not to overdress as it is to be warm because the resulting perspiration dampens the clothing and may lead to chilling. A hat with a brim is necessary because the sunlight at high altitudes is intense. The worst sunburn we ever had came during an early spring sojourn in the mountains when the bright sun and the reflection from the snow seared and blistered our faces.

But as all mountaineers know, one's efforts to reach the high country are rewarded by the exhilaration of attainment and the grandeur of scenery below and beyond. On a mountain top he is at once impressed with his power and humbled by his insignificance. Nowhere else can he ever feel quite the same way.

# INDEX